W9-CQV-160

"OH, WHAT FUN IT IS!

Here are all your favorite cartoon characters right out of the longest running comic strip in American political history."

—*The New Rebublic*

"MORDANTLY, APOCALYPTICALLY FUNNY . . .

this account has had time to marinate—probably in acid—and the results are fascinating. That power corrupts is scarcely hot news, but Ehrlichman shows the process in devastating detail."

—*Cosmopolitan Magazine*

"BRIMS WITH ORIGINAL, TELLING ANECDOTES . . .

about the leading contenders for Oval Office favor . . . will amuse, outrage, inform and captivate Nixon watchers . . . delicious gossip."

—*Publishers Weekly*

"JUICY . . .

John Ehrlichman has produced the most readable, gossipy account of the Watergate years."

—*Toronto Star*

John Ehrlichman

Witness to Power

The Nixon Years

PUBLISHED BY POCKET BOOKS NEW YORK

POCKET BOOKS, a Simon & Schuster division of GULF & WESTERN CORPORATION
1230 Avenue of the Americas, New York, N.Y. 10020

Published by arrangement with Simon and Schuster
Library of Congress Catalog Card Number: 81-18432

ISBN: 0-671-45995-3

First Pocket Books printing November, 1982

10 9 8 7 6 5 4 3 2 1

POCKET and colophon are registered trademarks
of Simon & Schuster.

Printed in the U.S.A.

CONTENTS

Preface

ONE THOUSAND AND three times during the years 1969–1973 I took notes as I talked with Richard Nixon. Some of those notes are a single page, but most of them ran two to ten pages.

Spasmodically I made memoranda of remarkable events, too.

For seven years all of this material was held by the Government and I was not permitted access to most of it. Finally, in 1980, I was admitted to the Archives and was permitted to copy some of those records which had been seized in my White House office the day after I was fired.

This is not a history book. It recounts *what I knew* in those early 1970s, occasionally elaborated with later developments if they help to round out the narrative.

The Nixon dialogues come from my notes. If the Nixon tapes are ever released, I'll be seen to be less than a *verbatim* reporter, but I have the substance correct, I know.

This is primarily an account of people and events as I perceived them eight to ten years ago. I haven't followed every account with the parenthetical phrase "(or so I thought then)," but I trust the reader will supply it when required. It is obvious that many things I believed were untrue.

Richard Nixon was a Presidential candidate when I first met him in 1959 and for the next ten years that I knew him. Such a person is not like ordinary Americans. The aspiration demands enormous sacrifice. A candidate is rarely at home; he seldom sees his family, rarely has time to enjoy a concert, a novel or his garden.

Presidential candidates are hybrid humans, from whom are plucked the normal joys, emotions and experiences of life, that they may single-mindedly run the race without distraction or disability.

Then, when one of them is elected, we wonder at the man in the White House who is so strangely different from the rest of us. We fail to recognize that he is an animal which has been groomed to run a special race and has forgotten how to do almost everything else.

When Richard Nixon sat down in the big chair in the Oval Office that first day of his Presidency he *was* the President. He needed no on-the-job training. He knew from his time as Vice President how the White House worked. And most important, he had a sense of direction and purpose; he knew where he wanted to take the country.

But during the time I was there with Nixon I saw him buffeted and battered by events and by the demands of individuals and groups. When I left, in May of 1973, Nixon was a different person than he'd been in 1969. That is not an extraordinary fact, given the circumstances of those four and a half years. Yet the bookshelves are jammed with writings that picture Nixon and his Administration with an unrelieved and unchanging sameness, cutting a cross-section at a moment in time and extrapolating both forward and back. Any Presidential administration is a dynamic process, changing every day—in both character and direction. Because Nixon was the man he was, facing a hostile Congress, leading a country at war and lashed by scandal, a suggestion that things were much the same in 1973 as they had been in 1969 is misleading.

War, racial unrest, economic instability and politics were strong, shifting winds which often required us to tack and maneuver as we navigated the course Nixon set for us.

And the primary reality was that we were dealing with people. Richard Nixon's family and close friends affected him every day he was President. Nixon's staff and cabinet were constant influences on him. So were the congressional leaders. One part of this book—Part II—is about some of the people who were a part of Richard Nixon's life during the time I knew him, from 1959 to 1973.

Part III is about the Congress, the press, the economic Establishment and other institutions, and about some of the issues that changed Richard Nixon during those years.

Parts I and IV are an account of how I got into all of this, and how I got out of it. I certainly didn't stay the same, either, and this book is to some extent an account of how I changed.

I did what I did, and I do not intend to deny it. But at the same time, I did not do some of the things imputed to me in the Watergate Legend, and I feel equally obliged to state my denials, along with my admissions. Some of the scars still hurt, and I can't be sure that I'm truly objective; but since this is a personal, impressionistic account, perhaps that doesn't matter.

JOHN EHRLICHMAN
Santa Fe
March 1981

Part I

CHAPTER ONE

The Circus

RICHARD NIXON SELDOM spoke to anyone while riding in an elevator. Nevertheless, the first time he ever spoke to me was in a hotel elevator in Milwaukee. He really didn't want to, and his acknowledgment of my presence was perfunctory. But I was one of his new advance men, recruited by H. R. Haldeman for the 1960 Presidential campaign, and they both knew that Nixon had to say something to me. You couldn't send the new man home from his first campaign advance unless he could tell folks that he'd met his candidate. There was no need to let him into the Vice President's suite for an intimate little chat, but he did have to be introduced. So I was introduced.

In the late fall of 1959, while in New York on business, I had visited the Haldemans at their home in suburban Connecticut. I hadn't seen them for a long time. Jo, Bob, my wife, Jeanne, and I had been friends as undergraduates at UCLA, after I returned from World War II.

All of us left Los Angeles after graduation. I went to Stanford law school. When Jeanne and I were married in my second year there, we had a reunion with the Haldemans. They were living in San Mateo, between Stanford and San Francisco, where Bob worked for an advertising agency. Later he was transferred to New York, and the growing Haldeman family lived near Greenwich.

That fall, when we met in Connecticut, Bob was working part time in some of the Presidential-primary states for Vice President Richard M. Nixon. The day after our Sunday brunch he was to leave for a week in New Hampshire to set up Nixon's arrangements for a campaign trip into that state.

The work he was doing sounded exciting to me. I had been an interested political bystander for years, following the conventions and campaigns in the papers and newsmagazines, and attending candidates' rallies when they took place in Seattle. Once, for two days, I made a campaign trip with a friend who was a Congressional candidate. We went to the Clark County Fair near Vancouver, Washington, where he shook hands while I held his coat and passed out campaign buttons. It was competitive, a little risky, easy and interesting to talk to the people, and I liked it.

But ever since I'd run for student-body president in high school—and been resoundingly defeated by the captain of the football team—I had had no desire to run for public office. At UCLA I'd discovered the safer joys of behind-the-scenes politics, and I'd had some success at it there.

When Haldeman asked if I was interested in doing advance work for Nixon, I wanted to do it. Nixon was Eisenhower's Vice President and I knew what any news reader knew about him, but little more. A fine woman I had worked with in an administrative office at UCLA had quit to become one of Nixon's secretaries (Loie Gaunt still works for him, thirty-six years later), but that was the closest I'd come to him. I was neither his strong supporter nor even an active Republican, but I knew nothing about Nixon that would cause me to have doubts about working for his election.

Moreover, I was feeling an itch. In 1959 I was 34. I had led a lively life until I was about 25; I went to war when I was 18, flew twenty-six rough missions over Europe as a lead navigator of the Eighth Air Force, then came back to UCLA. There I was Assistant Dean of Students and ran the Interfraternity program while I finished college. For several months after graduation I was employed by old William Randolph Hearst at his baronial Beverly Hills estate, tutoring one of his grandchildren.

After three years of law school, my wife, our new son and I moved to Seattle. By 1953 I was a partner in a small firm, trying many lawsuits, fathering children, teaching Sunday school and living up to the expectations of my father's formidable siblings. In all respects I was what family, church and community expected me to be, and it gave me a large measure of satisfaction that I was.

But at the same time, I stood in the lee of my Uncle Ben, one of those self-taught and self-made community leaders who inspire the admiration of all who hear the story of their humble origin and rise to wealth and influence. Through Ben I came to know the city's shakers and movers, men like Eddie

3

Carlson and Dan Evans and Jim Ellis* who were shaping the courses of great corporations, cities and states.

And I began to itch to be a part of some real action of some kind. I was more and more the creature of my growing clientele, working long hours, evenings and weekends to represent their interests; I handled their problems well enough, and my income was substantial, but I was bored.

My father once told me of a friend who survived the stockbroker's life by going off for a while every year to Ringling Brothers' Circus to be a clown. Then he'd return, refreshed, to make money for his clients once again.

That Sunday in Connecticut, Bob Haldeman was suggesting that I run away to the circus for a little while, and it was irresistible.

My wife was less delighted. She had a houseful of young children and a growing sense that husbands had all the fun; my good news thoroughly reinforced her suspicions.

During the pre-primary months I made a trip to Chicago and Milwaukee to watch Bob Haldeman advance a Chicago fund-raising dinner, then to do my own first advance in the Milk City under Bob's eye. (Milwaukee was called the Milk City because of the color of the brick used in its early buildings. When you advance a political stop you're always on the lookout for such local tidbits to feed to the candidate's speechwriters.)

A Republican boss of the old school, Vincent Mercurio, introduced me to the realities of local politics on that trip. Every candidate's schedule is a compromise between conflicting interests of the candidate and the local sponsoring organization. A skillful advance man keeps the local people working enthusiastically while refusing to allow his candidate to devote his time and dwindling physical strength to local events that will do *him* no good. An adroit local leader like Mercurio uses the candidate to generate enthusiasm in his organization and pay off debts to individuals ("Listen, John, after the speech I want that the Vice President should just stop by the hospitality suite and say hello or thank you to a few people—it will do him a lot of good.")

---

* Dan Evans was Governor of the State of Washington; Ellis is a lawyer and civic leader in Seattle; Carlson became head of United Airlines and during my criminal trials made it possible for my attorneys and me to live at the Mayflower Hotel in Washington.

Once in a while, a local boss will run off with the candidate in the middle of an event while the advance man's back is turned. Ohio is a vital Presidential state. Its sometime Governor, James Rhodes, would agree to almost anything when an advance man came to town. But as soon as the candidate stepped off his airplane, Rhodes would grab him by the arm and lead him through Jim Rhodes's own schedule, to suit Jim's purposes. Very early one morning he hauled Nixon out to the Ohio State Fair grounds to give prizes to agricultural journalists. ("It will do him a world of good with those people.") En route we narrowly averted a detour Rhodes had ordered to take Nixon down the fair's brand-new plastic shoot-the-chutes, seated on a gunnysack. ("I just don't understand you fellows; you should have let him do that. It would have done him a world of good.")

Vince Mercurio's Milwaukee Lincoln Day Dinner went pretty well. Back at the hotel after a triumphal exit, Nixon, Haldeman and a couple of Secret Service agents went into a waiting elevator; the hotel manager and I stood by the door wondering whether to get on or not. Haldeman pointed at me and beckoned. As we rode up, Nixon looked down at the floor, dourly.

"Mr. Vice President, this is John Ehrlichman, who advanced this stop," Haldeman said.

Nixon looked at me intently. "Oh, yes. Fine. How are you?" Then he was gone, eyes down, deep in thought.

During the 1960 campaign I saw Nixon many times, but it was to be 1962 before I would have any sort of real conversation with him. Haldeman explained to each of his advance men that we must not intrude; the Vice President should never be engaged in unnecessary conversation under any circumstances. There would be plenty of time for chitchat after the election. That was fine with me. Nixon the individual barely interested me then. I was out for the campaign experience.

Before the August 1960 Republican Convention in Chicago, Nelson Rockefeller was on again, off again. Early in 1959 he had begun a run for the nomination, then had withdrawn from contention. In the spring of 1960 he reconsidered and began again to travel the country, making speeches and wooing convention delegates.

Robert Finch, Vice President Nixon's administrative assistant, who was managing his primary campaign, called me in Seattle one spring day to ask me to go to North Dakota to watch Rockefeller campaign across that state. Finch wanted to know what Rockefeller said and did; he stressed that he particularly wanted the names of North Dakota delegates Rockefeller and his people were working on.

Another Vice Presidential aide, Charles McWhorter, was (and still is) an encyclopedia of Republican politics. From him I received the names of several Nixon loyalists in Fargo who could be counted upon to help me find a vantage point from which to observe Rockefeller at work.

It turned out that McWhorter's contacts, Barb and Jim Dawson, John Paulson and Bob Owen, were helping to organize things for the Rockefeller visit, although their sympathies lay with Nixon. The first night in Fargo I was invited to a reception they staged at the home of a small, foul-mouthed banker. When I was introduced to him as a visiting Seattle lawyer, this little man told me he had raised my hometown Senator, Warren Magnusson of Washington, as a foster son, sponsored him both financially and politically and sometimes acted as Magnusson's bag man. (This little man's voluble, profane claim to fame was extraordinary to me that night. But over and over in the following years, I heard similar stories from people claiming some connection with famous politicians. A lot of very wealthy and successful people get their jollies from these vicarious political connections. That partly explains why fat cats gave the huge sums they did to Nixon and other candidates.)

Nelson Rockefeller was in the center of the banker's living room, shaking hands with well-dressed Fargo people as they were brought to him by aides. I moved around the edge of things until I noticed I was standing next to Mary Todhunter Clark Rockefeller, Nelson's patrician wife. She stood alone in a corner, holding a drink, watching her husband with undisguised disapproval. He was grabbing shoulders, shaking hands and slapping backs, grinning broadly, thoroughly enjoying himself.

Mrs. Rockefeller and I turned away from him at the same time and looked at each other. She shook her head.

"Isn't this awful?" she asked.

Barb Dawson managed to sign me on as a driver in the long motorcade that was to accompany the Rockefellers across North Dakota to Bismarck. Among my passengers was a Republican candidate for lieutenant governor who appeared certain that I was part of the staff Rockefeller had brought from New York. En route we stopped at Congressman Mark Andrews' farm for breakfast. Andrews and his wife, Mary, knew of my assignment, but Nelson Rockefeller, Hugh Moore and the rest of the New Yorkers with whom I ate in the Andrewses' small living room evidently thought I was a North Dakotan. I had decided before arriving in Fargo that I would not lie to anyone about my identity or what I was doing there, if I was directly asked. But no one asked.

During the three days I was there I managed to pick up some good political information for Finch from friendly local people in Fargo and Bismarck. The candidate for lieutenant governor, himself a delegate, told me everything he knew. Three days after Rocky left North Dakota and I returned to Seattle, Nixon's regional campaign staff came to North Dakota to undo whatever Rockefeller's visit might have gained him.

I visited Bob Finch in Washington shortly after my North Dakota adventure. It was perhaps some measure of Nixon's relationship with President Eisenhower that the Vice President had offices in the Senate Office Building, rather than in or near the White House. His quarters there were no larger than those of the average Senator; Bob Finch and Rose Mary Woods, Charles McWhorter, Loie Gaunt and six or eight other aides were crammed into the three rooms. On a tour of the cubby-holes and partitioned crannies I met, in quick succession, people who would importantly reappear during Nixon's White House years.

Finch, of course, was to have an unhappy term as Secretary of Health, Education and Welfare. He introduced me to L. Patrick Gray, a retired Navy officer, who was doing office chores for the Vice President. At another desk was Major Robert Cushman, U.S. Marine Corps, one of Nixon's military aides, who was to be Nixon's 1969 choice for Deputy Director of the CIA.

Several months later Finch sent me to Los Angeles to observe John F. Kennedy's organization in action at the Democratic Convention in the new Los Angeles Municipal Sports Arena. Finch told me Nixon was convinced Kennedy would be the nominee, in spite of strong efforts by Lyndon Johnson, Stuart Symington and a people's movement that was trying to revive Adlai Stevenson as a candidate. Finch sent me to his old friend the Mayor of Los Angeles, Norris Poulson, who was a Nixon ally. Poulson reached into his desk and produced several sets of Democratic Convention passes and badges. With them I could pose as a delegate, journalist or "distinguished guest" so that I could move freely around the floor of the Democrats' convention and into the press areas and caucus rooms.

I kept my eyes and ears open, attended six or seven state caucuses and sat in the front row of the gallery to watch the struggle among Kennedy, Lyndon Johnson and Adlai Stevenson's ragtag supporters. I even managed to wander into John Kennedy's inner sanctum to watch his people at work. The Kennedy operation was slick, well financed and ruthless in its treatment of Lyndon Johnson's Southerners and the uncredentialed mob that was trying to stampede the convention for Stevenson.

I wrote Finch a long report of my impressions. Some of them weren't very prescient; I left Los Angeles believing Kennedy had lost the South. (Southern delegates told me bitterly that they felt they had been steamrollered. The selection of Lyndon Johnson as Kennedy's Vice Presidential running mate seemed to me crassly expedient. I didn't believe it could be sold to Southerners, or anyone else.) But I also came away with tremendous respect for the Kennedy organization.

Almost at once Haldeman asked me to go to Chicago to help prepare for the Republican Convention at the stockyards. There, under Haldeman's direction, I worked at both the hotel and the auditorium, arranging the Vice President's airport arrival, parade and hotel appearance—in short, I did straight advance work. (I realized afterward that I had known almost nothing of what was really going on. That year I saw and understood more of the Democratic Convention than the Republican. I certainly had better credentials and could move around the convention more easily in Los Angeles. I was far from the inner circle of Nixon aides who engineered his flight to New York to meet with Nelson Rockefeller, for example. I first learned of that from television news. Nor did I know any of Nixon's campaign plans until I was called into a meeting Finch and Haldeman were having with four delegates from Hawaii.)

After winning the nomination, Nixon decided to begin his campaign in Hawaii. It was then a new state, and Nixon would be the first Presidential candidate ever to campaign there. It would be the ultimate "historic first."*

---

* There was a running gag on any Nixon campaign; everything that happened was "a historic first." Every campaign speech claimed at least one, however mundane. The Hawaiian trip to four islands was Nixon's first stop as nominee, Hawaii's first Presidential campaign, and Oahu's, and Maui's and Kauai's too.

During that trip Nixon also had his first meeting with Harry Bridges, the left-wing leader of the International Longshoremen's and Warehousemen's Union, a powerful political force in the Islands. While the crowd at the huge Nixon rally in the brightly lit Kapiolani Park amphitheater cheered and shouted during the warm-up entertainment, Nixon and Bridges met in the dark behind the bandshell. What they said was not for an advance man to know—I arranged the time and place, made sure Nixon arrived, then hurried off to make sure the motorcade cars were parked in the right place.

We had learned all about positioning motorcades at our advance men's school. Haldeman was very fussy about motorcades. To teach us how he wanted things done, he had brought his men into Washington during the summer for a day of lectures and a brief meeting with Vice President Nixon, who dropped by to see us.

The approved advance man's style around Nixon was super-cool. One recruit, a friend of Herbert Klein's, began taking pictures of Nixon as the candidate thanked us for the hard work we were about to do for him. Haldeman glowered at the photographer, but the Nikon didn't stop.

After Nixon left, nothing was said, but the offending amateur was immediately transferred to Klein's press operation, where he could be as uncool as he wished. On the 1960 tour, Haldeman's advance men were nameless and faceless, as unobtrusive as possible, always concerned for the candidate, never thinking of their own comfort or of their eventual scrapbooks.

We were each given a thick manual of procedure, which was to be amended almost daily by telegrams changing the kind of car Nixon would ride in, the type of podium he used, what the sign on the side of the Nixons' car should say and the hotel-room arrangement. In 1960 Nixon involved himself in such minutiae, often to the exclusion of really important things. He barraged Haldeman with complaints about the campaign schedule and logistic details, and as tour manager, Haldeman was the conduit. My advance man's manual bulged with telegrams changing and rechanging the precise specifications for platform microphones, press arrangements and marching bands.

After one particularly long campaign day, ending with an airport reception featuring an endless line of dignitaries at the foot of the stairs to greet the Vice President with hearty handshakes, a high school band to be thanked and a huge crowd to be addressed and then "worked" along the fence, Nixon finally made his way to his limousine. He turned to Haldeman as they drove away and said, with exhausted seriousness, "Bob, from now on I don't want to land at any more airports."

In September of 1960, Haldeman pulled me out of Des Moines to go into New Jersey, where there was serious trouble. A young Washington, D.C., lawyer had been sent in to advance a fourteen-hour campaign motorcade which was scheduled to take Nixon into Elizabeth, Paterson and Bergen County and other important Jersey population centers for rallies. New Jersey was a key "battleground" state for us. In Newark I discovered that our advance man, John Warner, had so offended thirteen Republican county chairmen that they were threatening to cancel the entire motorcade.

Warner was extraordinarily pompous for a young man. He had married into the very wealthy and influential Mellon family; no doubt his style went with that social territory, but it wasn't winning the hearts and minds of the New Jersey politicians he encountered.

I spent days with Ray Bateman, a young New Jersey legislator, mending those damaged political fences. The Nixon motorcade ran as scheduled, thanks to Bateman's skill. Sixteen or seventeen years later Bateman narrowly lost the New Jersey governor's race to Brendan Byrne. In spite of New Jersey, Mr. Warner was to be given posts in the Nixon Administration—Secretary of the Navy and Bicentennial Chairman—at the insistence of the Mellons and their relatives the Scaifes, who were contributors of millions of dollars to Nixon campaigns.*

I went from New Jersey to fifteen other states to set up campaign stops, motorcades, rallies and even a balloon ascension (Nixon wouldn't get into the balloon basket to have his picture taken) in cities from coast to coast.

The campaign was, for me, a kaleidoscope of airplane meals—it was always Chicken Kiev on United Airlines that year—hotel suites, rallies, telephone calls, motorcades and finally, tense exhaustion.

Nixon ended the 1960 campaign at the Ambassador Hotel in Los Angeles. I had been there for a week arranging for rooms, press facilities and a "Victory" ballroom while Nixon and the rest of the tour dashed to Alaska and three or four other states. He had rashly promised to campaign in all fifty

---

* John Warner, of course, subsequently was divorced from Cathy Mellon and married Elizabeth Taylor. In due course, their marriage was blessed with a seat in the U.S. Senate from the Commonwealth of Virginia.

states, but that weekend before the election there were several still unvisited. I overheard heated debate among his advisers; some argued that he must keep his pledge, even though the remaining states had few electoral votes and could not determine the ultimate outcome. Others urged Nixon to focus on key states in the last few days; they didn't think many people really cared whether he kept the fifty-state pledge.

In 1960 Nixon made virtually every campaign decision himself; he decided to go to Alaska and the remaining states. He felt that the promise had to be kept. The final four days of the campaign were punishing; Nixon and the others arrived at the Ambassador on Monday, in the middle of the night, totally exhausted. I later learned that Finch and the other insiders had private poll results showing Kennedy had pulled substantially ahead in the final week. Why Nixon decided to trek off to Alaska, instead of trying to turn the tide in California, Illinois or another swing state, I don't know. That remains for him to explain.

A few times I had a glimpse of the Dwight D. Eisenhower problem. Nixon and his strategists repeatedly tried to schedule the popular Eisenhower to make an appearance with Nixon at televised rallies and other campaign events. All kinds of excuses were given for Eisenhower's refusals, principally his health. I gathered that Nixon seldom talked with the President directly. Bob Finch and others negotiated with Herbert Brownell for Eisenhower's support, usually without success.

Nixon's big ticker-tape parade through New York was supposed to have Eisenhower as its centerpiece. Almost up to the moment the parade began our people were on the telephone with Brownell, begging for Eisenhower's appearance.

Rose Mary Woods frankly blamed Mamie Eisenhower for Ike's apparent reluctance to support Nixon openly. Mamie was characterized as bitter toward Nixon and overly protective of Ike's health. Whatever the reason, the lack of Ike's open support likely cost Nixon the election; the margin of defeat in the popular vote was less than 1 percent.

After the results were in, my wife and I went back to Seattle and I slept for two days. I had almost no sense of disappointment. My job had been done well enough. The exciting experience was just what I had hoped it would be. No one likes to play on a losing team, but I didn't identify my own fortunes with Nixon's. I never had any expectation of going into a Government he might form if he was elected President; when I went off to be an advance man, I really intended to return home, win or lose.

I had been impressed by Nixon's political instincts as I watched him during the early trips in 1960. Things were less hectic then, and he moved with sureness, turning situations to his advantage. I felt comfortable working for his candidacy because, I reasoned, such instincts would serve us all well if he was elected. But the last few weeks of the campaign had shown me a Nixon who was irritable, unwise and exhausted. And after the 1960 loss I returned to my Seattle life unsure of him.

CHAPTER TWO

The California Campaign

IN THE SUMMER of 1962, Rose Mary Woods called to ask me to make arrangements for the Nixon family to come to the Seattle World's Fair on a "vacation." The Nixon family was still very newsworthy; Nixon Day at the exhibition resembled a campaign stop. The press and crowds of people gathered around them wherever they went. Nixon appeared at a department store to sell copies of his new book, *Six Crises*. We had arranged for a friend's large yacht to take the Nixons overnight, after their Seattle appearances, through the San Juan Islands to Vancouver Island, Canada. Only the four Nixons, my wife and I were aboard, with a small crew. The trip was quiet, relaxed and memorable because it was the first time Nixon and I had ever had real conversations. Moreover, my wife and I had not yet become acquainted with Pat, Tricia and Julie. During a side trip (to Double Island to feed the raccoons), leisurely meals and quiet tours of Victoria, we talked for hours.

Nixon had by then decided to run for Governor of California. During our boat trip he barraged me with questions about urban problems, land use, highway location and conservation. Since my return to my law office after the 1960 campaign I had narrowed my practice to the legal aspects of land use, and I was soon immersed in planning and zoning, Federal highway controversies and some of the pioneer environmental litigation in the region. So Nixon and I talked about urban blight, the role of the State of California in land-use planning and how to clean up the air and the water. I catalogued the problems facing mayors and governors—highway location, school finance, historic preservation, urban renewal, parks and recreation—that he would be called upon to wrestle with. In my view, Nixon could have contributed much to California if he'd focused his talents on those not inconsiderable subjects. But it was evident they interested him only as campaign issues.

Nixon realized he had to understand such "local" issues if he was to campaign successfully up and down California. As we rode around Victoria in a horse-drawn surrey on a sightseeing tour, he quizzed me intensively about what we were seeing—restored neighborhoods, huge parks, a thriving business district.

Nixon first had to win the Republican gubernatorial nomination, and his bruising primary contest with Joe Schell, a rock-ribbed conservative of the old school, taught a lesson Nixon never forgot. His defeat of Schell and the do-or-die right-wingers who supported him was a costly victory; in the general election Nixon discovered that the archconservatives would not kiss and make up. It didn't matter that Nixon was to the right of his Democratic opponent, Governor Edmund "Pat" Brown. Schell's supporters refused to contribute money, come to rallies, work the precincts or—in many cases—go to the polls. Nixon had been flanked on his right while he was battling the more liberal Brown and the latter's supporters in organized labor and among the black, Chicano and Jewish voting segments. Sometime during that experience Nixon must have promised himself that he would never again alienate the politically active conservatives who can make such a difference in a close election.*

Bob Haldeman was manager of Nixon's 1962 gubernatorial campaign. He called me one summer day at my office in Seattle to beg me to come to Los Angeles to take over the scheduling desk; Nixon, he said, lacked confidence in the scheduler

---

* I think the Joe Schell experience explains, in a major way, why Barry Goldwater always had an open door to Nixon during his Presidency. Nixon's political philosophy was fundamentally conservative, but Pat Moynihan and others could and did talk him into nondoctrinaire decisions on specific issues. When the resident conservatives—notably Dr. Arthur Burns and speechwriter Pat Buchanan—or the commentators of similar persuasion complained that Nixon was straying or being led too far to the left, he would sometimes regret his tolerance for more moderate arguments. Occasionally he would actually reverse his field in response to conservative criticism, and at those times I would tip my hat to Joe Schell's ghost.

they had recruited. I could not suddenly abandon my law clients again, and I had little enthusiasm for Nixon's decision to run in California, but Haldeman was in difficulty and I was flattered that Nixon had expressed some confidence in me; I agreed to come part time.

The Nixon headquarters was on Wilshire Boulevard not far from Crenshaw. The campaign rented an apartment for me a few blocks north in one of those stucco–and–color-flood-lighted Los Angeles apartment houses with fake-looking palm trees and a swimming pool in the courtyard. The walls were thin, the rented furnishings uncomfortable, but it was only a short walk from headquarters and I wasn't there much. The second bedroom and living-room couch accommodated a stream of other transient campaigners, Nixon loyalists from other states who came in to lend a hand. Many of us saw the California race as a step toward another Presidential race, perhaps in 1968.

The California campaign staff in 1962 included a number of household-names-to-be. Bob Haldeman managed the campaign from a rented store building on Wilshire Boulevard. Down the street Herbert Kalmbach ran a field operation and did some fund raising in an old house. One of his field men was Dwight Chapin. Murray Chotiner, Bob Finch, Nick Ruwe and I did chores of all descriptions. Pete Wilson, one of our advance men, later became Mayor of San Diego and, himself, a candidate for Governor of California. Press Secretary Herb Klein had a young helper named Ronald Ziegler.

I usually worked nights at the campaign office when I was there. I could not miss seeing Murray Chotiner coming and going after hours with unidentified visitors. Haldeman told me about some aspects of campaigning I had not seen as an advance man. During that California campaign I heard and saw more dirty politics—on both sides—than in all of my 1960 national-campaign experience. The trash from our opponent's office wastebaskets was regularly collected by a friend of Chotiner's to be sifted through for information. At times I was shown Pat Brown's advance schedule, salvaged by the garbage gleaners.

Cash in large quantities was delivered to Haldeman to be used in a variety of projects; he told me cash was paid to buy editorial endorsements from local and ethnic newspapers.

The Brown campaign installed dozens of telephones to be manned by volunteers in a get-out-the-vote blitz. One evening they planned to phone thousands of registered Democrats to urge them to go to the polls. And Murray Chotiner planned to sabotage them. Someone had managed to secure the numbers of all the Brown phones from a telephone-company employee, along with some technical advice. In those days if someone called a number, then failed to hang up after the call, it was impossible to call out from that number. Trusted Nixon people with rolls of dimes therefore drove madly from pay phone to pay phone dialing the numbers on the Brown list. When a Brown volunteer answered, the Nixon caller would leave the receiver hanging in the booth, jump into his car and hurry to the next pay phone. Brown won that election largely because he was able to turn out the preponderant Democratic registration. I concluded from the vote count that we'd wasted a lot of dimes that night.

During one brief trip to Los Angeles to help with the schedule, I was called into a meeting with Bob Finch, one of his law partners and some Nixon advisers. Governor Pat Brown had charged that the Nixons had entered into racially discriminatory restrictive covenants when they bought their home in Beverly Hills. Since I specialized in real estate law, I was included in the meeting to plan Nixon's response to the charge.

Like so many California subdivision conveyances in the fifties and early sixties, the Nixons' contained a restrictive covenant against the sale of the property to any person other than a Caucasian. I saw from their signatures that Patricia and Richard Nixon had undoubtedly bought their California home subject to that discriminatory clause. And, I was told, the Brown campaign was already making maximum use of this deed, labeling the Nixons as racists.

I was taken to Nixon's pseudo-Grecian home in Truesdale Estates, on a hill behind Beverly Hills, to talk to Richard Nixon himself about the racial covenant. I discovered that his understanding of real estate conveyancing was sparse. It was my first realization that although he was then a member of a large, prestigious Los Angeles law firm, Nixon was an inexperienced lawyer who had forgotten much of what he had learned long ago in law school. He was a "business-producer" for his firm, not a practitioner. Later, in New York, he was to play the same role with an even larger firm. But when President, he would sometimes rather fatuously remind visitors that he had been a lawyer—sometimes he said he was a tax lawyer—and was no stranger to the courtroom.

He had signed the deed incorporating the racial covenants without reading them. Nixon would not admit he'd not read the covenants, but neither would he say that he had. In any case, he had signed documents agreeing to be bound by them. I told Bob Finch I could see no way around them. The Hobson's choice was to admit that he had signed something he hadn't read and have Nixon appear to be negligent, stupid or unbelievable, or to be silent and appear to be a racist. Nixon chose the latter course, perhaps upon the premise that deep in their hearts most of the people who would vote for him approved of such covenants and, doubtless, that there's a little bit of the racist in almost everyone.

Governor Pat Brown sued Haldeman, Finch and others during that 1962 campaign and they counterclaimed. Nixon sued some people too. Most of the substantive issues Nixon and I had discussed on Puget Sound and in Victoria were lost in the acrimonious rhetoric flying between the candidates. But even with all the mud-slinging I did have my first try at "working an issue" during that campaign.

California's interstate highway program was in high gear in 1962. Freeways were being cut through cities from one end of the state to the other, infuriating dislocated residents and businessmen, conservationists (later to be called environmentalists) and others. Pat Brown and his highway department were the protestors' natural targets; Richard Nixon was therefore their natural ally.

I put together a policy paper on highways and their location, got Nixon to approve it, then went to California several times to meet with the executive committee of a citizens' organization opposed to the Governor's freeway program. Nixon wanted the endorsement of that large group, and I wooed them assiduously. But most of them were liberals, of the bird-watching variety, and Richard Nixon was just too much for them to accept, even if he was right on their issue.

One trip took me to Monterey to see the leader of the anti-freeway coalition, a lawyer who practiced with a large Persian cat on his desk. With his support I spent days importuning the other leaders of the coalition on trips to Santa Barbara and Los Angeles, finally coaxing from them a lukewarm and equivocal resolution which, in the right light, might have been read as an endorsement of Nixon's highway policy, if not of Nixon himself. But by then the election was upon us.

Election night of 1962, the Nixon forces—campaign staff, contributors and hangers-on—gathered at the Hilton Hotel in Beverly Hills. Press rooms to receive the victory statements, hospitality suites for the fat cats and the usual ballroom festooned with balloons had all been provided according to H. R. Haldeman's specifications; but, as I later learned, Haldeman's heart wasn't in it.

For over a week Nixon, Finch and Haldeman had shared the realization that Pat Brown would defeat Nixon by a substantial margin. Haldeman had commissioned secret polls which showed Nixon behind, and losing ground every day. Even so, during that last week Nixon continued to campaign vigorously and Haldeman and his campaign staff spurred on the countless donors and volunteers. No one was allowed to be pessimistic, at least not in the hearing of any of the foot soldiers.

I was not privy to the discouraging polls; I genuinely believed the predictions of victory Herb Klein and Bob Finch and the others were passing out to the press and public.

Election night began in a gala Hollywood atmosphere in the public rooms downstairs at the Hilton. Haldeman ruled that I was permitted to come upstairs to the floor where Nixon and the others had their suites, but I was not invited into the candidate's presence. Instead, I watched my seniors, Haldeman and the others, come and go. I was a familiar figure, if not a confidant, and they talked freely around me. As the unhappy results began coming in, I deduced from their unguarded talk that as soon as he had arrived at the hotel on election day Nixon had begun greeting defeat with lubrication but without grace. Haldeman and the others had decided that in view of his deteriorating condition, there would be no Nixon interviews for the big TV cameras that were waiting at the far end of the hall on Nixon's floor. As the evening wore on I gathered that our candidate was good and drunk; Finch, Haldeman and Klein were apparently having some trouble keeping him away from the telephones in his suite and buttoned up inside his room.

About eight the next morning, Haldeman instructed that a few cars should be assembled at a side door to carry Nixon away from the hotel while Herb Klein held a diversionary press conference. As Nixon and six or seven of us walked quickly down the hall toward the cars, Nixon glanced through the open door of the press room and saw Klein, the reporters and assembled cameras. At once, on impulse, he turned and went through the door, up onto the low dais where Klein was beginning his concession to the victorious Brown. Herb was caught by surprise, but quickly recovered and mumbled some words of introduction as Nixon took over.

It was one time that Richard Nixon vented—in public—

what he was really thinking. He was hung over, trembling and red-eyed, but his voice was as strong as ever.

The press, he said, wouldn't have Richard Nixon to kick around anymore.

Nixon talked for less than five minutes, during which he announced his retirement from politics. Then he turned back to that open hall door and resumed his walk to the car.

After Nixon drove away, my wife and I had breakfast with Herb Kaplow, who had covered the Nixon campaign for NBC. Like Kaplow, the others who saw and heard Nixon that morning knew him well. They had been traveling with him for years and had seen him on hundreds of platforms. They sat within fifty feet of him in the Beverly Hilton that morning, under bright lights. They couldn't help seeing his condition. Kaplow talked about it at breakfast. Yet the coverage I saw of Nixon's last hurrah made no mention of his obvious physical condition. He was ragged, jangled and going through a rough morning after. But no one wrote it that way.

That press coverage must have seemed ironic to Nixon: they all wrote it as a bitter but rational retirement statement; the coverage sort of cleaned him up. As a candidate Nixon had complained throughout the 1960 campaign that the press refused to print what it knew about John F. Kennedy and his girlfriends. Instead, Jack and Jacqueline Kennedy were continually depicted as a close and loving couple—the ideal marriage. But in those days a politician's "private life" was rarely exposed by the press.

Nixon was convinced that most reporters applied a double standard—they protected their friends but would have torn him up if he'd ever strayed from the strait-and-narrow, as Kennedy and others did. For example, Wilbur Mills' drinking problem might never have been reported were it not for his own very public indiscretions. And there was widespread talk of the unreported sexual proclivities of Estes Kefauver and other members of the Congress, including Lyndon Johnson.

The reporters I talked to about their treatment of public figures stoutly denied that they treated Nixon any differently from other politicians. During the 1960 campaign a *Newsweek* reporter, Jane Brumley, was joking with some of our staff and other reporters about John Kennedy, Robert Kennedy and their sexual activities. When I next saw her I asked her to explain to me why she and the others didn't file stories exposing John Kennedy's sham "happy family" pose, against the background of his trips to Cuban bordellos and his onshore peccadillos.

Jane took the view that what Jack Kennedy did in bed had nothing to do with his fitness for high public office, and *Newsweek* wouldn't print any such story she might file. But as time passed, even some of Kennedy's close friends, like *Newsweek*'s then Washington Bureau Chief (and Jane Brumley's boss), Ben Bradlee, began to see the merits of printing stories about the private lives of politicians. By the time of Fanne Fox and Wilbur Mills, Mr. Bradlee had changed jobs and was sending his *Washington Post* reporters to listen at motel doors to confirm Elizabeth Ray's stories about Wayne Hays and other Congressmen.

After the 1962 Nixon defeat in California I resumed the full-time practice of law in Seattle. As the 1964 election campaign began to warm up, I watched with detached interest. My sympathies lay with Nelson Rockefeller, William Scranton and the other Republican moderates who were ineptly trying to derail Barry Goldwater, but I did nothing to try to get involved.

Shortly before the Republican Convention, in the summer of 1964, Bob Haldeman called to suggest that I come to San Francisco to help him arrange Nixon's part in the convention. The most recent Presidential candidate of the party is its "titular leader," according to political writers and the last-past candidates. However, the title really means nothing when it comes to arranging for that "leader's" rooms, cars, convention seats and other necessities of political life. So Nixon needed our help. He had persuaded Goldwater, William Knowland and the other convention planners that they should give him a chance to try to heal the divisions in the Republican Party. Nixon would deliver the major address the second night of the convention to try to bridge the widening gap between Goldwater's conservatives and his opponents. No one had anything to fear from Nixon. As he was fond of saying, politically he was "as dead as Kelsey's nuts," a New York lawyer and senior statesman with barely a showing in the Presidential polls.

Haldeman and I shared a small room in the St. Francis Hotel, not far from Nixon's suite, from which we attempted to ensure that Nixon's speech would be properly staged. Nixon (and we) had hopes that a show-stopping speech might revive him politically. Nixon and some writers had slaved over his text in New York, and he polished it as he waited in the hotel, refusing all interviews or other distractions.

I went to the Cow Palace intending to walk through the route Nixon would take from his car to a holding room (where he would wait until introduced) and up onto the platform. But the convention had begun, and I had no tickets or badges to admit me to the areas I needed to see. I was sent to the credentials office, where I discovered that the keeper of the passes was a former Nixon staff man, Jack Wooley. He had been the fellow in the Nixon scheduling office who was my telephone contact all through my advancing adventures in the 1960 campaign; he was now a Goldwater loyalist. Thanks to auld lang syne (and Wooley's suspicion that Nixon was still a force to be reckoned with) I came away with my pockets loaded with credentials of all kinds.

All that day the Goldwater people had been packing the hall with friendly folks, giving them ribbons and badges designating their wearers "Junior Sergeant at Arms." By late afternoon the legal, safe capacity of the Cow Palace had been far exceeded. At a side gate I found Senator Edward Brooke of Massachusetts and three black friends being turned away. I tried to talk them past the fire marshal, but Brooke lacked the magic spangled badges Wooley had given me. The Senator was mad and getting madder, so I went in and found Wooley to warn him of the senatorial problem he had at the side gate. Eventually Brooke and his party were admitted, but as a result of the overcrowding and incidents like Brooke's, Wooley earned a reputation for running the most fouled-up ticket and credential operation in modern Republican history.

Leonard Garment had his first taste of Republican internecine warfare that week. Garment was then one of Nixon's partners in the New York law firm where Nixon had found shelter after the 1962 defeat. Nixon had invited to San Francisco as his personal staff Len Garment; Patrick Buchanan, the speechwriter; Rose Mary Woods, Nixon's secretary, and her assistant, Shelley Skarney.

Leonard Garment joined me in Nixon's box at the convention in time to see and feel the power of conservative Republicanism, which in 1964 was epitomized by the Goldwater forces and the huge, fist-shaking William F. Knowland. Knowland was a U.S. Senator, and that night he was the leader of the cowboy-suited California delegation. Knowland was down in the front row, leading the charge against Nelson Rockefeller as Rockefeller tried to speak to the convention. Garment and I were deeply troubled when Rockefeller was booed off the platform by Knowland and the Goldwaterites.

Nixon's speech, on the other hand, was as well received as he had hoped it would be. He was generously welcomed, and after he spoke there was long and strong applause.

Later that night Nixon opened his suite and received some of the old Nixon troops. Haldeman had ordered food and a small bar, and we stood around and reminisced with Charlie McWhorter, Bob Finch and the others who came by to congratulate their twice-downed candidate on his apparent resurrection. As the evening grew late, however, Nixon became loudly celebratory.

It didn't take much alcohol to affect Richard Nixon under the best of circumstances. And after a speech, debate or other major appearance he seemed particularly susceptible. It took hours for him to unwind and come down from events in which he'd invested intense preparation and emotion. In the campaigns of 1960 and 1962 he had occasionally resorted to pills or liquor after major appearances to help him sleep. So this San Francisco episode should not have surprised me, but as it unfolded I was offended by it. At the end of the evening, when there were only eight or nine of us remaining, Nixon made some clumsy passes at a young woman in the group. No one made any attempt to rescue the embarrassed girl or deflect Nixon, and he persisted. She appeared as unwilling to offend him as the rest of us, but at last she escaped the arm he'd draped over her shoulder. She blushed brightly and left the suite. The rest of us soon said our good-nights and left Haldeman to steer Nixon to bed.

I returned to Seattle the next day, convinced that Nixon's drinking could cost him any chance of a return to public life.

After seeing Nixon briefly during several campaign trips he made to the Northwest to support 1966 Congressional candidates, I was invited to a small meeting in New York to talk about his political future. This nucleus of loyalists included Peter Flanigan, Maurice Stans and some other Easterners I did not know. Nixon was showing up well in the early polls versus Ronald Reagan, Nelson Rockefeller, George Romney and other possible nominees. It was the consensus of the gathering that he should make the run in 1968.

After the meeting I called Rose Mary Woods and asked for an appointment to talk with Nixon privately.

We met in his office at Nixon, Mudge, Rose, Guthrie and Alexander, a room I recall principally for its Vice Presidential decorations and its lack of any view of the New York skyline.

I told Nixon that it seemed obvious that he would be running again in 1968 and that I would be asked again to help him. He responded that he had not yet decided what to do. I said that, all things being equal, he would have my support, but that I was very much troubled by his drinking. I was in no position to ask him to stop, nor would I ever intrude that way into anyone's personal life. But, I continued, I didn't want to invest my time in a difficult Presidential campaign that might well be lost because the candidate was not fully in control of himself. Nixon asked if I thought that was why he had lost in 1960 or 1962; I said I didn't think so, although his impulsive press conference after the election in California in 1962 was one episode of the kind I feared should he run again.

Nixon didn't try to brush me off or change the subject, as I had anticipated he might. He said that if he decided to run he wanted my help. He felt it was not unreasonable of me to expect that he would keep himself in the best of condition in a campaign. Everyone had a right to expect that of him. He thanked me for coming to talk to him about it. I understood his reply to be an undertaking, *quid pro quo*. If he wanted me to work for him he would lay off the booze.

And as far as I'm concerned, he kept that bargain during the 1968 campaign.

CHAPTER THREE

The 1968 Convention

IN THE FALL of 1967, Richard Nixon called to ask me to come to New York for a three-day school for his advance men. His campaign had begun and he needed help. The New Hampshire, Wisconsin and Oregon primaries were only a few months off, and the Nixons would be on the political road constantly in the late winter and early spring.

The Nixon candidacy was strong in the primary states' polls. He was showing up well against Romney, Reagan and Rockefeller. If Humphrey was the Democrat, Nixon had a good chance to win.

I had to decide whether or not to go. My law practice had grown; but now there were enough young men working for us to do most of my work for a while. Our children were settled and busy in the Seattle suburb where we lived. I was away frequently looking after my clients' business all over the country; I rationalized that my absence would be nothing different for my family.

By 1967 I had an eight-year investment in Nixon's political career, and 1968 looked like the year when he might win one, after those losses in 1960 and 1962. There were things about Nixon that I didn't like, of course. But by now I had an equity in his candidacy, and he was my only entrée into the big political game I had learned to play.

I was more and more bored with my personal life and profession. Once again, to go off campaigning would be an adventure and a relief. At the time, I didn't admit to myself very much of how I felt about my Seattle existence. Consciously, I was dissatisfied with the level of challenge there. As in 1960, I saw others moving in what appeared to be the mainstream of public life, and I envied them. That much I could admit to myself. And that admission was enough.

My dissatisfaction was not anything that I talked to anyone about. I told my wife this new campaign was an opportunity and a duty (but perhaps, as she said later, she knew it was an escape). I simply told my family and partners that I had decided to go off to the political wars once again, and I left with their support.

John Whitaker, a geologist and an accomplished amateur politician, had opened a small office in Washington to handle Nixon's schedule. Dwight Chapin, Pat Buchanan and John Davies (on loan from AT&T) were the skeleton Nixon traveling staff who made arrangements, carried the bags, wrote the speeches and followed up with the endless thank-you letters to the local people who helped along the way. But now the staff would expand. Media experts, more speechwriters and a full-scale operations office would soon appear.

Thirty-four men were recruited to become advance men in 1967. Among them was Ron Ziegler, by then working with Bob Haldeman in Los Angeles.

In early 1968 I began spending several days a week in Oregon as Nixon's proconsul, trying to improve the performance of Nixon's local chairman and his volunteers. As we came closer to the day of the Oregon primary I advanced an elaborate campaign trip into the state for the Nixons, their daughters and young David Eisenhower, Julie's fiancé.

During that Nixon visit to Portland, Robert Kennedy announced his candidacy from the large Senate caucus room in Washington. When he declared for the Presidency he was surrounded by the Kennedy clan and the old John Kennedy crowd. Four or five of us sat with Richard Nixon as Bobby Kennedy made his speech for the television cameras. When it was over and the hotel-room TV was turned off, Nixon sat and looked at the blank screen for a long time, saying nothing. Finally he shook his head slowly. "We've just seen some very terrible forces unleashed," he said. "Something bad is going to come of this." He pointed at the screen. "God knows where this is going to lead."

Even before the Oregon primary I was tapped for a far more interesting job. The Republican Convention was to be held in Miami Beach in August of 1968. Bob Haldeman called me in February to ask that I join him there to meet with Peter Flanigan and others to do some early convention planning.

Since Flanigan's father was on the board of directors of the Hilton Hotels, Peter was indispensable to our first meeting with the owner of the Miami Beach Hilton as we sought to rent his hotel for the two weeks of the convention. Congressman William Cramer and other Florida allies of Nixon came by to give us advice on the local political situation (which was chaotic—the party was badly split). We walked through the convention hall and talked about the houses, trailers, offices, cars and boats we might need.

Haldeman and a number of his J. Walter Thompson advertising protégés were about to leave their jobs to work full time on Nixon's primary campaigns. Dwight Chapin, Larry Higby, Ron Ziegler and Ken Cole all came from Thompson (and eventually would take White House jobs). Longtime Nixon workers like John Whitaker, John Nidecker, Nick Ruwe, Roy Goodearle, Herb Klein and Murray Chotiner were assembling, along with Len Garment, Peter Flanigan, John Mitchell and a number of new adherents.

In early May, Bill Timmons and I opened a small office in an out-of-the-way building in Miami Beach. There were no signs on our door. I lived next to the very posh Bath Club, at Willard Rockwell's private beach hotel, The Flamingo, which he maintained for the use of his friends. For most of the spring I was its only guest. Rent-free, of course. Bill Timmons was given a house in Coral Gables.

Much of my time was spent negotiating exceptions from the convention rules to permit our people additional telephones, trailers and other facilities at the hall. We agreed to pay an arm and a leg for the rooms and facilities we needed at the Hilton. To prevent incursion by the press and our opponents, we took stringent security measures, including fencing off the fire escapes, to safeguard the top four floors, where Nixon,

Haldeman, Mitchell, Richard Kleindienst and our convention staff would have offices. I'm not sure what we thought we were protecting ourselves from, but with all the security guards, badges, credentials and checkpoints we made it impossible for anyone—often including ourselves—to gain access to the offices at the top of the Hilton.

As Timmons and I assembled a small group of helpers and began to tackle our list of logistical problems, we began to regret our choice of the Hilton as the Nixon headquarters. One day the manager called to say he'd be preempting our reservation of two sleeping rooms on one of the lower floors of the hotel. We'd reserved virtually the entire hotel to house our staff and major financial contributors. But the mortgage on the hotel was held by the Teamsters' union, the manager explained, and they wanted to house two of their friends there during the convention.

"Who?" I asked. "Well, as a matter of fact, it was a couple of journalists." "Who?" "Drew Pearson and Jack Anderson." "No! Of all the reporters in the world, not those two!" I yelled. Nixon would have a stroke on the very eve of his nomination; they were his deadliest foes. At last the Hilton manager backed down and peace was restored. But I wondered how Pearson and Anderson had arranged to have the Teamsters put the bite on the hotel. And I sometimes imagined the look on Nixon's face if he had happened to run into Pearson and Anderson in the Hilton elevator one day.

About a month before the convention, Peter Flanigan asked that I fly to Dallas to meet Ross Perot, to respond to Perot's offer of help. A small blond man in his late thirties, Perot was the principal owner of Electronic Data Systems Corporation, which had thrived from the day Perot left IBM to form his own computer company. He had decided to support Nixon for President, but Perot rarely did the ordinary. He would support his candidate not merely with money but by furnishing the campaign with some of his men, a hand-picked cadre of young former military officers who had been recruited and trained at the Perot Dallas headquarters to help run EDS.

Perot greeted me from behind an oversized desk. His office was decorated with polished wood plaques bearing Perot's credos. "EAGLES DON'T FLY IN FLOCKS" was one. There were carved eagles and statues of eagles all around the office.

During a quick lunch in the basement of his building, Perot restated his offer. He would furnish ten of his best men and pay their salaries and expenses through the campaign. But we had to agree to use them in responsible positions. Perot wanted his men to come out of the experience with some breadth of perception they could not have gained otherwise.

I was taken into an empty classroom to interview my prospects. But I was not to meet them yet. Perot had arranged for videotapes to be shown on a large screen, displaying some of his men talking about themselves. I viewed tapes all afternoon, then came back the next morning to meet several of the men I'd selected from the videotapes and three who were to be interviewed in person.

Perot gave us superb people. One, Vernon Olson, was to be my right hand all through the campaign. The others worked at a variety of other jobs. Thomas Meurer helped John Nidecker with the "rally" activities at the convention—demonstrations, balloon drops, even our poor, sickly elephant which chronically suffered from heat exhaustion—and Tom went on to become a premier advance man. I'm not sure that elephant care enhanced Tom's value to Ross Perot, but Nixon was surely fortunate to have Perot's men.* In the last days of the campaign Perot lent us two researchers to help plan what we should do to effect an orderly transition from Lyndon Johnson to Richard Nixon, because by then it looked almost certain that Nixon would win. The help they gave us was influential in structuring our transition policy apparatus and in organizing the early White House staff.

When the New York and Washington offices of the Nixon campaign began to arrive in Miami Beach for the convention on August 1, our months of preparation were put to the test.

First to collapse was our telephone system. The preeminent Nixon loyalist at American Telephone and Telegraph, John Davies, had prescribed a special switchboard at the Hilton to serve the telephones in our offices on the upper floors, the direct lines to our Nixon delegate-watchers at each of their thirty-five hotels, our trailers at the convention hall and our motor pool. But within hours it was evident that the system was totally inadequate. One of Haldeman's admen, Ken Cole, stepped in to deal with telephone-company engineers, because

---

* During the White House years, Ross Perot was a frequent visitor. He was included at state dinners and businessmen's conferences; from time to time he called to warn of some problem we faced that we might not have heard of. But he asked for my help only once. He called to tell me that he had built a small fishing cabin on the shore of a Bureau of Reclamation lake in Texas some years before, but now the Bureau was trying to cancel his lease. It was my pleasure to try to save his cabin for him.

John Davies was totally absorbed with new telephone problems at the convention hall.

Dick Kleindienst, Nixon's field strategist, had talked Nixon into meeting with a series of the state delegations, and one of Kleindienst's people had selected the Palace Room at the Hilton for these stroking sessions. But there were other events already scheduled in that room, and the Hilton would charge us a huge price to "tear down" the room for the Kleindienst meetings. We suggested to Kleindienst that we save money by moving his delegation meetings to the American Scene Room, but he adamantly refused. Engraved invitations had already been sent to each delegate in Kleindienst's name. He had invited them to the Palace Room.

Finally Peter Flanigan came up with the answer. As in Shakespeare, an equally sweet rose resulted when Bill Timmons' sign painter prepared two signs, merely switching the names of the rooms. Just for Tuesday morning the American Scene became the Palace.

When the Nixon headquarters staff all arrived in Florida, we could see that there were signs of bad blood in our home office. Former Congressman Robert Ellsworth had been executive director of the Nixon effort in its early stages, and Ellsworth was still listed as one of Nixon's political advisers. But Ellsworth and John Mitchell were not getting along well.*

In Miami Beach the elevators, lobbies and halls of the Hilton were jammed day and night. Our elaborate badge system was intended to ensure that the offices on our working floors were protected from all that congestion, but it took a long time to get by the checkpoints where credentials were examined. And the area between the hotel entrance and the elevators was often impassable with wall-to-wall humanity.

One cause of our problems was that John Mitchell had brought us about twice the campaign staff we'd been told to expect. At the last minute we were housing our unexpected

_____

* Once Nixon was in the White House, Bob Ellsworth and another political operator, John Sears, were hired and then fired within months. Ellsworth was given the NATO ambassadorship (a kind of way station en route to the exit—a departure route that Don Rumsfeld later also took), while Sears was merely bounced. Behind both the Ellsworth and Sears firings one could see John Mitchell's fine hand and his considerable influence on Richard Nixon. Nixon once told me he no longer trusted Bob Ellsworth—he just didn't feel comfortable with him. It seemed clear to me that John Mitchell shared, if not inspired, those sentiments.

colleagues in third-rate hotels up and down the beach, revising our ticket lists and padding our credentials requests to try to get them into the convention.

Maurice Stans, Herb Kalmbach and their fund raisers had first claim on several hundred choice suites and rooms in three hotels on the beach where they housed their fat cats. As Kleindienst and the political operation looked to the care and feeding of the delegates who would cast their ballots at the convention, Stans and his people saw to the well-being of those who would finance our campaign. A hospitality suite was established on one of the lower floors of the Hilton where Stans, Mitchell and Lucy Winchester, among others, greeted the big contributors with food and drink at all hours. Buses transported them to the convention. The candidate would personally greet them at a special reception.

I spent my early-August days dealing with crises. Our bus contractor rebelled. Nixon decided at the last minute to add an early-morning press conference to the Tuesday schedule, so we needed a room, chairs, lights and a public-address system that worked. John Volpe, Governor of Massachusetts, had not been provided with a limousine. Richard Nixon's brother Don had bulldozed a Hilton room clerk into giving one of his friends a room that had been promised to one of Maury Stans' fat cats. (We moved Don's friend to some rooms we had about fourteen miles north.)

When the delegates began to arrive in Miami Beach our convention crew welcomed each one, individually. Ed Morgan was a new Nixon advance man from Phoenix, where he practiced law. He and the Cudlip brothers (from Grosse Pointe, Michigan) were put in charge of a gigantic greeting operation. Ed and the Cudlips, with some thirty volunteers, operated out of a suite of hectic, overcrowded offices they somehow scrounged at Miami International Airport.

The week before the convention, Ed and his staff called each delegate at home to learn his exact travel plans. When Mr. and Mrs. Ed Gopher of St. Paul got on flight 298, their arrival time and gate number were assigned to two members of the "Sunshine Squad." When they stepped off their plane, Mr. and Mrs. Gopher were greeted by a small brass band and fifteen or twenty young people holding hand-lettered signs reading "WELCOME GOPHERS," "WELCOME ED AND GLORIA," "MIAMI LOVES NIXON DELEGATES" or perhaps "GO, GO, GO-PHERS," and the two local Miami Nixon supporters assigned to the Minnesota couple would present them with "NIXON'S THE ONE" red-white-and-blue airline bags crammed with gifts, guidebooks and Nixon brochures. The local people escorted the Gophers to a free bus festooned with Nixon decorations. Someone retrieved their luggage and helped with airline problems. Drinks and snacks were served aboard the bus as it crossed Biscayne Bay to Miami Beach. The local hospitality-squad members offered to show the Gophers around after they accompanied them to their hotel rooms.

Producing the signs and rushing the hired band from gate to gate as the thousands of delegates and alternates arrived was a monumental job. One room at the airport was stacked high with the used personal signs no one had time to dispose of. Morgan, the Cudlips and their volunteers developed an *esprit* and effectiveness that were the envy of our rivals.

Recruiting volunteer help had been one of our major tasks in the months before the convention. We lured Miamians with promises of tickets to the convention. By signing them up early we made it difficult for the late-arriving Rockefeller and Reagan organizers to find local Republicans who would work for them. The Rockefeller organization partly solved its problem by bringing in young New Yorkers in a steady stream of railroad trains. What a budget they must have had!

As a matter of fact, we hired people too.

Haldeman had created an operation designed to co-opt much of the available network television coverage at the convention. At all hours there were pro-Nixon events staged to tempt the attention of network television producers; we hired that indisposed elephant, stilt-walkers, acrobats, flotillas of small boats and legions of beautiful young women who successfully attracted the cameras.

Wilt Chamberlain, the basketball player, was ensconced in a suite at the Hilton to give interviews and make appearances for our candidate. As he towered above the convention crowds, he was the ultimate in visible black support. But the young staff man assigned to look to our big ballplayer's needs rendered periodic, horrified reports of Mr. Chamberlain's appetites, requests, tastes, demands and insatiable requirements. One tangible manifestation was his hotel bill, which included thousands of dollars of charges from the men's haberdashery at the Hilton.

By any measurement, our convention operation was a success. In spite of spasmodic problems, people were housed, fed and given the equipment to get our man nominated. Before it was over I had been asked to run the campaign tour, train the Nixon and Agnew advance men and help plan the candidate's schedule.

So, with a wave to my law partners, I went from Florida to New York to rent airplanes, walkie-talkies and all the other equipment we would need to take Richard Nixon back and forth across the nation from Labor Day to Election Day.

CHAPTER FOUR

Campaigning

THEY JUST DON'T campaign for President the way they used to. But I suspect they will again sometime; campaign reform comes and goes.

In the 1960 campaign, there were dirty tricks on the Nixon side and also on the John Kennedy side. But the Nixon campaign staff always felt a bit outclassed; the Kennedy fellows were really much better at the dirty stuff than we were.

Nixon's 1960 campaign managers were Leonard Hall and Robert Finch. James Bassett and Congressman Robert Wilson handled scheduling and the advance work. Hall was a Long Island politician of the old school, allied with Nelson Rockefeller and identified with the orthodox Republican Party organization, such as it was. The others were old Nixon friends from California. Finch was on Vice President Nixon's staff, had worked for him for years and was being groomed by Nixon for some always-elusive elective office. Finch was elected once—he became Lieutenant Governor of California under Ronald Reagan in 1966—but he was really cut out for the Congress. He was photogenic, could give a pretty good speech and had an easy smile. In Congress it seems to help if you're a little scattered and disorganized, and Bob Finch was that. He had no talent whatever for running a campaign, or running the Department of Health, Education and Welfare, or running anything else requiring much consistency and firmness.

Between the 1960 campaign and 1968 there was a major change in the cast of characters. Bob Finch, Bob Haldeman and Rose Mary Woods survived. Some of the 1960 advance team—John Whitaker, Ned Sullivan (a relative of Pat Nixon's), Nick Ruwe, Roy Goodearle and John Nidecker—

were also asked back to help. Whitaker became the 1968 scheduler. A few, like Herb Kalmbach and Dwight Chapin, had signed on during the 1962 gubernatorial campaign and were early recruits for the 1968 effort.

The 1968 field organization, the regional and state-by-state political technicians, were veterans of the 1964 Goldwater campaign—Richard Kleindienst and Robert Mardian, for example—and their friends.

Some Senators, Congressmen and state officials were recruited, but few of them had been Nixon workers in 1960.

William Safire and Raymond Price had done writing chores for Nixon over the intervening years, and they were back. Peter Flanigan, a young prince of Wall Street, and John Mitchell, Leonard Garment and Tom Evans, Nixon's law partners, took roles once held by Herbert Brownell, Walter Williams, Fred Seaton and Robert Hill, all of whom had been political powers around Nixon in the Eisenhower years.

Only Maurice Stans, Eisenhower's budget director, and William Rogers, his Attorney General, bridged the two administrations. Stans served as finance director of the 1968 Nixon campaign and then became Nixon's Secretary of Commerce, and Rogers became Secretary of State.

In the staffing of the 1968 campaign, many old Nixon loyalists were shunted to insubstantial or honorary roles to make room for more able and efficient newcomers. Bob Finch, manager of the 1960 campaign, had a standing invitation to ride along on the 1968 campaign plane and was given an office and title at the New York headquarters. But aside from occasional assignments from John Mitchell and tasks Finch invented for himself, there was nothing for him to do. (During his White House tenure, after leaving the Department of Health, Education and Welfare, Finch was vested once again with an impressive office and title, but no portfolio.)

Murray Chotiner had managed Nixon's Senate campaign against Helen Gahagan Douglas in California in 1950. Chotiner was a dark, slick-haired political operator who managed to find a niche in every subsequent Nixon campaign, notwithstanding his notorious reputation for dirty tactics. Nixon knew that Chotiner's very presence would inflame some of the press corps; Chotiner's long tenure resulted partly from Nixon's chronic reluctance to do away with an old supporter and partly from Nixon's pleasure in irritating the reporters who found Chotiner so objectionable. As President, Nixon hired Chotiner as a White House "special counsel" to do political chores and also to do things for Nixon no one else would.*

Chotiner was a fellow who always seemed to be in the process of divorce, while enjoying the company of yet another beautiful blonde. He spoke softly and slowly. The press pictured him as a ruthless and tough politician, and I had expected him to be a dese-and-dose pol with a big cigar; but his manner was just the opposite.

In 1968, Chotiner obtained the services of someone who looked and acted enough like a reporter to be accredited to the Humphrey campaign (and again to the McGovern campaign in 1972). Almost every day Chotiner's "mole" on the Humphrey press plane would send us lengthy reports describing the morale, internal operating problems and off-the-record or unreported comments of the opposition campaign staff and candidate and (often more important) the candidate's wife. This operative was known as Chapman's Friend. Those daily bulletins seldom provided truly important or valuable information, but they often served up tasty gossip. Confusion or distress among the Democrats encouraged us. Once in a while our press secretary would give a favored reporter an anonymous tidbit from Chapman's Friend and later we'd see it on the network news or in a wire-service report as an inside story from the Humphrey campaign.

Such espionage was a part of all the Nixon campaigns I was involved in. But while all this was going on in Nixon's campaigns, the counterspies were always hard at work. In 1960 a giant Nixon rally in San Francisco's Union Square was thoroughly sabotaged by John Kennedy's merry men. In the middle of Nixon's speech the microphone and lighting cables were cut by someone who crawled under the platform and clipped them neatly. One of Governor Pat Brown's fellows still brags about the sabotage he did on Nixon motorcades in 1962. In the 1968 campaign, we had all kinds of trouble from coast to coast: organized heckling, sabotaged public-address systems and ambushes of rocks and eggs.

In 1968, Nixon demanded that his staff conduct his cam-

---

* Chotiner's presence on the White House staff ultimately created a specific embarrassment to Nixon, and Nixon told Haldeman to send Chotiner away. Murray Chotiner did as he was told; he became a Washington lawyer—but we continued to hear from him. He lobbied effectively for his clients and, occasionally, did political errands for the White House from the outside. Nixon spoke sentimentally of him even after he had fired him, but it was obvious that Murray had used up his equity in some specific way I was never told about.

paign as if we were in an all-out war. As tour manager of the campaign, I had countless talks with Nixon about the jeering and heckling that drowned him out at rallies. The press sometimes reported that Nixon coolly refused to let the shouting bother him, but in the privacy of his cabin on the airplane it was obvious that he was extremely upset by the opposition's tactics.

His solution was to order me to have the Secret Service rough up the hecklers. But I assured him that our Service detail, with whom I worked very closely, would not risk the charge that it had stifled "legitimate political dissent." So, as an alternative, Nixon wanted me to create some kind of flying goon squad of our own to rough up the hecklers, take down their signs and silence them. At times my advance man would report that a local police department, sympathetic to Nixon, had offered to ensure our freedom from hecklers. We always accepted such offers—in fact, we sometimes solicited them. If local police wanted to give the bum's rush to screamers and chanters, they were shown our gratitude. Occasionally, we would even pay cash money for that kind of help. In 1968, especially in October, the disruptions became so constant and boisterous that we considered canceling our remaining public rallies. But we decided we couldn't do that; those were the events which produced much of our television news coverage. Instead, when the event was important, we went to elaborate lengths to screen those attending.

Ed Morgan, surely the wittiest and most resourceful of all our advance men, devised a screening system that should find its way into campaign annals as the best of its kind. The Nixons and the Agnews were scheduled to gather on the platform of Madison Square Garden for a nationally televised rally of gigantic importance on October 31, 1968. The Nixon campaign was paying a fortune to buy the network television time and another fortune for promotional advertising to attract a huge TV audience. The word came loud and clear: there was to be *no* heckling on *our* paid television time in *our* rented arena. It was up to the campaign staff to ensure that the TV viewer saw only wild enthusiasm.

I delegated the problem to Ed Morgan and offered him the help of any of the campaign tour staff. He chose six of our most experienced men to work with him. He moved them into New York and spent ten days setting up The Great Madison Square Garden Rally Scam.

Admission was to be by ticket only. Morgan had thousands of extra tickets printed and distributed; the only way to be sure the press would say that Nixon spoke to an overflow crowd was to print and hand out ten times as many tickets as we had seats to be filled. Buses were hired to bring the Nixon faithful from the solid Republican suburbs of Westchester County, Suffolk County and northern New Jersey. These certified loyalists were provided with reserved seats between the television cameras and the platform. The twenty rows immediately in front of the speakers' rostrum were for the Youth for Nixon delegations from colleges and high schools in the area, Nixonettes in their uniforms and the paid staff people from our Washington and New York campaign offices. They could be counted upon to cheer lustily at all times.

The evening of the rally, as the thousands of general-ticket holders arrived at the Garden they passed through a couple of roped-off, one-way chutes manned by Morgan's men. Anyone who looked like a potential troublemaker was directed to a door on the right, while putative good guys went left. The right-hand door led to a one-way hall, then down a flight of stairs into a corridor which brought them to another door. Out the door was truly *out;* the traveler who was carrying a megaphone, a hostile sign or a McGovern haircut found himself on the street.

If the ticket holder returned to the entrance and complained, he was profusely apologized to, his ticket was reexamined and he was directed to an office in a nearby building. Apparently, he was told, there was a problem with his ticket. At the office he was courteously requested to wait in the reception room until someone in charge could help him. After the Garden was completely filled, Morgan phoned the office to close the operation down. Those still in the reception room were told to return to the Garden. There they were informed by fire marshals that all seats were taken and they could not be admitted.

The lower floors of the Garden, deep beneath the main floor, teemed with New York police, our private security officers, Garden security men and Secret Service agents. At least some of that army had sworn to remove bodily any demonstrators who threatened a dissenting voice. But thanks to the great Morgan ticket scam, there were only one or two hidden signs unfurled during the candidates' speeches, and they were far back in the unlighted recesses of the upper seating. There was no disruptive chanting or heckling; the television audience saw only the thunderous cheering of a friendly, enthusiastic crowd of enlightened American voters.

A candidate seldom enjoys the advantages we had in the

Garden that night. Usually he's on a makeshift platform out in the open, at a shopping center or in front of a courthouse. The television people are looking for something different; they have heard the candidate's basic speech a dozen times or more. So a clever heckler, or a bunch of placard wavers or chanters, have a good chance of showing up on the evening news.

We tried to persuade the film crews covering our trip not to shine their lights and point their cameras at those people. After all, the real story is the candidate's fabulous reception by the forty thousand other citizens at the rally, not the shrieks of the ten or twelve dissidents.

You suggest to your advance man that he suggest to the local committee that they devise some techniques of their own to deal with the problem. There can be no violence, of course. That would be unlawful—and besides, that would be the lead story on the news: "Violence today marred the visit of Candidate X to the usually peaceful town of PQR as eleven outspoken opponents of Mr. X were sent to the hospital with unknown injuries." No, local committees should be persuaded to think about bringing in a couple of hundred loyalists with their own placards and banners to come between the cameras and any protesters. If they want to chant, let's have our people chant louder; if they're drowned out, protesters usually quit. If they are outnumbered and surrounded, they'll usually go away.

All this strife is hard on a candidate. After five or six weeks on the road, doing six or more events a day, he's tired and edgy. He's having trouble thinking about what he's saying even under the best of conditions. When he's heckled or harassed he gets mad, and when he gets mad he's not an effective candidate. He may even appear to be an unpredictable and dangerous one.

Even Nixon's super-efficient 1968 campaign had its share of unforeseen adversity. After we'd made two campaign trips to Cleveland and its suburbs, Ohio Governor James Rhodes talked our schedulers into sending us to Cleveland a third time, late in the campaign. Rhodes wanted us to have a big, conventional evening rally in the civic auditorium in the center of the city. One of our best advance men, Charles Stuart, was sent into Cleveland a week in advance and did everything right to set it up and build a crowd.

It's a well-known fact of campaigning that Americans don't just go to political rallies; they are *gotten* to go. Our advance men were trained always to send buses to the suburbs to bring in our loyalists. Hundreds of thousands of handbills were distributed downtown at noon. Thousands of tickets were passed out. Sound trucks patrolled population centers. Radio, newspaper and television ads made our rallies inescapable.

Stuart did all that and more in Cleveland. But almost no one came.

The local Nixon organization had been exhausted by our other visits there. Everyone who could be induced to come and hear the candidate had already come and heard. So when I went over to the immense auditorium to double-check things an hour before the candidate was to leave the hotel, I found few signs of life. Usually by that time a hall will be nearly full, the band will be playing and the warm-up entertainment will be under way. But not that night.

Instead, there were hundreds of rows of empty seats and a tiny, huddled throng down in front. Perhaps two hundred and eighty people were gathered in the front section. We were going to have more journalists than that in our traveling press section over at the left side of the auditorium! As I looked at all that emptiness, the television people were setting up their cameras on the raised platform against the left wall. Their pictures from Cleveland would be all about how Nixon gave a campaign and no one came.

Chuck Stuart was beside himself. His committee had placed Nixon placards upside down on every other chair; as far as the eye could see their white sticks sat up in uniform rows like skeletons, but no one was there to pick them up and wave them.

I went down the checklist with Stuart: publicity, tickets, handbills, even the buses. He'd done it all. So I went across the street to tell Richard Nixon what he was about to experience.

There is a Nixon campaign legend about the time Bob Finch delivered Nixon to a Polish social hall for a hand-shaker with the ethnics, and the hall was empty. That happened because Finch got his dates a little mixed up. The Poles had all been there the day before. Having heard stories about Nixon's reaction to that empty hall, I was not looking forward to telling him how things were going to be across the street in Cleveland.

"There's almost no one there," I told him. He was keyed up, freshly showered and shaved, too much talc over his beard, thinking about what he was going to say that night. At first I thought he hadn't heard me. Then I could see him begin to focus on our problem.

"What about the entrance?" he asked. He was scheduled to

enter at the back of the hall and walk down the center aisle, shaking hands with the cheering throng. That was supposed to be tomorrow's television picture.

"I've changed it. Now you come out from backstage; but do you really want to do it?" I asked. "There can't be three hundred people in there, and the place holds thirty-five hundred."

"John, we've got to do it. I'll only talk a few minutes. Then I'll get off the stage and shake hands with the people. Get them all down front." He was calm, almost casual.

"That's where they are. Bunched down front."

"It's that goddamned Rhodes," he said grimly. "He insisted we come in here again. But he's not thinking about us; he thought this would help him. So he's got to be there too! You make sure he's up there on that stage with me, all the way through this."

And so he was. As Nixon was gamely speaking to his little band of loyalists I circulated through the press area over at the side. "So, what happened?" I was asked over and over. And I leveled with them: we'd just come here once too often and shouldn't have. I reminded them of the huge crowds we'd had before, one at a suburban shopping center that jammed the Cleveland highways in all directions for half a day.

Next day, although the networks reported a sparse crowd, they did so *diminuendo*. It would have been a major story if Nixon had decided to cancel or stay away from the event. But instead the press gave him a few points for his courage and equanimity.

Later they asked me what Nixon had said to or about Chuck Stuart, the advance man. I told them what happened when we returned to the hotel. Nixon had asked me to bring Stuart to see him. He knew Stuart must be feeling terrible, and he waved off the young man's apology. "These things will happen now and then," Nixon said. "If you've done all you can, don't worry. You fellows do a superb job. Our advancing is the best in American political history. We'll just put Cleveland behind us and go on to the next one. It," Nixon added wryly, "is bound to be better."

CHAPTER FIVE

The Family

IF RICHARD NIXON had held an ordinary nine-to-five job as manager of the small-appliances department of a discount store, he probably could have had a fairly warm and close relationship with his wife and daughters. His family problem was occupational in the first instance; for thirty years he was a politician of national stature. All during that time, the women of his family were a part of his political scenery. He saw their roles as ancillary to his, whether he was Congressman, Senator, Vice President, candidate or, after the 1968 election, President. In the 1968 campaign he told Bob Haldeman at length how Pat and the girls should be scheduled, where they should appear, how they should be introduced. Special aides and advance men were recruited for them. With Julie's fiancé, David Eisenhower, the family was a potent factor in the election campaign, and Nixon didn't miss a single opportunity to employ them to advantage.

But once they were all back on the campaign planes (christened the *Tricia*, the *Julie* and the *David*), Nixon would huddle with Bob Haldeman in the forward cabin. Pat would sit back in the staff section reading, next to Rose Woods or Helene Drown, a friend and former neighbor who was her traveling companion. David, Julie and Tricia had seats in the next cabin back. As the plane landed at each campaign stop the girls and David would walk forward, collecting Pat at her seat, assembling their coats and campaign smiles. When they arrived in the front cabin to line up behind him, Nixon would greet them, the airplane door would open and they would walk out to stand as a family, waving and smiling to the airport crowd.

Day after day, four, five or six times a day, the family would be assembled and disassembled, along with the camera tripods and loudspeakers. Sometimes Nixon complained to us when the family wasn't used to good advantage, and the staff would try different techniques. John Davies steered Pat Nixon through the crowds, Bill Codus looked after Julie, Tricia and David, while Dwight Chapin handled the candidate. I tried to oversee the whole ballet, steering them with subtle signals to be sure no one got out too far ahead or was left behind.

During the 1960 campaign I had had no opportunity to get to know Pat Nixon or the Nixon daughters. In 1962, when Jeanne and I took that short yacht trip with the Nixons on Puget Sound, I spent most of my time with Richard Nixon. However, in the 1968 campaign Julie, Tricia and David Eisenhower took a more active part and I began to perceive their individual personalities. As tour manager that year, I had some occasion to talk with Pat Nixon, especially when she had suggestions or complaints about the schedule or logistical arrangements. I discovered she could be strong and very definite in her opinions.

By 1968 she was telling her husband's staff what to do; she obviously saw herself as an experienced campaigner with an ability to sense what voters might be thinking. But her husband seldom included her in his deliberations on strategy or scheduling. He treated her as a respected but limited partner, skilled at giving interviews to local women's-page editors, an indispensable auxiliary in receiving lines and on stage at rallies, but not a heavyweight.

Nixon's attitude toward his family naturally became the attitude most of his staff took toward them. Pat Nixon's suggestions and complaints were tolerated without being much heeded by Haldeman and the rest of us. It was clear that Haldeman gave little weight to her opinions. But Pat Nixon was not slow to read others' feelings toward her; she knew who her allies were. When she didn't like the way things were going, she would complain to her husband or Helene Drown or Rose Mary Woods.

Bob Haldeman bore the brunt of Pat's dissatisfaction over campaign arrangements. She could become very much upset over small details; I recall her complaints about the manner in which one master of ceremonies introduced her and her daughters. She was quick to criticize our advance men, especially when she thought one was misleading the public. Pat Nixon and Haldeman maintained a correct, cool relationship during that campaign—a coolness that eventually carried over into the White House. As a result, I was sometimes enlisted to deal with Mrs. Nixon because the President wouldn't and Haldeman couldn't.

Pat Nixon did not adapt well to the White House, or "The Residence," as we were instructed to call it. At the outset she distrusted her new social secretary, Lucy Alexander Winchester. Lucy had been chosen by Mrs. Nixon, but not until I had interviewed the six or seven prospects and recommended Mrs. Winchester to her. Pat did not want to do the screening, she said; she had asked the President-elect to have me do it. Pat liked Mrs. Winchester, but she regretted not having made the choice herself. It was to be many months before Pat began to confide fully in her social secretary. (She never accepted the press secretary Bob Haldeman and Herb Klein chose for her, Mrs. Jerry Van der Heuvel.)

Pat reacted to her new White House challenges with a stubborn reticence. As the Vice President's wife she had done almost all her official chores herself. Now she spent many hours at a desk in her room upstairs in The Residence reading letters from the bags of mail sent to her in the wake of the November election. She refused to permit the efficient White House mailroom operation to process her letters, as it did the President's. She was uncomfortable with the idea that a reply might be a form letter, perhaps even signed by a machine.

Bessie Newton was one of four secretaries who had given the Nixons devoted service over the years. Pat decided that Bessie could help her with the First Lady's mail; for months the two women sat in Pat's bedroom reading letters, one by one, talking about possible replies and spooning out drops from that ocean of correspondence.

I was elected by the President and Haldeman to deal with the problem. Granted a late-afternoon appointment by Mrs. Nixon, I was received in the yellow oval room at the center of The Residence overlooking the south grounds and the Washington Monument. She was obviously wary and tense, but she tried to be gracious and attentive as I began my rehearsed explanation: the President was concerned, as were her friends, about how she was adjusting to her new situation. Doubtless her husband had spoken to her (I was almost certain he had not), but I wanted her to understand that many, many of us who counted ourselves her friends were close by to help in any way we were permitted. Perhaps she would feel the need of someone to talk to—even to share problems with. There was the mail, for example. I would be happy to try to ease that burden. If she liked, we could talk about it.

Pat bristled; she saw easily what this chat was all about, and she didn't like it. She explained icily that she had an obligation to all the people who cared enough to write her. She might be slow and old-fashioned, but she believed everyone deserved a personal answer and a personal signature.

But, I responded, she just couldn't hope to do it all. She could never catch up with the backlog.

She firmly nodded—one nod. It was obvious that the subject was closed.

Before I left, I added that I had one other thing on my mind: I was concerned about her health. She was very thin, and I hoped she would pay attention to her nourishment. In the same way that she owed her correspondents her personal attention, she owed her family and friends the best care she could give herself. If she was lonely or depressed, I hoped she would feel free to call my wife (whom she said she liked) or me.

There was no reaction. In a moment I realized that as far as she was concerned, I was entitled to none. I was vaguely prepared for tears, for outrage, even for a little sociopolitical psychology. But I was undone by her lack of any response at all.

As I walked back to my West Wing office down the wide, vaulted Residence hallway under the State Dining Room, I could not remember what I had said or done to make my departure. Somehow I had said goodbye, feeling I was a clumsy intruder, having neither reached nor helped her. I had nothing to report to the President or Haldeman.

Julie seems more open than her mother or sister, but she survived the Vietnam years at Smith College only because she was tougher than her attackers. Julie is quick-minded and articulate, a Richard Nixon in attractive packaging. If she thinks you are out to get her, she will come straight at you, smiling, either to charm you or to cut you off at the knees.

Tricia, the most retiring of the three Nixon women, spent the first weeks at the White House in her room. Her father complained to me that she was always there, curled up on her bed reading; she seldom came out even for meals. She had drawn her curtains against the traffic on Pennsylvania Avenue and had closed her door to the mobs of tourists who shouldered through the elaborate public rooms a floor below; neither her father nor her mother could lure her out. Several social functions listed her as a hostess, but she refused to attend. Both her mother and her father were concerned, but Tricia stayed up in her pink-and-white refuge.

The word got around. I heard about Tricia from the social staff and the housekeeping people in The Residence. Her solitary confinement was no secret to them, although no reporters had yet written about it. Tricia was asked to reign over the Azalea Festival in North Carolina in April following the inauguration, and the President had approved her doing so. That

41

was, he said, the kind of traditional social event a President's daughter ought to be supporting—good, clean young people, flowers and beauty. But no one could get the fairy princess to agree to come out of her tower. The festival management was pressing hard for an answer to its invitation so that its programs could go to the printer, and the President was hearing altogether too much about the festival from his wife and Bob Haldeman and the North Carolina congressional delegation.

So he asked me to have a little chat with Tricia. After all, Julie was involving herself with good works, and getting a good press. And Mrs. Nixon was honorary chairman of countless organizations and, for all her reticence, was gracing the many White House social events. Tricia's refusal to come out of her room could be embarrassing if the press got wind of it.

I had no illusions about Tricia; I told her father that I had sized her up as a very tough-and-troubled cookie. She didn't have the aggressive *savoir-faire* Julie had. Her retirement was her defense, and I thought she would fight hard to retain it. Nixon knew all that, but he also believed that a President's daughter had certain obligations.

I telephoned Tricia in her room and invited her to lunch in the White House mess. I wanted our talk to be on my turf—we were going to talk business. And I thought it might help her to see around us some of the people her age who were doing useful and important work in her father's service.

On the occasion of our luncheon Miss Nixon could not be faulted for her grooming. She arrived on time, dressed all in pink-and-white angora. But just before leaving her room she had apparently taken a couple of difficult pills. Nothing on the menu pleased her, so with her eyebrows arched she ordered a hamburger, and didn't eat it. She didn't swallow what I was saying to her, either.

I had swung from small talk to "How do you plan to spend these White House years?" and midway through that gambit I lost my audience. She said, very plainly, that how she spent her time was exclusively her business and, therefore, not mine. Oh, well, yes, I suggested, but it was also the President's concern. She shook her head. She had campaigned hard for him, all over the country. As far as she was concerned she had done what she could for him, but he and his staff were not about to run her life all the years he was President. She might do some social things, and again she might not. She might take a job. She might not. What she did and when, she would decide. Thanks for the lunch.

And so the young lady with the scoop nose and the pink angora sweater left me to finish my sandwich alone.

Richard Nixon and I agreed that I wasn't doing too well with his ladies, and for a while thereafter I was not called upon again to exercise my persuasive techniques. He asked Rose Mary Woods and Bebe Rebozo to try their luck from time to time, and they were evidently more effective. At last Tricia emerged from her room and found things to do in the nation and the world.

In late 1969, Tricia agreed to make a trip to England. Her journey was carefully planned and advanced by one of Dwight Chapin's people and by William Codus at the State Department, along with Tricia's own Secret Service detail. She would travel in one of the President's airplanes, and of course, she would stay at the elaborate official residence of our Ambassador to the Court of Saint James's, Walter Annenberg. The President was careful to send along with her a small, handpicked staff sensitive to Tricia's moods and temperament. The agent in charge of her Secret Service detail was William Duncan, one of the brightest and most discreet the Service had to offer, a particular favorite of the Nixons.

In a few days Bill Duncan called me from London with a problem. At that moment he was attending Ambassador Annenberg's gala party given in honor of the President's elder daughter for all of London society. He had stepped away from the ball because Tricia wanted the President to know—right this very minute—that his Ambassador was apparently intoxicated and had put his arm around her shoulder in a most objectionable and familiar fashion. Tricia had dispatched Duncan to the telephone for her father's help, while she hid in the powder room.

I suggested to Duncan that he tell Tricia her father was unavailable. Moreover, her best bet would be to attach herself to the Ambassador's charming wife for the rest of the evening. Beyond that, I emphasized, Bill Duncan was on his own.

When I hung up I recalled Nixon's exultation when he'd decided to make Annenberg his Ambassador to Great Britain. Walter Annenberg was a major contributor to Nixon's campaigns, as befitted a multimillionaire. He and his siblings had inherited a publishing business from their father, Moe Annenberg, who had cornered the racing-wire and racing-form business. Walter and his sister had gone on to publish newspapers, *TV Guide* and other magazines, and acquired a chain of television and radio stations as well.

When Walter Annenberg was being considered for the ambassadorial appointment we ordered a routine FBI field check on him. J. Edgar Hoover's report was four or five inches thick, and included a history of Moe, his race-wire empire and his manifold underworld connections. But the file contained nothing derogatory about his son, Walter.

According to Nixon, Walter Annenberg yearned for a prestigious appointment to certify his respectability to those who still remembered his father and the old days.

Nixon relished the idea of sending Walter to England; he pointed to the "unbroken line of the Eastern Establishment's stuffed shirts" who were sent to London as Ambassador by other Presidents. He, by God, would break the pattern. He'd send them the son of a racketeer and a Jew. That would send a signal to the Eastern, Ivy League blue-bloods who thought they owned that embassy!

So Annenberg had gone to London, and Tricia doubtless wished one of those fancy Ivy Leaguers had been the host at her big party. Should I tell the President about Duncan's call? I decided to let the Nixons compare notes on Walter Annenberg later, when Tricia got back home.

A day or so before Tricia was due to return, her father asked what plans were being made for her arrival at Andrews Air Force Base. In fact, no plans were being made. So Richard Nixon began to issue instructions. There was to be a group from the White House to greet her. Buses would take enough White House staff people and others to ensure a good crowd. Henry Kissinger should be there; it was, after all, a foreign trip by a member of the First Family. But Henry was to be specifically cautioned not to say or do anything to embarrass Tricia. (Nixon explained that Tricia was sometimes put off by Henry.)

In the press of other business, I found it impossible to be there for Tricia's return. Because I heard nothing to the contrary concerning the welcoming event, I assume Kissinger avoided embarrassing Miss Nixon.

Walter Annenberg survived very well. He served several more years in London, quite successfully. The Queen kept racehorses, of course, and she developed a warm place in her heart for the proprietor of *The Daily Racing Form*.

Pat Nixon grew in her role as First Lady. She eventually learned to trust and confide in her staff, especially the able and discreet Lucy Winchester; the piles of Mrs. Nixon's mail at last came under the jurisdiction of mail-answering experts and were answered to Pat's satisfaction. But for all the years I was there, a tension persisted between Mrs. Nixon and her staff on the one hand and the President's staff—particularly Haldeman's people—on the other.

Julie and David had their share of troubles too.

In the spring of 1970, the President agonized over whether or not to attend Julie's graduation at Smith College. David Eisenhower was due to graduate a week later from Amherst, and all things being equal, the Nixons might have moved to eastern Massachusetts for a grand week of family celebration.

But in April, Jerry Rubin, Rennie Davis and members of the Black Panthers were up there, recruiting demonstrators at Holyoke and the University of Massachusetts, organizing anti-Nixon protests on the assumption that the President would be coming.

At the end of April, Julie wrote me a sad little note urging that her father not come:

April 28th

Dear John,

I know you are getting sick of hearing about Smith graduation. It worries me that Daddy is so concerned about it. I truly think the day will be a disaster if he comes. Smith girls are furious at the idea of massive security precautions.

The temper up here is ugly. At a rally at M.S. one of the Chicago Seven led the audience of 10,000 in a chant of "fuck Julie and David Eisenhower." Also, please see enclosed article from the Northampton newspaper.

Please let me know what you think about this article and about RN attending graduation.

Sincerely,
Julie

Within a couple of days Nixon decided not to go. On May 4 he asked Ray Price to prepare a "frontal statement" in which the President would say directly that he could not attend the graduations of his daughter and son-in-law (the grandson of a great general and revered President) because lawless elements threatened to disrupt the events. Nixon hoped that good and decent Americans would strongly resent that kind of coercion by Davis, Rubin and the others. If Nixon couldn't go, he'd score a few points on his attackers anyway. As usual, he missed no opportunity to widen the gap between the antiwar activists and the good people of Middle America.

* * *

45

The Nixons did not have many close friends. Most of their truly social, nonpolitical friends of long standing were former neighbors with whom Pat kept in touch after moving to Washington and New York.

In both the 1960 and 1968 campaigns it was one of these California friends, Helene Drown, who traveled with Pat most of the time. She had no specific duties, but was intended to be Pat's companion and gofer. Helene soon found a niche she relished as conduit for Pat's complaints to the staff, a role she undertook with undue enthusiasm. Mrs. Drown is a waspish woman who managed to translate Pat's low-key requests and suggestions into mean-spirited demands. As a result, Helene Drown was always at war with Haldeman and me and the other members of the campaign staff. In 1968 some of my advance men took retaliatory delight in finding the worst of hotel rooms to assign to Helene Drown. More than once I ducked and ran when I saw her coming across a hotel lobby to complain about where they had put her for the night. Unfortunately, Helene Drown seldom made a remark to or about the campaign staff that was not negative or critical. Since Helene was the person closest to Pat, she had a predictable effect on Mrs. Nixon's morale. And of course, Pat's moods affected the candidate.

The Helene Drown syndrome was a problem that continued into the White House years. After he became President, Nixon spent a remarkable percentage of his time in office fussing and grumbling about Mrs. Drown, especially when we were at San Clemente, where Helene was close by.

Pat had found little of interest to do at San Clemente. She began inviting Helene Drown to stay at Casa Pacifica for days at a time, to keep her company. During those visits Mrs. Drown's negativism soon pervaded the First Lady's attitude, depressing her and making it so unpleasant for the President that he would hide in his upstairs study or go to his office on the Coast Guard property next door and remain there until Pat and her guest had retired to their rooms for the night.

One day in April 1971, Nixon had Rose Mary Woods call me into his San Clemente office, where they were talking to Bebe Rebozo. Nixon was beside himself. They described to me the latest Drown invasion at Casa Pacifica. To avoid the Drowns, Nixon had stayed in his office until late the night before. When he returned home his wife was waiting for him, and he was barraged with Pat's Drown-inspired complaints. Rose said she'd tried to suggest to Pat that the Drowns be asked to stay away for the President's sake. But Pat cut her off.

Rebozo wouldn't get involved with Helene Drown at any price. So I was called in to try to get rid of Mrs. Drown.

The four of us—Rose, Rebozo, Nixon and I—debated strategy. Rose suggested some tactful things I might say. Bebe shook his head; it would take dynamite, not tact, to get "that woman" out of the President's house.

Nixon began to spin out a script for me (as he often did, speaking as he would in my place):

"You know, this has been one of the two toughest decisions the President has had to make since he's been in office. [So far as my notes show, the Drowns were not to know what the other one was.] Helene must be out *this morning*, he has decided. I am calling at the President's request to relay his decision to you.

"You must not talk to the President about this. [Presumably I have called Jack, not Helene, on the basis that if one step removed is good, two steps are better.] If you go to him you will lose a friend.

"He has decided the Nixons will have no more houseguests at San Clemente. So this decision is not discriminatory against the Drowns. The Nixons must select their companions with great discretion. They are constantly bugged by their relatives; for example, Tom Ryan [one of Pat's cousins].

"Rebozo is different. Notice, he always stays at the San Clemente Inn [a motel up the street], not at the house."

Nixon was warming to his subject.

"Tell Jack that it is for the good of the country that Helene Drown gets out of my house!" he exclaimed.

Three months before, during the previous visit to San Clemente, Nixon had soliloquized to me at length about Helene Drown. Then he was thinking of having his lawyer, Herb Kalmbach, talk to the Drowns. "Perhaps," Nixon mused, "we could make Jack Drown an ambassador. Then Helene would be out of the country." Something had to be done to keep the Drowns away. Herb could tell them that no other Californians came to visit as they did. "He could say that countless Californians deeply resented the favoritism the Nixons were showing the Drowns. If they mention Rebozo, Herb should point out that Bebe is different: he handles the President's business affairs."

For a while I'd thought all this was just extravagant talk, but in April, Nixon was so genuinely distraught that I took his instructions at face value. I went back to my office and called Jack Drown.

Jack is a huge, tall, open-faced magazine distributor. His

smile is broad and genuine, his huge handshake is hearty and he's a good fellow to be with. I could find no pleasure in giving him bad news under any circumstances. But I called him and told him that Helene was a big problem for the President and that it would be better for her not to be at Casa Pacifica anymore. Jack reacted as I thought he would. He was obviously hurt and troubled, but he said he understood. He was sure neither of the Drowns had any desire to make things more difficult for Dick. He was sure Helene would leave at once and stay away. But he also implied that this ostracism was the doing of the White House staff and not the President. I assured him in the strongest terms that I was delivering Mr. Nixon's message, not anyone else's. But he was skeptical.

The Drowns stayed away for months. Then, during one San Clemente trip, Helene was back. Nothing was ever said by anyone about her fall from grace, nor was her restoration ever explained.

Richard Nixon despised the Washington social scene. He was particularly harsh in his criticism of the "Georgetown crowd"; he would purse his lips and mince the words when he talked about their "boring and time-wasting tea parties." As a Congressman and Senator he had been uncomfortable at the small Washington dinners he'd attended in the forties and fifties, and as Vice President he'd refused most social invitations. As President he refused all of them.

But occasionally the Nixons invited the Washingtonians they liked to small, formal dinners in the family dining room, upstairs in the White House residence. The guest list was limited to a few people who had extended kindnesses to the Nixons years before, and occasionally White House staff people were included, particularly if one of the guests might be expected to raise some piece of business.

In 1969, Alice Roosevelt Longworth and J. Edgar Hoover were the guests at such a black-tie supper. My wife and I were included because the FBI Director was my responsibility. I had heard a little about Theodore Roosevelt's outspoken daughter, then about 85 years of age, but I'd never met her. I was unprepared for her vigor and sprightly chatter.

She appeared frail and bony at first sight, but she was one of those elderly people whose strength and personality at once capture one's attention; in a moment I ceased thinking of Alice Longworth as an old lady. She had been a great beauty. Now she said things that were calculated to shock and surprise; she needed and wanted the limelight, just like every other political woman (and man) in Washington. But she was unfailingly courteous to the Nixons. It was obvious that she liked them.

All at once in the middle of dinner Mrs. Longworth looked around the upstairs family dining room and exclaimed, "By God, I had the measles in this room!" She had caught measles not long after her father had succeeded to the White House. A doctor confined her to her bedroom—the room that much later became the little dining room—where she leaned out the window, hatching plots to sneak her half-siblings past the nurse. One day, she told us, they successfully smuggled Alice's pony up the broad staircase, but he was captured before the children could hide him in Alice's room. (That staircase, formerly at the west end of the hallway, disappeared in some subsequent remodeling, but Mrs. Longworth showed me where it had once been as we toured the family quarters after dinner.)

Nixon's admiration for Alice Longworth's father, Theodore Roosevelt, had equipped him to reminisce with her in an intimate manner. Nixon knows encyclopedic details of the lives and careers of Roosevelt and Woodrow Wilson. During the first months of his Presidency, Nixon circulated copies of their essays and memoirs to some of the staff. That night Nixon and Mrs. Longworth exchanged Theodore Roosevelt anecdotes in the familiar manner of old family friends; there appeared to be an extraordinary affinity between them.

Another evening, the Nixons entertained Henry Ford II and his beautiful wife Christina in the same room. Christina Ford and Alice Longworth were both witty, strong women with extraordinary presence who eclipsed the First Lady. In such company Pat Nixon receded to near-invisibility. Her husband, on the other hand, enjoyed the company of such women, and was at his best in their presence. His dinner conversation could be very impressive, for it often came straight out of a briefing memorandum that told the Nixons all about their guests, their hobbies, philanthropies and other interests.

Bebe Rebozo ran a small garage and several coin laundries in Miami before he became a friend of the famous. I'm not sure how he really made the ascension; there are several versions of the story. But when he and Nixon first met, Rebozo was already a friend of Senator George Smathers of Florida. The tall and handsome Smathers is surely one of the most accomplished politicians of this age. On various occasions he was host to Nixon, Rebozo and young John Kennedy on his Florida beach. Smathers' questionable but successful primary campaign against former Senator Claude Pepper is sometimes cited as the progenitor of Nixon's strategy against Helen Gahagan Douglas in California. By the time Nixon became President, Smathers had retired from the Senate to become the dean of Washington lawyer-lobbyists and a habitué of the Key Biscayne Hotel, where he leased an oceanfront villa.

Rebozo arranged for Nixon's White House staff to use some of that hotel's other villas when Nixon was in residence at his Key Biscayne home, a few blocks away. I would sometimes see Smathers emerge, blinking at the afternoon sun, always with a different young lady of great beauty as his swimming companion. He was an inspiration, if not an example, to those of us beginning to enter middle age.

To be with Bebe Rebozo is to be with a genial, discreet sponge. He has cheerfully tolerated endless Nixon monologues with patience and equanimity. Moreover, Rebozo the garage mechanic, having become the owner of a state bank, a student of real estate and the folkways of the wealthy, can now carry his end of a conversation with anyone with unfailing pleasantness. Nixon has always found it effortless to be with Rebozo. Bebe makes no requests or demands. He is a bartender of some accomplishment. Above all, the cement of their relationship is the fact that Rebozo is completely loyal to Richard Nixon. And he does not gossip.

When I was trying lawsuits in the old days, I didn't want to talk about the day's courtroom battles when I came home to my family at night. In fact, I preferred to sit watching some inane television comedy that made no demands on my mind. Nixon wouldn't be caught dead watching TV sit-coms (although he actually watched more television than he would admit). Bebe Rebozo was Nixon's equivalent source of undemanding mental relaxation.

On our trips to Florida, Ron Ziegler and the White House press office worked diligently to establish that Nixon worked hard on the nation's business at Key Biscayne. Haldeman, Kissinger and I were often taken to Florida and, from time to time, were reported to have worked with Nixon on affairs of state. If such staff meetings at the house next to Nixon's took place, they were rare.

Usually on those Florida trips, Nixon and Rebozo would go cruising on Bebe's boat or simply sit by the water, drinks in hand, Nixon talking and Rebozo passively listening.

As the White House months passed, Rebozo called me with increasing frequency with suggestions or instructions from the President. When Nixon bought the San Clemente house, Rebozo was deeply involved in its remodeling. He flew to Los Angeles for meetings with the General Services Administration official in charge of the project. Over the months, he so successfully co-opted the GSA project manager that the GSA began carrying out Rebozo's instructions without question. If there was undue government expenditure, at either the San Clemente or the Key Biscayne house, Mr. Rebozo should be given full credit for his persuasive involvement.

Bebe was unselfish, but not entirely selfless. At times during the months when I was Counsel to the President, I was directed by Nixon to help Bebe with his personal problems. At one point he was engaged in a struggle with the Department of the Interior over some real estate in the Everglades. Another time he was the victim of investigative reporting by *Newsday*. On a few occasions he asked for help for his relatives. In each case the White House staff helped.

In the fall of 1969, Bebe Rebozo was concerned that the President's personal finances were not being well managed. Early in the year the Nixons' longtime arrangement with the business-management firm of Vincent Andrews & Co. had been terminated. Mr. Andrews had died some years before, and in the judgment of our staff the work performed by his son and other successors was not the best available. A close friend of Rose Mary Woods, Claudia Val, worked for the Andrews firm, and Rose had bitterly opposed any change of managers. Rebozo, Haldeman and I were subjected to Miss Woods's dark scowls and minor revenges for a while, but we persuaded Nixon to let Herb Kalmbach look after his personal affairs as well as a large cache of campaign money.

I thought Rebozo and Kalmbach were to have worked out the problems of money management between them. Herb had campaign "trust funds" on deposit in California, the unspent gleanings from countless fund-raising efforts in the late sixties. At one time Herb told me he had nearly $2 million tucked away.

Bebe held Nixon's personal money—the proceeds of Nixon's Fisher Island stock sale, the sale of the New York apartment and the sale of Nixon's law partnership. But Rebozo wanted Kalmbach's trust funds in his bank too.

In November 1969, the President ordered me to instruct Kalmbach to send Bebe all that old campaign money forthwith. I did so, but Herb appealed the ruling successfully and retained control of the trust funds in California.

At that time, those Kalmbach campaign funds were being used to finance "political" investigations by Anthony Ulasciewicz, the former New York police undercover man. I had hired Ulasciewicz because Nixon was asking for investigations—of the Kennedys, for example—that I simply could not ask government-paid investigators, such as Jack Caulfield, to do. Ulasciewicz was paid with Nixon money to do Nixon chores.

Later, the Kalmbach funds and other money Herb raised from Nixon supporters went to the Watergate burglars. It is entertaining to speculate who might have gone to jail in Kalmbach's place if those campaign funds had been transferred to the Key Biscayne State Bank in 1969, when Bebe Rebozo so badly wanted the deposits.

Rebozo was Nixon's principal contact with the Howard Hughes organization and also with the Mary Carter Paint people—the paint company that was later to be called Resorts International. Some individuals, J. Paul Getty and Bobby Baker among them, also found that they could easily reach Nixon's ear via Rebozo.

Florida businessmen and politicians often made their contacts in the same way. After lengthy study, my staff recommended that the Cross-Florida Barge Canal, a U.S. Army Corps of Engineers project, be stopped. The Corps had already dredged a long section of the wide canal, inflicting heavy damage on the ecology of northern Florida. Our study showed that by any test—cost versus benefit, economic return or the flow of commerce—the project couldn't be justified, particularly when the benefits were measured against the damage it would do.

Nixon had granted me a broad delegation of his prerogatives on the subject of the environment. The fact was that he didn't much care about the subject of environmental conservation or what I did about it, so long as I didn't create any political problems for him. So I exercised my delegated discretion and ordered the Corps to stop work on the Cross-Florida Barge Canal.

Florida commercial interests were not happy with the decision. After returning to the White House from a weekend with Bebe Rebozo, Nixon pushed my red call button and demanded to know why the hell I had stopped the canal. I briefly described how it was ruining the water table, destroying wildlife and knocking the ecology out of kilter. He waved all of that away. He had not had a good weekend in Florida; Florida's business people were unhappy.

I offered to deliver the staff's thick study of the pros and cons of the canal for his evening reading; but that was the last thing he had in mind. Instead, he asked me to call Bebe Rebozo and explain our reasons for stopping the Corps. Had I received this instruction early in my White House career, rather than later, I might have called Rebozo myself. But I had begun to learn a few things; I had a member of my staff call him instead. (Some years later, a judge held that the canal must be built—it was authorized by statute, and a President, not to mention an assistant, couldn't stop it.)

My last contact with Rebozo was months after I was fired and had left the White House. True to form, it was indirect. It became clear in the winter of 1973 that I would need to change lawyers; John Wilson could not represent both Bob Haldeman and me. So I approached William Frates of Miami, whom I had known for some time through one of his partners. Before he accepted the assignment and began to help me, Frates told me that he also represented Rebozo before Sam Ervin's Senate committee and in civil litigation. Since Rebozo's problems and mine were miles apart, neither Frates nor I thought that presented any problem. But Rebozo mounted the most strenuous objection to Bill Frates helping me.

Bebe Rebozo asserted that he and I had an adversity of interests; I was not really surprised, although I could think of no specific basis for that contention. But by then it was 1974, and I had been fired by his friend nearly a year before. The truth of things was beginning to emerge. I took Rebozo's assertion that his interests and mine conflicted as some corroboration of my own growing suspicions about Richard Nixon.

Frates refused to withdraw as my counsel. As the evidence appeared, it was Richard Nixon, not Rebozo, whose interests conflicted with mine. Once again, Bebe Rebozo had played the role of alter ego, this time unsuccessfully.

Part II

CHAPTER SIX

The White House Staff

In 1969, at the beginning of the Nixon Administration, John Mitchell was probably the man closest to the President. Mitchell started out riding high. Nixon put him on the National Security Council and gave him extraordinary assignments far beyond the scope of the Department of Justice, which Mitchell headed as Attorney General. A year later Nixon said of Mitchell, "There's a man who can do any job—John Mitchell. He's a tough son-of-a-bitch." But by 1970 I wasn't so sure.

When I first met Mitchell, I thought he was smart, tough, enigmatic and capable. He managed the 1968 campaign effectively, working at a bare desk in a shabby office in the New York Nixon campaign headquarters. His picture was all over the papers and magazines then, smoking his pipe, taciturn, aloof, a sort of Wall Street Gary Cooper. In his pictures he looked better than he did in person, however; the day I first met him, at the headquarters, he looked more like a tapir than a movie star. He was fleshy, with a cleft nose and an unhealthy complexion. He said a few cordial words to me about the convention, named some Seattle bond lawyer we both knew and in a minute sent me on my way to Miami Beach to set up the convention facilities.

I didn't see much of Mitchell through the rest of the campaign; he was in New York doing high-level political things and I was on the road seeing that things ran on time, chasing down reporters' lost baggage and keeping the candidate in a good humor.

On election night, John Mitchell, Bob Haldeman and I kept the long vigil with Nixon in his half-dark suite in the Waldorf Towers until the Illinois votes were counted and California came in and we knew he'd won. (I felt I was in the wrong place that night. Nixon was remote and uncommunicative. Mitchell was constantly on the telephone relaying information, and Haldeman was programming the public-relations effort. There was nothing for me to do, so I sat in the shadows and watched Nixon do his electoral calculations on a yellow pad.)

The next day, Mitchell and I were among the six men who were asked to go to Florida with the President-elect. (The others were Bob Haldeman, Bryce Harlow, Bob Finch and Ron Ziegler.) At Key Biscayne I attended some meetings with Mitchell and ate a few meals with him, and I began to see that he wasn't as gruff and remote as he appeared. At that time he was a man with some tough personal problems* for which he didn't have the answers; he was withdrawn and quiet, but hardly forbidding.

Through the transition period, in December and early January, Mitchell helped Nixon recruit the staff and Cabinet for the new Government. He knew most of the governors and politicians from coast to coast; he'd played the kind of politics with them a bond lawyer must play to get and keep his lucrative legal business. He'd gotten rich certifying New York State bonds, Florida highway bonds and the indentures of most of the other states. Mitchell's personnel recommendations were nearly all from his own genus: the wealthy and successful who were known to one another as members of the good men's clubs.

After the inauguration, Mitchell's function changed. He not only assumed command of a Cabinet department but took on a major role as public spokesman for the Administration (and in both capacities eventually proved seriously wanting).

Thereafter as Mitchell tried to cope with his broad assignments, Bob Haldeman, as White House Chief of Staff, became the man in the White House closest to the President, and I, by virtue of a curious confusion, was also reputed to have a major influence.

In 1972, *The Washington Post*'s Sally Quinn began an article about Bob Haldeman:

One of those high White House officials was asked about President Nixon's chief of staff, H. R. (Bob) Haldeman. The official went on

* The day after the election, Nixon had asked Mitchell to be his Attorney General. But Martha Mitchell was in a sanatorium, drying out, and Mitchell declined Nixon's offer. Nixon subsequently asked me to be Attorney General, but I also declined. I was totally unprepared for the offer; felt I was unequipped for the responsibility as I understood it then, and I said so. Nixon accepted my decision, and went on to suggest that I be director of the Central Intelligence Agency or chairman of the Republican National Committee. I considered those proposals equally unrealistic, and I said so. Shortly thereafter, Nixon suggested I come with him for a year as White House Counsel, and I agreed.

for several minutes describing his sense of humor, personality, professional demeanor and other traits, then hung up. Later, he called back.

"I made a mistake," he said. "I was talking about Ehrlichman."

The confusion between Harry Robbins Haldeman and John D. Ehrlichman, the President's chief adviser on domestic affairs, is understandable.

They were roommates [we weren't] at U.C.L.A., and were strong Republicans [he was, I wasn't] there. Both are Christian Scientists [I was then, he wasn't—he is now] who don't drink or smoke [I didn't—he did], are secretive about themselves and their work, extremely loyal to the President, powerful in the Nixon Administration.

The mistakes in Miss Quinn's story were about average for Haldeman–Ehrlichman stories during the White House days. Most people who don't know us think that Haldeman and I are just alike.

Richard Nixon had the same problem; he was forever calling me Bob. He'd start out to tell me to do something: "Ah, Bob—ah—Bob—ah—John—" Haldeman once wrote that Nixon never could remember how many children the Haldemans had, or their names. In my case it was *my* name. Not only was I "Bob" much of the time, but Nixon never mastered the spelling of my last name. Notes to me came addressed to "E."*

Bob Haldeman signed up to work for Richard Nixon in 1956 because he genuinely believed in the man. He was certain that Nixon eventually would lead the nation as no one else could. As he came to know Nixon better, Haldeman realized that his political idol was far from perfect. By then Haldeman was so committed to Nixon that he was willing to draw upon his considerable personal resources to compensate for Nixon's shortcomings. Was Nixon irresolute? Haldeman would be his backbone, hiring and firing, saying no, demanding staff performance with icy firmness. When Nixon was reticent, Halde-

---

* In 1980—after six years of complete silence—I received a book from Richard Nixon in the mail. There was no letter or note; just *The Real War* with a little bookplate pasted in the front which read:

INSCRIBED BY THE AUTHOR
Richard Nixon
for
John Erlichman

When Bob Haldeman saw the misspelling he laughed. "Well," he said, "at least you know it's not a forgery."

man persuaded him to do the necessary public things. When Nixon's energy flagged, Haldeman shielded him from the unnecessary demands that would sap his strength.

The two became complementary, and by 1968 it was hard to tell where Richard Nixon left off and H. R. Haldeman began. It was evident that Richard Nixon believed he was a better candidate—and later, a better President—as a result of the merger. He grew totally dependent on the Nixon–Haldeman relationship. Virtually nothing Nixon did was done without Haldeman's knowledge. That is not to say that Haldeman approved everything Nixon said or did; but it was essential that he know, and have a chance to object, before it happened.

The President's family could not reconcile themselves to what had become of Nixon in this process. They complained continually about Haldeman. Nixon's secretary, Rose Mary Woods, had worked for him since 1952, when he became Vice President. She was dedicated to Nixon, but she lacked the ability to complement him as Haldeman could. So Rose Woods was moved to a secondary role when Nixon realized that Haldeman could supply much of what Nixon needed to become President. Haldeman could run a staff, manage media campaigns and protect Nixon from minutiae as no one else had ever done. The family and Rose Woods were unhappy. It was not that they were jealous—they just didn't like the change.

Haldeman was not the only Nixon alter ego/collaborator. Later, Richard Nixon was to find a new complementary personality in Charles Colson. In foreign affairs Nixon-Kissinger was perhaps the most effective of the complementary relationships, although it was the hardest for Nixon to tolerate. Nixon-Colson was the least attractive of the Nixon partnerships.

Much has been said of Bob Haldeman's loyalty to Richard Nixon. He was indeed loyal, especially to Nixon-Haldeman. Haldeman was an astute, if tolerant, observer of Nixon's mistakes and foibles. He was a sharp and outspoken critic of Nixon-Colson, but a willing bridesmaid to the Nixon–Kissinger relationship.

Charles Colson came along nearly a year after the White House staff was organized and operating. Colson may have been a number of unattractive things, but stupid wasn't one of them. He soon figured out exactly where he could operate in the White House and where he couldn't, and he was usually careful not to trespass—unless he could get away with it.

Colson also realized that Richard Nixon was frustrated. The

President was surrounded by old Nixon men who knew their boss well. Often we would simply refuse to do what he asked because we thought his orders were unwise or would result in harm to him. Colson felt the familiar Washington imperative; he wanted power and recognition. To move up in the White House he needed a pass-safe from the President himself, and the way to get that was to be the man who would do whatever Richard Nixon wanted done.

Colson's ostensible job was "outside liaison." He was to be the White House contact for special-interest groups and individuals who needed to be listened to. But Nixon soon discovered that he'd hired this new fellow who could be called in to take on the rough chores others wouldn't do. Before long Colson's small staff was growing, and the frequency of Colson's visits to the President was increasing.

Haldeman realized that a fifth* staff group was growing within the White House, and he did his best to keep it under his control, but Nixon too often overruled him. On paper, Colson reported to Haldeman; in fact, Colson reported to the President. The Colson staff grew to twenty-three people, with Nixon's personal approval, while everyone else was under an injunction to make drastic staff cuts. As time passed, each of us—Kissinger, Shultz and I—found Colson operating in our substantive areas at the President's specific instructions.

But that was later. At the outset it was Nixon-Haldeman. The Nixon–Haldeman partnership worked well for me most of the time. I had become accustomed to working with Nixon through Haldeman. (When the established White House system later included my direct access to Nixon, that made my work easier, because I could directly see, hear and feel the message. But access to Nixon had disadvantages too—countless hours of his rambling and rumination. Someone had to sit with Richard Nixon to listen. Usually it was Haldeman; sometimes it was Henry Kissinger, George Shultz, Daniel Patrick Moynihan or I, and later it became Ron Ziegler by default.)

Occasionally Haldeman took a few days off and I filled in for him. The Old Man, as Haldeman called Nixon,† would grind away on me for two or three hours at a time, and I grew to appreciate how Nixon-Haldeman truly worked. I was expected to sit with the President as he leaned back in his chair,

---

* The original four being those under Haldeman, Kissinger, George Shultz and me.

† Haldeman also called Nixon Rufus, The Leader of the Free World, Milhous and Thelma's Husband, depending on the occasion.

feet up, toying with his wristwatch and talking up and down a subject. If Nixon went to Red Beach for a swim, the Haldeman-substitute went along to listen and take notes. Once, at the Robert Abplanalps' island in the Bahamas, Nixon and I stood up to our necks in clear warm green water for two hours, little silver fish swimming around our legs, as he talked about the current political situation. At night he woke me up with phone calls, during which he would go over much of the same stuff he'd chewed on all afternoon.

The Haldeman role was to argue (gently) the opposite of the President's thesis, raising factual issues and suggesting further inquiry if it appeared necessary.

But once Nixon's decision had been made, Haldeman became the enforcer. Countless times I thought their joint effort had produced a bad decision and I said so. Nixon would accept my opposition and sometimes change his mind, but if I talked to Haldeman alone he would simply say, "Well, that's his decision—and he's right, you know."

Usually Haldeman stayed away from substantive policy, but he often sat in as Henry Kissinger presented foreign-policy issues or when I advanced domestic options to the President. Haldeman's interjections during policy talks were intended to air political considerations or effect clarifications (on Nixon's behalf), and he seldom expressed his own opinion. People were another matter; Haldeman had strong likes and dislikes, and he rarely missed a chance to criticize a colleague he didn't like.

Dozens of assignments, instructions and inquiries came from Haldeman every day. For example, one day this memo came from "H":

MEMORANDUM FOR: JOHN EHRLICHMAN
FROM: H. R. HALDEMAN

Billy Graham raised with the President today the point that postal rates for religious publications are being increased 400%, while postal rates for pornography are only being increased 25%.

Needless to say, the President was horrified to learn of this state of affairs and wants to know what we are doing about it.

Upon which I endorsed:

Shall we lower religious mail or raise the rates for porn?

And Haldeman replied:

> *You'll have to raise that question w/RN and BG—I am only qualified to report the horror, not to act upon it.*
>
> H

By 1970 the White House staff was divided into four units. Haldeman looked after a vast array of nonsubstantive activities. Everything from the mail room to politics was his concern. Kissinger and I tended to foreign and domestic policy, respectively, and economic policy was Shultz' domain.

Haldeman's personal staff included Dwight Chapin, the appointments secretary; Steven Bull and Alexander Butterfield, who ran people and paper into and out of the President's office, and Larry Higby and Gordon Strachan, who looked after Haldeman's creature comforts and paperwork and made sure people did what Haldeman asked them to.

Ron Ziegler's press office, Herb Klein's (actually Jeb Magruder's and Charles Colson's) communications apparatus, the political operators, all the speechwriters, the Counsel, the military aides, the communications agencies (phones, and so on), the mess, the garage and the congressional liaison people all reported to Haldeman.

The East Wing—Pat Nixon's office, including the social secretary and the housekeeper, chef and groundskeepers—although not strictly Haldeman's province, became so in effect. What happened at parties, dinners and Pat Nixon's press conferences was of vital concern to the President, and Nixon demanded that Haldeman oversee this area. At times, some of Mrs. Nixon's staff—and Rose Mary Woods—asserted Mrs. Nixon's independence in these matters, and there was friction. Unfortunately, the Nixon family usually left it to the staff to fight out these jurisdictional battles, and that allowed unnecessary animosities to develop.

Mrs. Nixon and Haldeman were unfailingly courteous to each other, but it was clear to me that Bob did not have a high opinion of the First Lady. He spoke of her as "Thelma" (her given name) or "Mrs. Nixon" most of the time. She was seldom "Pat" except to her face.

Bob Haldeman was Chief of Staff in the White House, and his staff reflected his predispositions. Both Henry Kissinger and I were allowed to choose our own policy people, but we took constant criticism for our choices from both Nixon and Haldeman.

The Haldeman staff was characteristically young, straight-arrow and ideologically pure. His people were male (except for the secretaries), white and middle-class.

I started out as Counsel with three young lawyers—Henry Cashen, Egil "Bud" Krogh, Jr., and Ed Morgan. Cashen and Morgan had been advance men in the 1968 campaign. Once in the White House, they served Richard Nixon well in many ways.

When I took charge of the Domestic Council, I delegated hiring to Ken Cole and my assistant directors, but I did some recruiting myself. The Council staff included a few professional women—three most of the time—and a couple of blacks. But I had more trouble because of the liberal tendencies of some of my people than because of their race, sex or previous condition of servitude. Dyed-in-the-wool conservatives—Pat Buchanan, principally—sniped from the sidelines at Barbara "Bobbie" Greene Kilberg, Ed Harper and Lew Engman because they weren't doctrinaire enough. Bob Haldeman didn't like Ed Morgan. Richard Nixon was deeply suspicious of Sally Ann Payton for a while.*

When Arthur Burns, my predecessor in domestic-policy work, left the White House for the Federal Reserve in 1970, his bequest was a small but militant staff of like-minded conservative thinkers. He suggested to the President that the new Domestic Council staff be formed around this nucleus.

Such aggressively doctrinaire people as Dr. Martin Anderson and Dr. Roger Freeman certainly have their place, both in and out of government. The conservative point of view deserves effective advocates. But I had begun to assemble a small staff of lawyers, educators and business people I had worked with either in Nixon campaigns or during the formative months of the Administration. I believed that the domestic-policy staff should be made up of nonadvocates, whose primary job would be to assemble *all* the facts and *all* the philosophical arguments for the President's consideration.

I think it's fair to say that Dr. Anderson (later Ronald Reagan's key domestic adviser), Dr. Freeman and the others making up Burns's residual legacy simply could not bring themselves to admit the existence of two possible views on most issues.

From the sidelines Pat Buchanan and other conservatives

---

* She finally made the grade with Nixon when he heard the perhaps apocryphal story that she had opened a meeting with the top male officials of the city government of Washington, D.C., thus: "All right, you black motherfuckers, here's what we're going to do now. . . ."

complained to the President that I was not using the people Burns had left behind. It was true. As gently as possible I was easing them out to make room within our spartan staff budget for people who could do the job as I thought it should be done.*

Daniel Patrick Moynihan's staff presented a similar problem at the other end of our limited political spectrum. When he ran the Urban Affairs Council, Moynihan assembled a cadre of very young, very bright liberals to work on urban problems. Some of them left soon after Pat's Urban Affairs Council was melded with the Domestic Council. Most of the rest worked for Moynihan until he resigned from the Cabinet. But when Pat left he urged me—among others—to take his young people aboard. I tried to use one or two, with no more success than I had had using Arthur Burns's people.

When Washington reporters asked me what qualifications I possessed to be the President's assistant for domestic affairs, the question was usually asked with a sneer. After all, I was only "a zoning lawyer" from Seattle, a place most of them had barely heard of. I had no prior Washington experience.

Before reporters had ever asked me that question I asked it of myself, more than once. During the 1968 campaign, I wondered what I was doing pretending I could run Nixon's tour; after all, I wasn't a politician. The answer was simply that Richard Nixon had confidence in me. If he hadn't, it wouldn't matter how much training and experience I'd had.

Every President adorns his staff with pedagogues and other superbly qualified big names. They are given large offices and a staff, and from time to time attend conferences and conventions, where they bring greetings from the President. We had science advisers who were winners of prestigious prizes. We had staff men who had been college presidents. There were practical politicians on our White House staff who had run a national political party or state organization, or held high elective office. Some of these were respected, famous and successful in their fields, but those who didn't win Richard Nixon's personal confidence simply languished. He rarely saw

---

* In 1972 Nixon ordered me to rehire Martin Anderson and instructed me to find something worthwhile for him to do. I was never told what led to this ultimatum, but I assumed that Nixon had been attacked on his right flank by Goldwater, Burns, Buchanan or one of the others. I did rehire Anderson, as a part-time employee, and he did some good, though doctrinaire, analysis for us. But I never got any praise from the right-wingers on the sidelines—only grief.

them except on ceremonial occasions, and then only briefly.

A very high percentage of the White House staff, the National Security Council staff and the Domestic Council staff was young; the majority were probably 30 or under. They were intelligent (or, at least, facile) and inexperienced in government at any level. Most had never worked in Washington or for the Federal Government before.

An example was Bud Krogh, the son of one of my uncle's best friends. I saw Bud often as he finished college, did a Navy tour and completed law school. He worked for my law firm during his summer vacations, and I hired him full time when he graduated. Bud was an attractive, hardworking and intelligent young man.

In the main, Krogh did do good work; he ran the Government's drug-abuse program, looked after the Justice Department and designed some major organizational reforms.

At the same time, he demonstrated such doubtful personal judgment on several occasions that it has to be said he materially contributed to the demise of the Nixon Administration. G. Gordon Liddy was Krogh's protégé. When Liddy worked at the Treasury Department, a time came when his boss, Eugene Rossides, was about to fire him. Earlier Liddy had worked on a law-enforcement task force that Krogh oversaw, so when he got into trouble Liddy came to Krogh for help. Krogh disliked Rossides. Unfortunately, he took the occasion to thumb his nose at Rossides by bringing Liddy into the White House.*

John Dean, my successor as Counsel to the President, was another representative member of the younger staff. He was young, impeccably dressed, apparently intelligent. *His* sponsor was John Mitchell, who urged him upon Bob Haldeman, since the then-vacant position of Counsel was part of the Haldeman organization. Because Dean came from the Justice Department with Mitchell's blessing, only the most cursory background check was done.

Dean's ex-wife was the daughter of a wealthy Missouri Congressman, and that was all of Dean's political background; unfortunately, John Dean's professional background was even shallower. He had practiced law very briefly with a good

---

* It's a fact that I never met G. Gordon Liddy as long as I worked at the White House. He wrote several good memoranda which I read, and once I telephoned him about one of them, but he always worked out of my sight. In mitigation of Krogh's lapse, it should be remembered that Liddy had one other sponsor who urged his employment: Gerald Ford, then the Minority Leader of the House of Representatives.

Washington firm. His personnel file would have disclosed that one of the firm's partners accused him of self-dealing in a radio-station license case and Dean was summarily fired. But apparently no one at the White House looked at the file before Mitchell sent him over to be the President's Counsel.

When Dean left that firm and took a job with a congressional committee staff, the law firm was persuaded to say that Dean's conduct there ought not to preclude his hire elsewhere.

During his time at the White House, Dean offered a close observer some clues. The young man lived beyond his salary. He owned an expensive town house in Alexandria next door to Senator Lowell Weicker. Dean's Porsche, Gucci loafers and tailored sports clothes should have raised more eyebrows than they did. I'm told that for a time one of Dean's flashy girlfriends was on his office payroll to "advance" his trips around the country and abroad.

In 1972 I received a tip from a member of the Cabinet about Dean's trouble with the law firm he had briefly worked for. Because Dean reported to Haldeman I would ordinarily have sent it on to him, but Haldeman was away, so I asked my staff to have Dean's personnel file sent over to me. The next day it arrived, but it was hand-carried into my office by Dean's assistant Fred Fielding.* Fielding explained that the file was "sealed." (In fact, it was in a large envelope wrapped around and around with cellophane tape.) John Dean was out of town and would not be back for several days. Why did I want the file? Fielding asked. I repeated what I'd been told and said I wanted to look at the law firm's statements in the file. Fielding tucked the package firmly under his arm and said he'd have Dean call me. This was an old allegation that was easily explained, Fielding assured me.†

I let Fielding talk me out of looking at the file, and the next day Dean called to assure me that there was nothing to the rumor. A few days later he came in to explain, with the deepest sincerity, how the law firm's partners had misunderstood his motives.

When I later learned that Dean had financed his honeymoon with trust funds, I was not too surprised. His explana-

---

* Haldeman's nominee for "Deep Throat."

† In view of this episode, I find it ironic that Fred Fielding was appointed to review conflicts of interest and ethics problems during Ronald Reagan's transition and became Counsel to the President early in the Reagan Administration.

tion about "borrowing" the money reminded me of the way he'd talked himself out of the previous allegation.

Dean was more open about his romantic pursuits. In fact, he revealed in vivid detail a great deal more than one wanted to know about his premarital bouts with his friend Maureen. Thinking back to the time when John Sears, a White House aide, was fired on suspicion of conducting the most discreet of flirtations, I had difficulty accounting for the tolerance Dean was accorded. It may be that Haldeman was not privy to Dean's romantic chronicles.

CHAPTER SEVEN

The Cabinet

AT 8 A.M. on January 22, 1969, Chief Justice Earl Warren swore in the new Nixon Cabinet. Nixon had deliberately set that unreasonable morning hour to demonstrate to everyone—including the Cabinet members—that the Nixon team was going to work early, often and hard. ("In view of the fact that we started at eight o'clock in the morning . . . we will call it a working Cabinet.")

This Cabinet had first gathered in Washington a month earlier, to be dramatically unveiled on live television. The Secretaries and their families had been secretly stashed in the Sheraton Park Hotel so that Nixon could reveal them to a waiting nation on prime-time television on December 13. The logistical problems involved in spiriting those twelve families past staked-out reporters and into their hotel suites were monumental, and they were all mine. I recruited a team of the campaign advance men to schedule the arrivals, with one man to look after each family; we had Hickels from Alaska, Blounts from Alabama, Kennedys from Chicago and Finches from California, with kids of all ages.

After the television extravaganza, Nixon spent the following day with the Secretaries and their wives while some of our campaign team took the Cabinet children on a gigantic guided tour of Washington, ostensibly conducted by Tricia and Julie.

At the Sheraton Park I had organized a day of lectures and discussion—a short course on how to be a Cabinet officer—for the husbands and wives, plus the Agnews and Nixons. The group heard experts talk about press relations, conflicts of interest, Congressional relations, how to work with the White House, protocol and etiquette, and heard much from the President-elect about how he intended to change things.

Nixon led off with a rambling speech in which he exhorted his Cabinet to work hard, seize their departments from the control of their dastardly bureaucracies, save time for their families and stay in touch with the American people. The President made it sound as if he intended to give his Cabinet full freedom to run their departments without White House interference. At the time, that might have been Nixon's real intention.

But before too many weeks it was obvious that he'd changed his mind. Some of the men he'd selected for the Cabinet soon embarrassed him by what they said or did, and he began to instruct them via his senior staff: Bob Haldeman, Dr. Arthur Burns, Daniel P. Moynihan, Bryce Harlow and Henry Kissinger. Nixon knew he was reneging; but as he said to me, none of his Cabinet had been elected—only Richard Nixon had been elected, and only he would have to stand for reelection. If he had to pay the political price for his Cabinet Secretaries' mistakes, then he, by God, had the right and obligation to correct those mistakes.

If Bob Finch had been given a free hand at HEW, Nixon would have been held liable for a civil rights policy he didn't believe in and refused to defend. Moreover, Finch and John Mitchell disagreed philosophically, yet their responsibility for civil rights problems overlapped. When there was conflict between Secretaries, only the President and his staff could resolve it.

None of that was discussed at that first Cabinet session; it might have been better if it had been. The Cabinet men undoubtedly began their jobs with the euphoric and erroneous idea that Nixon reposed great, almost unbounded confidence in each of them. At the time Nixon probably *believed* that he did, but essentially he didn't. He wanted to be reelected and he wanted a place in history as a great President. Because he wanted these things he couldn't possibly give the Cabinet free rein.

Nixon had known some of the Cabinet—HEW Secretary Robert Finch, Secretary of State William Rogers, Secretary of

Commerce Maurice Stans and Secretary of Defense Melvin Laird—for a long time. Some, like Secretary of Labor George Shultz and Secretary of Agriculture Clifford Hardin, he had never met. They were a mixed lot, disparate in ability and personality. Within a year Budget Director Robert Mayo, Treasury Secretary David Kennedy and Transportation Secretary John Volpe had totally lost Nixon's confidence, and both Mitchell and Finch—two of the supposed rocks upon which Nixon had built his Cabinet—were warring with each other and waning in Nixon's esteem.

Conflict characterized the Cabinet's teamwork from the beginning. Early in the term, Treasury's Customs agents and Justice's narcotics agents violently disputed who had jurisdiction over foreign drug busts. In one instance they began shooting at each other when both competing forces showed up at a suspected heroin laboratory.

John Mitchell adamantly defended his narcs, and David Kennedy refused to yield Customs' jurisdictional claims. So the President designated me to adjudicate the dispute, because law enforcement was a part of his Counsel's bailiwick. I met with Kennedy and Mitchell one Saturday morning in the Roosevelt Room, across the hall from the Oval Office. David Kennedy had been briefed to the nines by his staff; he knew all about all the statutes, regulations and executive orders that applied to the disputed jurisdictional question. He was fully informed about what the Justice Department narcs had done wrong, and he came out swinging. But it wasn't a fair fight. Mitchell was Nixon's man, and Mitchell knew it, and I knew it. After all the talking was over, I urged Secretary Kennedy to compromise, but he wouldn't budge. So I adjourned the meeting and went upstairs to draft a memorandum for the President to sign.

The Justice Department won the dispute, because Nixon had more confidence in John Mitchell than he did in David Kennedy. (But in later years, when John B. Connally was its Secretary, the Treasury Department began to win all its jurisdictional battles with the Department of Justice.)

Nixonomics was another area that got off to an uncertain start. The Triad and the Quadriad were committees of economic advisers who met with the President at his convenience. Of all domestic subjects, the economy commanded more of Richard Nixon's attention than any other. (And of course, it was not exclusively domestic in character.) Arthur Burns, John Connally and George Shultz were the most influential of Nixon's economic advisers. All held Cabinet rank, but so did others who were less persuasive. These three brought talent and experience to the problem, and their strong personalities had a lot to do with the course of economic events.

One of the less influential Cabinet members was Robert Mayo, our first Budget Director. Mayo had been a subordinate of David Kennedy's at a Chicago bank before Kennedy became Secretary of the Treasury. That troubled Nixon.

"Kennedy is weak and Mayo thinks he's still under him," the President said. "Our economic people don't have that bulldog attitude they need. Paul McCracken is a decent man, but he's not strong either."

Mayo was a pudgy, bespectacled banker whose mannerisms and odd sense of humor thoroughly alienated Nixon during the development of the budget in the fall of 1969. The more Nixon showed signs of annoyance with Mayo's *bonhomie,* the more Mayo compensated by trying to be more humorous and engaging.

By late November, with only three weeks remaining to make all the final Federal budget decisions, Nixon refused to spend any more time with his Budget Director. I was appointed go-between, carrying Mayo's questions and Nixon's answers back and forth. When Mayo tried to see or telephone the President, Nixon would tell Haldeman to refer Mayo to me. It was awkward, procedurally and personally.

Once the budget was issued in January 1970, Nixon avoided convening the economic quadriad because Mayo was a member. Instead he would see Arthur Burns, David Kennedy and Paul McCracken, singly or in a group of three.

Finally, in early March, Mayo demanded a showdown meeting with the President. Nixon gathered Henry Kissinger, Bob Haldeman and me to lend him support when he confronted the well-rehearsed and organized Mr. Mayo. Mayo came in grimly, sat down and began to recite a list of grievances:

He had been denied all access, Mayo first (correctly) claimed.

Second, Ehrlichman's new domestic-policy operation was going to conflict with the function of Mayo's Budget Bureau.

Third, Kissinger persisted in putting Mayo on committees of *under*secretaries. Mayo had Cabinet rank. He should be on committees of Secretaries.

Fourth, the budget and budget message just prepared had, for the first time in history, been completed without the Budget Director's talking directly with the President. Important decisions could get garbled if the President insisted upon working that way.

Mayo announced to the President that he had been offered "another opportunity" and was thinking of resigning during the summer, if his relationship with the President and the rest of us couldn't be worked out.

Nixon said he would give Mayo's complaints full consideration. Then, when only Bob Haldeman and I remained in the office, Nixon flashed an embarrassed smile. "I guess Mayo has got to go," he said.

Once the decision was made to replace Mayo, Nixon began to play his fill-the-vacancy game in earnest.

Caspar Weinberger, who had been Ronald Reagan's hard-nosed budget director in California, would be the new Deputy Director of the Office of Management and Budget, Nixon said tentatively. Hickel would be moved out of Interior. Nothing would be done until July, however. In July the Nixon Cabinet would set a record of longevity, surpassing that of Woodrow Wilson's Cabinet. He'd hold them all together until he'd broken the record.

Two weeks later Nixon changed his mind. Mayo should leave at once; never mind the Wilson record. Bob Haldeman was sent to tell Mayo that he "lacked the President's confidence." Haldeman delivered the coup and reported that Mayo might be gone in about three weeks.

Nixon shuffled some new pieces. He might put John Mitchell on the Supreme Court. "Do you think he can be confirmed?" he wondered. "Pat Moynihan will be leaving in time to teach at Harvard in the fall. He has taken a lot of heat from his wife, poor fellow; she just doesn't like Washington. We should move Don Rumsfeld; we'll make him an assistant to the President. He's wasted at OEO."

Bryce Harlow will leave in November, Nixon noted, in time to return to Procter and Gamble and retain his retirement and other fringe benefits.

Hickel is asking if the President had confidence in him? Stall him: "The President has confidence in all the members of the Cabinet; he'll tell you if ever he doesn't."

Nixon felt guilty about firing Mayo. Haldeman should talk to Mayo again: "Tell him that after the elections in November he might become U.N. Ambassador or we'll put him at the CIA. We don't want him rattling around bad-mouthing the President."

Nixon yearned to recruit his old law professor Kenneth

Rush; perhaps he could join the Cabinet or direct the CIA.

"Should we hold a vacancy on the Federal Reserve Board for Bob Mayo?" Nixon rambled. "Maurice Stans is griping that he and the others in the Cabinet are too remote from the President. He shouldn't say that. Perhaps Weinberger should succeed Mayo as Director of OMB."

In the summer of 1970, Bob Mayo left and George Shultz took his place. Hardly anyone noticed that Mayo was gone.

I sometimes wondered what George Shultz said to his wife, Obie, when he went home after a routine day with Richard Nixon and the White House staff.

George had been Dean of the School of Business at the University of Chicago. He was taking a sabbatical, doing research at Stanford, when Nixon picked him to be his Secretary of Labor. Shultz had no practical political experience (other than as a member of a university faculty), but he had been an arbitrator and negotiator in major labor disputes and was considered an authority on industrial labor problems. Shultz was an economist by education, however, and before long he was being included in meetings with the President on economic subjects that went far beyond the scope of his Department of Labor.

Nixon found Shultz both expert and congenial. George rarely confronted Nixon with overt disagreement; like others who were successful with Nixon, if Shultz considered a Presidential decision unwise he would either loyally try to make it work—putting the best face on it he could—or loyally disregard it, hoping Nixon would eventually change his mind.

Shultz was a tough, determined ex-Marine who could be stubborn beyond reason, but I usually found him easy to work with. When he came from Labor to the Office of Management and Budget—at the time of the reorganization of the White House—he and I had to figure out how to mesh the gears of the new Domestic Council with those of the old Bureau of the Budget, which had become his OMB. George's large inherited staff had been at Budget a long time, as career government experts. My Domestic Council people were new to government, impatient with its processes and primarily devoted to Richard Nixon's political well-being. The OMB people knew everything—about what was going on in the departments and agencies, about what had happened during the years before we got there, about how things worked in Washington and out in the regions. The domestic-policy staff needed to know those things to produce good work for the President.

At the same time, George realized that my people had a credibility with Richard Nixon that his careerists could never attain. John Whitaker, an assistant director of the Domestic Council staff, had been a Nixon loyalist for more than a decade, working in half a dozen high-level campaign jobs. If an issue had come to Nixon with Whitaker recommending "yes" and seven OMB men advising "no," Nixon would have gone along with Whitaker because he knew he could rely on him to look out for Nixon's political success, whatever the merits of the opposite argument might be.

Shultz and I agreed at the outset that there was great potential for rivalry and jealousy unless we kept our two organizations in very close touch. We devised a daily morning meeting of OMB's top six or eight people with the eight leaders of the Domestic Council staff. That session quickly became a vital White House clearinghouse. There, every morning at seven thirty in the Roosevelt Room, across the hall from the Oval Office, the substantive and tactical problems of the day were dealt with. George sat at one end of the conference table and I sat at the other with our principal assistants along either side. There was no agenda, and the only firm rules were (1) that we would adjourn promptly at 8 A.M. and (2) that every person at the table would be called upon to contribute, every morning. Any topic could be raised, but with so little time, no one earned any points for trivia. Nor was there time to debate.

Before long, the President's Congressional-liaison men were also sitting in with us every morning and we began calling on them in the daily round-the-table. Then others asked to come, because these sessions were virtually the only place in the White House where one could find out what was actually going on, as far as substance and policy were concerned.

The President's Consumer Adviser, Virginia Knauer, began coming to the seven-thirty meeting. Then we added Peter Flanigan and one of his aides, and Don Rumsfeld and someone from the press office. Even the Science Adviser attended every day. Some of these people didn't contribute much, but Shultz and I agreed that it did no harm to have them there, and it partly assuaged their pangs. The President rarely saw them, and this meeting was the next-best thing to a Presidential audience.

So five and sometimes six days a week the OMB leadership and my deputy and assistant directors met to mesh our efforts. And all through the budget process, beginning in the spring of every year, my staff sat in with Shultz' budget examiners, probing for early signals of future trouble and trying to forecast the issues we would be coping with in the departments and agencies a year later.

OMB under Caspar Weinberger (who advanced to Director when Shultz succeeded John Connally at Treasury) was harder for me to work with. Shultz had a talent for compromise and accommodation that had lubricated the surfaces between his staff and mine; Weinberger was less flexible. Cap Weinberger was inclined to take Nixon's orders at face value, whereas Shultz exercised some judgment. Nixon was fond of ordering personnel cuts ("cut the State Department by fifteen percent; do it by Friday"), and Cap was the sort who might salute and go out and begin to cut off heads left and right, without regard for Congressional reaction, our ability to get the job done or how the public might receive such a sudden "reduction in force."

At Treasury, George Shultz began to deal with the Finance Ministers abroad, playing a major role in international monetary affairs. But Richard Nixon also expected George to spend a couple of days a week in the White House, overseeing the domestic economy. And he was still Nixon's conduit to George Meany and other labor leaders.

Melvin Laird was a creature of the Congress, and that probably explains his appointment as Nixon's Secretary of Defense. Nixon first wanted Democratic Senator Henry Jackson for the job, but couldn't get him. Both Laird and Jackson were effective members of the Congressional elite, who could do the kind of downfield blocking on Capitol Hill that Nixon needed to ensure healthy defense appropriations and a free hand in Vietnam.

Congressional doves were going to try to impede him, the President-elect knew. He would need a coalition of conservative Democrats and Republicans to defeat the efforts of anti-Vietnam advocates like Stuart Symington, Frank Church and Les Aspin. Thus, a Secretary of Defense had to understand the Congress and be willing to play its games. And Laird was a consummate Congressional game-player.

Secretary Laird had personal ambitions that sometimes got in Nixon's way. At the time Nixon and Kissinger were taking a hard line with the North Vietnamese, hoping to coerce a settlement of the war, Secretary of Defense Laird was posing as a dove; he had one eye on the voters back home in Wisconsin. Nixon told me Laird hoped to be elected to the Senate, having already served in the House. To keep his dovish credentials with the folks at home, Laird was continually leaking stories to the press that he opposed the aggressive war policies of the White House.

Laird actually refused to carry out some of Nixon's instructions concerning the conduct of the war, particularly some of the Air Force operations. So Henry Kissinger and the President cultivated the Joint Chiefs of Staff. Instead of sending orders through the Secretary of Defense, Henry would send the President's instructions to Admiral Thomas Moorer, Chairman of the Joint Chiefs, bypassing Laird. Laird knew that was happening, of course, but he didn't object, since Henry's gambit left Laird free to disown the operations.

Nixon characterized Laird to me as a "sneak." Just how sneaky he was Laird revealed during the Green Berets incident.

The second week in September 1969, I was called out of a perfunctory meeting Nixon was having with Joe Blatchford, the director of the Peace Corps. Henry Kissinger was asking me to meet with Secretary of the Army Stanley Resor to hear about the possible court-martial of some of the elite Green Beret soldiers. It was obvious that the President had directed Henry to include me in order to get an outsider's opinion of what should be done; Kissinger simply did not invite other staff people into his jurisdictional bailiwick otherwise.

The Green Berets stood charged with murdering a Vietnamese who was believed to be a double agent. Nixon did not like the idea of court-martialing those superb soldiers for simply doing what soldiers are supposed to be doing in a bitter war. The President did not like to appear to be letting down his fighting men, so he was considering dismissing the charges. That upset Secretary Resor.

I had never met Stanley Resor before. He impressed me as an intelligent and sensitive man of rarefied breeding, not at all the sort of fellow I would have expected to find in charge of our Army. He briefly told me the facts of the case, which he obviously found to be distasteful. "To quash the court-martial of these men," he added, "would, in my view, be both immoral and political dynamite. It is bad enough we are over there [in Vietnam] fighting an immoral war."

Kissinger interjected to assure Resor that he too considered it an immoral war.

Resor continued: "The CIA and the United States Army simply do not do business as the men in this case did. Spies are not taken out and killed without due process of law." Right there I wrote in my notes, *Who'll believe that?"*

The next day, while at dinner with the President, Kissinger, Haldeman and Bryce Harlow at Camp David, I had a call from the Secretary of Defense. Stanley Resor was with him, Laird said, and had just told him that both General Creighton Abrams and Admiral John McCain felt it absolutely necessary for the Green Beret court-martial to proceed. Laird wanted the President to know (through me) that these two, the top military brass in Vietnam, believed the Berets would be absolved and that it was important to permit their trial to proceed to such a verdict. "Unfortunately," Laird said, "a great many people believe the Berets are assassins; an acquittal would clear the record." I said I would convey the message. But I wondered (and still wonder) why Laird didn't call Kissinger to the telephone. He was Laird's White House liaison.

When I returned to the table with Laird's message, Bryce Harlow predicted that committees of the Congress would hold hearings into the Green Beret case, whatever the President did. Bryce wondered aloud what his old friend Admiral McCain had *really* told Resor and Laird. Like the rest of us, Harlow sometimes found it hard to believe our Secretary of Defense. While at the table, Harlow, at the President's urging, picked up a Camp David telephone and tried to reach McCain, but was told the Admiral was flying to his office in Hawaii.

Less than an hour later, Secretary Laird called me again to ask why the White House was trying to call McCain. Before I could refer him to Harlow, Laird reported that a Pentagon reporter was going with a story that the White House had decided to quash the Green Beret court-martial. I took that as a typical Laird gambit to try to find out what was going on. Before I hung up I assured him that no decisions had yet been made.

I came back to our meeting smiling. "Mel knows Bryce tried to call McCain," I said. "How do you suppose he knew that?"

All of us knew. At that time Camp David's telephones went through an Army Signal Corps switchboard, not through the regular civilian "Admin Board" located in the White House. The Camp David operators were all Army enlisted men and their supervisors were Army officers. The only question was: how closely did Mel Laird monitor the President and the rest of us at Camp David when we called someone on his Army telephone system? Did he just keep track of whom we called, or did he also know what was said?

Before long, Bob Haldeman arranged for some of the civilian telephone operators to be brought to Camp David to operate the switchboard whenever the President was there. But the White House Communications Agency, the group which handled the President's telephone communications whenever he traveled, and which transmitted most of the cable traffic into and out of the White House, continued to be operated by Mel Laird's military.

From time to time Henry Kissinger complained bitterly to Nixon, Haldeman and me about Laird's unscrupulous tactics. But Henry didn't demand Laird's firing, as he did Secretary of State William Rogers'. Laird was so effective with his old Congressional cronies that everyone realized he was irreplaceable.

A prospective Cabinet member could be looked at by a President in two ways. First, a President might ask, does he or she have the talent, that mixture of art and science, that will enable him to get some things done? Second, will he (or she) and the President get along? Perhaps the second is the more important qualification. Outward Bound suggests that executives who are going to work together be required to go on a wilderness trip together first, to see if they are compatible.

If Richard Nixon, Wally Hickel and George Romney had backpacked together for four days in the Pecos wilderness, the first Nixon Cabinet would not have included either of those two former governors, I'd bet. They just didn't get along.

Early in the 1968 campaign I was on a United Airlines plane returning to Seattle from a Chicago political strategy meeting while Governor Walter Hickel of Alaska was up in the first-class section returning home from the same meeting. After the meal had been served, Hickel began "working" the coach section of the plane, slowly moving down the aisle shaking hands and talking to every passenger. He introduced himself, said a few words of praise for Richard Nixon and gave out Nixon buttons to anyone who would take one. By the end of the trip he'd shaken every hand on the plane.

When I reached Seattle I phoned Bob Haldeman to tell him about Hickel's performance, and Bob passed along my description to Richard Nixon. I don't know what impact that episode actually had on Hickel's political career, but I'm willing to bet it had some effect. That kind of symbolic effort meant much to Nixon. He wanted his people to step out and support him openly and vigorously.

Whatever else he was—or was not—Wally Hickel was vigorous. As a young man he had gone to Alaska from the Midwest, penniless and ambitious. What Wally lacked in education and refinement he made up in hustle. By the time he was

40 he'd made his first million in land development and had gravitated to politics.

Hickel was different from the others in the Cabinet, not only because Alaskans are different, but also because he had always been a small-timer. His entire Alaska state government amounted to less than the Department of the Interior—fewer people, a smaller budget and narrower problems. His own private land-development projects would have been small potatoes anywhere except in Alaska. He was the proverbial big frog in a small puddle until he came to Washington, and there he had trouble understanding the difference. I was sympathetic; I had the same problem on a little different scale.

Hickel was often abrupt and dogmatic; at times I found him difficult to work with simply because he was less experienced and less informed than his colleagues. Part of the responsibility lay with Hickel's staff, some Alaskans who did not prepare him well. But I formed a lingering suspicion that Hickel also had a reading deficiency of some kind that made it difficult for him to understand and retain written information.

John Whitaker was the White House expert on Wally Hickel. John helped get Hickel ready for his confirmation hearings, then tried to guide him in his relationship with Richard Nixon. When Hickel stayed on the track Whitaker laid for him, he was usually all right. But when Hickel went off on his own—usually out of stubbornness or vanity—there was trouble.

It is generally assumed—even by Wally Hickel himself—that his troubles began when he wrote the President on May 6, 1970, charging that Nixon lacked "appropriate concern" for dissenting young people who were protesting the Vietnam war. The most bothersome aspect of that letter was that Hickel gave a copy of the letter to a reporter even before he sent it over to the White House. Thus, even as John Whitaker was trying to ensure that neither Ron Ziegler nor Herb Klein played into Hickel's hands by releasing the letter from the White House, *The* (Washington) *Evening Star* was setting it in type for its next edition.

Years later one of Hickel's aides wrote me a letter with an account of what had happened that week at Interior. In reaction to the Cambodian "incursion," Kent State and the Vice President's attack on young demonstrators, one of Hickel's younger staff aides drafted a proposed manifesto for Wally Hickel to issue. Hickel rarely wrote or even read substantive memoranda that went out over his signature; he relied upon his staff to read him the gist of what he was sending. In this case Hickel liked the idea of speaking out, but he decided that he would send a letter to the President, rather than simply issue a statement to the press. Several of his staff collaborated on the text, and when it was signed, Hickel directed one of them to give a copy to a woman reporter for the *Star* who had impressed Hickel. It is generally assumed that that was the beginning of the end for Wally.

In fact, fully two months earlier, in early March 1970, Richard Nixon had begun to consider who might replace Hickel as Secretary of the Interior. Nixon was planning to dismiss other Cabinet Secretaries also.

Hickel had begun as the goat of the Cabinet. The media had savaged him for being an exploitive developer in a job that was supposed to belong to the conservationists and environmentalists. During his first year at Interior he sided with the oil companies in advocating offshore drilling and the Alaska pipeline, and the press had worked him over for that.

But when Hickel's youth letter hit the papers, he suddenly became the darling of *The New York Times, The Washington Post* and the networks. After all those months as a punching bag, Hickel liked the adulation more than a little. He was a "pop" hero. He gave interviews, and his staff did too, hitting the President for his unavailability to Hickel. We on the White House staff got most of the specific blame in these broadsides, but the President saw all of the favorable Hickel press attention as undercutting him at a time when he needed the broadest public support. His Cabinet, Nixon exclaimed, should be out there beating the drum for him, not leaking letters and attacking his staff in the press.

By May 21 it was definite: Rogers Morton would replace Hickel, the President told me. Four days later Hickel's proposed trip to Russia was ordered canceled. And by then Bob Haldeman's staff had reported that Hickel's letter had actually been drafted by a young White House Fellow, Mike Levitt, who was attached to the Interior Department for the year of his fellowship. Levitt went on Haldeman's list of things to take care of.

By Wednesday, May 27, Hickel had heard nothing at all from the President about his critical letter, and the silence was bothering him. About three in the afternoon he came to my office. "Am I in trouble?" he asked.

"I guess I'd better ask the President how much trouble you're in," I said.

"I'd like to see him."

"I'll see what I can do," I assured him.

In the late afternoon I talked to the President; then I telephoned Hickel. "Wally, the President says he thinks it would be a good idea for you to go home and run for Governor."

"Hell, John, there's only three days left to file up there. Even if I wanted to, I'm not so sure I could. Will he talk to me?"

"Yes, he will. He'll see you tomorrow afternoon. But he'll want to know all about your running for Governor of Alaska, nothing else."

"Okay," Hickel said. "I'll see what I can find out."

Hickel met with Nixon and me about four o'clock the next afternoon. He reported that if he were to run for Governor it would tear the Alaska Republican Party apart. During the night he had talked with the Chief Justice of the State Supreme Court and other Alaskan politicians. Several candidates had already filed and probably wouldn't back off. Hickel would precipitate a tough primary fight if he announced for the office now.

Nixon wouldn't retreat either. He assigned Bryce Harlow to try to clear a track for Hickel's Alaskan candidacy, then quickly left the office to unveil a portrait of President Madison before leaving for Knoxville and San Clemente. I left too, for a weekend in the Virgin Islands. Nothing specific was said to Hickel about his tenure beyond the President's obvious, if oblique, direction that Hickel ought to go home and run for Governor.

The next day *The New York Times* carried Hickel's denials: he would not resign and he would not run for Governor of Alaska. His office told the *Times* that Hickel and the President had discussed "sensitive areas." "This," the *Times* reported, "was interpreted as being Mr. Hickel's ideas on better communication with young people." That, of course, is not what they had discussed.

From that time on, Hickel's departure was certain; the only questions were when and how. Meanwhile, he was the lamest of lame ducks.

By October, Nixon had decided to let Hickel go soon, but he wanted it to appear that his grounds were not the fact of Hickel's May letter or its publicity. Instead, there would be an audit of the Interior Department. At Nixon's insistence, George Shultz appointed Arnold Weber to assemble a team of auditors from other departments and agencies to go into Interior's books. We had heard rumors of financial scandal at Interior. The auditors were to look at air charters, Hickel's office remodeling and charges involving the use of confiscated liquor. Weber estimated he'd need until the end of the year to do a thorough job. Nixon wanted his report by the end of November.

On November 7, during a weekend at Key Biscayne, the President convened a post-election bull session with Bob Haldeman, Bob Finch, John Mitchell, Bryce Harlow, Charles Colson, Don Rumsfeld and me. During that talk Nixon popped a surprise: he'd decided to immediately replace Secretaries Romney, Hickel and Kennedy. Rogers Morton would replace Hickel, and Bryce Harlow would take Morton's place as Chairman of the Republican National Committee. All of that was a big surprise to Harlow, who immediately declined the honor. The rest of the plan involved Rumsfeld's taking HUD, and Clark MacGregor and George Bush (both defeated for the Senate that week) taking jobs in the White House.

All of that was only a Nixon trial balloon, but the part about Hickel and Morton continued to fly. Two weeks later the President was saying "Hickel must go" more frequently than usual. On the twenty-fourth, Nixon said, "I'll see him tomorrow" and "Draw me up a talking paper."

On the eve of Thanksgiving, I ushered Wally Hickel to the Oval Office. It was a chilly evening, and for some reason, Hickel kept his overcoat on his lap all through the President's peroration. With relatively little hemming and hawing Nixon told Wally that he had decided to ask for his resignation. I kept my head down, taking notes, not anxious to look at either of them.

Hickel asked, "Will that be effective the first of the year?"

"No," Nixon said. "That's effective today."

Nineteen-seventy was a year of Cabinet changes. Before the actual switching took place, Nixon had talked about them endlessly, like a woman about to rearrange the living room. In early spring he told Haldeman he'd decided to move Robert Finch to the White House, replacing him as HEW Secretary with Elliot Richardson, who was then number two man at the State Department. Don Rumsfeld would be Director of the Office of Management and Budget, and Caspar Weinberger his deputy.

Nixon told me on May 25 that in November he would replace Secretaries Romney, Hickel and Kennedy; Rumsfeld would be temporary Director of OMB until January. Three days later, Nixon had decided to fire the Commissioner of Education, James Allen. On June 5 he moved Finch out of HEW and swore in Richardson, transferring his Science Adviser, Lee DuBridge, to the State Department in the process. (At Richardson's swearing-in, William Rogers leaned over to me and muttered, "Some trade: I give Elliot Richardson and get Lee DuBridge!")

The next day he decided to fire George Romney at once. Romney had issued a press release announcing he was taking a cut in salary to help balance the budget. "An ineffective grandstand play," Nixon called it. "That does it. He's got to go."* Two days later Labor Secretary George Shultz was picked to be Director of the OMB. The same day he offered Daniel Patrick Moynihan the post of Ambassador to the United Nations in New York. Pat said he'd think about it.

Once he'd decided to bring Bob Finch into the White House, Nixon fretted about what Finch could do there. On the premise that Finch was an administrator (more than doubtful in view of his HEW debacle) and a politician, Nixon proposed that Finch take over the White House political operation personified by Harry Dent and Murray Chotiner, but actually run by Bob Haldeman. Finch was enough of a politician to see the problems in trying to occupy that part of Haldeman's turf, so he laughed off the proposal by saying he was "too close to Chotiner and too far from Dent" to be able to give them instructions.

Nixon continued to be concerned about Finch. Bob had collapsed during his final crisis at HEW, and had been hospitalized with what the President's doctor reported was a psychosomatic paralysis of one arm. Nixon understood that to mean that Finch had undergone a kind of mental collapse, and he was determined that the White House should be a peaceful shelter for his longtime aide and ally. Finch really should be in the Senate, Nixon said. He should build up a base in California while he was in the White House; then he should move home and run.†

---

* Two weeks after Romney's announcement, Nixon gave me a research assignment: how could we go about lowering the President's salary by $25,000, to $75,000 a year? At the same time, what would it take to raise his pension in the same amount—$25,000? A lawyer dutifully wrote him a memorandum on how it could be done, but nothing more was ever said about it by the President.

† Nixon deeply immersed himself in California politics to try to make a place for Bob Finch in the Senate. About the time Finch came to the White House, the incumbent Republican, Senator George Murphy, was reported to be in poor physical and political health in California. Nixon decided that the old movie actor should retire—he'd probably be defeated in November—and Finch should run in his place. The only problem was that George Murphy didn't agree.

Nixon hoped that a sinecure in the West Wing could incubate the Senatorial chances of Don Rumsfeld too. He had represented a solidly Republican Congressional district in the suburbs of Chicago; in 1969 Nixon decided he wanted him in the Executive Branch without really knowing how he wanted to use him. Rummy Rumsfeld was handsome and bright, and that was enough; Bryce Harlow and I were dispatched to recruit him. Eventually the senior staff grew to realize that the ambitious Rumsfeld would decline every assignment that did not enhance his personal goals; but that didn't become clear until he had moved into the West Wing. There he and Finch performed odd jobs, unconnected with either Kissinger's policy process or mine. Occasionally the Rumsfelds and Finches went off in one of the White House airplanes on an "inspection trip" to a foreign land, and their return was followed by a ceremonial appointment with the President to "report their findings."

Nixon was trying to conceive of a new niche for Spiro Agnew too. Having unleashed him in mid-1969, Nixon feared his Vice President had become too outspoken for most assignments. In July 1970, four months before the critical Congressional elections, Nixon was wondering whether Agnew would help or hurt if he were sent out to speak for congressional candidates.

"Do you think Agnew's too rough?" Nixon asked me one day. "Could we just use him in fund raising until November? His style isn't the problem, it's the content of what he says. He's got to be more positive. He must avoid all personal attacks on people; he can take on Congress as a unit, not as individuals."

Some candidates were sending word that Agnew would not be welcome in their districts or states. Senator Robert Taft of Ohio said so publicly; Agnew would offend his black and Jewish constituents, Taft was reported to have said. Nixon ordered Bryce Harlow to call Taft and protest; that was no way for a Republican candidate to talk about the Vice President. The Harlow protest, although mild, was truncated. Taft hung up on Bryce.

In the early spring, one emissary after another was sent to talk Murphy out of running for reelection. Rogers Morton, Richard Moore and others struck out. Because it was Nixon's judgment that Finch could not win a Republican primary against Murphy, and since time was short and Bob Finch's HEW record would be difficult for him to defend, Finch remained in the White House as the President's protégé—without portfolio—for another two years.

We had inaugurated some praiseworthy Indian policies—self-determination being our central theme—and we were gaining some recognition, thanks to Bobbie Greene Kilberg, Len Garment, Brad Patterson and the other White House staff people who urged Nixon at the right times and in the right directions. Nixon decided that if Taft and the others wouldn't have Agnew, our new Native brothers might. Maybe the Native American vote could be won if pursued. "Let's put Agnew on at least six Indian reservations between now and November," Nixon ordered. "Let's tie him to Indians. And," he said, as if determined to solve all of his problems at once, "Pat [Nixon] should also do Indians."

Once the 1970 Congressional elections were behind him, Nixon renewed his effort to make staff changes. A Minnesota Congressman, Clark MacGregor, had run against Hubert Humphrey and been steamrollered. John Mitchell suggested that MacGregor become the President's assistant for Congressional liaison, and Nixon began to play with that idea. By early December, George Romney also was to be moved.

George Wilcken Romney had been a rousing success as Governor of Michigan. Before that he had been the Washington lobbyist and spokesman for the automobile industry for many years, and he even ran American Motors at a profit in the late fifties. But as Nixon's Secretary of Housing and Urban Development he was a frustrated and unhappy man.

It must be remembered that Romney and Nixon were adversaries for the Republican nomination in early 1968, until Romney did badly in New Hampshire. Everyone recalls his statement that he'd been "brainwashed" on a trip to Vietnam, but he was faring poorly in the state primary polls even before that. Romney came into the Nixon Cabinet under the cloud of having lost to Nixon in the primaries. Romney's record as a governor and industry leader counted for very little with the President. Romney was a moderate—an ally of Nelson Rockefeller—and a loser.

Nixon never explained to me why he picked Romney for the Cabinet. It may have been one of those strange reverse-spin appointments like Walter Annenberg's to the Court of St. James's, and like some others I saw later in the Administration's tenure. At the 1968 Republican Convention, George Romney, Michigan's favorite-son candidate, had refused to the bitter end to release his pledged delegates to Nixon. That was an incident Nixon could never forget.

As President-elect, Nixon needed a few moderate Republicans to balance the Cabinet. What better revenge than to put Romney into a meaningless department, never to be noticed again?

That's not how Romney saw his role. He was in the President's Cabinet, a distinguished American of impeccable rectitude, with a record of solid success in government and business. He had countless awards for his civic efforts. People eagerly sought his opinions on the issues of the day, and he delivered his messages forcefully. He was photogenic, a strong public speaker with an attractive family. Face to face, he could be persuasive. (But I've also seen him depend upon large note cards in making an informal presentation, badly dulling his argument.)

It soon became clear that Secretary Romney was not destined to be one of President Richard Nixon's confidants or advisers. The more reluctant Nixon was to spend time with Romney, the harder Romney pressed to have frequent appointments with the President. Romney wanted to come over to the White House to talk about HUD's Model Cities program; it needed reorganization and a new funding commitment. But Richard Nixon thought Model Cities an abomination. (Early in 1969 Pat Moynihan was Romney's White House liaison, and it may be that Nixon was not telling either Moynihan or Romney how he really felt about such HUD programs. But from November, 1969 I was telling Romney how it really was, and he surely associated the advent of that bad news with my ascendency.)

When Nixon flatly refused to see Romney, it fell to me to hear the Secretary's long discourses on HUD's problems. And I also heard, often and at length, of Romney's personal discontent. He became increasingly unhappy at the way Richard Nixon was treating him, all of which I faithfully reported to the President.

Nixon had decided to fire Romney (along with Volpe and Hickel) no later than mid-1970, but first he wanted to try to bring about some peaceful resignations. HUD's budget was squeezed hard during the early round of discussions in that late summer and early fall. That was intended to be a signal to George Romney that it was time to move on.

Toward year end, in a rambling evaluation of the Cabinet, Nixon talked to me at length about the whole crowd, beginning with Stans, Mitchell and Rogers. When he got to Romney, he said, "Make the change." I was to talk to Romney the second week in December, to "sell him on leaving." Nixon wanted me to "tell Romney how the President really feels." I urged Nixon to talk to Romney himself. It was unrealistic to expect the Secretary to take my "suggestion" and resign without the worst kind of backlash.

On December 7, 1970, Nixon had a big personnel day. At breakfast, John Connally agreed to become Secretary of the Treasury. At 11 A.M., the President finally decided George Bush would be Ambassador to the United Nations and Don Rumsfeld should be Chairman of the Republican National Committee. An hour later, Nixon saw George Romney but, instead of firing him, rather gently suggested Romney ought to consider heading a national program of volunteer action instead of HUD. Romney said he'd think it over until after Christmas.

From then on, that December day was all downhill. Spiro Agnew came in to complain to Nixon about not being given more to do. And at 3 P.M., Don Rumsfeld flatly rejected the idea of leaving his warm and comfortable White House office for the rigors of the Republican National Committee.

After Christmas, Romney pocket-vetoed the President's unforceful suggestion that he move on. And within three months he was at the center of a kind of left-handed Cabinet revolt. The March 1971 revolution was presaged by a much milder Cabinet uprising a year and a half earlier when Roy Ash's Commission on the Reorganization of the Office of the President had successfully persuaded the President to inaugurate the Domestic Council as a policy-sifting and -effectuating apparatus roughly comparable to the National Security Council.

The Cabinet had been invited to a briefing in the White House Residence, to be given by Roy Ash and some of his commission colleagues, including John B. Connally. Midway through Ash's explanation of the new organization, George Romney voiced his objection to the erection of another White House staff apparatus which, he feared, would only make it more difficult for Cabinet members to meet with the President, face to face, man to man, one on one, for substantive discussions.

Romney could not always control his temper, and he had a tendency to get more and more worked up as he listened to what he was saying and increasingly believed what he heard. That day in 1969 he got quite exercised.

Spiro Agnew chimed in. He too said he was concerned that the President wasn't seeing enough of the Cabinet (and, inferentially, the Vice President).

John Connally damped down the discussion as soon as Agnew sat down. Had Big John not stood quickly to say that the Commission's recommendations were the President's desire, and that it was not really an open question, Agnew might well have put the issue to the Cabinet and confronted Nixon with a difficult vote of no confidence.

Now, in March of 1971, some members of the Cabinet were so unhappy with Nixon and his staff that a similar threat once again arose. Nixon's obvious reluctance to spend time with some of his Cabinet members certainly underlay their discontent, but in 1971 the ostensible issue was the economy. Nixon was coping with the wage–price spiral by working with a handful of economic advisers, and he was not calling Cabinet meetings to take advice from Red Blount, John Volpe, Maurice Stans and George Romney.

On March 18, 1971, I got wind that George Romney had invited part of the Cabinet to an early-morning meeting the following Monday to hear the Chairman of the President's Council of Economic Advisers report on the wage–price problem. Obviously this rump session would have no plenary powers, but the very fact that it convened was a symbolic rebellion against the President, who refused to hold a general Cabinet meeting where economic issues could be discussed. Moreover, my informant said, the Chairman of the Federal Reserve Board, Arthur Burns, was invited to attend and participate.

About 6:45 P.M. I managed to get a few minutes with the President to tell him what Romney was up to.

"You go to that meeting of that damn rump committee," the President exploded. "You just walk in and sit down. It's an end run of the system! Arthur Burns *can't* be in on it. He can't be."

I reminded Nixon that he had avoided general Cabinet sessions where there could be freewheeling discussion of the economic problem. It was understandable that this group might gather to talk about it.

"All right," he said defensively, *"you* schedule a *Domestic Council* meeting on it! Get Agnew to chair the meeting. Have more of those meetings—have one every two weeks. Have one on the twenty-sixth, on the economy! You can even invite Laird and Rogers so you can call it a 'Cabinet meeting,' but the Domestic Council is in charge of the agenda. *You* structure it." If I sympathized with the Cabinet crybabies, I could put on the meeting without the President.

He would fight the "cabal," by God. I was instructed to find out Arthur Burns's role in organizing the Monday session. "I," said the President, "will see Arthur tomorrow—alone.

"Red Blount wants to run for the Senate. But if he's a part of something like this, we can't send him out on the road speaking. I'll decide next week whether Agnew or the President chairs your Council meeting on the economy," Nixon concluded.

The next day Romney's Cabinet cabal (Nixon liked that word) was still very much on the President's mind. In the midst of talking about who would be Undersecretary of the Interior, Nixon exclaimed, "What's wrong with that Maury Stans? Joining in a thing like that cabal? It creates a political problem; there will be leaks. Arthur Burns being there creates a problem. When you go to their meeting [he said to me] I want you to speak up about the importance of people staying in the process."

Bob Haldeman was told to call Paul McCracken and say that the President wanted to see the paper McCracken planned to deliver at the Monday meeting. "Any papers done by my Council of Economic Advisers should come to the President," Nixon declared.

"Make this point at their breakfast," the President instructed me: "that they are nothing but a damn secret splinter group. Then there's the Burns problem. I'll take a political approach when I meet with him today. That may appeal to him. Maury Stans should talk to Arthur too. Maury should try to get him aboard. Get Maury and Cliff Hardin in here at least once a month, and include them in all the social stuff; that goes a long way. But," Nixon continued warmly, "that Romney and that Volpe! They are seriously juvenile types."

Then, addressing the problem of Cabinet meetings, the President said, "We'll have no more unstructured Cabinet meetings. There'll be no hair-down political talk with those people. The meetings will be just substance, and we'll do more social things like dinners at Camp David and church services. I've wasted a lot of time on the Cabinet problem. We should put more emphasis on the subcabinet and the Administration wives—that's a good thing.

"The boats and Camp David—that has now been done, as far as the Cabinet is concerned. No more. The Cabinet has no divine right to use those things.

"We'll have a one-hour Cabinet meeting every two weeks, at which I intend to say less. You can turn it over to me for five minutes at the end. Four out of five meetings should be on domestic issues. Those [Secretaries of domestic departments] are the Cabinet asses we want to pat with these meetings."

The Cabinet Committee on Economic Policy should be rejuvenated by George Schultz, Nixon said. (In fact it had been a moribund concept from its beginning.) "Do you know what this rump session is all about?" Nixon asked, suddenly inspired. "It's a jealous reaction to all the publicity George Shultz has been getting lately about his enormous economic influence. Well, we'll have a Cabinet meeting next Friday. And have a meeting Wednesday of the Administration women [the wives of appointees]. I'll do a drop-by and talk to them."

On Saturday, I had my assistant, Tod Hullin, call Romney's executive assistant to say that the President had instructed me to attend the "Cabinet committee" meeting Monday morning. I figured I'd better warn Romney and give him the weekend to figure out how to be graceful. If I surprised him, he might lose his temper and compound his foolishness.

As it was, he could barely contain his unhappiness when I walked into his huge conference room at HUD. Evidently he'd not warned Paul McCracken or some of the others that they were going to have a skunk at their Monday-morning garden party. Paul was extremely flustered. There was very little revolutionary fervor displayed. It was too early in the morning for much passion—and, too, I was a sort of wet blanket.

Red Blount made a vigorous little talk about the damn unions and their wage demands which, he said, were driving up prices and causing inflation to increase.

Paul McCracken's paper dealt with causes of inflation, notably the Davis-Bacon Act (a requirement that contractors pay the "prevailing wage"—usually the top wage in the area—on all Federal contracts) and what might be done to ease inflationary pressures.

Arthur Burns spoke drily about the need for a wage/price stabilization board and for more study of an "incomes policy" (which I understood to be economese for wage and price controls). All in all, it was a rather flat and arid meeting, held at an enormous table, much larger than the Cabinet table, so the participants were physically separated by vast distances. I concluded that Romney had a lot to learn about staging revolts. He needed a small, warm room, an evening meeting and one or two rousing speakers to get things really rolling. And he needed a big man on the door to keep the skunks out.

Just after noon that same day, George Shultz and I had a meeting with the President. We talked about the Interior Department's new undersecretary, formation of a construction-industry wage board, reorganization of the Corps of Engineers and whether military hospitals should perform abortions for military dependents. (Nixon ordered they should not.) Welfare-reform negotiations with the Congress needed some Presidential guidance. Much of the administrative responsibility for welfare would be moved to the Labor Department, Shultz proposed. ("Good," Nixon said. "It's like having an alcoholic bartender for HEW to run welfare.")

The fateful meeting on milk-price supports with John Connally, Cliff Hardin, John Whitaker, Don Rice, Shultz and me was scheduled for later in the day. (Most of John Connally's later troubles arose from that session.)

At last I reported on the rump Cabinet session I'd attended that morning. I gave Nixon a list of who had attended and a synopsis of what everyone had said. "George, try to get Arthur Burns off this wage-price–board thing he's talking about," Nixon said. "Let's not let him talk us into something that will just fail." Nixon said he'd decided to ride out the economy until May 15, then review the first third of 1971 and measure the trends. "My guess is we'll have a good second half. Unemployment at five point eight percent or six percent will be okay. We've got to avoid heating up the economy, but the Fed's got to keep the money supply up."

Shultz urged the President not to let anyone stampede him. He had a sound budget and should hold to it. The Fed should be kept at 5 to 6 percent positive money supply.

The Cabinet met the following Friday, and Nixon talked at great length about the economy in a rambling monologue that precluded any give-and-take.

But no one—not George Romney, nor Richard Nixon—ever mentioned the Cabinet Cabal again. And the President didn't bring up Romney's departure again until the summer of 1972.

What went wrong with the Nixon Cabinet? Surely something did. Most of the Cabinet members were discontented most of the time, and many of them failed to manage their departments well. There was constant friction between the White House and the Cabinet. The President, from 1970 on, spent a significant percentage of his time worrying about the Cabinet and tinkering with it. And so did some of us on his staff.

At root were the President's own shifting and variable concepts of the Cabinet—of what it should be and do—and what the President expected from it.

At first, during its selection, he wanted the Cabinet to symbolize that all elements of the body politic were to be represented in the Nixon Administration. There would be liberals as well as conservatives, ethnics and even Democrats. At the same time there was some rather vague intention that the Cabinet would perform a collegial advisory function.

But very soon Nixon changed his view; then he looked on the Cabinet principally as managers of their respective bureaucracies. A good Secretary keeps things under control. Cabinet members were to be spokesmen, too. They should be out in the country making the case for the President and his policies. A good Secretary is a good P.R. man.

From the outset Nixon could never understand why a Secretary needed to be courted and cultivated. There was no reason for a Secretary to be anything but loyal and eternally grateful. Nor was there a reason for a Secretary to need to see the President all the time.

In the spring of 1970, after one of his rare meetings with Agnew, Nixon complained that his Vice President had become an advocate of the "crybabies" in the Cabinet. Agnew had lectured him on the need for the President to have his department Secretaries in more often for consultation.

"The damn crybabies just want therapy, of course," Nixon said. "They'll say, 'Oh, help us' and 'protect us.' Imagine that damn Agnew!"

Indignantly Nixon went through the names of the Secretaries Agnew had wanted him to call in for consultation. "Hickel? He can wait. So can Romney. Stans? Yes, but no more than thirty-minute meetings. The same for Volpe and Blount. Hardin can wait."

The President would invite a Cabinet member to the White House when the President thought it was necessary, but a Secretary should never invite himself. A good Secretary should be discreet and considerate of the President's needs.

Cabinet officers should always remember that they were not elected to their positions; the President was elected—by all the people—and he appointed the Cabinet. If a Secretary makes political waves it's his President who gets wet. A good Secretary hews to the President's policies.

The President expected his staff to discriminate among the Cabinet members. "You should rely on the good Secretaries and run the others," he told me one day about halfway through his first term. "I do the same thing," he said. "Some of what they send me I just sign; some of what I get I always read before I decide to sign it."

The Cabinet is the President's political family, and it will participate in the social events the President decides to have. The President intends for these occasions to be warm, mutually pleasant and finished early in the evening. The loyal Cabinet families' attendance precludes the necessity of inviting potentially more critical outsiders. A good Secretary has an attractive family which admires the President and makes no indiscreet demands upon him.

Eventually, Richard Nixon began to consider some of his Cabinet—not John Connally, but some of the others—to be extensions of his staff, to be used to articulate public-relations campaigns and to give advice only when it was specifically called for. The Nixon Cabinet came to be essentially *ministerial*. This was because, as time passed, it appeared that whenever discretion was granted to the Secretaries they failed to do things the way Richard Nixon wanted them done. Since Nixon was the one who had to go back to the people after four years, to explain why things had gone as they did, he reacted to their "failures" by retaining almost all of the discretion.

Thereafter, when discretion was delegated, it would go to people close at hand, the nonideological people who understood what Richard Nixon wanted, the people who were loyal to him and had demonstrated that they would never embarrass him. That is, discretion would go to certain people on the White House staff.

CHAPTER EIGHT

John Mitchell and the Nixon Court

IN 1968 EARL WARREN, Lyndon Johnson and Abe Fortas had tried to put together a two-step maneuver involving the Supreme Court. Had it worked, Chief Justice Warren's resignation would have become effective, "at the pleasure of the President," upon the confirmation of Fortas as Warren's successor. But as the 1968 election approached, Senate Republicans and conservative Democrats—at Nixon's urging—blocked Fortas' confirmation; so Chief Justice Warren's resignation was on the

President's desk and on Nixon's mind from the moment he was elected.

John Mitchell was in charge of finding the President the candidates who would become the Justices of "the Nixon Court." Nixon and Mitchell agreed that the nominations should rescue the Court from the influence of the Ivy League. Nixon's Court would be "strict-constructionist" and "constitutionalist," not a collection of social engineers like William O. Douglas. There would be no racial or ethnic slots, either—no more "black seats" or "Jewish seats."

Mitchell was told to find nominees who came from the meat-and-potatoes law schools, from the areas of the country Nixon thought of as his constituency (above all, not the Northeast). Mitchell advocated appointing judges with some experience on the bench whose track record could be examined by his staff before he made his recommendation; that was fine with Nixon.

But the first nominee, Warren Burger, was a Richard Nixon discovery, not a Mitchell recruit. Burger was one of three Republican judges on the Court of Appeals for the District of Columbia who naturally would have been considered for the Supreme Court. The others were George McKinnon and Roger Robb.

Nixon had served with McKinnon in the Congress, and he liked him. Several times Judge McKinnon was invited to the White House just to chat with Nixon, and on occasion he was invited to kibitz in policy meetings. But Burger more nearly personified the Chief Justice Nixon was looking for. Burger looked like a judge, talked like a judge and, most important, wanted a seat on the Supreme Court so passionately that he would have agreed to almost anything to get it.

Burger was a politician. He had been the chairman of the Minnesota delegation at the 1952 Republican Convention which swung from Taft to Eisenhower (and Nixon) at the pregnant moment. For that he became an Assistant Attorney General and an Appellate judge in the ensuing eight years of the Eisenhower-Nixon Administration.

Within a few days of his inauguration, Nixon had Warren Burger come to the White House to administer the oath of office to some of the President's appointees. Nixon then took Burger into his office for a long talk—for which Burger was not entirely unprepared. He had brought with him to the White House a copy of a speech he had given on crime, law and order and the administration of justice which *U.S. News & World Report* had reprinted.

After Nixon and Burger had talked for some time, the President sent for me to join them. Nixon handed me the *U.S. News* reprint and told me to disseminate it—to Mitchell, Pat Buchanan and Arthur Burns—and to "keep in touch with the Judge." I didn't have to do much to comply, because Burger was a past master at keeping in touch. From then on I received little notes from time to time signed *"W.E.B."* about the Supreme Court, law enforcement and the President's policies, along with excerpts from articles for me to read. Nixon told Attorney General Mitchell to talk to Burger at length, to make sure he would be Nixon's kind of Chief Justice: a strict law-and-order man, a politician who could and would produce results, a Justice dedicated to undoing the excesses of the Warren Court.

Burger convinced Mitchell and Nixon that he was all of that, and more. He was even willing to create another vacancy when Nixon wanted one. If Burger was confirmed as Chief Justice he would serve for a time and then step down, Nixon told me a few days prior to Burger's confirmation. The President said he had Burger's promise that Burger would retire before Nixon did so that Nixon could then appoint another, younger Chief Justice to carry the Nixon mandate far beyond the Burger and Nixon years.

The President expected to make a major change in our relations with other countries, and foreign affairs were important to him. Second in importance was his ability to change the domestic situation through the creation of a long-lived strict-constructionist Supreme Court, composed of young Justices who would sit and rule in Nixon's own image. He guessed he'd always be thwarted by Democrats in the Congress; the likelihood of winning broad domestic legislative changes—a Nixon New Deal—was slim or nonexistent. But if he could get his Supreme Court nominees confirmed by the Senate, fundamental domestic changes could be effected by the third branch of the Federal Government. The nomination of Burger was his first and perhaps his most important step toward that goal.

From the time Nixon arrived at the White House he continually played his shuffle-the-people game with the Supreme Court. As I sat listening to him he would daydream about whom he might put on the Court in place of Black or Harlan or Douglas. At times his choices were Secretary of State William Rogers; John Mitchell; William French Smith (Ronald Reagan's choice); Congressman Richard Poff; Senator Robert Byrd of West Virginia; Robert Finch ("of course, he's not strong enough"); Jewell La Fontant, a black Chicago lawyer

("How about that? A black woman. Too bad she's not Jewish"); Secretary of Health, Education and Welfare Elliot Richardson (the Ivy League epitomized) and even Spiro Agnew.

Some of these selections were not entirely apolitical. I was sent to tell Elliot Richardson he was a prime candidate for the Court in 1971. Richardson was at HEW then, and Nixon suspected him of disloyalty. The President's welfare-reform legislation was blocked in the Senate Finance Committee, and Nixon was convinced that the only way to get it moving was to make conservative gestures toward Chairman Russell Long and the Republicans on the committee. They needed reassurance, Nixon reasoned, that this welfare reform would not become a giant giveaway scheme. But Secretary Richardson was all over the Congress, wooing the support of Senator Abe Ribicoff and other liberals with generous alternatives, in spite of countless White House meetings called for the purpose of keeping Richardson and the other HEW people informed of the President's desires. When we received reports that Richardson was undercutting our conservative strategy, Nixon tried to win Richardson's loyalty with the hint that if he was a faithful team player, his next move might be to the Court. So I delivered the message, which Elliot Richardson received without a blink.

When we returned from the President's first European trip in March of 1969, Nixon secured Chief Justice Warren's agreement to "retire" in the late spring. The President began to make plans for ceremonies and dinners to send Warren on his way, all the while conjuring with the names of possible replacements he had collected.

From the beginning Nixon was interested in getting rid of William O. Douglas; Douglas was the liberal ideologue who personified everything that was wrong with the Warren Court. Removing both Warren and Douglas would be a strong signal to the people of America that Richard Nixon kept his campaign promises. John Mitchell had begun to gather information about Douglas' nonjudicial sources of income, and some of it looked hopeful.

Meanwhile, the Justice Department was hearing rumors of Justice Abe Fortas' dealings with financier Louis Wolfson. By May 1969, *Life* magazine had written an exposé of Fortas' agreement with Wolfson, and Nixon cleared his desk of other work to focus on getting Fortas off the Court. Suddenly *Life's* Fortas disclosures were an unexpected gift that promised Nixon another vacancy on the Court.

Warren was the guest of honor at an elaborate retirement

dinner at the White House in April. All his children had been the President's guests, along with present and former Justices, prominent citizens and the Cabinet. Nixon had been extraordinarily gracious in toasting Warren that evening, revealing none of his dislike for his old California rival. Warren was cordial in his response. Perhaps he would help with Fortas, Mitchell suggested. Warren had every reason to feel gratitude for the manner in which his retirement was being handled by the President.

John Mitchell was sent to give the outgoing Chief a chance to show his gratitude. All the evidence the Justice Department had gathered was shown to Earl Warren. It went beyond the *Life* magazine story and included material Wolfson and others had furnished, showing that Fortas had contracted with Wolfson's foundation for life, that Wolfson wanted Fortas to get him a pardon and that Justice Fortas, while on the Court, had corresponded with Wolfson about his benefactor's problems with the Securities and Exchange Commission.

Within a few days Warren had done the job well; he had persuaded Abe Fortas to resign, and suddenly we had *two* vacant seats on the Court.

Nixon had already decided that Warren Burger would replace Earl Warren. Burger had been invited to the Warren retirement dinner, but I believe the decision was still a closely held secret; only John Mitchell and I had been told by the President. As soon as Fortas was gone, however, a quick FBI check was run on Warren Burger, and John Mitchell was told to inform Burger that he would succeed Warren as Chief Justice.

Nixon wanted to be sure that this nomination received the maximum attention. It was highly symbolic; the Warren era was over and a Nixon Court was coming into being. The selection of Warren Burger was to be one surprise that stayed secret, so that it would have unforgettable media impact. Nixon knew that when a Washington story dribbled out in leaks and speculations, the eventual official announcement rarely commanded headlines, TV leads and the attention of the commentators.

The President asked me to find a way to get Burger and his family up to the family quarters in the White House without the gate-watchers among the press seeing them. If Burger was recognized, the wire services and television would be speculating on his appointment before Nixon could announce it, and the impact of his prime-time spectacular would be dulled.

I asked Ed Morgan to smuggle in the Burger family, and as

always, Morgan delivered with flawless execution. Midway in the planning the President insisted on knowing—and second-guessing—every detail. But about five in the afternoon Morgan sent cars from the White House garage in all directions. Ed Morgan's car and one other eventually went to the Burger farmhouse in suburban Virginia and brought the new Chief, his wife and their children to the basement of the Department of the Treasury building, just east of the White House.

Early in my tenure as Counsel, the Secret Service had shown me the utility tunnel, bomb shelter and other underground rooms beneath the White House. The tunnel could be used to walk under the street to the Treasury, although it was primarily a conduit for pipes and cables. Morgan and I had decided to walk the Burgers into the White House basement that way, then cram them into the little elevator for a nonstop ride to the family floor.

At the appointed moment, Ed took the nondescript and unrecognizable children of the Burger family to the East Room (which was jammed with reporters and White House staff) so that they could watch as their parents walked in with the Nixons. The whole exercise went well, and the President got the surprise, headlines, commentary and coverage he was looking for.*

When Warren Burger was easily confirmed by the Senate on June 9, John Mitchell was told to quickly provide his list of prospects to fill the second vacancy, the Abe Fortas seat. This nomination would be the one to send a signal to every conservative and every Southerner; the nominee must be a bona fide son of the Old South. With this one we'd stick it to the liberal, Ivy League clique who thought the Court was their own pri-

---

* Nixon put a high premium on well-executed plans. Haldeman, as campaign tour manager in 1960, gained Nixon's confidence in large part because his plans were carefully made and superbly carried out. I followed in Haldeman's footsteps. When Ed Morgan showed resourcefulness and precision, he was marked as a man who could be counted on. Later, when school desegregation and busing became Nixon's premier domestic concerns, he specified that I was to take Ed Morgan off his other assignments and appoint him to look after those politically vital problems.

In 1969 a few columnists derided the new White House staff because it was largely Nixon's old campaign crew wearing new hats. But the President-elect had great confidence in the ingenuity and reliability of people like Morgan, Haldeman and John Whitaker. We could always go out and find an expert on meat prices or special education or health economics to help our people analyze and understand a specific issue. But loyalty, versatility and reliability were Nixon's first criteria, and he counted on his old campaign people to take charge of his major projects.

vate playground—people like Erwin Griswold, Robert Morgenthau and the Kennedys—Nixon exulted.

By mid-August, Mitchell had proposed and the President had nominated Clement Haynesworth, the Chief Judge of the Fourth Circuit Court of Appeals, a Southern gentleman in every respect.

A month later Birch Bayh, the ambitious young Senator from Indiana, declared war on Haynesworth with a barrage of allegations, charging that the Judge had adjudicated cases in which he had a financial interest. *The Washington Post* and the television networks began to dredge up innuendo and rumor, including Haynesworth's passing acquaintance with Bobby Baker, Lyndon Johnson's notorious Senate aide.

By October 1, the nominee's chances had so deteriorated in the Senate that Bryce Harlow was recommending that Clement Haynesworth withdraw his name. The whip count was 52 against and 48 for confirmation, and "festering." Harlow reported that Senator John Williams of Delaware was about to openly oppose the President's nominee, and "if Williams goes, Griffin and Cook will go too, and it's lost for sure." Senator Margaret Chase Smith had written the President opposing Haynesworth. Senator Charles Mathias was asking for an appointment to see the President to express his doubts about the nominee. The rest of the Republican side threatened to cave in too, although the press continued to report that the White House remained confident.

The President assigned Attorney General John Mitchell to work on Senator John Williams. "The President is on the line for Haynesworth," Mitchell was to say. "This is his first big issue in the Senate. You can't let him down."

Democrats for Haynesworth, men like his home-state Senator Fritz Hollings and Senator James Eastland of Mississippi, warned Bryce Harlow that the Republicans must hold firm. No Democrats were going to bear the brunt of the liberal attack on Haynesworth unless all the Republicans were standing solidly with the President.

The President assigned Mitchell, Harlow and me to meet with Senators Roman Hruska, Robert Griffin and Marlow Cook to get them to rally their fellow Republicans. Those three told us they would try, but they confirmed that Haynesworth's chances were eroding badly.

One afternoon Nixon went over his own tally with me. He began with the Democrats. There were 16 Southerners; "Haynesworth should get all of them. Dodd and Tydings should be all right. Among Byrd of West Virginia, Jackson, Pastore and McGee there should be two votes. So let's say we have twenty Democrats.

"That means we need thirty-one of the forty-three Republicans. We know we've lost Margaret Smith, Goodell and Packwood. Ed Brooke wrote that he's against us. We probably don't have Javits or Case. The dominoes are John Williams, who knocks over Bob Griffin, who takes along Cook and Boggs. Prouty and Aiken? I don't know.

"Mitchell has got to tell our Senate leaders to begin to lead up there. The President's leadership of the nation is being put in question. Haynesworth is a good product. Mitchell's got to explain to them that it is the President who is being challenged up there. If the Republicans desert, then the Democrats will. It's up to our leaders.

"Fritz Hollings says he counts sixty for Haynesworth as of this morning, if there are no more losses," Nixon told me. "What they are doing to Haynesworth," he continued, "is grossly unfair. He's no different from other judges who have a little wealth. It's a double standard because he's our nominee.

"Tell Burger to write a letter to every Federal judge, by God. This Haynesworth case should be an example to them: he owned some stock;* otherwise he's an innocent man. Tell them the President sold all his stock. Say I strongly recommend they all sell all their stocks so that the courts will be above suspicion. Everyone can put his stock in blind trusts or sell it."

By October 8, Senator Robert Griffin had leaked to the press his intention to oppose Haynesworth. Bryce Harlow explained to us that organized labor had rallied its troops during the week everyone was in recess for the funeral of Senator Everett Dirksen. A wave of anti-Haynesworth mail and telegrams was pouring into the Senators' offices now.

Nixon's reaction was typical: "We can stimulate mail too. There should be letters and wires from the Farm Bureaus, Southern bar associations, the National Rifle Association and our other friends; they have got to be energized. Get pro-Haynesworth speeches into the record; we've got to build a wave of support for our man."

Tomorrow Senator Birch Bayh will attack Clement Haynesworth with five new charges, Harlow reported. "All right,"

---

* Haynesworth was shown to have owned a few shares of a corporation interested in the outcome of litigation he decided.

Nixon replied, "have the Justice Department react. Clark Mollenhoff should prepare a one-page response. Get Bill Rehnquist over at Justice to analyze Bayh's charges."

Nixon began to focus on Everett Dirksen's replacement in the Senate, someone named Smith, because his vote on the Haynesworth nomination might be crucial. Smith was a colorless Illinois hack who had been chosen Senator to satisfy some local political debts; but he was a vote for Haynesworth, so he was important.

(Congressman John Anderson of Rockford, Illinois, had phoned to ask the President to pressure Governor Ogilvie to appoint Anderson to the Senate vacancy, but Nixon was not about to do so. Anderson was notoriously unfaithful to Nixon's interests in Congress, although he was nominally the number three man in our Republican leadership. Nixon could see no reason to ask Illinois Governor Ogilvie for a favor unless by doing so he could get an extremely reliable Senator to succeed Dirksen. Anderson's pleading phone call was taken by Bryce Harlow; it simply wasn't worth the President's time.)

John Mitchell was instructed to go see the new Senator Smith; he was to say that Smith was in fact the deciding vote on Haynesworth and that his President was counting on his loyalty.

Nixon recalled that Charles Evans Hughes, Louis Brandeis and John J. Parker had had trouble being confirmed by the Senate, but he couldn't recall why. So Bryce Harlow was assigned to have someone research those and other Supreme Court nominees, for whatever help history might afford Haynesworth. Perhaps we could show that men in as much trouble as our man turned out all right once they were confirmed.

On October 9, the President saw the need to boost the Haynesworth nomination with something from the White House. But he felt it should not be a full-scale press conference; instead he would invite the White House press "regulars" into the Oval Office along with William White and reliable commentators like James Kilpatrick, together with "that little Nashville fellow" whose name he couldn't remember and some other Southern reporters.

And there was need for a dose of Presidential credibility. So Daniel Patrick Moynihan should hold a small press backgrounder in which he was to confide that Richard Nixon never planted questions or resorted to automatic, manufactured answers at his press conferences. Pat Moynihan was to point out to the reporters to whom he dropped his secrets that Richard Nixon's answers were short and crisp, the product of a tough mind. By way of contrast, Moynihan was to say, some staff people needed five to seven minutes to respond to a press question. They didn't realize that the evening news may carry only thirty seconds and that you had to impart substance, feeling and style in just that time.

This typical Nixonian soliloquy was, I think, pure hubris. There was little chance that Pat Moynihan would have agreed to such an assignment under any circumstances, and even less that he would have committed *his* credibility to the Haynesworth struggle, even so indirectly. But it made Nixon feel good to issue such orders. I had long before concluded that he didn't care whether they were followed or not.

In fact, the President's press conference with the regulars didn't take place until October 20. By then Harlow had produced research on Brandeis, Hughes and Parker which Nixon used with some effect in a strong statement supporting Haynesworth:

"If you want to go back and read what really can happen in cases of this sort, I would suggest you read the debate over Louis Brandeis and also the confirmation of Charles Evans Hughes in which they poured on him all the filth they could possibly amass because of his connection with insurance companies.

"The Brandeis case was not a very proud moment in the history of the United States Senate. There was anti-Semitism in it and there was also a very strong partisan attitude towards Woodrow Wilson."

Parker, from North Carolina, had been rejected by the Senate in 1930 (and was a friend and partner, we later learned, of Haynesworth's father).

The liberals' opposition to Clement Haynesworth rankled and itched. It was inevitable that the President would try to scratch the itch. If they were going to get one of ours, Nixon decided, perhaps we should be going after one of theirs. "Very well, talk to Jerry Ford now," the President instructed me. Ford should do nothing until "the next day after the vote" on the Haynesworth nomination. But then Ford should "move to impeach that sitting Justice who has been charged" with improprieties verging on the criminal. It was time to go after William O. Douglas.

Within a few hours I had conveyed Nixon's message to Ford. I found Jerry Ford to be vague and unfocused much of the time, and on this occasion our talk ended with no assurance that Ford either agreed to or understood his assignment to bring about Douglas' impeachment.

The President wanted to be sure Senator Bayh and Haynesworth's other enemies didn't miss the point, so to be certain they got the message, I was instructed to hint at Douglas' impeachment when I appeared at an off-the-record reporters' gathering a few days later. Things said at Budge Sperling's breakfast group or some of the lesser luncheon gatherings of reporters immediately became prime gossip around town and soon found their way into print, even though the ground rule was "off-the-record"; White House occupants have all used these forums for pumping up trial balloons or sending messages.

In no time at all my hint that Nixon might seek Douglas' eye (or seat) for Haynesworth's began to appear in the columns. And shortly, Jerry Ford began making speeches calling for Douglas' impeachment.

Whatever merit the impeachment might have had on its own, our transparent attempt to link it to Haynesworth's nomination did Haynesworth no good. In fact, Ford's friend, and Michigan's Senator, Robert Griffin loudly claimed that the linkage was enough to turn him against Haynesworth.

The more trouble Haynesworth had in the Senate, the more Nixon flayed his propagandists to produce a groundswell of favorable public opinion to which the Senators would have to give heed. He saw the problem as one to be handled by Pat Buchanan, his conservative writer, and Harry Dent, the Southern political expert. And Herb Klein should be calling all the Southern news editors. Every Southern paper should be praising the Haynesworth nomination. He would be the first Southerner appointed to the Court since Hugo Black.

Pat Buchanan should confide in the conservative columnists: President Nixon was under great political pressure to nominate a "lib" (that, he said with a nod, was a euphemism for "Jew" when you're talking about the Court), but the President resisted that pressure. Buchanan was to say that as far as President Nixon was concerned there was no religious or ethnic test for nomination to the Court—"not Jewish, Italian, Negro, Catholic or Protestant." The only test was: is the nominee a "Constitutionalist"? Haynesworth was that—he met that test—and he deserved the support of every conservative. Haynesworth would vote "consistent with Burger." He would not zigzag like some of them. Buchanan was to tell them that.

But of course, all the nose-counting and press contacts and

White House statements and John Mitchell's trips to the Senate were not enough to save Clement Haynesworth's nomination. On November 21 he was rejected 55 to 45. Seventeen Republicans voted against him.

On December 4, 1969, Haynesworth was asked to visit the President; I was designated to join them, presumably to take notes for the President's file. Those notes show that Nixon introduced me to Haynesworth as his "chief counsel" (although I'd moved from Counsel to Assistant for Domestic Affairs the month before. Doubtless Nixon thought it a better "touch" to have a counsel—a lawyer—in attendance since Haynesworth was a judge). "John was one of your main supporters," the President explained, less than truthfully.

Nixon and Haynesworth sat in wing chairs on opposite sides of the fire. The judge was smaller and thinner than he'd appeared on television. He spoke quietly, with a slight speech impediment sometimes halting his courtly Southern drawl.

"I thought we should get together to make our game plan," Nixon began. "We'll go out to the cameras and I'll say that you were my nominee for the Supreme Court and you've not been confirmed because you were subjected to the most brutal and vicious attack. An ordinary man might now leave the Court of Appeals and retire from public life. But this morning we've talked and I know that you are no ordinary man. Despite your terrible personal ordeal, I have asked you to stay on the Court of Appeals. Your judgment, experience and integrity are needed there, and I'm glad to be able to announce that you will continue to serve there."

"That sounds fine," Haynesworth said softly.

The door opened and a White House photographer came in.

"We'll just have a picture for your personal files," Nixon said jocularly.

When the photographer finished snapping the two seated men, Nixon said, "This has been an ordeal for you. You could say 'Chuck it all,' but the Court needs you. Our courts never had more mediocre people than they have today."

"I am," said the Judge, "very concerned about the unfair attacks upon John Mitchell regarding his failure to thoroughly investigate my fitness."

"You should tell him that," Nixon nodded. "You know, never before has a President engaged his White House staff as I did in support of your nomination."

"I'm grateful," the Judge replied. "While this experience has not been pleasant—I feel like I've been beaten over the head—I've come through whole. I believe my prestige with the

Bar is higher than before. And I'm most grateful for the trust of the White House staff and John Mitchell. They were staunch and unflagging."

Nixon said to Haynesworth, "Warren Burger was a staunch supporter of yours, you know."

"Yes, I know. He called me a number of times. We have a warm relationship and I'm delighted. You know," the Judge said, smiling, "when *The New York Times* and everyone was on us so hard, my wife just despaired one morning, and she asked me, 'What will we do?' So I said to her, 'Why, if this keeps up, I'm going to go home and run for Sheriff of Greenville County, Miss Dorothy.' You know"—Haynesworth grinned as he stood to leave—"they are after me to run for Governor down there. How about that?"

As Judge Haynesworth had predicted, with the collapse of his nomination came widespread criticism of Attorney General John Mitchell. He was seen to be the manager of a flawed operation; Haynesworth's vulnerability to Bayh's conflict-of-interest charges should have been discovered before the nomination went to the Senate, his critics charged. Mitchell's responses to these attacks were so heavy-handed and ineffective that Richard Moore, a Nixon political adviser and sometime speechwriter, was assigned to guide Mitchell's image-making.

"The President supports Mitchell," Nixon soliloquized to Haldeman and me. "I want everyone to see that. Have him come in for a meeting."

So Mitchell came in, and was given another chance to fill the Fortas seat with a true Southerner. Mitchell went back to the Justice Department and put together a list which included Judge G. Harrold Carswell. Carswell's name had first come to John Mitchell in April of 1969 when Warren Burger had sent Mitchell some judicial recommendations at the President's suggestion. Burger was lobbying hard for a seat on the Supreme Court and he wanted to be helpful; so he assembled the names of some judges who had impressed him, including District Judge Carswell.

Mitchell liked Carswell's looks too. When there was an opening on the Fifth Circuit Court of Appeals in 1969, Carswell was nominated to fill it. His confirmation by the Senate was routine.

Since Carswell had so recently been through that confirmation process, Mitchell reasoned, the Senate Judiciary Committee—Birch Bayh and the others—could hardly give his Supreme Court nomination the hard time they had given poor

Haynesworth's. Mitchell obtained Nixon's tentative approval of Carswell, but Nixon insisted that Mitchell line up a majority of Senate Judiciary Committee members before the nomination went up.

On January 19, Mitchell phoned Bob Haldeman to urge that the White House announce Carswell's nomination immediately. Mitchell had discussed Carswell with the Republicans on the Judiciary Committee, and now Senator Roman Hruska intended to talk over the nomination with all the Senators in the Republican caucus that afternoon at three o'clock. Then the name would be certain to leak all over town; it surely would be in the *Post* next morning.

"You'll have to telephone the fellow," Haldeman told the President.

"Can't someone else call him?" Nixon asked.

"John Mitchell called him to see if he'd take it, but *you* really have to offer him the nomination as a matter of form," Haldeman insisted.

"Well, okay, if I must," Nixon said. As he reached for his telephone, he hesitated. "What is his name?" he said vaguely. "I'll call him later." Eventually that day the call was made, Carswell agreed to serve and his nomination was announced.

Once again the battle lines were drawn in the Senate. A majority of the Judiciary Committee voted to send the nomination to the Senate; but on the Senate floor Carswell was, as Bryce Harlow reported to the President in late March, "in increasingly bad shape. His condition is critical. The situation is dangerous." Even Nixon loyalist Senator Hiram Fong would vote against Carswell. "They think Carswell's a boob, a dummy," Harlow told Nixon. "And what counter is there to that? He is."

John Mitchell's strategy was to bet all his chips on Senator James Eastland, the crusty old chairman of the Senate Judiciary Committee. Although Eastland was a Democrat, he was a Southern conservative and Mitchell's close ally. But Eastland wasn't doing much for Carswell, and Nixon's Senate-liaison men could find little indication that Mitchell and the Justice Department were exerting much effort either. So a meeting was called to review the situation. Nixon wanted a full accounting the next morning of what Justice planned to do to resurrect Carswell's chances. When Mitchell sent Richard Kleindienst to the President's meeting, instead of coming himself, I figured that our Attorney General didn't really have his heart in the Carswell battle.

"John Mitchell is on the line here," Nixon began. "The

President is not going to lobby each one of these Senators for this nomination. I'm not going to have Richard Schweiker in here, for God's sake. Marlow Cook has a fellow he wants to be a judge; he'll end up trading me that man for Carswell. Prouty has one too. Tell them they get no judge if they don't vote for Carswell. Tell them that. Who else do you want me to see? Dodd?"

"Dodd is for recommitting the nomination to committee," Kleindienst said.

"No one gets in to see me without a firm commitment to Carswell," Nixon said. "At least John Sherman Cooper is firm for Carswell. What about Saxbe?"

"He's for Carswell, but he's soft."

"Who else is soft?"

"Mathias, Schweiker, Case and Goodell are all against us."

"Sure!" Nixon said vehemently. "They are never for the President on any issue." He turned to Bob Haldeman. "They are never to be invited to the White House again, for any reason. Charles Percy too. Never to the White House again."

Nixon and Kleindienst ran down the tally. (Hatfield? He's okay. But weak. Pearson? He's getting a lot of heat from Kansas.)

"All right," Nixon asked, "now, just who is running this Carswell nomination?"

"It looks like Justice won't," Haldeman said.

"Well, the White House shouldn't," Nixon added. "In the Eisenhower Administration the Deputy Attorney General had all the political responsibility. Things like this must be run out of Justice." He was talking to Mitchell through Kleindienst. "There's got to be one man in charge over there. Who will it be? Rehnquist?"

"He's not a nut cutter," Kleindienst replied uncomfortably.

Nixon nodded. "It's got to be Kleindienst," he said with finality.

After Deputy Attorney General Kleindienst left the room, Nixon summed up the Carswell situation for us: "We'll probably lose it," he said.

Nixon knew instinctively that he should keep some distance between the Carswell debacle and the White House, but he couldn't let the fight alone. On March 31 he called for Ron Ziegler to plan a public-relations initiative, but the Press Secretary was at home ill. So Gerald Warren, Ziegler's deputy, came in and was told to tell the press that the President advocated applying what he called the "Haynesworth Test" to the present Supreme Court and to all of those Senators who were criticizing Carswell for belonging to racially segregated clubs. "Let them all declare what fraternities and clubs *they* belong to. What racial covenants do *they* have on their homes? What segregated resorts do *they* take *their* families to?" Warren did not repeat the President's rhetorical questions to the press corps. He had enough trouble with the Harrold Carswell nomination as it was.

On April 8 the Senate rejected Carswell, as by then we knew it would. Nixon was angry, but he saw a chance to cap the whole Haynesworth-Carswell Southern gambit with a last statement that might recoup some of his losses by permanently memorializing his commitment to "Southern values." He sent for Pat Buchanan and asked him to prepare a short statement for the television cameras later that day.

Meanwhile, he told John Mitchell to give him the name of a conservative Northern judge. By the quick choice of a Northerner he would dramatize what he was about to say to the Southerners.

After reading what Buchanan had prepared, Nixon had second thoughts about going before the cameras. Perhaps Ron Ziegler could just hand out the text of the statement. Pat Buchanan's language was sharp enough to capture heavy media attention, but it was too blunt and harsh to be heard coming from the President's own mouth on the evening news.

Nixon sat back and began to amend the Buchanan draft. He lined out Pat's reference to "The Old Confederacy" as a synonym for the South. Pat had written: "To the men and women of the [South], let me say that today I share your personal feelings about the act of discrimination that took place in the Senate yesterday."

About four o'clock, better satisfied with the draft as he'd revised it, the President called for Ziegler. He wanted the eleven-paragraph statement duplicated and handed out at once. And, he added, the President would come in and make a shorter statement for the cameras. Ziegler already had the camera crews standing by in the press room, in case that was what Nixon ultimately decided. So at 4:20 P.M., in plenty of time to capture the top position on the evening network news, the President paraphrased his handout for television. In doing so he omitted the reference to "regional discrimination" at the end of the statement.

The release said, in part:

I have reluctantly concluded—with the Senate as presently constituted—I cannot successfully nominate to the Supreme Court any
Federal Appellate Judge from the South who believes as I do in
the strict construction of the Constitution. Judges Carswell and
Haynesworth have endured with admirable dignity vicious as-
saults on their intelligence, their honesty and their character. They
have been falsely charged with being racist. But when all the hypocrisy is stripped away, the real issue was their philosophy of
strict construction of the Constitution—a philosophy that I
share—and the fact that they had the misfortune of being born in
the South. After the rejection of Judge Carswell and Judge
Haynesworth, this conclusion is inescapable.

Four of the present members of the Court are from the East, one
from the Midwest, two from the West and one from the South.
More than one-fourth of the people of this nation live in the
South—they deserve representation on the Court.

But more important than geographical balance is philosophical
balance—the need to have represented on the Court those who
believe in strict construction of the Constitution as well as others
who believe in the liberal construction which has constituted the
majority on the Court for the past fifteen years.

With yesterday's action, the Senate has said that no Southern
Federal Appellate Judge who believes in a strict interpretation of
the Constitution can be elevated to the Supreme Court.

As long as the Senate is constituted the way it is today, I will not
nominate another Southerner and let him be subjected to the
kind of malicious character assassination accorded both Judges
Haynesworth and Carswell. However, my next nomination will be
made in the very near future; a President should not leave that vacancy on the Court when it can be filled.

Buchanan evidently knew who the next nominee would be.
His proposed draft had said: "My next nominee will be from
the Midwest; and he will fulfill the criteria of a strict constructionist from the second highest Federal bench in the land."

Nixon didn't want to tip his hand; he rewrote: "My next
nominee will be from outside the South and he will fulfill the
criteria of a strict constructionist with judicial experience
either from a Federal bench or on a State Appeals Court."

Before the cameras he added, pointedly, "I believe that a
judge from the North who has such views will be confirmed by
the United States Senate."

So far, John Mitchell was batting 0 for 2. After all, Burger
was Nixon's discovery, not the Attorney General's. Mitchell's
next nominee, Harry Blackmun, came from the same list as

Carswell: Chief Justice Warren Burger's April 1969 list of recommendations.

Harry A. Blackmun met all the President's criteria, and besides, he could be expected to follow closely the new Chief Justice's lead. They were the closest of friends and colleagues, beginning years before, when they were young men back home in Minnesota; then at the Mayo Clinic, where Burger was a trustee and Blackmun its lawyer, and more lately as fellow Federal Appellate judges.

The day after Carswell was rejected—the day the President's "discrimination" statement was made to the cameras—Nixon decided to let Mitchell offer the seat to Blackmun. The little Minnesota judge was sent for, and the following day, Friday, he met with Mitchell, then with Nixon.

On Tuesday, April 14, Ron Ziegler told the press that Blackmun was the nominee. In the next six weeks the Senate confirmed him, and near the end of May I received an invitation to attend Harry Blackmun's installation at the Supreme Court.

I had gone to Warren Burger's coronation because the President had attended and addressed the Court; that was an extraordinary event in itself, and the known tension between the retiring Chief Justice, Earl Warren, and Nixon made it doubly interesting. Warren's swan song from the bench had a few barbs in it for Nixon, but Nixon's remarks were generous and bland. He could afford to be generous on that occasion; he had begun to turn this Court around, and as he spoke, he could look up there and count three more seats he would probably be filling before his first term was over.

I went to the Blackmun inaugural because I was curious about the mood of the other Justices. There was a tea-and-cookies reception after the short swearing-in session, and I chatted there with Justices Potter Stewart, William Brennan and Byron White and the Chief Justice. I was looking for signs of trauma, and I imagined that I saw some: everyone said he was grateful that Blackmun's confirmation had gone so smoothly. No one mentioned Haynesworth or Carswell, but they were obviously the ghosts at the reception. Stewart, Brennan and White were clearly not overjoyed to see the White House at their tea party. Although they were polite, no one invited me home to meet the wife and kids.

As the Blackmun nomination glided through the Senate, the Nixon-Ford project to unseat Justice Douglas was still pending business in the House of Representatives and being taken more seriously by all concerned. Douglas hired a lawyer to represent him before the House Judiciary Committee, and we began to hear reports from Warren Burger of Douglas' bitter resentment of the impeachment effort.

In mid-April, Bryce Harlow told the President that the Speaker, John McCormick, intended to bottle up the Douglas impeachment, either in the Judiciary or the Rules Committee, where it would die. Nixon might be able to pry the resolution loose, but he'd have to decide to make a major fight of it. Nixon began looking up and down the Supreme Court bench for easier ways to make a Nixon majority. It was obvious that Douglas' health was poor, and Justices Black and Harlan also had physical problems. Thurgood Marshall didn't overwork himself, but he was not in good shape either. Time was on the President's side. He decided not to press the Douglas impeachment, but he would wait awhile before calling off Jerry Ford and the others. It was not a bad idea to keep Douglas worried for a while, Nixon thought.

Warren Burger is a man with aggrandizing tendencies. One day in 1970 he invited me to come to his chambers for lunch; he had an idea he wanted to discuss. The two of us ate near his office in an ornate little dining room furnished with antiques which, he told me, he had personally collected.

Since the President gives an annual State of the Union address to a joint session of the Congress, Burger observed, it seemed appropriate and even necessary that the head of the third branch of Government, the Chief Justice, similarly address the Congress on the State of Justice. He described to me how he would tell Congress and the nation of the conditions in the courts, the prisons and the legal profession. The networks could televise his speech, if they wished. Would the President urge the Congressional leaders to invite Burger to make such an annual address? I said I'd find out.

When I reported Burger's ambitious idea the President didn't much like it, but he also didn't want to be the one to turn it down. He instructed me to tell the Chief that since this was a question for the other two independent branches of the Federal establishment, the President would simply defer to the decision of the Chief Justice and the Speaker.

Both Nixon and Haldeman expressed concern to me that an annual State of Justice speech might dilute the impact of the President's State of the Union. We were not about to sponsor *The Warren Burger Show* on prime time. Burger tried to sell his idea all over the city of Washington, without success.

It was also brought to my attention that Chief Justice

Burger's personal establishment was not to his liking. Although Burger expanded the limousine service and security force at the Supreme Court, the Justices didn't have the Air Force planes, the Army helicopters or the countless conveniences the Secret Service provides to the President.

Several times in his first two years on the Court, Burger called me to ask for the use of one of the airplanes that are kept at Andrews Air Force Base for the President's use. On one occasion Burger wanted to be flown to Europe. Another time he was going to an airport that had no commercial air service. Each time, Nixon decided to turn down the request, and I had to tell the Chief Justice.

There was surely no shortage of aircraft at Andrews. The President's fleet included 707 transports, business jets, twin-engine KingAires and turboprop Convairs. But Nixon rarely allowed the use of his air fleet for errands like Burger's. Customarily, Congressmen were invited to fly to a funeral of one of their colleagues, and the senior White House staff had unlimited use of the planes for trips in the line of duty. Otherwise, the planes were used only to ferry the President's family and friends to Key Biscayne and San Clemente, and for the extensive courier service between those places and Washington.

Burger did not permit minor disappointments over speeches or airplanes to impair his friendship with the President. As an aspect of his campaign he sent a steady stream of notes and letters to Nixon, many of them through my office.

During the evening of April 30, 1970, he even delivered one of his notes in person. The President made a prime-time television speech that evening, explaining the Cambodian "incursion" he had ordered. As usual when there was a major speech, I stayed at the office, eating dinner from a tray as I watched the telecast. I was getting ready to leave after the speech when a gate guard phoned to say the Chief Justice was on his way in with a letter for the President. I walked down to the small basement lobby and there was Burger, all dressed up, carrying a thick, square envelope addressed to the President. He just wanted to drop it off, he said, because he wanted the President to know how much he supported him in this latest move in Vietnam.

I called the President to let him know Burger was there; Nixon asked me to bring the Chief Justice to The Residence.

As Burger and I walked through the West Wing, along the portico and down the wide ground-floor hallway in The Residence, he told me how stirred and pleased he had been with the President's decision to invade Cambodia and with the night's speech.

The President greeted us at the elevator on the family floor and took Burger to say hello to the group assembled in the sitting area at the end of the broad hall. Pat Nixon, Bebe Rebozo and Julie and David Eisenhower rose as we approached. That evening Burger stayed with the President for some time. I left almost immediately to go home.

The President and John Mitchell made a constant effort to keep in touch with Burger. The President had a notion that Burger's decisions on cases before the Court were not always worked out with sufficient clarity. On several occasions Nixon, Mitchell and I openly discussed with the Chief Justice the pros and cons of issues before the court. After a breakfast meeting with Burger on December 18, 1970, I made notes of the subjects we covered:

—The Chief Justice's back was bothering him. The President and Attorney General recommended their back specialist, a Dr. Ryland, to whom Nelson Rockefeller and Henry Kissinger also had been going for treatment.

—Burger described the tremendous advantage Justices Douglas and Black had over Burger and Blackmun when draft decisions were discussed in the Court's conferences, "because they had participated in [deciding] the landmark cases."

—A recent criminal case, decided 5–4, was "a real turning point" in his relationship with the rest of the Court, Burger said.

—The President pointed out to the Chief Justice the enormous importance of the "school cases" before the Court. They discussed the issues of forced integration of the schools, the relative merits of "tracking" and desegregation in Northern schools and the President's intention to "set the course" for the country. (Nixon and I had discussed several times the probability that if he took strong, clear positions on these issues, Burger and a majority of the Court would follow his lead.)

—Burger urged his State of Justice speech before the Congress again. He seemed much more interested—I wrote "preoccupied" in my notes—in court reform and in how to get the Speaker to agree to his joint-session spectacular than in the substantive issues Nixon was anxious to discuss, but he did not seem to consider the President's lobbying to be improper.

On other occasions Nixon and Burger talked about Nixon's view of the death penalty, the rights of criminal defendants and similar law-and-order issues.

Some of Burger's notes and calls kept us informed as to the illness and frailty of Justices Black and Harlan. At last, about 3 P.M. on September 17, 1971, Burger telephoned me to say that a messenger was bringing the President a letter from Hugo Black. "This is it," Burger said. His voice conveyed excitement and triumph.

Black's two-paragraph resignation arrived a few minutes later. At once the South began to rise again, urging that the President renew his try to put a Southerner on the Court. A Virginia Congressman, Richard Poff, began to be talked of as Black's replacement. Poff was the ranking Republican on the House Judiciary Committee, a small, serious man, about 50 years old, from downstate Virginia. Nixon liked Dick Poff, and he liked Poff's positions on the critical issues: busing, housing and abortion. Poff had loyally supported the Administration politically and in the Congress, and as soon as his name was mentioned the ACLU and ADA attacked him (which didn't hurt his chances with Nixon). He was at the top of the list of the President's prospects.

Another Virginian, Lewis Powell, was also being talked about, but the President thought he was too old. We were looking for men in their 40s or 50s, who would be on that "Nixon Court" for a long time.

When the Fortas seat was being filled, Nixon had Ron Ziegler tell the press that we were going to promote only people with judicial experience. Now there was an unannounced change; the list included legislators and lawyers too. A reporter asked Pat Nixon whether the President would consider a woman for the court, and Pat was widely quoted as saying she was working on her husband to appoint a woman. Evidently she or someone had persuaded him that he ought to find a woman if he could. Names of women judges and lawyers were gathered, but Nixon considered and rejected Shirley Hufstadler and some other women as lacking the necessary Constitutional fundamentalism. At the same time, he told me he would appoint a woman if Mitchell could find him one.

John Mitchell was still the keeper of the list, headed by Dick Poff, but all at once it became *two* lists. Six days after Black resigned, Mr. Justice Harlan joined him in retirement. His letter elated Nixon.

Dan Rather appeared on CBS news to tell the American people that the President had known of the Harlan resignation far in advance. "The letter has been written for weeks," Rather confided. Rather was wrong again. Actually we had no advance notice; the timing of Harlan's resignation had taken us all by surprise.

Now there were two seats open and it truly would be the Nixon Court. The White House began to feel the crosscurrents as never before; Senate liberals, the ACLU and some journalists began to make war on every conservative whose name was rumored to be under consideration. As the pressure mounted, we began to hear those on Mitchell's lists accused of everything from theft to bigotry.

The public attack on Richard Poff included an accusation that he was a racist. Reporters and investigators descended on his hometown to dissect his public statements and investigate his personal affairs. By October 2, Poff had notified John Mitchell that he had decided to withdraw his name from consideration "for personal reasons." Both sides were investigating him, it seemed, and they were going far beyond his professional life into subjects he didn't feel like talking about. If it was a choice between a seat on the Court and retaining some private life, he'd prefer to forget the seat on the Court.

At first Nixon was tempted to cast Poff's withdrawal as another bigoted attack on a good Southerner. His immediate reaction was to direct me that the press should be told "the President regretted this malicious and false attack on the race issue." It was to be the Haynesworth-Carswell statement replayed.

I suggested that this gambit might simply invite the ACLU to reply specifically, perhaps hurting Poff with the public disclosure of things he wanted to keep private. Nixon relented. He decided that we would ask Dick Poff to issue a statement saying whatever he thought appropriate and the White House would follow his lead. If Poff didn't mention the racism charge, we wouldn't. "Besides," Nixon said, "all of that might inflame the South"—as if that were not exactly what he had in mind.

Nixon then ran down his list of remaining prospects. Lewis Powell of Virginia became a stronger possibility, despite his age. Nixon rambled, trying to reconcile the conflicts in his mind. If Poff was nominated, you couldn't have two Virginians; but with Poff out, we had to consider Powell. He was 64 then, thus "too old." The Nixon Court would be "the President's legacy," and his appointees had to be young. Still, Powell was healthy, vigorous, a good lawyer and, Nixon thought, right on the important issues. Moreover (although he didn't say it out loud), the President was feeling the pressure to name someone soon.

Mitchell had found* an Arkansas lawyer who was only 50 who had represented the school board in opposing integration of Little Rock's schools. Herschel Friday was his name, and he was now high on Mitchell's list. Mitchell told Nixon that Mr. Friday thought right on the key issues and was vigorous and articulate.

The President still wanted to nominate a Southerner. Hugo Black had told his wife that the present Senate would never confirm a Southerner. When the President had phoned to talk to the Blacks after receiving the Justice's resignation, Mrs. Black had told Nixon of her husband's support for what he was trying to do. But Black believed it a hopeless effort; Bayh and the others would keep all Southerners off.

Later that afternoon (October 2, 1971), Nixon was again toying with the idea of nominating Vice President Agnew to the Court.† He found "the Agnew thing intriguing," he told me.

"The Senate would clobber him," I said.

Nixon nodded. "They would attack me by rejecting him, and then Agnew would be useless; with a Senate rejection he becomes used goods," Nixon said. Nothing more was said about Agnew.

Senator Robert Byrd of West Virginia would be flattered to be considered, Nixon reasoned. There should be some public speculation about Byrd for the Court. He had gone to law school at night and had never practiced law, but it should "get out" that Nixon thought so much of Byrd's ability that he would consider him for the Court. Byrd then would be much easier to work with. "He's a very vain man, of limited ability," Nixon mused. As I asked questions, it became clear that Nixon had no intention whatever of nominating Byrd, but he wanted Byrd to hear that his name had been on the President's list—a very short list.

William Rehnquist had been the White House's lawyer from the first days of the Nixon Administration. Deputy Attorney General Richard Kleindienst had recruited him from

---

* Chief Justice Burger wrote Mitchell on October 13, 1971, renewing an earlier conversation, urging that he consider Herschel Friday, Powell and Judge Frank Johnson of Alabama. While Burger would welcome a *qualified* woman to the court, "only a handful of women were going into the law schools twenty-five and thirty-five years ago, and therefore, there is not now the large reservoir of talent as is true with respect to men."

† Once before, Nixon had talked of offering Agnew a Court seat so that John Connally could be appointed Vice President.

their home state, Arizona, and designated him to head the Office of Legal Counsel at the Justice Department.

When I became Counsel to the President, I was told that William Rehnquist and his staff would be available to brief and answer any of the legal questions that arose in the White House. I was delighted. Bill Rehnquist and I had been law students at Stanford at the same time, and I knew him to have been a superb student. In 1969, when I was Counsel, I sent him more than a few tough questions, mixed issues of law and politics, and he handled them well, with a sensitivity to the President's objectives and to the practicalities of our situation.

Bill Rehnquist and I talked often. After I moved to Domestic Affairs we served on some policy committees together. Occasionally we met socially, at the public school our children all attended or at some party.

After the Carswell defeat I advanced Bill Rehnquist's name as a candidate for the Court, but neither the President nor John Mitchell would consider him seriously. They dismissed him as an insider, too close to Mitchell and the President, and without a distinguished legal or judicial reputation.

After Dick Poff withdrew his name, Mr. Friday, the Arkansas school-board lawyer, and a Los Angeles woman judge, Mildred Lilley, became John Mitchell's top recommendations. The President had heard about Judge Lilley but didn't know either one of them.

The circumstances of Poff's withdrawal again suggested that, as in the Haynesworth and Carswell disasters, Mitchell was not adequately investigating his candidates before submitting their names to the President. So the President decided to have some independent checking done on Mrs. Lilley and Mr. Friday before giving Mitchell the go-ahead on their nominations.

"Who do we have who can find out about these people?" Nixon asked me. I suggested Egil Krogh of my staff. Krogh worked regularly on legislation and the problems of law enforcement with the Justice Department. But Krogh protested that he was swamped with work just then. He suggested that we use John Dean, then Counsel to the President, and David Young, a young lawyer who had been Henry Kissinger's aide and body servant for a couple of years and was anxious to be given other assignments.

I told Young and Dean as much as I knew about the President's Supreme Court criteria and the kind of information he would like to have about Herschel Friday and Mildred Lilley, and I sent them off to Arkansas and Los Angeles without much expectation that they would discover anything new or interesting. John Dean, in that error-laden and ghostwritten book *Blind Ambition,* surmises that he and Young were sent out as part of a big power move on my part to discredit and weaken his old hero, John Mitchell. Like most of what Dean wrote, that is demonstrable nonsense. I spent enormous time and energy trying to help Mitchell with his Justice Department problems. The President himself issued instructions for me to convey to his Attorney General almost every day. Our object was to help Mitchell perform well and look good.

Over the years, Nixon was outspokenly critical of Mitchell's mistakes, and Richard Moore, Egil Krogh and I spent countless hours trying to repair them. Matters customarily managed by the Justice Department were moved into the White House at Nixon's direction. For example, Lewis Engman became the Administration's antitrust manager for a time after Nixon decided Mitchell either could not or would not conduct the Antitrust Division as the President wanted it done.

I had plenty of other things to do; I didn't need the added burden of being Mitchell's keeper. And I surely didn't want his job.* But over the nearly four years of Mitchell's tenure, Nixon's confidence in him steadily waned as a result of one disappointment after another. It is not remarkable that the President was looking for a "second opinion" on Mitchell's recommendations.

Dean called from Little Rock, Arkansas, to report that Herschel Friday's nomination was going to present problems. After talking with him at great length, Dean described Mr. Friday as a rather ordinary lawyer, unencumbered with strong ideas or opinions about the issues of the day. Friday personally did not feel strongly about school desegregation; he had had a school-district client opposed to integration, so that was the side he had taken in the Little Rock case. Law-and-order issues didn't excite him much. In fact, Dean didn't think anything at all excited Mr. Friday much.

In Los Angeles, Judge Mildred Lilley looked better to Young and Dean. But the American Bar Association thought her unqualified for nomination to the Supreme Court.

When he heard these reports, the President decided not to nominate either of Mitchell's choices. Instead, he turned to Richard Moore, by then on the President's staff, for help in finding new candidates. Nixon went back over names on lists he had worked with when there had been other vacancies. He

---

* I had been offered it by Nixon in 1968 and had turned it down.

was feeling pressure; the longer he waited the worse it would get, with the press badgering him and the Congress telling him what he ought to do. He had to find two people quickly.

By Wednesday, October 20, he was considering a perennial candidate, Ronald Reagan's counsel, William French Smith* of Los Angeles. Smith was an Ivy Leaguer, and that bothered Nixon. He asked Dick Moore to find out where Smith had gone to school and whether Smith had been a law-review editor. Moore went to the law library at the Department of Justice and discovered that William French Smith had graduated from Harvard but had not been on the law review there. At the President's request, Moore also looked up the legal pedigrees of Lewis Powell of Virginia and the Fordham Law School's Dean William Mulligan.

While he was at the Justice Department, Moore dropped by to say hello to Mitchell. He found Richard Kleindienst in Mitchell's office too. Immediately before Moore's arrival the President had telephoned Mitchell to say that he was seriously considering Assistant Attorney General William Rehnquist as one of his nominees.

The Attorney General, Moore told me, was "ashen." The phone call meant that Nixon had rejected Mitchell's recommendations, Judge Lilley and Herschel Friday, and had decided to develop a nomination list of his own. It was a devastating vote of no confidence in John Mitchell.

The next day Nixon asked Dick Moore to find out what I thought of Bill Rehnquist. Moore already knew that Bill and I had been at law school together and that I was enthusiastic about his possible nomination, and he told the President how I felt.

That same day, October 21, the President announced that he would nominate Lewis Powell and William Rehnquist to the Court. By early December they had been confirmed, and they soon joined Warren Burger and Harry Blackmun as the Nixon appointees.

In August 1972, about two months after the burglars had broken into the Watergate headquarters of the Democrats, the Chief Justice invited my wife and me to dinner at his home. It was one of those curious experiences that happen only in Washington, where the public *persona* does not always jibe

---

* Ronald Reagan's Attorney General, 1981–.

with real life; where one's fame can quickly outstrip the financial means or the inclination to live like someone famous.

The Chief Justice and his wife lived in an old farmhouse on a fair-sized property in a Virginia suburb of the District of Columbia. Tract housing encroached on them from every side.

The guest of honor was the Lord Chief Justice of England and Lady Widgery. His Lordship was sporting a red dinner jacket, the ladies were all in long dresses and the rest of us—a former Attorney General, some judges and a retired general—were in dinner jackets and black tie.

The Burger house was not spacious. It was a warm summer evening, and we were all squeezed into a tiny dining room where hired waiters and maids, with platters of catered food, tried to negotiate the narrow spaces between our chair backs and the old, papered walls. The table was a forest of wineglasses and candelabra. Before, during and after each course there was a discussion of the wine that had been or was about to be served. The Chief had a story to go with every sip. This one had been found in the cellar of a small inn near the Pyrenees; the next one had been bought at auction (with each bid and counterbid remembered and recounted).

As the candles burned, the room warmed from uncomfortable to unbearable. After dinner, everyone toasted everyone in a Champagne of remarkable pedigree.

Just as the ladies were about to retire, the Chief Justice of the United States, taking inventory, noticed that my wife, Jeanne, had drunk *none* of her wine. At her place were all the glasses, goblets and tulips, as full as when the waiters had first decanted. Burger was dismayed.

"Are you unwell, my dear?" he asked Jeanne. She looked startled.

"Your wine," he pointed. "Was it not to your liking?"

"Oh," she said. By now everyone's attention had been drawn by Burger's look of distress. "It's just that I don't drink," Jeanne confessed. "I'm sure it's very nice."

"Indeed it is," crooned the Chief, making a very long reach for her first wine. "Don't drink? Don't drink *wine?*" One after another, in the order of their arrival, Burger drank the untouched wines, then polished off the Champagne as Mrs. Burger tried to gather the ladies for a retreat to the parlor. No priest could have consumed the Mass-end residue of a sacramental wine with greater religious fervor.

That was my final and most lasting memory of Warren Burger the man.

CHAPTER NINE

The Vice President

ON NOVEMBER 14, 1972, a week after Richard Nixon's land-slide reelection, he was sitting in the corner of the tiny den in Aspen Lodge at Camp David, his back to the windows. Haldeman was beside the desk. I was near the door, between Nixon and the fireplace, facing the windows. It was a rainy day, the clouds low on the hilltop like fog. The trees were bare and gray in the steam rising from the swimming pool just outside the windows.

The President had been rambling. He'd decided on the three prayers to be given at his inaugural ceremony—Catholic, Jewish and Protestant—and he'd dictated other inaugural instructions to Haldeman.

He wanted his Presidential Library Foundation to hire Julie at $1,000 a month to work on documentaries. She would need a film editor who was a Nixon advocate, not merely a technically competent professional. (She was never hired.)

Spiro Agnew had been reelected as well. "He's the first question we have," Nixon said. "I'm not sure he's the one to succeed me in 1976—but we may be stuck with him. He wants it, but we will not help him."

His mind slipped off to budget questions. We'd withhold money from clean-water programs, keep the school-lunch program, flush Model Cities down the drain, hold the budget back to the $250-billion level, cut education and the National Science Foundation by half . . .

"We must get control of the CIA. The DIA and NSA [Defense Intelligence and National Security agencies] are a big waste; cut their budgets. It won't affect our muscle. Cut twenty-five percent of the Pentagon personnel. Cut the White House staff; make it slim and lean. Cut the Secret Service—I don't need all that. Fix it so fewer people talk to the President. . . ."

Back to Spiro Agnew: "We have to make a basic decision about him." I nodded. "By any criteria he falls short. Energy? He doesn't work hard; he likes to play golf. Leadership?" Nixon laughed. "Consistency? He's all over the place. He's not really a conservative, you know."

"Maybe," Haldeman suggested, "the Vice President needs your 'benign neglect.' "

"Yes, that should be our strategy," Nixon nodded.

"Do you want him to continue to handle intergovernmental relations?" I asked.

"No," Nixon replied. "He shouldn't have it. He'll just take the gravy and leave the President all the negatives and the problems. He has such a poor staff, too. Give Agnew the Bicentennial to look after.

"We've got to build two or three [Presidential] candidates for 1976," Nixon continued. "In about April [of 1973] let's begin that process.

"I suppose I've got to talk to Agnew about the reorganization," the President said with reluctance. "I'll see him briefly and then I'll send him to you fellows for a detailed review of the plan."

"He won't like that much," I said. I knew Agnew hated to be filled in on things by me.

Nixon nodded. "Can we ask his staff to resign? They really should, you know; they are of such poor quality."

"I'd rather see his Secret Service detail go," I said. "They are the living example of genetic selection. He's gathered around him the biggest bunch of hoods in the Service."

"There's not much to be done about that," Haldeman said. "Spiro likes them."

Nothing more was said about Spiro Agnew that day. We were beginning the process of reorganization and cabinet selection that would keep us up on Camp David's cold mountain for the next sixty days.

Six months later, at my very last meeting with President Nixon, in May 1973, we also talked about Agnew. By then there were rumors that Agnew was in trouble, and Haldeman had told me a few of the details in deep confidence.

"I'm going to have to get rid of him," Nixon told me. "They've got the evidence. Agnew has been on the take all the time he's been here!" The President was distressed for several reasons. Aside from the obvious ways that Agnew's conduct complicated the Watergate crisis, Nixon genuinely believed that as long as Spiro Agnew was Vice President, most Representatives would think twice before voting Articles of Impeachment against Richard Nixon.

Nixon called Agnew his "insurance policy" when someone raised the subject of the President's physical safety. "No assassin in his right mind would kill me," Nixon laughed. "They know that if they did they would end up with Agnew!" But in May of 1973 it seemed certain that Agnew would be replaced soon.

There had been a few early warning signs that Spiro Agnew was more than casually interested in which contractors were awarded government business in Maryland and on the Eastern Seaboard, but we had missed seeing them.

On March 31, 1970, the Vice President told Nixon that he was concerned about the way the GSA awarded its contracts in the Eastern states. Agnew asserted that "our friends" were being discriminated against. Someone (presumably Agnew) should monitor this important form of patronage.

When nothing came of this gambit, Agnew made another move, and in response Robert Kunzig, the GSA Administrator, called to ask me what to do.

That same day I was sitting next to Bob Haldeman at a Cabinet meeting. To fight boredom, we sent notes back and forth on a pad of paper. I wrote:

> *Do you know about the V.P. taking over all GSA patronage for Md., Pa., Va., W. Va.?*
> *—Appointments*
> *—Architects*
> *—Favors for Congressmen*
> *—Construction, etc.*
>   *To be cleared with Blair?*

Haldeman replied:

> *By whose order?—When?—Why?*

I answered:

> *Agnew's assistant called Kunzig [the GSA Administrator] in last week and ordered it.*
> *Add: District of Columbia*

After the meeting Haldeman said he would check, then relay the President's desires to Kunzig. But so far as Haldeman knew, there had been no decision to give Agnew such sweeping control of the GSA.

To me this was simply another case of Agnew trying to grab some of the White House levers. It didn't occur to me that Agnew might be seeking to profit financially from such control; I ignored the signals.

Obviously, Spiro Agnew was a problem that required constant vigilance; more attention than I, for one, was able to give.

One morning in early September 1969 I had to leave the senior staff meeting early to go see the Vice President. Peter Flanigan had alerted me that Agnew's Space Advisory Committee was about to make some recommendations to the President that Flanigan knew Nixon could not live with. Peter had been unsuccessful in dissuading the President's science adviser, Lee DuBridge, from agreeing with the staff of Agnew's Advisory Committee that there should be a very costly manned mission to the planet Mars in 1981. So Flanigan had asked for a meeting with Agnew, the ex-officio chairman of the committee, in the hope that we could persuade him to kill it.

I had read a briefing paper on the question the evening before, and it seemed obvious to me that Agnew and DuBridge owed it to the President not to include a proposal our budget couldn't pay for. A Mars space shot would be very popular with many people. If the committee proposed it and Nixon had to say no, he would be criticized as the President who kept us from finding life on Mars. On the other hand, if the committee didn't recommend it, we avoided the problem altogether.

DuBridge was perhaps to be forgiven for failing to understand such a political argument, but I saw no excuse for Agnew's insistence that the Mars shot be recommended. At our meeting I was surprised at his obtuseness. It was, he argued, a reasonable, feasible option. That was what his committee was supposed to come up with, and that was what they intended to do.

I had been wooed by NASA, the Space Administration, but not to the degree to which they had made love to Agnew. He had been their guest of honor at space launchings, tours and dinners, and it seemed to me they had done a superb job of recruiting him to lead this fight to vastly expand their space empire and budget.

I finally took off the kid gloves: "Look, Mr. Vice President, we have to be practical. There is to be no money for a Mars trip. The President has already decided that. So the President does not want such a trip in the Space Advisory Committee's recommendations. It is your job, with Lee DuBridge's help, to make absolutely certain that the Mars trip is not in there."

Mr. Agnew was not happy to be told what to do by me. He demanded a personal meeting with the President. This was a matter for Constitutional Officers to discuss.

I overlooked the obvious innuendo that I was lying to Agnew about what the President had decided. "Fine," I said. "I'll arrange it at once, and someone will call you."

Flanigan and I left Agnew about 9:45 A.M. At 10:00 A.M. the Vice President called me. He had decided to move the Mars shot from the list of "recommendations" to another category headed "Technically Feasible."

When I saw President Nixon later that day I told him about our session with Agnew and his telephone call.

"Good," Nixon said. "That's just the way to handle him; use that technique on him anytime." Nixon looked at me vaguely. "Is Agnew insubordinate, do you think?"

Nixon found early that personal meetings with Agnew were invariably unpleasant. The President came out of them amazed at Agnew's constant self-aggrandizement. Nixon recalled that as Vice President he had seldom made a request of any kind of Dwight Eisenhower. But Agnew's visits always included demands for more staff, better facilities, more prerogatives and perquisites. It was predictable that as Agnew complained and requested more and more, Nixon would agree to see him less frequently.

At first, in 1969, I was sent to see Agnew when Haldeman realized he and the Vice President did not get along well. The President's idea was that a high-level staff person should listen to Agnew (when an appointment with the President had been requested) and try to deflect his imprudent demands; I was expected to arrange for the ministerial tasks to be done by our staff, and I was supposed to show Agnew why his other demands ought not to be pressed in talks with the President. None of that worked, of course.

Spiro Agnew had been the Governor of Maryland; we thought it natural that he would take responsibility for our relations with governors, mayors and county officials. But it turned out that he was only an excellent conduit for their complaints—especially the gripes of Ronald Reagan, John Bell Williams and a few other conservatives. Notwithstanding Agnew's 1968 love affair with the Presidential candidacy of

Nelson Rockefeller, Rocky soon gave up on Agnew's liaison and began calling me directly. I tried to wean Rockefeller back to Agnew until the Governor went to the President and insisted that I be his avenue to the President instead of Agnew.

"Agnew doesn't play them well," Nixon explained to me.

More than once I was called to Agnew's office to hear his complaints. If he were going to be able to do the intergovernmental relations job for the President, he'd say, he had to have more help from the White House staff, not the sort of resistance he was getting. The budget people, the Congressional-liaison staff and my domestic-policy experts were to be told that a Vice Presidential "request" was to be given heed. I tried to explain that such staff people usually were following established Presidential policy, which probably didn't please the mayor or governor Vice President Agnew had on the phone. That was why they were calling him. His job was to sell our policy to them, not theirs to us.

Before long Agnew lost his zest for the intergovernmental assignment. He dabbled in taxation, health and other substantive issues, but found them to involve hard, dull study.

Speechmaking and traveling were less taxing and more interesting. He could take the texts prepared in the President's speechwriting shop, change a phrase here and there, and hit the road to attack the "effete corps of impudent snobs" who came on television after a Presidential speech to provide their "instant analysis" and who, "by the expressions on their faces, the tone of their questions and the sarcasm of their responses, made clear their disapproval."

By October 1969 the press was reporting the President's disenchantment with his Vice President. The reorganization of the Executive Office of the President was well under way, and Agnew had allied himself with those in the Cabinet who opposed the change.

Late in the morning of October 27 the President called for Bryce Harlow, Haldeman and me. Harlow was to go to Agnew with a warning.

"Say," Nixon dictated, "that the President pointed out to you that it is traditional in this town to try to divide the President from his Vice President. I'm an expert. For eight years the press tried to divide me from Eisenhower, without success. They are playing the same game now. He can't let it happen. And," the President added, looking at Haldeman and me, "the staff is *never* to criticize the Vice President."

Two weeks later the President was informed that Agnew

was engaged in battle with the State Department. He wanted to go to Vietnam, Formosa and seven other Asian countries and State was afraid to let him go.

"I'm sort of afraid to have him go too," Nixon said deadpan, repeating his joke about the assassin's dilemma. "If they kill Nixon, they get Agnew. I'd hate to have anything happen to him."

At other times Nixon was more sanguine that he could get some good work from his Vice President. In 1970 he directed that planning for a new health program be an Agnew project: Health experts were to be added to the Vice President's staff, along with a speechwriter and TV specialists. Agnew then chaired a series of interdepartmental meetings on health issues, but he seemed incapable of organizing the work and guiding the staff to a result. I watched the Vice President closely during this health project, trying to discover the cause of his mental constipation.

I concluded that the man was exceedingly narrow; new thoughts were unwelcome to him. As a result, his health project did not gather for the President all the practical alternatives for a final choice. Instead it became a narrow reflection of Spiro Agnew's preferences. One by one the resource people dropped away from the effort (as did I), and it languished. Eventually the quest for a health program was reassigned to Ken Cole, Jim Cavanaugh and a new working group, and some excellent options were forwarded to the President. Spiro Agnew had struck out on health.

In March of 1970, Nixon was concerned lest Agnew involve himself in the civil rights problem. Again, Harlow, Haldeman and I were called in, and Bryce Harlow was sent off with orders for Agnew. To mollify the Vice President, Haldeman and I were to stay out of the new arrangement: "You, Bryce, are to clear any of his statements on school integration or civil rights," Nixon said. "Tell him I'm very pleased with the way he's handled himself, so far. But he's not to have any press conferences. Anything he wants to say that's not under the Lyndley Rule* must be okayed by me in advance. Tell him I don't want any new ground broken. Say: I'd hate to have to repudiate something he said."

At times Nixon and Agnew were closer. In May of 1970 Pat

---

* A press rule of nonattribution which, in Washington, is seen more in the breach than the observance.

Moynihan wrote the President about a riot in Augusta, Georgia:

If you will accept the idea there is a "standard" riot, Augusta's was in most respects standard. (Again as best one can tell from newspaper accounts.)
- A summer day. (Late spring will do in the South.) A fairly crowded slum, close to or involving fairly extensive commercial outlets for consumer goods.
- Rumors spread of a police atrocity. (In this case a young prisoner was killed in jail. The rumor was the police had murdered him.)
- Gatherings. Dispersal by the police.
- Nightfall. Beginning of fires and looting.
- Killing and wounding. (In this case six killed.)

Moynihan anticipated more riots in the South and made some recommendations toward their amelioration—a Presidential statement condemning violence, plus investigation and reactivation of the Federal "urban disturbance network." He concluded:

I am dead in earnest. Southern racial violence would be a disaster. But if it should occur in an atmosphere in which the national government could be said to be implicated—and unless you act rather forcefully this will be said and believed if such violence occurs this summer—it would be a calamity of historic proportion. That it would destroy the administration goes without saying.

A copy of Pat's memo went to Spiro Agnew, and within a week Agnew wrote me a response which I sent to the President:

May 26, 1970

MEMORANDUM FOR
    THE HONORABLE JOHN D. EHRLICHMAN

Returned herewith is the Moynihan memorandum copy. Also enclosed are copies of FBI reports of May 19th concerning recent disorders in Southern cities.

While I usually respect Pat Moynihan's judgments, and always his sincerity, I find his conclusions on this subject disturbing and even somewhat frightening. We must not fall into the usual trap of separating and dissecting a fragment of a disorder. It has become fashionable in the liberal community to totally disregard the unlawful and outrageous acts which may have led to isolated instances of police overreaction and to focus on a single result which serves their thesis.

It is obvious from these reports that none of the incidents arose out of improper police conduct. They all began with the usual civil rights propaganda techniques. We have had enough maudlin sympathy for law-breakers emanating from other areas of government. The only thing that keeps the country together is the steadfast resolve of the White House not to be trapped into such attitudes. In my judgment, nothing makes the average American any angrier than to see the pained, self-righteous expressions of a Muskie or a Percy as they attach like leeches to the nearest Negro funeral procession.

Please be certain that these opinions reach the President. This is a time when he must not crack under the steady onslaught of pressures in this direction. The polls show that the people are with him and not with the whiners in the Senate and in the liberal community.

/s/ *STA*

Nixon underlined the sentence about Muskie-Percy types and noted *"E—I agree"* next to the final paragraph.

As a response to the Kent State shootings and the other college-related violence that peaked following the Cambodia "incursion," the President appointed a Commission on Campus Violence. The chairman was to be William Scranton, the former Governor of Pennsylvania.

I had several meetings with Bernard Segal, the Philadelphia lawyer who was president of the American Bar Association, to assemble a list of names from which the President could choose eight committee members. I asked for names from Bob Finch, Pat Moynihan, Leonard Garment, John Mitchell and others. We were interested in having some black members because there had been a number of cases of violence involving black students, most notably at Jackson State College in Jackson, Mississippi.

I urged the President to put Joe Rhodes on the Commission. Joe had been president of the student body at the California Institute of Technology when I first met him. He'd managed to lead Cal Tech into a number of progressive changes with a minimum of confrontation, and I admired the way he'd gone about it. In 1969 and early 1970, Joe and I talked occasionally about what he was seeing on campus. When he won a fellowship from Harvard we kept in touch. There was no secret about his views on the war, Spiro Agnew and Richard Nixon. But our differences were put rationally, and all our talks were completely honest on both sides. I didn't talk about people like Joe Rhodes to reporters; I saw no advantage in grandstanding the fact that I was in touch with a few students.

The Scranton Commission was not going to be a whitewash—that was obvious from its makeup. James Ahern, a liberal police chief, and Benjamin Davis, a retired Air Force general, were the law-and-order element. Bayless Manning, dean at Stanford Law School; Jim Cheek, president of Howard University; Martha Derthick, a professor from Boston College, and Joe Rhodes represented the colleges. Erwin Canham had been editor of the *Christian Science Monitor,* and Revius Ortique, Jr., was president of the all-black National Bar Association.*

Davis, Rhodes, Cheek and Ortique were black. When they were approved by the President and announced, the press made a beeline for Joe Rhodes, the only student named. And Joe said some things that made headlines on June 16, 1970.

In May, during a visit to the Pentagon, the President had made an offhand comment that students who torch and destroy their campuses (a visiting professor from India had lost everything during a Stanford protest riot that week) were "bums." That catchy appellation quickly ran away from its context, and most students grew to believe Nixon had called all campus protesters bums.

Against that background, Joe Rhodes told *The New York Times* he would "try to figure out . . . who gave what orders to send police on campus [at Kent State and Jackson State] and [if they were] thinking about 'campus bums' when they pulled the trigger."

Spiro Agnew was in Detroit that day and saw the wire-service reports of Rhodes's remarks just before he held a press conference. Agnew fearlessly led with his chin: "Unless the *Times* reporter is in error," he said, "Mr. Rhodes should resign immediately. He clearly does not possess the maturity, the objectivity and the judgment to serve on a fact-finding body of national importance."

Agnew tried to find daylight between the President and me: "My remarks should in no way be interpreted as an implied

---

* The Scranton Commission's counsel was Matthew Byrne, who became the trial judge in the Daniel Ellsberg case three years later.

criticism of a Presidential appointment. Having used a relationship of mutual trust with Presidential adviser John Ehrlichman for his own political gain, Rhodes is no longer entitled to the cloak of dignity that a Presidential appointment would throw around him."

That day I had taken the domestic-policy staff to Camp David for a planning session, but I spent much of the afternoon on the telephone, talking about Rhodes and Agnew.

Agnew belatedly realized he had given the President a narrow choice between Joe Rhodes and Spiro Agnew, and he scrambled to shore up his demand that Rhodes must go. Agnew's constant ally Governor Ronald Reagan had also been hit by Rhodes in the same press conference (Reagan was "bent on killing [campus] people for his own political gain"). Agnew called me as soon as he returned from Detroit to report that "Ronald Reagan is furious at Rhodes." Agnew called John Mitchell, too. Agnew called me back to ask if I intended to remove Rhodes from the Commission. I said I could not. Then I called Joe Rhodes to tell him what was going on.

Near the end of the day, the President called too. I said it was unfortunate that Agnew had created such a difficult choice. But it seemed to me there were only two options: the President could toss off the only student on the Commission because he'd misconstrued the "bums" remark and opposed the war and Spiro Agnew was after him, or he could repudiate his Vice President. Nixon said he'd sleep on it.

The next morning William Scranton called to urge that Rhodes be retained. A few minutes later Spiro Agnew's aide called to say the Vice President was "too busy" to come to Camp David to make his scheduled talk to our domestic policy meeting.

A headline in *The Evening Star* that day (June 17) was "PRESIDENT REBUFFS AGNEW ON STUDENT." Nixon had sent Ron Ziegler to tell the press he would not remove Rhodes.

In my view that was the only possible way Nixon could have gone. Agnew was exceedingly foolish to have issued an ultimatum which would have required the President to repudiate a bright black student at the very time we were trying to quiet the colleges.

At his first meeting with William Scranton to set the Campus Disorder Commission's course, the President urged Scranton to have a meeting with the Vice President. "He does have some ideas about this," Nixon said, "and he doesn't have horns. At all costs you don't want him in an adversary position. And you know, Rhodes was wrong about Reagan. No one in California has been killed on a campus by any officer."

"I've told Rhodes to say nothing more to the press," Scranton said, "but I'm sorry the Vice President said what he said about Rhodes."

"I am too," Nixon said. "Reagan called me and he was very mad. John Mitchell called twice. I don't rebuff my Vice President—I don't do that—but before he had a press conference he should have called Ehrlichman or someone. He didn't, did he?"

"No, sir," I said. "He didn't."

Nixon gave Scranton a free hand, with one qualification: "Just don't let higher education off with a pat on the ass."

Thursday, June 18, the President summoned Bob Finch, Don Rumsfeld, George Shultz, Bob Haldeman and me aboard his yacht for dinner. He wanted to talk about Spiro Agnew. The Vice President proposed to deliver a speech the following Saturday which harshly blasted the Congress. Those on the staff who had seen drafts of the speech warned the President that it was a very bad idea.

"I want you people to program Agnew," Nixon said after reviewing his current Vice Presidential troubles. I looked around the table; he had the wrong group. I reminded Nixon that Haldeman and I had both struck out with Agnew before, and by now Agnew must be furious with me over his Rhodes embarrassment. We couldn't program Agnew to leave a burning building. The other three were liberals, in Agnew's way of looking at people. I doubted that they could do what the President wanted done. Shultz wasn't willing to agree, but Finch and Rumsfeld were.

As we talked about who might do some good, the President eliminated Pat Buchanan and John Mitchell. Pat couldn't and John wouldn't.

In thinking then about what *motivated* Spiro Agnew, I realized that I didn't have a clue. I didn't take his Presidential aspirations seriously. He wasn't a Nixon team player. Maybe he was just a dedicated public servant who wasn't too bright.

The Congress had voted to lower the voting age to 18. Nixon was debating whether to veto the legislation, canvassing his legislative lobbyists as to whether a veto might be sustained.

"It probably ought to be vetoed," Nixon mused. "That would be the best politics. Agnew and Reagan both want me to veto it. Rockefeller says sign it. I could stump around the country like Agnew and Reagan, attacking the eighteen-year-olds, and get sixty-percent support, but it would divide the country. There's no political mileage in signing it, and we could demagogue the hell out of a veto; we won't win many blacks or young people, you know. But we do have an obligation not to have the goddamned country blow up."*

Just after the Fourth of July the President directed that "no one" (translation: me) was to talk to Joe Rhodes until further notice. "And there's to be no more discussion about Agnew among the White House staff."

But the next day Nixon decided to make another try at programming Spiro Agnew. He summoned Bryce Harlow, Bob Finch, Bob Haldeman, John Mitchell and me to renew the Agnew deliberations. At last it was decided that Harlow should volunteer to take the Agnew assignment until the November 1970 election. Harlow reluctantly agreed.

With Harlow in place, reviewing Agnew's schedule, speech texts and press briefings, the President began to send Agnew out to help Republican Congressional candidates and speak to conventions such as that of the American Legion.

On November 1, 1970, Nixon and Agnew met in the Oval Office along with Ron Ziegler, Dick Moore and me. Pat Buchanan had been assigned to write Agnew's campaign material. Nixon intended to give Agnew some things to say, so Pat was there to take notes.

Agnew startled me by artlessly opening the meeting: "Mr. President, as I travel around I get a great many questions about our 1972 ticket."

Nixon nodded. "Of course, this far ahead the President can't say anything. Just say we're only thinking about November of 1970. You can say, 'The President has shown great confidence in me so far, and I hope it will continue.'

"Ron," Nixon said, changing the subject, "I want you to get out immediately that the President is delighted with the Vice President's campaigning. He's had a big impact, good crowds, and from reports we've had from all over I'm impressed with the intensity of the Vice President's campaign.

"Then I want you others to do some backgrounding," Nixon said to us. "The President is grateful to the Vice President. The President knows how hard this kind of campaigning is. He's having a big impact. He's partisan, but we're not doing a high-road, low-road operation. I'm not so partisan because

---

* The President signed the bill.

I'm the President of all the people. I work with both parties in the Congress even when some of them are sincerely wrong."

Nixon had some pointers for Agnew on the economy. Then he turned to California. "I want you to hit that Tunney. He told a deliberate lie about our intending to close the Ames base. He's not fit for office."

"Oh, Mr. President," Agnew said in his high singsong, "I won't be too gentle with him."

A month after the 1970 election, the President was feeling overworked. I was preparing him for his brief part in the launching of our housing program. He was bucking.

"The people responsible for these damn programs should sell them!" he exclaimed. "It's less effective to use the White House all the time. And it offends the Cabinet. You have to remember how my time is committed."

I pointed out that this appearance would be very brief.

"Don't keep saying that, John," he snapped. "I know, I know, I have to do the damn thing. It's all right," he said in a Jack Benny voice, with a big Benny sigh. "I'll just work twenty-two hours a day instead of twenty."

Then he thought of Agnew. "Let the Vice President attend these things. He can handle revenue sharing and health. He should preside at the Domestic Council meetings, too. That will force him to attend them. But leave him off the International Economic Policy Council. I don't want him in that."

Six months later, in late July 1971, the President interrupted our daily meeting to tell me his latest Agnew problems. The President had recently announced that he would be making his historic trip to China. Now Agnew, in Africa on a tour, had told the leader of one nation that he disagreed with the President's China policy. Agnew said he didn't think the forthcoming trip was a good idea.

The President was very agitated. "It is beyond my understanding," he said. "Twice Agnew has proposed that *he* go to China! Now he tells the world it's a bad idea for me to go! What am I going to do about him?"

"I think you ought to drop him next year," I replied.

Nixon nodded. "I've had Bob [Haldeman] arrange for Bryce [Harlow] to let Agnew know I'm thinking about someone else." Then Nixon recounted his long July 19 talk with John Connally about the Vice Presidency.

But by the early summer of 1972, John Mitchell had persuaded the President to give Agnew "four more years."

* * *

A final note on the Vice President's helpful suggestions.

Agnew called me about the Bicentennial once in 1972. He'd had an inspiration: the chairmanship was vacant, and he had just the man. How about a nationally renowned—no, *world*-renowned—figure; an ethnic—an Italian—an able executive? How about Frank Sinatra?

I gulped. "I'll refer your idea to the President," I promised. But I'd seen Sinatra's thick FBI package, full of innuendos about connections with organized crime. I couldn't imagine trying to get him through a Senate confirmation.

When I told the President about Agnew's idea, Nixon just laughed.

I called Spiro Agnew back to tell him Sinatra was not acceptable, and I could tell the Vice President was very disappointed. He told me how well he and Sinatra would work together. I'm sure that at the time, Agnew still hoped to be Vice President on July 4, 1976. And I fully expected him to be. But he didn't press hard for Sinatra's appointment. Perhaps Agnew was husbanding his strength for a battle he could foresee. Or perhaps he already sensed he was beaten.

CHAPTER TEN

Hoover

THE DIRECTOR OF the Federal Bureau of Investigation was 74 years old when I first met him, briefly, at the Hotel Pierre in New York during the late-1968 transition. His appearance surprised me. His big head rested on beefy, rounded shoulders, apparently without benefit of neck. He was florid and fat-faced, ears flat against his head, eyes protruding. He looked unwell to me.

During this meeting at the Pierre, the President-elect rather ostentatiously told Hoover, "Edgar, you are one of the few people who is to have direct access to me at all times. I've talked to Mitchell about it and he understands." Hoover nodded. It was obviously no less than he expected. He too was traveling the comeback trail. He had been frozen out of the

White House by the Kennedy brothers. Because he had cultivated his relations with Lyndon B. Johnson from the time L.B.J. was a rising power in the Senate, things had been a little better for him during the Johnson Presidency.

But Hoover had bet on Nixon's return to office as the surest way to stay in power. Hoover and Nixon had kept in touch during all the years Nixon was out of office. Rose Mary Woods had been Hoover's Nixon contact for the exchange of information and advice between them. Whenever Nixon traveled abroad as a private citizen, the FBI agents who posed as "legal attachés" in U.S. embassies were instructed by Hoover to look after Nixon. Hoover fed Nixon information during those years via Cartha De Loach, an assistant director of the FBI, and through Lou Nichols, a retired Bureau assistant director who had become a distillery executive. But Hoover was more than a source of information——he was a political advisor to whom Nixon listened.

As far as Nixon was concerned, his grant of direct Presidential access to Hoover was symbolic. It bestowed on Hoover the access the Kennedys had denied him. But once the gesture had been made, it became Bob Haldeman's assignment to create a process to protect Nixon from Hoover exercising that access. The last thing Nixon wanted was Hoover walking in on him whenever the Director felt like it. Perhaps because Haldeman feared that Rose Mary Woods had become too close to Hoover, she was not designated Hoover's White House contact. Instead, I was called in one day in January 1969 to be told by the President that I would be his liaison with Hoover. I was to go to Hoover's office and establish myself as his friend and White House confidant.

There had already been a hint that this was coming. One day, a week or so earlier, Hoover had come up to my office; the President had sent him up after one of their meetings to have me follow through on his promise that Hoover was to have the money he needed to finish the new FBI headquarters. That huge building on Pennsylvania Avenue, then under construction, was a monument to Hoover's mastery of the Congressional appropriation process, but the President's Bureau of the Budget was objecting to the additional money that would be needed to meet Hoover's elaborate specifications. Hoover had come to see Nixon for redress. In due course, I straightened matters out with a phone call.

I took Hoover that good news the following week, when I went to the Justice Department to see him. It was a measure of my naiveté that I was afraid there would be no basis for common understanding between a boy from the country and the legendary J. Edgar Hoover. As it turned out, it was Hoover who wooed me, and he did almost all the talking.

My staff had cautioned me that every meeting in Hoover's office was secretly filmed or videotaped. But they did not prepare me for the Wizard of Oz approach that his visitors were required to make.

Signs directed me to Hoover's foyer in the Department of Justice building, where the reception desk held television monitors and other electronic gear. I was greeted by several FBI agents (short haircuts, narrow lapels, quiet ties, shined shoes) and a very tall, muscular black man whom I was to see again months later.

I was ushered through double doors into a square, lightly furnished anteroom, remarkable for its plaques, framed citations, mounted trophies, medals, tablets and certificates which jammed every wall. There were awards from the Boys Club, service clubs and police associations featuring torches, eagles, flags and gavels. I was led through a second room, windowless and similarly decorated. There must have been fifty or sixty awards on each of the four walls. I was quickly taken through it and yet a third trophy room to the double doors of a large office decorated in blond wood and red leather. Inside, a very large desk, bare of papers or files, was backed with several flags. J. Edgar Hoover was nowhere to be seen. My guide opened a door behind the desk, at the back of the room, and I was ushered into an office about twelve or thirteen feet square, dominated by Hoover himself; he was seated in a large leather desk chair behind a wooden desk in the center of the room. When he stood, it became obvious that he and his desk were on a dais about six inches high. I was invited to sit on a low, purplish leather couch to his right. J. Edgar Hoover looked down on me and began to talk.

An hour later he was still talking. There were two of these getting-acquainted sessions with the Director, early in 1969, and both of them were rambling, nonstop monologues. The Director had strong and definite views on a great many subjects and I was massively exposed to all of them: Black Panthers, domestic Communism, the Congress, the FBI budget, Hubert Humphrey and his supporters, Russia, Bureau training, Bureau procedures and morale, the Kennedys, the need for more FBI agents abroad, and much more.

High on all Hoover's walls in that small office was a soffit which concealed indirect fluorescent lighting. Often during these harangues I tried to identify a wavering purplish light that came from behind a segment of the soffit. And of course, I looked all over for the eye of the surveillant television camera, but I never found it.

After the first session the President asked me how we'd gotten along. "Great; Hoover did all the talking," I said. Nixon nodded. "I know. But it's necessary, John. It's necessary."

Because I was Counsel to the President, my office was the place to which all FBI communications with the White House came. My administrative assistant and secretary sifted out most of it, bringing me only the most important or peculiar Bureau paperwork. In general, the FBI investigative work I saw was of poor quality. The Bureau dealt excessively in rumor, gossip and conjecture; sometimes a report was based on "a confidential source"—the Bureau euphemism for wiretapping or bugging. Even then the information was often hearsay, two or three times removed. When FBI work was particularly bad I sent it back to Hoover, but the rework was seldom an improvement.

During that first year, the President was continually calling for intelligence about domestic violence and bombings. He wanted to know who was doing it, and what was being done to catch the saboteurs. I soon discovered that our best source of information was the New York City police department intelligence unit, not the FBI. Jack Caulfield, a former New York policeman on my staff, was able to secure far better data for the President from the NYPD than we could get from Hoover.

Early in May 1969 the FBI Director passed the word to Nixon (via John Mitchell and Rose Mary Woods) that he had most disturbing information about a coterie of homosexuals at the highest levels of the White House staff. Nothing could grab Nixon's attention faster than that allegation; he immediately called Hoover for the details. An FBI source, an investigative reporter of marginal repute, had names, places and dates, Hoover said. The story was that H. R. Haldeman, Dwight Chapin and I were lovers. The informant supplied specific dates on which we were supposed to have held our trysts at a particular resort. Hoover said the reporter intended to publish his information unless Hoover assured him the story was untrue.

By May 27, Murray Chotiner had heard the story and was able to tell Bob Haldeman who the "reporter" was. He turned out to be one of Jack Anderson's part-time legmen who peddled stories from the periphery of the legitimate Washington press corps.

For the next month Haldeman was careful to keep track of where he, Chapin and I were each day (and night), in case there were new allegations.

On June 24, Attorney General John Mitchell told the President he was hearing the story too. The rumor was reaching serious proportions. He suggested the President protect himself by having Hoover look into the allegations.

Hoover suggested to Nixon that he designate one of the FBI's most discreet executives to conduct an investigation at once. I'm not sure what else Nixon decided to do, but I was immediately required to submit to interrogation by Assistant Director Mark Felt, who came to my office on June 26 with a stenotypist. I had good alibis for the dates alleged—I was elsewhere with other people, including a satisfactory number of women. I answered all Felt's questions under oath, and he left me. But I was not sure I had convinced him of my sexual orientation. He was coolly noncommittal. Later I was told by Bob Haldeman that Hoover had been satisfied the charge was false; Haldeman said Hoover had sent word to the President and had also passed a message to the Jack Anderson reporter that he had been misinformed.

When I was told by Bob Haldeman that Hoover had "cleared" us of the homosexual charge, my early reaction was one of gratitude. I had been upset by the accusation, and I was at first a little put off by Nixon's quick assent to Hoover's investigation. I felt Nixon should have taken our denials as conclusive; after all, Haldeman, Chapin and I had worked for him, on and off, for nearly ten years.

Much later I wondered about Hoover's motives. There is no doubt that by granting us his "clearance" in that episode, Hoover had won the gratitude of the President's Chief of Staff, Appointments Secretary and Counsel. Particularly in the light of later revelations, and my own experience with the FBI when I became a target of its 1973 Watergate investigation, I have come to wonder if Hoover may have had a part in contriving the accusations.

In September of 1969, J. Edgar Hoover invited the President, the Attorney General and me to dinner at his home. John Mitchell and I had been accepting invitations to some Washington parties and receptions, but Nixon consistently refused to go out, even to the homes of members of the Cabinet, so it surprised me a little to hear that he had agreed to dine with Hoover.

We rode out to Hoover's home in the President's limousine.

It was a bizarre invasion of that quiet Northwest residential street, with the Presidential motorcade, police cars and motorcycles in the lead, Secret Service cars behind, complete with the President's doctor and all the impedimenta. The entire entourage waited outside all through the evening.

Hoover came out of the house to lead the three of us into his tiny front hall. It was nearly filled by the black man I had first encountered at Hoover's office. Now he was wearing a houseman's white serving jacket as he held the door open for us. To the left was a dingy, almost seedy living room, where the houseman served us drinks. Here, as in his office anterooms, every square inch of Hoover's living-room walls was covered with framed photographs and mementos. Most of them had been there for years and were brown or faded. Among the mounted Texas Longhorns and plaques from civic groups, I saw pictures of Hoover with familiar faces of the thirties and forties: Hoover and Tom Mix; Hoover and the Presidents— Roosevelt, Truman, Herbert Hoover. There were old-time movie actresses whose names I couldn't recall. Four or five hundred photographs crowded the living-room walls, their narrow wood frames touching.

When the President was settled, Hoover's longtime friend and housemate, Clyde Tolson, looking pale and pasty, came down the narrow hall stairs and shambled into the living room. Tolson was introduced to each of us, chatted briefly, but then excused himself. When he was gone, Hoover told us, at length and in detail, about the deteriorating state of Tolson's health.

Dinner was served by the huge houseman and a little maid in a small, crowded dining room overlooking the backyard. The menu had obviously been planned with great care. Steak had come from the Murchisons' ranch in Texas. Fruit had been specially flown in. Chasen's Restaurant had sent its Texas-style chili from Beverly Hills.

Hoover told us Chasen's flew him this chili regularly. Nixon told Hoover about the cottage cheese he had flown in each week from Knudsen's Dairy in Southern California to the White House.

There was even more lively dinner conversation, about espionage. The Russians had long planned to build a new embassy in Washington. Hoover was doing his best to infiltrate the construction project and plant some bugs in the walls as the building went up. He complained that the State Department was going to permit Russian workmen to come in to do the construction. If Americans did the work, Hoover's men could get onto the job site disguised as workmen; it would be very helpful if the Russian workers could be excluded from this country. Nixon promised to see what he could do about "the little shits at State."

Hoover regaled us with stories of late-night entries and FBI bag jobs at other embassies. I was fascinated by these tales of FBI derring-do, but it seemed to me there was also a very serious motive behind Hoover's storytelling. He was trolling these subjects in front of Nixon and Mitchell because he wanted their reactions to the FBI activities he was describing.

Later, in domestic-policy work, I was to learn instinctively to do similar fishing. I'd raise a subject in conversation with the President as informally as I could, not asking for any specific decisions. But often he would rise to the bait; he would speak his mind on the issue, and I would take away important guidance to pass along to a Cabinet officer or staff working group engaged in early planning for legislation.

Later, in thinking back to that dinner, I realized that Hoover had every right to believe that both his superiors, Nixon and Mitchell, approved of FBI bugging, taps and bag jobs. He told us about FBI operations against domestic radicals and foreigners, and our reactions were enthusiastic and positive. The Bureau has made much of an order Hoover issued in the late sixties mandating the discontinuance of FBI illegal entries. Maybe so. But he certainly never mentioned that order at dinner in October 1969.

All through this conversation I could not keep my eyes off the dining room's strange appointments. Hoover had decorated the spaces between the windows with groups of tall Plexiglas tubes about three or four inches in diameter, lighted from their bases with different colors. They were filled with a watery fluid and with blobs of a plastic material that apparently became warm at the lighted base, then rose through the fluid, contracting as they cooled, finally achieving a mass that caused them to drift back down to the base to begin their rise once again. There were six or seven of these tubes, with red, purple, yellow and green dough bobbing slowly up and down, as the Director went on and on recounting the Bureau's triumphs over Weathermen and the NKVD.

After dinner we were led down the narrowest of basement stairs to "the recreation room" for an after-dinner drink. Again, every inch of wall space held some framed memento. In this room the prevailing motif was horse racing. There were pictures of Hoover with winning horses; Hoover with jockeys;

Hoover in his box at Del Mar with movie stars, heavyset men, even a child.

Near the door was a small bar. All the walls over and near this counter were decorated with girlie pinups of the old *Esquire* vintage. Even the lampshade of a small lamp on the bar had naked women pasted on it. The effect of this display was to engender disbelief—it seemed totally contrived. That impression was reinforced when Hoover deliberately called our attention to his naughty gallery, as if it were something he wanted us to know about J. Edgar Hoover.

Nixon had enjoyed the dinner conversation, but he was not comfortable in this strange basement. After one drink, he exercised the Presidential prerogative; he said good night and we left. Several film crews and a dozen reporters were waiting in the street for the President to emerge. We were greeted with bright lights, shouted questions and scattered applause from Hoover's neighbors who had come out to the sidewalk to see what was going on. Nixon welcomed the press coverage. He had instructed the White House press office to tell the press where the President was having dinner.

Nixon was sure he benefited politically from his close association with Hoover. In Nixon's mind, the rock-ribbed conservatives in the country were like the redoubt upon which an old infantry commander anchored the right end of his line of battle. As long as it held strong, he was secure; he could not be flanked.*

A couple of months after Hoover's dinner party I was invited to join Nixon and Hoover in the Oval Office. I had moved from Counsel to Assistant for Domestic Affairs, but it was to be several months before John Mitchell would send us a new Counsel and I could transfer my FBI-liaison role to John Dean.

Hoover came to the Oval Office to visit and stayed to unload a mélange of opinion, information and bias. It was a typical Hoover–Nixon conversation, vintage early 1970.

Nixon urged Hoover to involve the FBI more deeply in prosecuting organized crime. The Director responded that on that day 1,057 cases against organized-crime figures sat un-

---

* This may explain why Barry Goldwater was always able to influence Nixon. The Senator articulated and personified that conservative political element. When I heard that Goldwater had softened in his defense of Nixon in 1974, I began to look for the President's resignation. I suspect that if Goldwater and a few other conservatives had held firm, Nixon might have fought the impeachment. But he believed he could not stand when his right flank was crumbling.

tried because the Justice Department had not assigned enough attorneys to the prosecutions. Over 400 cases waited in New York City alone. In his view, there was no reason for more FBI activity until the backlog was cleaned up.

Actually, the FBI was not working on organized crime because Hoover didn't want it to. Mitchell was of the opinion that Hoover feared his agents might be bribed if they worked "O.C." files. Whatever the reason, both Mitchell and Nixon were unsuccessful in asking Hoover to turn his agents loose on the Mafia. (In December 1972, after Hoover died, Nixon criticized him for this timidity in his later years. "Hoover wanted to avoid controversy," Nixon said. "He kept the Bureau out of drugs, the riots and organized crime.")

That day in 1970, Hoover wanted to tell Nixon about Black Panthers, not the Mafia. He had a date with his favorite appropriations subcommittee in a few days to tell his friend Chairman John Rooney about internal subversion. "Who finances the Black Panthers?" Hoover asked rhetorically. "I'm going to name names. They get their money from Leonard Bernstein and Peter Duchin and that crowd."

"We should get that information out," Nixon said. "We should disseminate transcripts of your testimony."

"Mike Wallace did an hour show on the Black Panthers on CBS," Hoover continued. "He made them heroes. That Eldridge Cleavenger [*sic*] was saying someone should kill J. Edgar Hoover and the President."

"That," Nixon noted, "is the kind of thing that set Oswald off."

"I will also discuss the financing of the anti-Vietnam groups—the Moratorium and the so-called New Mobe," Hoover said. "They also get money from some wealthy people in this country and from some foundations. But we suspect—and can't yet prove—that the Panthers and the Students for a Democratic Society get millions of dollars from the Soviet Union via the Communist Party of the United States. You know the SDS has been down in Cuba cutting the sugar-cane harvest."

Nixon ordered that some way should be found "to stop our own people from violating our foreign policy." He wanted legislation to go to Congress the following week forbidding Americans to help the Cuban economy.

Hoover could not get Eldridge Cleaver's name right. He reported that "Cleavenger" was trying to return to the United States from his foreign refuge. FBI agents would pick him up when he arrived.

Agnew, Nixon instructed me, should be told to "hit the Black Panthers and hit those students who went to Cuba" in his next speech. "He should make simple arguments."

They deplored Mike Wallace and CBS giving the Panthers a prime-time forum. "That CBS," said Hoover, "is crooked from top to bottom."

The Carswell nomination was in trouble in the Senate at that time (February 26, 1970). Nixon saw the Senate's mounting opposition as "a challenge to the President."

"It's a half a dozen Senate jackals who are behind it," said Hoover, nodding. "The Senate is out of touch with the country."

During the first week of 1971 the President began to evidence some concern about Hoover. Pat Gray had been moved from HEW to Justice as an assistant Attorney General, to help bolster John Mitchell, but Gray, Nixon's old staff man in the 1950s, was also having trouble with Hoover.

Nixon told me to have Pat Gray "butter up Hoover." He continued: "Tell Hoover that Pat Gray is the President's friend. Hoover is a question. Have Haldeman include an approve/disapprove question on Hoover the next time he polls."

But it was to be another eight months before Nixon felt compelled to end Hoover's long career. In part, his decision rested on Hoover's failure to carry out the President's wishes in the Pentagon Papers case. There is no room for doubt that the FBI was less than diligent in pursuing that theft and leak.

In my White House file was an internal FBI report, smuggled out to Robert Mardian, Mitchell's assistant Attorney General, evaluating the Bureau's effort in the investigation of the Pentagon Paper thefts. That FBI internal audit makes clear that Hoover assigned a very low priority to the project, notwithstanding the President's obvious agitation, Mitchell's clear instructions and repeated calls from Egil Krogh and others at the White House. At most, two inspectors were assigned to the case, and very few agents were devoting their time to it.

Mitchell told me, soon after the publication of the Pentagon Papers story, that Daniel Ellsberg's father-in-law, a toy manufacturer named Louis Marx, was a close friend of Hoover's. Marx would bring toys to the Bureau at Christmas for the FBI agents' children, Mitchell said. When Charles Brennan, a high-ranking Bureau executive, approved a proposal that FBI agents interview Marx about his son-in-law Daniel Ellsberg, Hoover learned of it too late to prevent the interview. Mitchell phoned me to report that Hoover had suppressed the report of the Marx interview, and retaliated by demoting Charles Brennan, ordering his transfer to a remote Bureau office.

I passed the Brennan story on to the President, along with Bud Krogh's complaint that the Bureau was dragging its feet in the Ellsberg investigation. As a result, Nixon authorized Krogh to use "his people," Howard Hunt, G. Gordon Liddy, et al., to find out what Ellsberg was up to. (Because Ellsberg was Henry Kissinger's former protégé and a former Defense Department official, he was in possession of retaliatory-missile plans and other critical defense information; the President and Kissinger were pressing hard to find out why Ellsberg had stolen and released the Papers and what he was liable to do next.)

Over the following weeks, principally because of what he was hearing from John Mitchell and me about Hoover, Nixon reluctantly, but finally, decided it was time to replace J. Edgar Hoover. His decision was not quickly arrived at. Hoover was under heavy attack in the press and from his political enemies. The television news and newsmagazines were scoring on Hoover, and because Nixon would not insulate himself from the FBI Director, the Administration was constantly on the defensive. Hoover's problems were Nixon's problems.

Hoover seemed to me like an old boxer who had taken too many punches. He stayed in the fight past his time, feebly counterpunching. But he had lost his judgment and vigor. He had become an embarrassment.

At last, in the fall of 1971, I was called to the Oval Office to help Nixon prepare to confront Hoover and ask for his resignation. Nixon had decided it had to be done, but he didn't want to do it, and he wasn't sure how to go about it. He rambled around and through the arguments for and against Hoover's leaving. He knew that no one else could fire Edgar; only the President could make it stick. Yet he had to do it in such a way that Hoover would remain his loyal friend—he couldn't have Hoover out in the country at loose ends, criticizing the President.

I took notes of Nixon's ramblings, as I usually did, until he finally asked me to summarize how I would tell Hoover the bad news if it were my job to do so. I spun out a sugar-coated pink slip that sounded good enough; Nixon asked me to go back to my office and dictate it just as I had delivered it to him, so that he could use it as the basis for his talk with Hoover. He told me he intended to have Hoover over for breakfast in The Residence the next morning. He would fire him then.

I went upstairs, had the scenario typed out and sent it through the paper mill in a sealed envelope.

The next morning Nixon and Hoover met alone at the White House residence. Haldeman and I had been separately told that Nixon had decided to fire the Director. When I saw Haldeman later in the day, I asked what had happened. Haldeman didn't know; Nixon refused to talk about it.

The next day, when I asked, Haldeman replied, "Don't ask. He doesn't want to talk about it. Don't ask him." It wasn't hard to guess that at the last minute Nixon had flinched. Later that day Haldeman conveyed further instructions: I was to forget that the Nixon-Hoover breakfast had ever taken place; I was not to say anything to anyone about it.

The dimensions of Nixon's surrender became clear when an FBI courier mistakenly left at my office a letter that Hoover had written the President a few hours after their breakfast.

For two years Hoover had battled both John Mitchell and Bill Rogers, the Secretary of State, to be permitted to install FBI agents in more of our embassies abroad. Hoover hated to rely on the CIA for news of what was going on abroad. And his "legal attachés" were valuable to Hoover in other ways. He expected all his foreign-based agents to do a thorough public-relations job for junketing Congressmen when they came through, to help the Congressional wives with their shopping, to act as guides and arrange for purchases to be sent home. Good Congressional relations meant healthy FBI appropriations.

Hoover's letter confirmed that far from being fired at breakfast, he'd talked Nixon into increasing his overseas force by about 20 percent, with new offices in Manila, Rio de Janeiro, the Dominican Republic, Australia, Malaysia and India. He had deftly bypassed Mitchell and Rogers.

In December 1972, Nixon finally told me a little about that confrontation with Hoover. "It was," he said, "a total strike-out. Hoover hinted that the President would have to force him out. Mitchell was surprised." Evidently Mitchell had assured Nixon that Hoover was ready to leave.

In his memoirs Nixon briefly describes his Hoover breakfast. He says Hoover made it clear "he would submit his resignation only if I specifically requested it. I decided not to do so."

Having watched Nixon try to fire Wally Hickel and others (including me), I suspect that Nixon once again found it impossible to say the words "You are fired." Herb Klein survived because he insisted that Nixon personally fire him, and he figured that Nixon could never do it face to face. It was not surprising that Hoover too had learned about that immunizing formula.

About six months later Hoover died, and we all went to his elaborate funeral. Nixon cemented forever his connection with Hoover on that day, with his attendance at the rites and his public statements. He even ordered that the enormous, unfinished FBI building be named for Hoover.

That same day Nixon instructed Assistant Attorney General Pat Gray to seize all Hoover's secret personal files and deliver them to the White House. But Gray was too late; Hoover's secretary had gotten there first.

After his reelection in 1972, the President had several meetings with his new Attorney General, Richard Kleindienst, to exhort him to restaff the Justice Department, including the FBI, as Nixon was doing in the Cabinet and White House. The Supreme Court fights, the civil rights struggles, the ITT controversy and Watergate had shown the Justice Department to be a weak link, and the President was determined that it become our strongest.

By the end of 1972, Nixon had misgivings about his choice of Pat Gray for Director of the FBI. He was uneasy about Gray's handling of the Watergate investigation and his reluctance to clean out the FBI's old hierarchy. Kleindienst vigorously urged Nixon to stick with Gray. Nixon preferred Jerry Wilson, the big police chief who had successfully reduced crime in Washington, D.C. But Kleindienst argued that Pat Gray was a loyal and capable politician, and that those were far more desirable attributes than Wilson's criminological abilities.

"Are there any good young judges?" Nixon asked.

Kleindienst mentioned Federal Judge Matthew Byrne* of Los Angeles. "He's a Democrat, but he's objective. I don't know of any others," Kleindienst added.

Later in 1972, talking with Kleindienst, Nixon spoke of Hoover and the controversy that had built around him, and of his enemies. Nixon looked somber; he knew that Hoover's enemies—the Panthers, the antiwar activists and the liberals, the Senate "jackals" and the networks—were *his* enemies too. "They would have driven him out, you know," Nixon said. "He died just in time."

* See p. 342 for an account of how the FBI job was offered to Byrne.

CHAPTER ELEVEN

The Brothers

RICHARD NIXON HAS two brothers, Edward and F. Donald Nixon; they are the survivors of a family which, collectively, had a profound influence on the young Richard. In a negative sense, they were important to Richard the President, too.

While she lived, Hannah Nixon was one of the major forces in Richard's life. I first saw Hannah when she attended the 1960 convention in Chicago. She sat there at the old Stockyards Convention Hall like a small bird, watching keenly, surrounded by a dozen of her relatives and the Ryans, Pat Nixon's relatives, as Richard Nixon was nominated to be President of the United States. Hannah was a slight woman, old and bent, quiet, and definite in her Quaker-based opinions. The rest of the relatives were a mixed lot.

As President, and since, Nixon has made generous rhetorical use of Hannah. For that and the other obvious reasons, people are entitled to be skeptical as to just how much he cared about her. Any politician who jerks tears with the line "My mother was a saint" evokes raised eyebrows and snide references to apple pie and motherhood. However, the fact is that Hannah's approval was always important to Richard while she lived, and after her death he talked about her often and admiringly in private.

Ed Nixon is perhaps the son who is most like their mother. Like her, he is thin and quiet, stubborn yet reasonable and intelligent. Ed is tall and bony, much too serious and anxious to please. His wife, Gay Nixon, is a good-looking schoolteacher of considerable wit and common sense. For a time, Ed and Gay permitted themselves to be swept along by the more attractive aspects of Richard's campaigns and his Presidency, and during the White House years I would occasionally see them at social events and political dinners. They had worked hard to get Richard elected, and seemed to enjoy the fruits of their labors, but they never lost their balance.

Don Nixon is a florid, pear-shaped fellow, given to wearing white sports jackets and colorful neckties. (By a not-too-remarkable coincidence, some of his clothes were tailored by the designer who created the White House policemen's fancy new uniforms in 1969—those Graustarkian white tunics, black trousers and shiny black hats.) Don bears a fainter resemblance to Hannah than do Ed and Dick; he has that remarkable nose, but he is fair, with blond hair. He does not have the jowls or the dark, overhanging brows of his brothers. Nor does Don have their social rectitude.

In another age F. Donald Nixon might have been a patent-medicine salesman or a carnival barker; when I first met him he was the modern equivalent, a "consultant."

Rose Mary Woods, Nixon's secretary, was responsible for looking after the Nixon and Ryan relatives during the Vice Presidential years. At the 1960 and 1968 Republican conventions, one staff person—usually John Whitaker—looked after their tickets, rooms, cars and other logistical needs. But when Nixon became President, Rose Woods, John Whitaker and Nixon had other things to do; family relations deteriorated. By 1969, Nixon and his brothers had almost nothing in common. Their mother had died. Ed was living near Seattle and Don was in Southern California; Richard Nixon had become a New Yorker. Once he began the 1968 campaign, he barely had time to keep track of his wife and daughters, much less his brothers, whom he seldom saw. Ed took campaign jobs in 1968 and 1972 to help out, but also because campaigning paid better than the job he had in Seattle.

Don Nixon and Hannah had been involved in a transaction with Howard Hughes in the late fifties which continued to embarrass Richard Nixon in 1960 and in his subsequent campaigns. When Richard was Vice President, Don was in the drive-in-restaurant business in their hometown, Whittier, a suburb of Los Angeles. As Don told me, his drive-in restaurants (featuring, believe it or not, the Nixon-burger) began to fail in the years Richard was Vice President "because Don was very busy helping Dick." That, of course, is nonsense. Don was asked to do very little, because he was always a potential embarrassment to the Vice President. Don talked loudly, extravagantly and incessantly, so the Nixon campaigns always discouraged his participation.

There were folks willing to help the Vice President's financially troubled relatives (as there usually are), and I've heard several versions of who first approached whom to bail Don out. Before long, Hannah had managed to borrow about

$200,000 from an accountant to help Don's floundering business. Hannah pledged as collateral an empty lot she owned in Whittier which was worth about 10 percent of the $200,000.

If they hadn't known it before the loan, the Nixons soon learned that the lender was an agent for the Hughes Tool Company. Because the loan was made just at the time the Howard Hughes organization was enmeshed in antitrust problems with the Eisenhower Administration's Justice Department, Drew Pearson and other reporters played it as a scandal. But Hannah, Don and Richard Nixon would never accept any suggestion that the loan transaction was unsavory.

Things turned out well for Howard Hughes. The antitrust matter was eventually dropped during the John Kennedy years. But in 1961 (after Richard Nixon's 1960 defeat) Don Nixon's restaurant business finally failed. Although Don's corporate debts were eventually forgotten, he could never erase the suggestion that his brother the Vice President had gotten him a loan from Howard Hughes in return for government favors.

While professing pride in Richard's political success, Don and his wife, Clara Mae, clearly resented it. He would often complain to me about the countless hardships he suffered because he was the brother of a President. But all through the White House years Don did his best to capitalize upon this relationship, often to Richard's acute private embarrassment.

When Richard won the 1968 election, Don boasted to friends that he intended "to make a million in the next four years," and he surely tried. If Don is not wealthy now, it is principally because he lacked the wit to reap the benefits of being a Presidential brother. And I must admit to having been one of several people who derailed him now and then as he tried to turn his vicarious advantages to cash.

When brother Dick became President, Don could not stay away from the flame. Although the Howard Hughes organization had countless activities dependent on Government contracts—aerospace, and airline permits, for example—Don did not seem to understand the potential peril of his appearing once again to do business with Hughes. We could not convince him that the slightest hint of a contemporary connection between Hughes and a Nixon would resurrect all the old innuendo surrounding Hannah's loan.

Our problem was compounded because the Hughes apparatus included an extraordinary exploiter named John H. Meier. Don was not Meier's first political conquest. Hubert Humphrey and his family had succumbed to Meier's attentions, and Meier continued to cultivate them right up until the time he jumped to Don Nixon. In July of 1968, as Humphrey and Nixon contested for the Presidency, Meier went to Washington (at Howard Hughes's expense) to meet with Hubert Humphrey.

But Meier was nimble. As soon as Nixon beat Humphrey, Meier went back to Washington, but this time he took along Clara Mae and Don as his guests.

An IRS report (which came to me in July 1972) showed that John Meier in fact charged the Hughes organization for the trip he and Clara Mae and Don Nixon made, just two weeks after the 1968 election. Meier wrote on his expense report that the purpose of their Washington trip was "for consultation with President-elect Richard Nixon on November 21, 1968."

Although I don't know for certain, it seems very doubtful to me that Meier ever saw the President-elect. He certainly did not see him in Washington on that trip, since Nixon stayed away from the capital all through the transition and up until hours before his inaugural.

Whether any business was actually done or not on that Washington trip, it seems certain that Don's family name alone assured the junketeers a fine time in November 1968. A fellow named Nixon couldn't buy a drink in those days in any of the better bars of Washington.

Don Nixon and John Meier talked the same language; theirs was the lexicon of the big deal. At the time of his brother's election, Don had a job with a company selling food service to factories and airlines. But after the election, Don opened an office where he could also be "Donald Nixon and Associates." He drove a large, fancy car belonging to a steel company which retained him as a "consultant," with no defined duties. He accepted $1,000 a month from another conglomerate on a similar basis.

As the President's Counsel at that time, I was concerned with problems of conflict of interest. One of my first brother problems, even before I became aware of Don's various "deals," was the matter of a hotel bill. Don had checked out of an expensive Washington hotel after his brother's 1969 inauguration leaving instructions that his bill was to be sent to the Government! On February 7, 1969, the sizable hotel statement found its way to me, after passing through the hands of several bureaucrats who were not about to give the new President's brother any bad news. So I was the one who wrote to Don stating plainly that neither the transition government of the

President-elect nor the new Nixon Administration had any appropriations for Don Nixon's personal expenses.

Within six weeks I was on the telephone to give Don a further lesson on his relationship to the Executive Branch. He had tried to telephone the Secretary of Commerce, Maurice Stans, to arrange for some of Don's acquaintances to come to Washington to get a Government loan. Stans' office called me to complain about Don's intervention.

I phoned to tell Don how careful he must be not to give the appearance that someone in the President's family was urging Commerce to make a Government loan. Just a call from someone like Don "resulted in large waves" in any of the departments.

Don always assured me of his purity of motive when he was caught playing the big shot with the Government. He was only trying to help Dick. The supplicants he was helping were Dick's good friends. Dick didn't have time to see them all, so Don just did what he could to help the President's longtime supporters. Try as I might to explain to Don how improper his intervention appeared, I could never seem to get through to him.

I wasn't the only one who recognized Don's potential for trouble. Drew Pearson and Jack Anderson had been watching and writing about Don since the Hughes loan episode in the fifties. Now they kept track of Don's comings and goings in Washington and at the White House because they knew of Don's predilections.

By the spring of 1969 I was hearing all kinds of stories of Don's dealings with John Meier, his solicitation of business from international airlines and other potential problems for the President; if I were going to discharge my responsibility to the President, I had to know at first hand what Don was doing. So I asked him to come east to review all his "activities" with me.

When Don came to the White House, I asked him about his connection to the Hughes organization and John Meier. I knew something was going on because Bebe Rebozo had reports from some of the Hughes people he knew. Interestingly, the Hughes executives were as concerned as we were. They didn't want to be accused of attempting to influence the Administration through Don. (That was, perhaps, more a measure of their low opinion of Don Nixon than a testament to Hughes's reluctance to influence the Government.)

Don denied any connection whatever with Meier or

Hughes. His denial to me was so loud and red-faced that I felt intuitively he was lying. I urged him to drop the phony consulting jobs with companies having business with the Government. I explained why the airlines to which he sold food services found him such a fascinating fellow: their overseas licenses were all granted by his brother the President. Don's employer—The Ogden Corporation—had many other activities which did not involve Government-regulated carriers. I urged him to transfer to one of them.

Don expressed bitterness at his lot in life. Here he was, being told by his brother's minion how he ought to change his whole life. And what did he get out of all Richard Nixon's great success? Nothing.

Don could not admit to himself that the reason people were cultivating him, giving him cars and money, was that he was Richard Nixon's brother. He had spent a lifetime in the shadow of Richard the super-achiever. As his brother ascended through Congress to the Senate and the Vice Presidency, Don was going into bankruptcy. Don's ego must have needed a lot of shoring up during those years. If he now had trouble sorting out fantasy from reality, perhaps it was not too surprising.

But I didn't psychoanalyze Don; I just gave him the sermon: he was to get off the gravy train at once, leave John Meier alone and lead a life of quiet rectitude.

Within a few days the President, Bob Haldeman and I again talked about Don's connection with Howard Hughes. I described Don's voluble but unconvincing denial of his frequent contacts with John Meier of Hughes. Don had given his brother the same denials when he met with him.

At that time, in 1969, the President and Henry Kissinger were having the FBI tap and in a few cases follow some White House staff people and journalists in an effort to find out who was leaking Kissinger's secrets. The President began to talk to me casually about adding Don to that list, to discover what Don was up to. But Nixon didn't like the idea of the FBI and J. Edgar Hoover knowing too much about his brother. He could not add Don to the Kissinger surveillance list if the FBI was going to do the work. On the other hand, having Don monitored by someone was clearly a good idea; we ought to know what sort of problems he was creating for us.

So Nixon instructed me to have the CIA put a "full cover" on Don, reporting to the President through me. The Agency could be counted on to keep a confidence, if J. Edgar Hoover could not.

I talked to the Deputy Director of the CIA, Robert Cushman, about Don, because Nixon had instructed me to give Cushman the assignment. When Cushman was a junior Marine intelligence officer he had been detailed to the CIA (where he once shared office space with E. Howard Hunt). Later, in the late fifties, he became one of Vice President Nixon's military aides. On becoming President, Nixon had appointed his former aide to the CIA hierarchy as one way to keep track of CIA Director Richard Helms. Cushman was, we then thought, Nixon's man over there at the Agency.

Cushman did some checking and called me back to decline the Don Nixon assignment. The law specifically forbade the CIA to engage in such domestic surveillance activities, and the Agency was afraid to undertake such a project, he said.

Nixon remained reluctant to enlist J. Edgar Hoover's help, but the longer he thought about it, the more he wanted to know what Don was engaged in, so we turned to the Secret Service. In early May 1969 I asked one of its executives, Pat Boggs, to come see me. When I explained what the President wanted done, Boggs agreed without hesitation. It turned out that Lyndon B. Johnson had paved the way for us years before. His brother, Sam Johnson, also suffered from that executive-sibling syndrome so embarrassing to Presidents, and Johnson had frequently caused brother Sam to be tailed by the Secret Service to keep track of his activities.

Beginning May 27 and until July 8, 1969, Secret Service agents trailed Don Nixon around Southern California and to New York, New Orleans and Las Vegas. Every three or four days I received a written report of where Don went, with whom he met and sometimes, what the agents had been able to overhear them saying to each other.

To do the job right, the Secret Service recommended, Don's phones should be tapped as well. I didn't feel I could authorize such a thing, so I asked Richard Nixon if that was what he wanted done. It was. So with the President's permission, the Service also tapped Don's telephones at home and at his office. Some of the telephone "logs" confirmed our worst concerns. In spite of Don's denials, it was clear that he was up to his ears in the kinds of "really big deals" with John Meier and others that might eventually embarrass his brother.

The very first Secret Service report indicated that in late May, Don had escorted John Meier and his family to the Disneyland Hotel for a vacation. Several times Don and Meier had engaged in what the log called "heavy conversation" while the others were sight-seeing.

The logs disclosed that Don was in some financial trouble. Moreover, for nearly two years he had successfully stalled an Internal Revenue Service audit of his tax returns, offering first one excuse and then another. In 1967 he had persuaded the IRS to postpone the audit until after Richard Nixon's campaign ended (the IRS apparently granted the delay so that its agents could know whether they were auditing a Presidential sibling or just another citizen). In January, February and April of 1969, Don was granted further delays "because he was traveling." In June, he was supposedly so heavily involved in the corporate reorganization of Ogden Foods, of which he was a nominal vice president, that he didn't have time for the IRS. Moreover, he was, he said, busy with some of his brother's affairs—the Nixon Foundation and the proposed Nixon Presidential library—so he was granted another audit extension. Apparently the IRS didn't check his allegations; actually he was only peripherally involved in Ogden's corporate affairs and had almost nothing to do with the Nixon Foundation and the Presidential library.

But in June the Secret Service reported that its agents had overheard Don trying to persuade his doctor to hospitalize him in case his requests for postponement of the tax audit were denied. And Clara Mae Nixon had been heard telling friends they were seriously short of money.

Meanwhile, Don was flying to Miami and New Orleans trying to sell food service to airlines.

Air West was Howard Hughes's recently acquired airline. Don had somehow involved himself in Hughes's planned takeover of Air West, then claimed he should have a multi-million-dollar finder's fee for his alleged part in the merger. When no one took Don's claim seriously, another item was added to his litany of grievances. In June of 1969, Don approached the new Hughes Air West management to urge them not to change food-service suppliers. And in the record of his telephone conversations with one of the directors of Air West there was talk of a secret "Vegas land deal" between Don and that director.

On June 15, Don had a call from a well-known United States district judge (now deceased) whose court was in Southern California. The judge wanted the President to appoint him to the seat on the U.S. Court of Appeals for the District of Columbia that had been vacated by Warren Burger when he was appointed Chief Justice. The California judge, a cousin of a prominent U.S. Senator, said he intended to be in touch with the White House staff about his desire to succeed

Burger. But he asked that Don "put in a good word" for him—obviously intending that Don speak directly to the President. Don Nixon agreed to do so; he was in the real political big time now, influencing the appointment of Federal judges! (Nothing came of it.)

The Secret Service reported that one of the big hotels in Las Vegas planned a gala opening of its gambling casino in July 1969, complete with Hollywood stars and other headline makers. Don had been recruited by the hotel's owners to secure the attendance of political celebrities at the lavish party. They particularly wanted Senator Everett Dirksen to come. Don was overheard making many phone calls trying to persuade Washington personalities to join him at the big Vegas party. (Dirksen turned him down cold.)

I decided to tell Don I'd heard from someone that he planned to attend the hotel opening in Las Vegas. I told him I hoped I might talk him out of it. I said the sponsorship was potentially embarrassing. Although there was no definite evidence that the hotel operators were part of organized crime, the Las Vegas scene was full of shady characters. The publicity couldn't help him, and it couldn't help the President. I said I hoped he had sense enough to stay away.

On June 26 the Secret Service heard Don tell a business associate that I had found out about the casino opening. Don reported that he had put me off with the excuse that he had legitimate business with the hotel people. But Don told his caller he had decided not to go to the opening.

By the end of June his callers were hearing Don blame me for his loss of that finder's fee for the Air West acquisition by Hughes. He felt I was interfering in his "legitimate" business deals, and he had decided that he would no longer be pushed around. He would go to the Las Vegas opening, regardless of what I thought.

On July 2 and 3, Clara Mae and Don were guests of the International Hotel in Las Vegas for its glittering, star-studded opening. Few politicians were there, because Don hadn't been able to attract any. But the President's sister-in-law and brother were photographed at all the casino parties, and the hotel got yards of publicity out of their presence. And Las Vegas was the seat of the Hughes empire. When he arrived in Vegas, Don called John Meier at home to say that he "can no longer meet openly with the Meiers, but will continue to see them privately."

Two days later he and Meier agreed to meet secretly on July 8. They made plans to do a "big land deal" near San Diego.

Meier flew from Las Vegas to Orange County, near Don's home, using an assumed name. When the two met, they were followed and photographed together by the Secret Service.

With that turn of events, the Secret Service was asked to discontinue its surveillance. The President had incontrovertible proof of Don's often-denied Howard Hughes connection.

As this surveillance went on, I had been intrigued by the Secret Service logs and reports. This was the first time (but was not to be the last) that I was called upon to read reports of a person's unguarded conversations and activities. But my prurient curiosity was a little dampened by my discomfort in reading about the Don Nixon family's ordinary comings and goings. Clara Mae's domestic complaints were crass and certainly not titillating. And there was no joy in stripping back Don's facade and having the pathetic realities of his life so starkly revealed.

Don had no idea that he was under surveillance. A couple of times he talked to me about his suspicion that his telephone was tapped, both before and after it actually was. He suspected Jack Anderson of overhearing him, but not his brother Richard.

We were learning, in 1969, that we were in control of a discreet information-gathering machine of considerable effectiveness. The FBI taps and surveillance that Kissinger and Nixon had placed on journalists and staff people had been effected without discovery. Now the Don Nixon project had worked perfectly.

Later we were to learn more about Don and his associates from the intelligence-gathering arm of the IRS.

During the six weeks of the Secret Service surveillance I received seven written reports and a handful of photographs of Don Nixon with John Meier, along with several oral reports about subjects "too sensitive" to include in a written report, including information about Don's eldest son, Donny.

As the reports came in I took them to the President, sometimes summarizing their contents for him orally, sometimes simply handing them to him for reading. He spent a long time looking at the photographs of Don and John Meier walking together.

Finally, in July 1969, we talked about what to do about Don. The President said he wanted me to talk to his "poor, stupid brother" again, to confront him with the evidence that he had lied to us about Meier. I suggested that Don might so resent being followed and photographed that he would try to get revenge. The President's brother was a compulsive talker;

with the impetus of righteous indignation he might generate vast press attention.

At last it was decided that the President would summon Don for a personal conversation. (I later learned that the President had enlisted Bebe Rebozo to help. Rebozo knew Robert Maheu and Richard Danner, both of whom worked for Howard Hughes. They would be asked to order John Meier to stay away from Don.) Meanwhile, I would talk to one of the officers of the Ogden Corporation, Don's employer; I would try to persuade them to have Don moved to a job that did not involve soliciting business from Government contractors or licensees.

I telephoned Ralph Ablon, Ogden's chief executive officer, who invited me to lunch at "21" in New York. I explained our brother problem to Ablon in unvarnished terms. I found him to be both pleasant and helpful. He agreed to do what he could.

Later he called me to say that the Ogden Corporation was unable to find anything suitable for Don. When Don's abilities were taken into account, whatever they gave him to do would be nothing but a sham. Although Ablon was no Nixon supporter, he said Ogden was willing to "carry" the President's brother, and I thanked him for the offer. But I felt it would be very unwise to be in debt so deeply to a stranger.

The brotherly confrontation between Dick and Don was postponed for nearly two months. The President went off on a trip around the world—to the splashdown of the first moon-walking astronauts, followed by visits to Asian countries, Romania and England.

Meanwhile, Don Nixon was getting ready for his forthcoming meeting with his brother. He resigned his "consultancy" with the steel company and gave up the new Lincoln Continental sedan it had furnished him. And he prepared a two-column analysis of his difficulties with Richard Nixon, headed "PROBLEM" and "SOLUTION." Richard Nixon's indifference to his relatives was the principal "problem"; the solution to Don's troubles, he proposed, was a public-relations program by which he might win the hearts and minds of the American people.

When the brothers finally met on Sunday, August 31, Don handed Dick his typewritten sheet. As they talked, the President made notes on it. Don had evidently decided to take the offensive; he demanded a full-scale investigation of his business affairs to dispel, once and for all, any lack of confidence "on the part of [the President's] staff in me." This would, he wrote, "provide a report to you, me and your staff as to the true nature of my business dealings." It would "establish once and for all with certainty that there is no intrigue and no misconduct." Don called for "mutually acceptable ground rules as to what activities I can engage in."

Under the heading "Family Relationships" Don attacked:

PROBLEM
Embarrassing lack of ordinary outward concern on part of the President toward the families of brothers and in-laws.

Don's corresponding demands were

SOLUTION
Acknowledge the birthdays and holidays with cards, notes (needn't be gifts). Make occasional courtesy phone calls, inquiries and send notes, etc. as to family matters.

The President wrote *"RMW"* (meaning Rose Mary Woods; she would once again be given the task of cranking out birthday notes.) He also wrote *"Astronaut menus, memos."* (Perhaps there were some party favors left over from the state dinner that could be sent out to cousins and nephews.)

The third heading, "Coordination of Nixon Brothers in 1972 Campaign," introduced a theme we were to hear often from Don:

PROBLEM
Complete absence of a well thought-out approach to the problem of bad publicity generated during each campaign.
                                    Hughes Loan
                                    Business dealings
                                    innuendos
                                    half truths, etc.

Don's solution asserted that his problems were mostly a matter of public relations and the failure of the President to back him up:

SOLUTION
Accept the fact that whether we like it or not, the entire Nixon family is involved in the campaign.

Therefore: Start image building now to counteract the certain personal attack on me to come in 1972. Appoint some-

one who is an expert in this field to work with us in anticipating and handling the press—and making the most of the opportunities that do present themselves. Extend your personal support to the family where political strategy dictates silence.

On September 4 the President handed me Don's manifesto, particularly referring to Don's last entry: "Report re: IRS."

Beside it Don had typed: "Satisfactory, but no friends on IRS."

Don had at last submitted to an IRS audit on the previous Monday. On Sunday, during their talk, Don complained bitterly to the President about the IRS agents' sarcastic attitude toward him.

When the President transmitted Don's IRS complaint to me, I was treated to a recapitulation of Richard Nixon's not inconsiderable catalogue of IRS grievances as well. When he was out of office, 1960–1968, the Kennedy brothers had had the IRS audit him, Nixon reminded me. "As a tax lawyer," the President understood about these audits, but the Kennedy-inspired audit of a former Vice President of the United States had been, in his opinion, a vicious, retaliatory action. Nixon wanted me to let the IRS commissioner, Randolph Thrower, understand that the President would not now tolerate his own family's being similarly persecuted. The President instructed that the two offending agents were not to be fired. They should be "otherwise dealt with."

I called Don to ask for some further details in writing, preferably from the accountant who had attended the audit conference. I was skeptical. In a few days I received the signed statement from Don's certified public accountant which I quoted in a memorandum to IRS Commissioner Thrower:

In my 15 years of experience in dealing and negotiating with agents, I am forced to characterize the conduct of the two agents on August 25 as being without precedent, completely unprofessional, cynical, and sarcastic toward the taxpayer. This attitude prevailed from the moment they entered the office. Their conduct toward me was proper, courteous, and professional.

I then wrote the IRS Commissioner:

The President asked me to call this to your attention. However, he also asked me to remind you that neither his brother nor any other member of his family should receive any different treatment from any other taxpayer in the country. It is precisely for this reason, with the expectation that all taxpayers should be treated with the utmost professionalism and courtesy, that this matter is called to your attention.

At the bottom of the accountant's statement Don Nixon had handwritten:

They were looking for info to put me in McNeil Island. Looking for unreported income.

—but I didn't pass along that observation to the Commissioner.

I sent the complaint off to Thrower, but I had that same feeling of uncertainty I'd developed in coping with other Don Nixon problems for nine months. I still believed it likely that there was more to the story than I'd been told.

And there was. Thrower replied that Don had not even attended the August 25 conference between the CPA and the IRS agents. The agents had admittedly been derogatory of Don because they had been trying to audit him for two years without success. They had been stalled outrageously, and they knew it. And they said so.

In an abundance of caution, Thrower took the two agents off Don's audit anyway, and he replaced them with another IRS agent from the Los Angeles area.

As a result of Don's other complaints, I was given a list of instructions by the President. If he had a P.R. problem within the family, he knew how to solve P.R. problems. From now on:

—Haldeman was to assign a military aide to Don and Ed Nixon at all White House social functions.
—Haldeman should recruit Clifford Miller, a Los Angeles public-relations expert, to work on the Nixon family image.
—I would inform Don there was no present indication he was guilty of any misconduct and I should draft guidelines for his future conduct. And I should call Don and read him the FBI report on one of his business associates (not Meier) about whom there were some doubts.
—Willard Marriott should be asked to hire Don, since Marriott would probably protect the President's interests better than might Ralph Ablon of Ogden Corporation.
—A family list should be prepared at once, cataloguing the

President's relatives and all their birthdays and anniversaries. Haldeman must appoint someone to see to the sending of birthday and other cards.

—Each child in the family should immediately receive a collection of mounted inaugural medals. Adults should be sent Presidential cuff links or women's jewelry.

—Don Nixon should be sent souvenir menus and favors from the astronauts' state dinner for him to distribute to the others.

—And Don should be given the American flag that had been standing with the battle flags behind the President's desk in his office in San Clemente.

—The following Monday, Don would bring seven or eight of their relatives to San Clemente for a tour of the President's home and office. Dwight Chapin must organize it and provide everyone with souvenirs.

That, the President concluded, should meet his "poor, dumb brother's" grievances, at least for the time being.

About the time I was calling Don to tell him that his brother wanted us to agree on guidelines to keep Don out of further trouble, Don and John Meier were busy getting into more.

Francis Meloy,* Ambassador to the Dominican Republic, telephoned me in late October to warn me that the President's brother Don might be heading the President into serious embarrassment in that warm, pastoral island.

John Meier had put together a Dominican extravaganza which, if everything went right, had a good chance of enriching Mr. Meier and the President's brother. The U.N. Ambassador of the Dominican Republic, Dr. Luis González Torrado, was the impresario of a four-day junket for Meier and his party, which included Alaskan Senator Mike Gravel; a political consultant to the Democrats, Joe Napolitan; one Anthony Hatsis, listed as "geologist," and, of course, Don Nixon. The presence of the President's brother ensured that the quality of their reception by the Dominicans would be presidential.

The day after their arrival, Don Nixon and Meier had a private meeting with the Dominican President's National Development Commission. The following day, a Dominican newspaper, *El Nacional*, published the substance of Don Nixon's remarks made before the Commission. He and his group were,

---

* Sadly, Meloy was the U.S. Ambassador killed by terrorists in Lebanon years later as he tried to mediate among the battling factions in Beirut.

the paper said, prospective investors in the Las Cañitas copper mine and in some tourist facilities on the beach in the Macao area. Don and the others had offered some $200 million as an investment, the story reported. The next morning *El Caribe* ran a story headlined: "NORTH AMERICAN GROUP IS INTERESTED IN THE LAS CAÑITAS MINES."

After various ceremonies and receptions, including the investiture of Meier in the Order of Christopher Columbus as a Knight Commander, on Saturday everyone went for a cruise on a navy frigate as guests of the Dominican Navy Chief of Staff. Along with lunch, there were meetings with businessmen and a helicopter trip to those Macao beaches referred to in the news reports.

Don, Meier and Hatsis left Santo Domingo on October 26. Several local papers then published a written statement by Don Nixon stressing the purely unofficial nature of his visit and his firm denial of any interest in Dominican investment. That statement was, of course, the product of close collaboration between Meloy and me in our many telephone calls during Don's visit.

Francis Meloy did an effective job of explaining to Don how his wheeling and dealing down there looked. The Dominicans wanted more U.S. aid. If they could gain favor with the Nixon family by granting mineral concessions at Las Cañitas, they'd be glad to trade. Latin American governments were accustomed to such arrangements. Don told Meloy he was surprised that anyone would believe he had such motives. He had been terribly misquoted. He was badly misunderstood. So Meloy asked Don to sign our statement to the press disavowing any interest in Dominican investment. Don resisted, but Meloy insisted. At last Don signed.

There are several postscripts to Don's Dominican detour. A subsequent IRS investigation of John Meier's activities turned up a large cash payment to the Dominican Ambassador to the United Nations who had arranged for John Meier's medal. The money came from the proceeds of a Howard Hughes mineral-leasing transaction. One can only wonder if Meier engineered his Knight Commander's medal with Howard Hughes's money.

Several years later, another IRS report alleged that John Meier had in fact invested in Dominican mineral rights. His partner, according to the IRS, was Hubert H. Humphrey's son Robert.

And finally, in June of 1971, for no apparent reason, President Joaquín Balaguer of the Dominican Republic wrote me a three-line note, thanking me for my "help and genuine sympathy for the problems" of his country. I don't know why he wrote me, but I like to think it's because Frank Meloy and I derailed Don Nixon before he could work out one of his big deals for the Dominicans.

In early November of 1969, the President asked me how the job search for his brother was coming. The President suggested that Don Kendall might hire Don Nixon at Pepsico. A few days later Herb Kalmbach, the President's lawyer, reported that Willard Marriott might be willing to carry Don on the Marriott payroll if the President personally asked him to. The Marriotts owned hotels, restaurants and amusement parks, as well as airline food services, so they might find something for Don to do that didn't involve the Government. I quickly arranged for the Marriotts, father and son, to come to talk to the President about Don. They suggested that Herb Kalmbach and President Eisenhower's old friend George Allen sit in too.

About that time, Bebe Rebozo wrote me a long letter forwarding information about Don Nixon and Meier he'd been given by Hughes's people. John Meier had been fired by Hughes. He had violated "special instructions" to stay away from Don Nixon. But, as Rebozo wrote me, Meier and Don Nixon each still found the other irresistible:

It appears that "JM" and "DN" may be working as a team. One supposedly with the land development and exploration contacts; the other is assumed to be an intimate advisor to the White House with access to administrative agencies of the government.

At one time they made a very determined effort to place coin machines in various Hughes plants in Southern California. They put considerable pressure on management to replace machines that were already in there; however, they were not successful.

It appears that the reward (whatever it may be) must be substantial. Otherwise, why would JM continue to violate special instructions about his association with DN? In other words, he deliberately jeopardized and finally lost a dignified and well-paying position because he apparently could not afford to give up his deals with "DN."

Rebozo passed along an evaluation of John Meier:

This fellow appears to be an opportunistic intellectual who, because of his contacts, has been able to feather his nest substantially. He obviously has a phobia [sic] for recognition and has managed to get on innumerable committees, etc.

For quite some time, he has exaggerated his position in the Hughes' organization, in a continuing quest for recognition. This has, on occasion, proved embarrassing to his employers.

Rebozo wrote me that when Meier returned from the junket to the Dominican Republic, he told fellow Hughes employees that Richard Nixon had made the trip so much more comfortable for him by writing the U.S. Ambassador there to extend to Meier "every possible consideration," including a special briefing. (This, of course, had not occurred.)

The President, Meier claimed, had also written Meier, congratulating him on his "work for the Dominican Republic." Someone at Hughes asked Meier to bring in the President's letter for Hughes management to see. Rebozo reported:

When asked to show the letter, he said he would bring it the next day. The following day, when contacted, JM said that DN had told him not to discuss the N family with anyone without prior approval. Therefore, he declined to show the alleged letter.

Before this moment of reticence, Meier had told associates at Hughes that he and Don were "financially interested in five oil wells in the north slope of Alaska."

Rebozo's letter closed:

In summation, it is obvious that the problem basically is that these two individuals are both self-serving promoters to the point where truth and integrity are completely disregarded. One is trying to cash in on a family relationship, and the other on a vastly overstated business relationship. This totally irresponsible alliance can only lead to trouble sooner or later.

Now you have the problem, and you can solve it. Let me remind you however, that assassination is illegal.

At 3 P.M. on December 5, the President met with the Marriotts and asked them to hire his brother. Whereupon the Marriotts took Don onto their payroll, the IRS quickly finished its audit of Don without further difficulties arising and I turned to some of the other problems of the country.

Part III

CHAPTER TWELVE

The Congress

I BEGAN MY service to the President-elect with a mission to the Congress in December 1968. There is, I discovered, the Congress of the civics books—perhaps to some extent the figment of college professors' imaginations—and there is the real Congress.

I went to Washington in the second month of the "transition," that time between election and inauguration when the President-elect and his small staff—made up mostly of carryovers from his campaign organization—are swamped with the work of forming the new Administration. It was some measure of the confusion of the times that rather than Bryce Harlow or another person with some experience on Capitol Hill, I was sent on this Congressional errand.

Nixon had appointed a prestigious inauguration chairman, who in turn had hired dozens of people to produce an extravaganza. They had been given the Pension Building, a classic Civil War–era Government building in a depressed and depressing quarter of Washington. The day I first visited it in December, flocks of pigeons were flying around the soaring ceiling.

In makeshift cubicles the Nixon-Agnew Inaugural Committee employees were organizing fancy-dress balls and a parade; others were allocating invitations, selling tickets and bargaining for hotel rooms and rental cars. It was a very commercial operation. Everything was going to cost the celebrants money except the reception for Spiro Agnew. Tickets to the balls were expensive. And the Committee was selling costly medals, license plates and other inaugural trinkets, too. When I arrived I was ceremoniously presented my very own souvenir license plates and a silver medal with Richard Nixon's profile on it. I was very much impressed with the Committee's generosity, but I never did figure out what to do with either of its gifts.

Haldeman had sent me from New York to try to unsnarl a problem: The President-elect couldn't get enough tickets to his own swearing-in. Nixon had more than the usual number of requests for tickets; Republicans didn't elect a President very often, and they all wanted to come to see one sworn in. Nixon had more than the usual number of relatives, too, and they all wanted front-row seats.

I was told to go to the Congress and persuade someone named Mark Trice that the President-to-be required a more generous allocation of tickets. Trice was Secretary to the Senate Minority, an appointee of the Minority Leader, Everett Dirksen. Trice's office, one of those hideaways in the Capitol building, was down several small passageways, up a narrow, curving flight of steps, at the end of a windowless hallway. I couldn't have found it on my own in a month of searching. Trice was a tall, bald stork of a politician, and he was perched in one of the more elaborate Capitol Hill nests.

Mark Trice knew why I had come. The entire Nixon allocation—seats for family, staff, friends and political creditors—was to be about seven hundred. Haldeman reckoned we needed about five thousand as a bare minimum. So Trice began to acquaint me with the realities of inaugural politics. In a reedy twang he lectured me about the needs of the Members. Senators and Congressmen too have families, staff and supporters to be accommodated. Presidents came and went, of course, but the Congress flowed on like the great rivers of the Midwest. And after all, the swearing-in was put on by the Congress in its own backyard.

There were thousands of tickets and thousands of seats, but the Congress and the Inaugural Committee would sell many of them, Trice explained, to pay for the construction of the elaborate press tower and inaugural platform and for rental of the chairs themselves. Trice calculated that the Members would need all but seven hundred of the remainder; we were lucky to be getting that many, he said.

I thought it logical that the President-elect be provided with as many tickets as he needed to his own inauguration. But Mr. Trice repeated that the inaugural ceremony was really a Congressional event, not Presidential. The inaugural *parade* was the President's. Congressmen who wanted to see the parade down in front of the White House would be coming to us, hat in hand, to beg seats in *our* grandstand. The swearing-in was in front of the Capitol (or in back, depending on how you look at it), and that is Congressional territory. Seven hundred tickets was the best he could do.

I suggested, with some intentional display of annoyance, that perhaps we would just move the swearing-in to the south lawn of the White House. Maybe the President-elect wouldn't show up at the Capitol. Trice blinked; he ventured that "old Nick Nixon"* wouldn't really do anything that drastic. That would be dreadful. Perhaps Senator Dirksen should call the President-elect direct, to discuss this problem. I said I thought that would be a good idea.

Ultimately Everett Dirksen called and agreed with Bob Haldeman that the President-elect should have another three thousand tickets. And we were granted extra standing room. So some of our partisans had to stand in the cold to watch the ceremony, but at least they were in places where they could see.

In view of my head-on collision with Mr. Trice I was not completely surprised when, on that cold inaugural morning, my wife and I were ushered to seats on the platform directly behind the largest white pillar. In the formal photographs of the President being sworn in, I can be seen peeking around that large post while my less disputatious colleagues enjoy fine views from among the Members and other dignitaries.

Richard Nixon was a man of the Congress, as he often reminded us. But the Congress of the Nixon years, 1969–1974, was dominated by the Democrats, and the Republicans had not controlled either house since Eisenhower's time.

I had met a few Congressmen while campaigning for Nixon over the years. My old school friend Paul N. McCloskey, Jr., was now a liberal Republican from Northern California. But I'd never encountered Congress *en masse* or even in committees, and I was unprepared for it. When I arrived in Washington I thought our Republican leaders would *want* to help the President with his legislative program. At last they had a Republican in the White House with whom they could work to turn the Government around and do things for the country.

I expected to find the legislative leadership vested in men of vision and ability. Doubtless there would be a certain amount of partisanship, but the Congress would put the country's interests first.

And I expected the Members to manifest a degree of self-

---

* Nixon has gone through several name styles over the years. There is a certain vintage of Congressional staff and membership who are given to calling Richard Nixon "Nick." He has been both Nick to the House of Representatives and Dick to the Senate. After the 1968 election he informed us he was dropping his middle name and its initial.

lessness, putting their duty ahead of perquisites, vanity and ego-sensitivity.

I was prepared to deal with Congressmen on the basis of these preconceptions; but wise and experienced people like Bryce Harlow warned me that they were misconceptions.

A few weeks after my clash with Mark Trice, I met with the ranking Republican members of the House and Senate judiciary committees. One of them was Senator Roman Hruska of Nebraska, who was also the father of the young woman I had hired to be my personal secretary. (During the transition Jana Hruska had begun to assemble the staff and facilities I would need in the White House. When we moved in she had things operating smoothly the first day.)

Jana's father and his House counterpart, Congressman Richard Poff of Virginia, wanted to persuade me that the new Administration should hire some of the people who worked on the minority staff of their committees. Specifically, they thought I would be interested in some of their lawyers for the White House legal staff. While they were trying to be helpful, I'm sure, it is also true that neither ranking member would have been hurt by having his protégés working at the White House.

I had a brief private meeting with Hruska and Poff; then they brought in the young men they were urging on me, and for the first time I met John W. Dean III and his staff colleagues.

But Hruska and Poff were too late to sell me staff people. I had already hired two talented lawyers who had worked for me during the campaign—Ed Morgan and Henry Cashen—and also young Egil Krogh from my law firm in Seattle. I thought I could get along very well with three associates.*

When I assumed responsibility for the President's domestic policy work in late 1969, I learned more about the real Congress, because I began to see more of Congressmen than I had in the previous months when I had served as Counsel. In the new job I had meetings with the "Republican leadership," usually in the ornate offices of Senator Hugh Scott or Congressman Gerald Ford. Occasionally I went to breakfasts and

---

* Evidently Hruska and Poff were more successful at selling their boys to our new Justice Department. John Mitchell, the new Attorney General, and his Deputy, Richard Kleindienst, hired Dean, Don Santarelli, Wally Johnson and others from the judiciary-committee staffs for fairly important jobs at the Department of Justice. With Mitchell's sponsorship, Dean and Johnson eventually worked their ways into the White House.

lunches to meet the rank-and-file Members and to talk about our domestic legislation.

Since the Eisenhower days the Republicans in Congress had been the loyal opposition, seldom offering fundamental legislation. As the minority, they did not bear much responsibility for what went on in the Congress. Now, suddenly, here were these Nixon outlanders coming around insisting that Jerry Ford and Hugh Scott, the leaders, actually mobilize their partisan fellows. We were asking the leaders to lead, to push Nixon's legislative packages. Moreover, the rank-and-file Members themselves began to feel the heat from the White House. Our lobbyists were calling on them to stay in town and vote correctly. Most Republican Congressmen and Senators didn't like all that activity very much. But few of them would say they blamed the new President for their discomfort; instead they took potshots at Bryce Harlow and Pat Moynihan and me.

It was a time when there was almost no leadership in the Congress. Nixon saw that vacuum as an opportunity, and he stepped in. Even when Congressional leaders do appear, a President can lead the legislative herd because he can mobilize public opinion better and can command the vast resources within the Executive Branch. Congress is a huge committee of individuals, only slightly interdependent, each answering to a small, discrete political constituency. Each Member is politically cautious, suspicious of his Congressional leaders and incapable of commanding much television time. Any President is therefore capable of acting and forcing the Members to react.

The Members consume time in enormous quantities in their quaint Congressional processes. They recess; they junket; they arrive late and leave early; they attend conferences out of town, fly off to give speeches, sip and chat and endlessly party.* And only sometimes do they focus on legislation.

Congressional strategists use time as they use money, to bargain for support. The successful ones—like Senator Russell Long—never do now that which can be done within minutes of an immovable deadline, when a better deal can be struck by the fellow who blinks last.

The Nixon White House and the Congress were different

---

* The House of Representatives was not often in session. The four full years I was in Washington, their record of days in session was as follows:

1969	1970	1971	1972
186	164	163	135

worlds. We went to work every day—often on Sundays. We operated on schedule. There was an elaborate Haldeman staff *apparat* which enforced assignment deadlines, followed up with memos and phone calls, insisted on prompt performance and ratted on you if you were late. Domestic legislation came off the Domestic Council assembly line according to a schedule that dovetailed with the Ziegler news plan, the President's activity calendar and the Haldeman PR strategy.

Moreover, Nixon was the first President in decades not to have either house of Congress under the control of his party, although by 1969 party loyalty had waned and other factors were more significant in the definition of the Nixon–Congress relationship.

From 1952, Nixon had always been a coalition politician; he was not elected President by his party alone. In his dealings with the Congress he necessarily allied himself with senior, conservative Democrats to win critical legislative votes. He had more trouble with his own leaders in the Senate than with half the chamber's Democrats.

In the second year of Nixon's Presidency, Majority Leader Carl Albert became Speaker of the House of Representatives. Albert was elected by the Democratic majority, and he personified the lack of real Congressional leadership of which Nixon frequently complained. He was a diminutive Oklahoma Congressman who, if the police reports were accurate, had a considerable drinking problem.

The Metropolitan Police and the Secret Service kept the White House fully aware of Albert's social troubles. The little Speaker would go out of an evening, often to the Zebra Lounge, there to drink, not wisely but too well. Sometimes he picked fights; once he tried to drive a car home, disastrously. At times the police picked him up, but they did not arrest him; they took him home in a friendly fashion. The detailed police reports of these encounters always promptly found their way to the office of the President's Counsel, thence to the President's desk.

Nixon felt sure that this police information should be used to enlist Albert's cooperation, but Bryce Harlow, Assistant to the President for Congressional Liaison, wanted nothing to do with blackmailing the Speaker. It rankled Nixon that the media, especially the television news organizations, refused to report Albert's escapades. Even the Washington papers gave Albert's social life scant notice. Nixon complained to me that the public had a right to know that its third-ranking Constitutional officer was a drunkard, and that the press applied a double standard because Albert was part of the Washington (Democratic) Establishment.

"If that were me, there outside the Zebra Lounge, drunk and running into things, the cops taking me home," Nixon said, "my picture would be on every television station in the country. Isn't there some reporter with the guts to run this story?" Nixon assuaged his outrage by ordering Charles Colson and Murray Chotiner to find some willing journalist to do a column on Albert's drunkenness. So far as I know, neither one successfully planted an Albert item.

At my first meeting with our Republican leader in the House of Representatives, Gerald Ford, I was not impressed. We were meeting because the staff of the White House Domestic Council was assembling the President's legislative program in a series of packages, attacking a wide range of national problems. Nixon proposed to send them to the Congress in a steady stream.

In the Johnson years, Jerry Ford had spent most of his time out of Washington making hundreds of speeches for local Republicans, or for a lecture fee. It was clear in our first conversation in late 1969 that Ford wasn't thrilled to be harnessed to the Nixon Administration. Furthermore, he seemed slow to grasp the substantive information we were trying to give him. I came away from his office with the impression that Jerry Ford might have become a pretty good Grand Rapids insurance agent; he played a good game of golf, but he wasn't excessively bright.

As our proposals began to move to Congress, I discovered that Ford, when he disagreed with Nixon's policies or programs, just didn't work on our bills. For example, he was one of several Congressmen in the thrall of the Association of General Contractors and the rest of the highway lobby. When the President proposed legislation to tighten up and eventually terminate the interstate highway program, our leader, Jerry Ford, quietly helped scuttle our efforts.

Bryce Harlow, Nixon's premier assistant for Congressional liaison, was one of those lifetime students of the Congress who correctly realized Ford's place in it. He helped me to understand why Ford had become the Republican leader. Bryce conceded that Ford wasn't a brilliant legislator, but in that Congressional herd of mediocrities he couldn't have been the Republican leader if he had been. Flashy and bright Congressmen are distrusted by the others.

Ford worked hard to win the loyalty of his Congressional troops; he traveled long distances to speak at their hometown fund-raisers and rallies. He looked after their perquisites and creature comforts. And he instinctively knew the mood and tempo of the House, because he was just like most of them. He could forecast with some accuracy which legislative proposals would and would not be accepted by his colleagues. Over the years my regard for Ford grew. Somehow, perhaps instinctively, he had achieved his maximum potential in the Congress. (When he became President he exceeded it, obviously.)*

The Republican leader in the Senate was Hugh Scott of Pennsylvania, a rotund, owlish Pennsylvania machine politician who maintained a liberal voting record. Scott could discourse brilliantly on Chinese pottery. And he could explain at length the reasons he could not get his colleagues in the Senate to support the President's legislation. I saw more of this hack than I wanted to. The White House liaison men who worked the Senate would let me know when it was absolutely necessary to go to the Hill to meet with Scott. Our lobbyists saw him every day and had to maintain cordial relations with him. When they needed someone to lean on him I often played the heavy as they, demanding help for our legislation, could not.

Hugh Scott and Richard Nixon were unhappily yoked. After one legislative disaster, in which one of the President's bills passed in the House but was killed in the Senate, Nixon summoned Jerry Ford and Hugh Scott to the Oval Office. Three of us from the President's staff were asked to attend.

Nixon began the meeting by praising Jerry Ford's diligence and adroit management of the defeated legislation in the House. He suggested there would be rewards for Ford's good work.

Then he began to describe his disappointment in the action of the Senate. To my surprise, as Nixon warmed to his subject, he began to really chew on Hugh Scott. He described Scott's shortcomings as a leader, a Senator and a human being, with precision and elaboration. There was much to be said on that subject, and the President said it all.

Nixon hated face-to-face confrontation, so his dissection of Hugh Scott was extraordinary. For a long time the President

---

* After the 1972 election, Nixon invited Ford to Camp David to explain to him how we intended to revamp the Cabinet and Executive Office of the President. After Ford left, I remarked how much more understanding I had for him in 1972 than I'd had in 1969. Nixon nodded. "But Jerry has changed," he said. "He has had some responsibility—we required him to work—during these past four years, for the first time in his life."

had felt frustration and anger at Scott's posturing, his insistence upon his personal prerogatives, his press leaks and his duplicity—assuring us he was pushing the President's legislation while (we knew) he was really bad-mouthing it to his colleagues.

Ford and the rest of us felt awkward sitting there while Scott was worked over. Scott reddened and fiddled with his pipe, but he said nothing in self-defense. Finally Nixon ended the meeting and we filed out of the room, whereupon Scott ran for his limousine and fled the scene. I never again saw Nixon in such a mood. It was rare and, in Scott's case, completely appropriate. I hope there is a tape recording of that woodshed session somewhere. It was A Historic First.

Nixon had pretty fair legislative results in 1969–1971, considering that Congress was dominated by the Democrats. Bryce Harlow and his staff were hardworking and effective lobbyists. When Bryce retired, Bill Timmons of his staff was his logical successor, but the President began to hear from the Members that he should appoint someone of more "stature" than Timmons. While Haldeman's personnel people made lists of prospects, Timmons accepted the job on a temporary basis and did the work well.

At Nixon's urging, Clark MacGregor, a tall, middle-aged Congressman from Minnesota, ran against Hubert Humphrey for the Senate in 1970. When MacGregor was defeated, Nixon passed the word that some Federal job should be found for him. The premise was that MacGregor had tried to knock off Hubert Humphrey for us, so we owed him.

MacGregor's friends in the Congress urged Nixon to make MacGregor the Assistant for Congressional Liaison. They enlisted John Mitchell to push for their man. We began to receive some anti-Timmons lobbying too, primarily in news columns fed by MacGregor allies. At last Nixon decided to appoint Clark MacGregor, over Timmons, to run the Harlow staff.

MacGregor launched a much-publicized campaign to bridge the widening gulf between the White House and the Congress, while the President watched with some amusement—up to a point. Like Rogers Morton and Melvin Laird, MacGregor had been one of the prime Congressional sources of leaks and gossip for columnists like Rowland Evans and Robert Novak. His name began competing for space with Kissinger and the President's in the Washington papers as Mac-

Gregor became a prime "off the record" White House source. Nixon ceased to be amused, and Haldeman was told to stanch MacGregor's press leaks.

MacGregor had buttons made up for White House people to wear which said, "I LOVE CONGRESS." Somehow, I didn't get around to wearing mine much.

(It was a rare week when my interoffice mail didn't include a lapel symbol that someone wanted me to wear. Nixon had Haldeman distribute little American flags to everyone on the staff. I didn't feel I needed to demonstrate my patriotism in my buttonhole, so I dropped mine into a drawer. After a while I'd collected several dozen. Sometimes I saw the President staring at the place on my lapel where a little flag should be, but he never said a word to me. Instead, Bob Haldeman would later remind me that the President expected everyone to show the flag, and Larry Higby would send me six or seven more lapel flags in case I had lost mine.)

As part of their "I Love Congress" campaign, Clark and Barbara MacGregor invited Senators and Congressmen to have dinner with some of the White House people in the recreation room in the MacGregor basement.

The dinner I attended was a remarkable affair. Some of my colleagues wore their "I LOVE CONGRESS" buttons and went around smiling at Congressmen. I met a few Members I hadn't met before, including the late Democratic Whip, Congressman Hale Boggs of Louisiana, who was moving among us uncertainly with a large water glass full of gin. Boggs had a reputation as a mean and heavy drinker. Not long before, he'd had a fistfight in the men's room at a Washington hotel banquet. By the time the MacGregor dinner was served, Boggs was spoiling for a fight. To my surprise, the MacGregors had artlessly seated one of Boggs's deadly political enemies across the table from him. The Republican Senator from Colorado, the late Peter Dominick, was a handsome, smart patrician with a serious back ailment which made it painful for him to walk. Somehow, in the distant past, he had crossed Hale Boggs. At dinner Boggs began to berate Dominick loudly; it was futile for Dominick to try to ignore him, so for a time he deflected Boggs's insults with humor. Finally Dominick got mad; he and Boggs shouted back and forth across the dinner table as everyone watched. Just in time, MacGregor eased Boggs out of the room to avoid a fight. Mrs. Boggs (later a Congresswoman) excused herself and took her husband home. At times like that Congress was hard to love.

* * *

Nixon demanded a high level of service from those whose job it was to be attentive to the Congress. Besides the lobbyists, we maintained a "hospitality" office responsible for arranging White House tours for the Congressmen's constituents from back home. An elaborate procedure was created to ensure that a letter from a Member got speedy attention and a thorough reply. The social secretary worked closely with the lobbyists, Henry Kissinger and me to be certain the right Members were invited to the President's receptions and dinners.

The morning after a White House social event, Nixon's desk would be dotted with little scraps of paper—notes he'd made during talks with Congressmen as they came through the receiving line. When I sat down for our morning meeting, Nixon would pepper me with questions and complaints he'd picked up the night before. Within a few hours my staff would produce answers to enable the President to telephone those Congressmen that same afternoon with a complete follow-up.

With both houses of Congress controlled by the Democrats, the President went to great lengths to bring some Democrats into the various *ad hoc* coalitions he had to build to win passage of his legislation. Nixon could effectively woo Congressmen when he wanted to. Wilbur Mills, a Democrat and the longtime Chairman of the House Ways and Means Committee, was vital to the passage of our legislation on taxation, revenue sharing and welfare reform. Mills was a student of taxation and finance, smart and diligent, and he was the captain of an able committee staff. He was a real Congressional power.

Nixon made sure that George Shultz spent time with Mills. Nixon saw Mills whenever necessary too, and he went the extra distance with the Chairman.

In 1971, Nixon heard that Mills was ill and telephoned him in Arkansas. Mills was in traction, suffering with back trouble.

Nixon recommended Dr. Ryland, "that miracle worker" who had been sent to the President by Nelson Rockefeller.

In the midst of their conversation Nixon found he was talking to a little girl. Mills had handed the telephone to his granddaughter ("Hi, honey. Take good care of Granddaddy. We need him here") and Mills's 86-year-old mother ("You can be proud of your son") for chats with the President of the United States of America.

That was time well spent, and Nixon performed well in those situations. All this wooing paid dividends; it is the currency of the Congress. Over the years Wilbur Mills moved Nixon's welfare-reform legislation and won Congressional approval of our revenue-sharing proposals in spite of the opposition of John Byrnes, our senior Republican on the Ways and Means Committee. Other senior Democrats, including Senators John Stennis and Russell Long, frequently gave Nixon their vote. In fact, Nixon felt closer to those conservative Democrats than he did to Republicans like Edward Brooke and Ogden Reid.

In the Ninety-second Congress, 1970–1972, there were eighteen Democrats in the House who supported the President in key votes at least 80 percent of the time. By contrast, there were that many Republicans who didn't support Nixon half the time. Eight Democratic Senators had Nixon-support ratings between 83 percent and 100 percent in that Congress. Only 22 Republicans were above 80 percent, while 9* were below 50 percent.

Senator Charles Percy, the Illinois Republican, for example, was wholly independent in opposing the President's legislation to build the anti-ballistic-missile system.† On the domestic side, he was one of the sponsors of a bill to create a quasi-governmental housing corporation; he was getting some mileage in the press as the savior of Government housing. At lunch with the Senator one day I was very blunt—at Nixon's specific direction—in establishing the linkage between our support for Percy's housing idea and his support of the President on A.B.M. It was evident that Percy had enjoyed his freedom from pressures of that kind during the years the White House was Democratic. He was very much offended that the President's man would try to trade for his vote—or so he said. And later, in backgrounders with the press, he harshly criticized me, not Nixon, for the attempt.

All through his first term Nixon was criticized for inadequate attention to the Members of both houses of the Congress. Bill Timmons once tabulated the number of hours the President actually spent with the Members, compared with Lyndon Johnson, Kennedy and other Presidents. Nixon saw more Members for more hours, Timmons said.

---

* Stevens (42.1%), Mathias (36.3%), Pearson (35%), Schweiker (30.4%), Percy (28.6%), Brooke (21.7%), Hatfield (20%), Case (13.6%) and Javits (13%).

† On average, over *four* years, Percy's support of the President's key legislation was less than 30 percent.

But when Congress adjourned in 1972, Timmons did another tabulation which showed that there was some basis for the later complaints he had been getting. Comparing the four years of Nixon's first term, the President's contact with the Congress had tapered off considerably.

Here is Timmons' tabulation:

	1969	1970	1971	1972
GOP LEADERSHIP MEETINGS	24	16	13	15
BIPARTISAN LEADERSHIP MEETINGS	10	4	9	5
CONGRESSIONAL HALF-HOURS*	15	39	9	0
BILL SIGNINGS (MEMBERS INVITED)	8	14	6	12
MEETINGS WITH SENATORS	125	121	94	23
MEETINGS WITH REPRESENTATIVES	87	115	69	30
PHONE CONVERSATIONS WITH MEMBERS	204	140	180	61
MEALS WITH MEMBERS	26	20	22	12
EVENINGS AT THE WHITE HOUSE*	0	3	1	2

---

* "Congressional half-hours" had been special appointments for Congressmen to come in and chat with Nixon. They began in late 1969, flourished in 1970, then dwindled.

"Evenings at the White House" were to be informal social gatherings and entertainment for the Members and their spouses.

Other Presidential activities at which Nixon might see Congressmen also declined in frequency. The White House church services went from 12 in 1969 to 7 in 1970, 8 in 1971 and 1 in 1972. Similarly, state dinners numbered 11 in 1969, 8 in 1970, 9 in 1971 and only 4 in 1972.

In 1971 and 1972, Nixon spent more and more time out of Washington, in California, in Florida or at Camp David. There were occasional Congressional meetings at the Western White House at San Clemente, but only individual Members or small groups were asked to visit the President there.

There was a Republican leadership meeting almost every Tuesday the President was in Washington. About eight in the morning, ten or twelve Members would come, to sit around the cabinet table in the room next to the Oval Office with Nixon, Spiro Agnew and a few members of the Cabinet, the White House lobbyists and some of the White House staff. The President usually assigned some of us to put on show-and-tell explanations of our legislative proposals with elaborate charts and pictures.

Our dynamic legislative leaders drank coffee and occasionally took notes, but they rarely were given a chance to say anything. Nixon deliberately scheduled the sessions early in the morning because he knew the Members were not often called upon to emerge into the early-morning light. He thought it would be good for them to realize that down at the White House people worked hard, beginning early in the morning.

One Senator from a Northeastern state invariably fell asleep at these sessions. That elderly Member slipped lower and lower in his smooth leather Cabinet chair, snoring gently, as George Shultz, Henry Kissinger or I explained full-employment deficits or liquid-metal fast breeder-reactors. Everyone pretended not to notice the slipping sleeper. Just before disappearing under the table the Senator would awaken, startled; pull himself up against the chair back and fall asleep again.

An atmosphere of Congressional tension began the election year 1972. Although every poll showed Nixon a probable winner over George McGovern by a large margin, Nixon did very little to assist Republican Senators or Congressmen who faced reelection. It had been decided that the President would campaign by "being Presidential." He would seldom venture out of Washington, but he was photographed and televised frequently at his desk doing his job for all the American people. That strategy didn't mesh well with visits to help beleaguered Republican Congressmen who were running in their home districts. So relations with the Congress were not improved during the 1972 campaign.

After the election, the President virtually disappeared behind the fences of Camp David. Aside from one brief visit with Gerald Ford, he had no personal contact with the Congress until he delivered his State of the Union address to a joint session in late January 1973. Almost immediately the President went to San Clemente, and it was there, about ten days later, that he began asking questions about the select committee the Senate was forming to hold hearings on Watergate.

Professional Washington lobbyists who go to work for a President can't afford to offend Congressmen. Once the President leaves office the lobbyist must return to representing a private clientele, and his effectiveness will depend on his good, continuing relationship with the Members. As Clark MacGregor did, the White House lobbyist rationalizes this potential conflict. It is good for the President to have an aide who gets along with every Member, he argues. If the President instructs his aide to get tough with a Member, the aide disregards the instruction because, of course, he best serves the President by doing so. And incidentally, when one leaves the President and the White House, one can go to work for the corporations. Great are the rewards of good Congressional relations.

At the same time, every President needs some staff people who do not intend to make Washington their life careers. He needs people immune from such considerations of self-interest, who will make it possible for the President to prod and goad, boldly trade for votes or send a little chill of fear rippling through the legislators.

I was one of those. When it was in the President's interest, or in the national interest or, happily, both, I could level effective and widely noticed criticism at the Congress. I commanded a measure of television time to blast the members for sloth or overspending. That went with my job, as far as I was concerned.

I have no doubt that the Ervin Committee was incubated in the smoldering antipathy Senators felt for Nixon and some of the staff. It was impelled by a mixture of the ordinary partisan desire to embarrass the opposition and a genuine desire to further individual Senatorial careers. And of course, it was aided by an abundance of evidence, a disjointed and dispirited defense and unprecedented television exposure. The Senators were not very capable, and their staff work was mediocre, but that didn't matter. The networks made them look good, and even worse staff work by the White House made them look better.

It was the first time in history that Presidential assistants and others on the White House staff were haled before a committee of the Congress on television to account for their conduct of the Presidency. Off camera, I had spent the months of May, June and July 1973 appearing before other committees of the Senate and House to testify about the CIA's conduct. Later I was called to testify before a House taxation committee investigating Nixon's taxes, too. In all these forums I encountered the hostility of the Members, who believed they had been scorned by some of us on the White House staff over the previous four years.

I could understand their resentment, but it did not much concern me; I had been carrying out the President's wishes. In doing so, I wasn't thinking about the well-being of the Congress. Nor was I much concerned about any long-term personal career dealing with the Congress. When I sat down before the Ervin Committee to testify, I reaped some of the bitter fruit of Nixon's Congressional relationship, but it was only one of a constellation of factors at work on me that day. In a sense I was in the middle, between the President I had worked for until the previous April and the Members. But I didn't see it that way then. I saw myself as the President's advocate, just as I had been for nearly five years before then. And the Members were our adversaries.

It was too late for conciliation, of course. Nor did I feel like just sitting in the witness chair, abiding the Senators' posturing and acting for the cameras.

So I took them on.

CHAPTER THIRTEEN

Domestic Affairs

IT HAS BECOME accepted "fact" that Richard Nixon was preoccupied with foreign affairs, to the exclusion of domestic issues. Theodore H. White has written that Nixon says no domestic problem needs the President; every one could be solved by the Cabinet. Writers have built on the misinformation of other writers, layer after layer, until this nonsense has become doctrine.

The truth is that Nixon liked foreign affairs better. Domestic controversy involved the unsolvable, passion-laden issues no one could enjoy grappling with, and the damnable special-interest groups who always demand and demand more but never show gratitude.

Foreign-policy activities—ambassadors ceremonially presenting their credentials, or the exchange of toasts at a summit conference with the Russians—all massage a President's ego. A visit to a sewage-treatment plant in suburban Chicago (to show support for a Clean Water Act) somehow didn't make Richard Nixon feel like the leader of the Free World.

But the point is that President Nixon *did* visit sewage plants and energy generators, and he sent the first environmental legislation to the Congress. Much of the time Nixon was immersed in deliberations on the nation's domestic economy (and foreign economic problems too), reform of the post office, tax reform and crime.

Nixon believed some of these domestic issues were potent political medicine; he insisted on personally making all the decisions on abortion, race, aid to parochial schools, labor legislation, drugs, crime, welfare and taxes, for example.

Others—notably the environment, health (except cancer research), campus unrest and antiwar demonstrations, hunger, transportation, consumer protection, youth, housing and revenue sharing—he delegated to others to look after.

One of the reasons I was so slow to leave the White House when my instincts told me I should in 1970 and 1971 was that I had been given *carte blanche* in so many areas of domestic affairs. I was permitted to speak for the President. Indeed, Nixon insisted I not bother him about many things. He preferred to stay away from the environment issues, for example—free to criticize, taking the bows when things went well, disowning me when EPA closed a plant or ordered expensive retrofit for a factory.

Revenue sharing was one of our major domestic-policy initiatives. The idea actually had been hatched by Brookings economist Joseph Pechman and the Democrats years before, but they were never able to sell it to the Congress. Arthur Burns dusted it off, and we refined it somewhat after Arthur left the White House; it made good Republican sense. By dismantling many of the Democrats' old categorical grant programs (such as sewer grants to cities) we could promise that the funds formerly granted under those programs would be sent to the cities, counties and states with no strings attached, so that the local government could decide its own priorities. The old grant programs incurred overhead at both ends: the cities had to do a ton of paperwork to qualify for a grant and the Feds did an equal amount, along with endless reviews, inspections and the imposition of Federal conditions and regulations. Most of the overhead could be cut, with substantial savings.

We launched a campaign for revenue sharing, strongly abetted by Nelson Rockefeller, who rallied the city, county and state officials to lobby for it. Most Members of Congress wanted to perpetuate the old grant programs. Every time Ashtabula, Ohio, got a Federal grant, the local Congressman announced it and made it sound as if it were he who had gotten the money for the home folks. Since revenue-sharing money would be distributed according to a set formula, there was no way for the Member to take credit.

Revenue sharing had Hill trouble from the beginning. John Byrnes, the ranking Republican on the Ways and Means Committee, declared war on it at the beginning. So did Wilbur Mills, the Chairman. That Committee would either pass or kill our proposal. So we began to put on slide shows and bombard the Hill with literature to reach the rank and file. The Cabinet and the White House domestic-policy staff made dozens of talks. The President invited every member of Congress to breakfast, over several weeks, and we put on our show there to demonstrate with maps and charts that every one of their Congressional districts would benefit from the $5 billion of general revenue sharing and six kinds of special sharing—for education ($3 billion), transportation ($1 billion), law enforcement ($1 billion), urban development ($1 billion), rural development ($1 billion) and manpower training ($1 billion).

The thaw in Congress was long and slow. As our sustained effort began to cause some movement, however, I discovered one day that while Wilbur Mills was gradually turning our way, we had lost *the President's* support! During budget discussions he brusquely decided that he would reduce the projected budget deficit by abandoning revenue sharing. That could "save" billions, he reasoned. What he knew, but would not admit, was that if there were no revenue-sharing reform the old grant programs would stay on the books, pumping out billions of dollars every year. There were great economies in revenue sharing, just in the overhead savings alone. And there was the promise of a long-range reduction in Federal spending too, as the sharing formulae were tightened in future years.

Moreover, hundreds of us, from Rockefeller to the Cabinet to our allies in the Congress, had invested countless hours and immeasurable political capital in this fight. I couldn't imagine the President making a sudden change of policy that would abandon them.

Over the years I've been asked if I *ever* said "no" to Richard Nixon. The press has painted some of the staff as fawning sycophants who, for one reason or another, were unable to disagree with the President. To be sure, you had to pick your time and do it skillfully if you were going to disagree with Richard Nixon and remain effective. But I did it many times.

I flatly disagreed with Nixon's decision to abandon revenue sharing, and I told him so. Almost every time we talked about the budget, he'd propose dumping revenue sharing, and sometimes I just sat still until he moved to another subject. He knew my view, and my silence was enough to reaffirm it. At other times I explained why we couldn't abandon our friends. Or I argued the merits of the proposal.*

In this instance, my allies and I were effective in saying no. Revenue sharing survived, and much of it became law.

The Federal Government—the three coordinate branches—relies on the President to propose the answers to most of the nation's problems. The Courts deal with cases as they are litigated; if there's no legal proceeding, a judge can't reach out for a problem even if he's got a good idea how to solve it.

A Congressman can reach for the problem, but he's only one of 535, and he finds it almost impossible to mobilize a consensus among his colleagues unless he's both a senior superstar and a master tactician. The Congress is a huge, unwieldy committee that is only as good as its leadership.

The Executive Branch is unwieldy too. It is huge, ponderous and badly organized to deal with modern problems. When a department's Secretary identifies a problem and tries to solve it, he or she often discovers that several other departments or agencies over which he has no control are also possessed of some jurisdiction over the problem. A health issue may involve the Department of Health and Human Services, the Veterans Administration, the Environmental Protection Agency, the Department of Defense and the Department of Labor—all at the same time. So who takes the lead? In a confused situation like that, usually no one at the department level does. It's up to the President. If he doesn't begin it, it doesn't begin. If someone else does begin it, the White House will end up refereeing jurisdictional battles.

That puts a huge additional load on the President and his small staff. Not only must he decide vital issues, but he actually must overcome the organizational mess and *initiate* problem-solving across departmental jurisdictions.

The press and the Congress complain all the time about the

---

* In 1979, Henry Kissinger and I talked about the problems historians are going to have with the thousands of hours of White House tapes—and the problems *he* and *I* are going to have with them. At times we will be heard responding to Richard Nixon's truly outrageous statements with silence or even acquiescence, when an outsider might have yelled or pounded the desk in outrage. But a Nixon assistant in our position knew he had to come back the next day with other problems that deserved serious consideration. We thought we owed it to the country to stay effective in our dealings with Nixon. So we often finessed.

growing size of the White House staff. (Actually, the growth of the Congress' staff is faster, larger and more costly.) There is one simple solution: for the Congress to allow the President to reorganize the Executive Branch to eliminate the jurisdictional thickets that now demand so much of his time.

In early 1971 we sent to the Congress four reorganization bills designed to do just that. The Cabinet would have been reduced to eight members, and the four new consolidated departments would have embraced related functions, so jurisdictional questions could be resolved by a Secretary, rather than the President.

Although President Nixon was ready to reorganize the Executive Branch, the Congress and the Washington Establishment weren't willing to let him. The Establishment—Federal bureaucrats and their lobbyist clients—had long-standing relationships which might be fatally disrupted by all the moving, consolidation and elimination of duplicate functions.

The Congress and its staff had similar (and similarly profitable) affection for the Executive *status quo*. Our radical change would have required the elimination of countless subcommittees, their staff people and their chairmen. A profound Congressional reorganization would have followed, and few Members could see any personal gain in that.

So our bills languished. One was given a brief and perfunctory hearing by a House committee, but then all four disappeared in the Congressional quicksand of self-interest.

After the 1972 election, the President moved by Executive Order as close to the proposed reorganization as he could get; but the Watergate crisis washed the experiment away in the summer of 1973.

Herb Klein and others have written some perfect silliness about these reorganization attempts. In fact, the proposals were efforts to strengthen the Cabinet, which was enmeshed in an archaic organization. Our proposals would have had the effect of decentralizing much of the decision-making in the Executive Branch.

Klein wrote that the 1973 reorganization was a power grab by Haldeman, Kissinger, Shultz and me. Perhaps from his very obstructed viewpoint in the old Executive Office Building, that's all he could see. But the truth is that the senior White House staff had all the clout it needed without a reorganization. In that period we were over our heads with work and hoped that a reorganization would move some of that load to Caspar Weinberger, James Lynn and other able Cabinet members.

Perhaps underlying Klein's criticism of the January 1973 reorganization was the President's contemporaneous decision to put Ron Ziegler in charge of Herb Klein's Office of Communications. That resulted in a front-page story in the January 9 *Washington Post* tracing Ziegler's rise in favor with the President and Klein's probable departure. Although Klein denied to the *Post* reporter that he would be leaving soon ("The President has asked me to stay on. I have no immediate plans to make a change"), Bob Haldeman had already told Klein that the President wanted him to leave.

At the same time, I stepped aside. I intended to resign before the end of 1973 (I knew nothing then about the Senate Select Committee's intentions), and I urged that Ken Cole take over the Domestic Council staff at once so that we would have a full year of transition. I believed it could take that long for Nixon to accept Cole and rely on him as completely as he must for Cole to succeed.

Nixon and I agreed that I would focus my attention on the reorganization, to try to make it work effectively. I would also take responsibility for energy, private housing and one or two other policy problems before I left.

But two months later, in mid-February 1973, Nixon pushed me back into the Watergate mess, and by the end of April I was gone.

Those who have written about my political philosophy have located me all across the spectrum. Perhaps the appellation I was most comfortable with was "pragmatic." But whatever it was, it was evidently not obvious. The right-wingers said I was much too liberal; there is an archconservative newsletter called *Human Events* which was always predicting my early departure and sticking long pins into my effigy. At the same time liberals accused me of excessive conservatism.

Characteristically, the liberals on the White House staff were rather passive, perhaps because they worked for a President whose philosophy was *a priori* conservative. But the conservatives were militant battlers who would take my scalp (or the heads of my staff) if I gave them half a chance.

In the fall of 1970 the conservatives nearly got me. From October 10 to October 23 I was frozen out—the Assistant to the President for Domestic Affairs couldn't get an appointment to see the President, nor could I get answers from him to my memoranda. Domestic-policy work came to a halt. Haldeman just shrugged when I asked him what was going on. So I sat in my office and pretended I was still useful, although in fact my usefulness depended entirely upon my access to the President.

At the end of the first week—October 20—I finally received a memorandum from Nixon enclosing a September 25 *Washington Post* column by Kevin Phillips, a young conservative columnist who was a protégé of John Mitchell's. Nixon's note said that Phillips' column was "a correct view" and I "should take action to correct [my deviation from] it."

Phillips, the author of a book, *The Southern Strategy,* was calling for Nixon to move to the right in his domestic policies:

POST-SOUTHERN STRATEGY

Although television and newspaper reporters enjoy dwelling on his flamboyant phraseology, Vice President Agnew's autumn campaign tour has a greater purpose than devising exotic names for liberal Democrats. Administration efforts to create a Republican majority seem to be entering a new Northern, blue-collar and Catholic phase.

Beginning with the President's Labor Day fete for union leaders, the political events of September—Agnew's tour, Mr. Nixon's campus unrest speech, his meeting with Chicago Poles, and announcement of forthcoming visits to Italy, the Pope, and Ireland—appear to mark the launching of what might be termed a "post-Southern strategy."

Because Southern support remains vitally important to Mr. Nixon's re-election plans, this should not be misread as a non-Southern strategy. It is rather a post-Southern strategy predicated on the surmise that 1972 GOP Presidential success in Dixie has already been fairly well assured.

Even in the Deep South, polls taken this month suggest that Mr. Nixon has not suffered too much from school desegregation. (One taken in Mississippi shows the President about as popular as segregationist Governor John Bell Williams.) Nixon strategists are beginning to hope that George Wallace, whose imminent remarriage is now rumored, may decide to stick to homestate and hearthside in 1972.

In addition to Dixie, the second, long-identified trend group of the emerging Republican majority consists of Northern blue-collar workers and Catholics.

This group is now moving to the strategic fore in White House plans because (1) Southern GOP presidential inroads seem basically secure and (2) the increasingly controversial radical influence in the Democratic Party of the Northern industrial states is alienating blue-collar and ethnic conservatives.

The objective of the post-Southern strategy was stated by Vice President Agnew in Illinois: "The time has come for someone to represent the workingmen of this country, the forgotten man of American politics. . . . The President and I are applying for that job."

Quite obviously, the South and the West cannot win elections by themselves, and the blue-collar strategy is aimed at shaping a new kind of GOP majority for 1972 in New Jersey, Pennsylvania, Ohio, Illinois, Missouri, California, and other indicated battlegrounds of the new GOP politics.

The fulcrum of Republican appeal is more or less the "social issue"—law and order, permissiveness, campus anarchy, racial engineering—described by Richard Scammon and Ben Wattenberg in their new book, *The Real Majority*.

As Scammon and Wattenberg suggest, the "social issue" may be on a par with the cyclical realignment issues of 1896 and 1932. By moving towards a me-too position, the Democrats are probably giving way to history.

Most importantly, by acknowledging the conservative and generally Republican "social issue" as centrist and paramount, Democratic leaders are allowing U.S. policies to be substantially redefined so that the Republican right-of-center becomes the center and the Democratic left-of-center becomes—fatally—the left.

However, the pre-September Republican record is one of ineptness and ambiguity. Exertions on behalf of expanded welfare, the Philadelphia Plan, and suburban integration, as well as the activities of the Presidential Commission on Campus Unrest have all detracted from the Nixon administration's ability to use the "social issue," and lessened pro-Republican realignment. Mid-1970 opinion surveys have profiled a generally dubious public view of administration actions regarding campus anarchy and race relations.

Thus, it is not enough for Vice President Agnew to simply attack the Democrats as soft on radicalism. The administration cannot build a lasting new GOP coalition until it can articulate a positive philosophy and program to replace liberalism's failure to meet the needs of Middle America.

So there was the reason for the Big Freeze. Nixon was sitting down there in his office ruminating on the direction in which his domestic policies were going, and he was signaling his unhappiness with that direction (as Phillips saw it) by refusing to see me.

I laid aside my other work and wrote a response to the Phillips column:

October 21, 1970

MEMORANDUM FOR

THE PRESIDENT

I agree with page 3 at top

RE: Kevin Phillips' column "Post Southern Strategy"
Washington Post September 25, 1970

Not page 5

Phillips asserts in this article that the Administration has been inept and ambiguous on "The Social Issue" as shown by "mid-1970 opinion surveys on campus anarchy and race relations".

It follows, he says, that as matters now stand the Administration cannot build "a lasting new GOP coalition" for want of a positive philosophy and program to replace liberalism's failure to meet Middle America's needs.

He cites exertions on behalf of expanded welfare, the Philadelphia Plan, suburban integration and the Scranton Commission as detracting from your ability to employ "The Social Issue" among Middle America.

I have been told that you believe this is a correct view and that I am to "take action to correct this".

Having read the article carefully I am of the opinion that Phillips seeks to move you into adoption of a totally "conservative" domestic program on questions apart from The Social Issue. To my view this effort would impair rather than enhance your use of the "social issue" in the next two years. I think his assertions miss the central point of Scammon's thesis.

Scammon and Wattenberg defined the Social Issue as having four elements:

-- Crime
-- Race
-- Youth-lash
-- Values (pornography, obscenity, etc.)

As Scammon says,

"... The social issue is not a straight right/left or liberal/conservative issue."

Yet I think Kevin mistakenly tries to equate the Social Issue with pure conservative positions on <u>non</u>-social issue questions. He knows that the Administration has bought the Scammon analysis. He is using it to lever us to substantive positions more in agreement with his views, on the questionable basis of "mid-1970 opinion polls" not otherwise identified or detailed.

Scammon, on the other hand, sets out a number of 1968 campaign-period polls which were favorable to you on the Social Issue issues.

The latest Derge poll available to us indicates strong approval of your handling of student dissenters and protestors. However, the poll is not structured to bear directly on the questions raised by Kevin Phillips' article. We should insert questions in the next poll from which we can derive better information on this important issue.

Scammon wrote his book as much or more for Democrats than for Republicans. His advice to them is: Capitalize on the economic issues (higher benefits of all kinds, expanded medicare, and be for the little guy. Say: "It's time to get America moving again.") They should neutralize the Social Issue by finessing race questions and coming out strong for law and order.

Republican strategy, says Scammon, is the mirror image.

Hold fast on the elements of the social issue. Finesse the
social issues "like school integration by indicating Republicans
are all for civil rights and actually move ahead - but at a
slower, more "reasonable" pace... Be for moderate integration
and against busing.

"On the Economic Issues show that Republicans, too, can be
the party of the workingman. Programs designed to help the
middle-income working class are desirable: tax relief; aid
to schools (somewhat less tied to racial issues than earlier
Democratic programs); tax sharing with states and cities
and counties and suburbs, etc. Say, "It's time to get America
moving again."

In short he advises both: <u>Go to the center:</u>

> "There is evidence to suggest that there are
> elements in each of the three parties that
> currently advocate a <u>move to the fringes</u> and
> away from the center. There is a shorthand for
> that, too: <u>defeat.</u>"

<u>My point is simply that the Social Issue strategy is a
centerist strategy</u>, not a liberal or conservative strategy.

It appeals to the broad middle of the voting spectrum and well
may repel those on the right and left wings.

Young Kevin's column either shows he misunderstands or
misuses the concept to impeach some non-conservative
initiatives deliberately designed to furnish some zigs to go with
our conservative zags in the same way we have included
Moynihans with our Dents (rather than trying to recruit
only those non-existent middle-of-the-roaders).

Very few initiatives will be truly in the center. They will
fall on one side or the other. Our domestic policy job, as I
have understood it up to now, was to insure some balance.
As we can, consistent with the Social Issue concept, we will
try to co-opt the opposition's issues (e.g., Muskie's
environment) if the political cost is not too great.

But we will not blur your position on crime, youth, values or race.

Phillips criticizes four policy positions specifically in the article. Criticism is due on one, is unsound on two and the fourth is now a tactical dilemma as to which I have a suggestion:

1. Welfare:

   Our welfare reform effort has been a good zig, without damage to the Social Issue, with promise of strong blue-collar appeal.

2. Philadelphia Plan:

   While anti-labor and pro-black, the legislative battle drove a wedge between the Democrats and labor which has stretched the membrane. The Plan itself is not widely understood in non-labor circles, in my view. Labor understands it and hates it. In due time, if we administer it without undue zeal it can become a "slow and reasonable" approach to civil rights such as Scammon describes in his advice for Republicans.

3. Suburban Integration:

   This is a serious Romney problem which we will apparently have as long as he is there. There is no approved program as such, nor has the White House approved such a policy. But he keeps loudly talking about it in spite of our efforts to shut him up. And he is beginning some administrative maneuvers in that direction.

[handwritten notes in left margin: "This may be questionable politically unless same moderation on work requirement", "OK", "Stop this one"]

4. <u>Scranton Commission</u>

You are well positioned on youth, universities and allied subjects but you are said to be committed to respond to the Scranton report soon. The press widely printed your promise to Scranton to read and reply, which you are said to have given him when he last came in to see you.

RECOMMENDATION: That you refer to the Report in a campaign speech, say you've read it and had it analyzed. Quote a couple of passages critical of students and administrators "that everyone here will agree with". Finesse the question of blame because indictments are now outstanding in Ohio. Joke about everyone advising the President these days. Reaffirm your position on violent dissent and move on to other subjects.

Then never comment on the report again and don't see Scranton again.

SUMMARY:

(1) I assume our domestic course is down the center, except on the Social Issue elements. If not, and particularly if you intend the pure conservative line which Phillips peddles in this column, someone had better straighten me out.

(2) I will have some polling done on these and some other specific issues and programs when Derge does his next one to see how we're really coming through to the public.

(3) We'll analyze the election results carefully for lessons on this subject.

(4) In Florida perhaps we can talk some about Romney, the use of Presidential Commissions (if any), our civil rights strategy and other accumulated questions in this area.

John D. Ehrlichman

At the same time, I told Bob Haldeman that I'd be resigning shortly.

"Why?" he said with genuine surprise.

"It's been over a week," I said, "and unanswered questions are piling up. If he's not going to deal with the domestic side through me, then he'd better get someone else. The problems aren't going to go away."

Later on Wednesday, October 21, Haldeman reported that he'd delivered my Kevin Phillips memo to Nixon. On Thursday, Haldeman said, "Don't quit yet—you really scored with that paper." But still I was not invited in for a talk.

On Friday, Nixon called me to his office and we spent ninety minutes going over my accumulated questions and reports. Just before he called, I received a Xerox of my memorandum back, with Nixon's handwritten notations beside some of the principal points.

Nothing was said during our conversation about my leaving—or staying—but Nixon asked my advice on Cabinet changes. And as if to propitiate me, he indicated that two of my most burdensome charges would soon be going.

"Hickel will go, for sure," Nixon said, "and Romney will go too, if we can find a good black to replace him. I want Morton at Interior; he's so big and strong-looking. He gives a good image."

Soon I heard that Haldeman had reported to John Mitchell that in the President's opinion, the Attorney General's boy Kevin Phillips had "flipped." And after that I was never frozen out again, although there were times when I would just as soon have been unincluded.

The racial issue was both a problem and an opportunity for President Richard Nixon. First, he had to be positioned where the majority of Americans would agree with him. That was not as difficult as finding ways to tell the country clearly where the President stood. Once the folks realized Nixon was with them on busing and housing, they would prefer him over a liberal like George McGovern, Nixon was sure.

A Constitutional amendment to ban busing would be very visible, but it would be hard for people to understand and might not be taken seriously. The President alone could not stop busing, but many people thought he could. The compromise device Nixon adopted was a loud call for a law requiring a moratorium on all court-ordered busing until Congress could attack school desegregation on a comprehensive basis. Whether Congress passed the busing moratorium was not as important as that the American people understood that Richard Nixon opposed busing as much as they did.

As we approached the 1972 election, Bob Haldeman canvassed the staff for forecasts of election issues and how we should manage them.

In May, Charles Colson wrote a long paper advocating a platform based on "The New Populism": (1) we're for the blue-collar little man, not big business, (2) we're against the present tax system and (3) we're against Big Government.

On busing, Colson wrote:

The fundamental problem with our position on busing is that it is not clearly perceived. People know the President is against busing but in the South they know they have already instituted busing plans, which the moratorium won't help, and in the North they see the courts rushing forward with new busing orders. Nowhere is the gap between rhetoric and performance any clearer than in this area and I would submit this one really fuels the credibility issue.

In part our program is not understood because the moratorium is in fact offensive in the South (they believe it will stop busing in the North, but do nothing about busing that has already begun in the South) and it is not clear in the North that it will do anything. If Congress acts on the moratorium and the courts respect the statute, then we will have something to run on in those areas affected but we still have a problem in the South. If Congress does not act, we have got to run against the Congress, once again, with a major effort in key areas. If Congress rejects the proposal, the President should consider calling for a constitutional amendment making it very clear, especially in the South, that existing busing plans *can* be undone.

Our whole objective here is to simply get our position clearly understood nationally. Once it is understood, then we need not campaign on it as a national issue, but rather exploit hell out of it in key areas. I would argue that busing, unlike a lot of other issues is clearly voter motivational. It is one of those issues in particular areas that is absolutely decisive in a voter's mind. He will put up with anything else if he feels that we not only are against busing, but can and will do something about it.

The key voter blocs Colson wanted us to go after were Catholics, organized labor—and: "Finally, we have the whole open-housing issue. Freezing Romney in place or even selectively rolling him back could pay enormous political dividends."

That is, we'll go after the racists.

That subliminal appeal to the antiblack voter was always in Nixon's statements and speeches on schools and housing, and it always bothered me. Richard Nixon was against busing, against desegregating schools quickly, against public housing insofar as "public" meant putting mixed-racial projects into white neighborhoods.

For years HUD Secretaries had been trying to locate housing projects in the white-ethnic neighborhoods of Chicago, but Mayor Richard Daley and his political machine had successfully resisted all attempts. At last a Federal judge ordered an end to the delays. Daley came to see Nixon, and I was asked to join them. After Daley had explained his problem, Nixon told me that our Department of Housing and Urban Development was to find some other place for the projects. We weren't going to crack the Polish and Italian neighborhoods, the President promised the Mayor. There would be no publicity about it, but both Nixon and Daley knew they had a deal.

I didn't know enough about the courts' decrees to argue with anyone then; when I saw the Chicago court orders, I realized that HUD had very little leeway. But I told George Romney and the Attorney General what the President's wishes were, and left it up to them to figure out how to stay out of trouble.

President Nixon was convinced that the majority of Americans did not support open housing, affirmative action, busing to achieve racial balance, Model Cities, the Equal Employment Opportunity Commission and the other Federal civil rights activities. But mere politics alone did not explain the President's motives for slowing things down and changing the Federal thrust. Of course, he saw, with Colson, that there was political gain in it. It offered him rapport (and the chance for more important coalitions on defense subjects) with senior Senators and Congressmen. Russell Long, John Stennis, George Mahon and Wilbur Mills were attracted to Nixon's civil rights position; they were Southerners first and Democrats second.

But more central was the fact that Nixon genuinely believed all of these Federal programs simply would never do any good. He was against busing because he didn't believe black children would gain anything in the process and certainly the white kids would be disadvantaged by it.

Twice, in explaining all this to me, Nixon said he believed America's blacks could only marginally benefit from Federal programs because blacks were *genetically inferior* to whites. All the Federal money and programs we could devise could not change that fact, he believed. Blacks could never achieve parity—in intelligence, economic success or social qualities; but, he said, we should still do what we could for them, within reasonable limits, because it was "right" to do so.

I was appalled but not surprised.

Throughout his public life Richard Nixon signaled to the American people where he stood on the race issue. He was never as blatant as George Wallace or Lester Maddox, but he delivered a clear message that was hard to miss. Nixon always couched his views in such a way that a citizen could avoid admitting to himself that he was attracted by a racist appeal. There were plausible reasons to be against open housing that had nothing to do with the fact that most public-housing-project dwellers are black. Busing is bad because it wastes education money, not because it mixes the races.

"Do they understand my position?" Nixon kept wondering. He was certain he'd set the correct line on racial issues, and he knew it should attract wide support, but did it? The polls were not reassuring.

So we issued several major policy papers, some delivered on television by the President himself. The seminal policy statement—on school desegregation—was laid down in March of 1970. A statement issued on public housing came as a result of sharp differences between George Romney at HUD and some of us at the White House and at Justice over the Federal role in dictating land use within a city or county. Another major policy paper settled the question of the tax status of private schools that engaged in racial discrimination.

These were major announcements which attracted enormous press attention and comment. They hardly complied with the doctrine of the low profile. But Nixon was convinced he would suffer politically—with the voter and in the Congress—unless his position was "perfectly clear."

I welcomed the occasion of these pronouncements for several reasons. They engaged the President totally for a few days. The process of setting down on paper exactly what he wanted his policy to be resulted in his permanent abandonment of some extravagant and imprecise Presidential rhetoric with which I would otherwise have had to live.

All the ideological factions of the White House staff came creeping out of the bushes at a time like that. We encouraged everyone to contribute—on paper—and all the views were considered and tabulated. For example, the "option paper" on tax exemption for white-flight private schools that Peter Flanigan put together for the President described three possible options and noted who had recommended which one. In response, Nixon asked why Bryce Harlow was for No. 3 and not

No. 1. Harlow was thought to be opposed to desegregation in all its aspects. Yet No. 3 proposed tough treatment for discriminatory schools. So Harlow wrote a paper on the politics of the issue that supported the choice of No. 3, the option Nixon ultimately selected. (It resulted in a statement flatly denying tax exemption where any discrimination occurred.)

These opportunities to air pent-up opinions were good for the White House staff. From Len Garment and Ray Price clear across the spectrum to Harry Dent and Pat Buchanan there was a healthy, vigorous, good-spirited argument which persisted until Richard Nixon signaled that he'd made his final decisions.

And these major statements helped George Shultz and me in our dealings with the Cabinet and their department people. When policy was murky or in dispute there was room for defiance. Highly visible Presidential policy declarations made compliance by Government employees easier to require. But we rarely achieved such visibility except on the passion issues: race, abortion and the war.

In meetings with Bob Finch, John Mitchell, Bryce Harlow and the rest of us, the President clearly spelled out his racial policies. He insisted that the Government's civil rights enforcers moderate their zeal. Nixon was constantly vigilant for news of some appointee's undue enthusiasm. When James Allen, Bob Finch's Commissioner of Education, made news in advocating more stringent enforcement in school desegregation, he was fired.

Leon Panetta of California had become Robert Finch's civil rights enforcer in the first batch of HEW appointees. And at once, Panetta became a symbol for Richard Nixon of all that was wrong with HEW and Finch's management of it. Almost daily the President's news summary contained a new story of HEW's interference with some city, state or businessman, and with increasing frequency, Leon Panetta and his civil rights lawyers were the instigators.

Nixon thought himself to be, in his own words, "one of the greatest desegregators" of schools in the country. (And in fact, he was.) But he wanted it done his way, with conciliation and understanding and not in a fashion that would abrade the political sensibilities of Southerners and conservatives.

Both Attorney General Mitchell and Secretary Finch had been giving interviews and making speeches about the deadlines to be imposed on Southern school districts to end segregation. Mitchell had been saying the deadlines were flexible,

Witness to Power

The inset is the staff badge at the 1968 convention, intended
to keep sinister spies from our control center. That pile of
baggage on Park Avenue in New York City was because my
baggage truck didn't show up. See how patiently and
calmly the Tour Manager deals with the crisis as takeoff

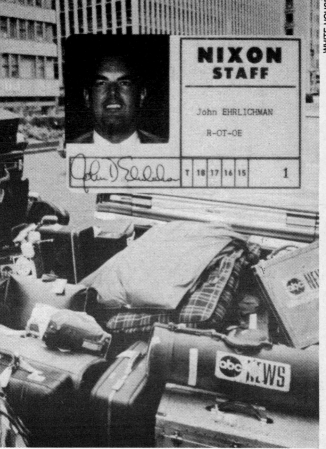

time approaches! The 1968 campaign usually ran on time and rarely lost a bag (thanks to David Shields, who knew every suitcase by its first name). And, incidentally, Nixon won the election.

REPUBLICAN EXECUTIVE COMMITTEE OF ALLEGHENY COUNTY

The Richard Nixons
are coming to Pittsburgh
Saturday, September 7

★ ★ ★

**Come one, come all
and greet the Nixons at
the Greater Pittsburgh Airport
4:30 p. m., Gate 16**

REPUBLICAN EXECUTIVE COMMITTEE OF ALLEGHENY COUNTY
Elsie H. Hillman, Chairman

A typical handbill, distributed by the thousands, used along with ads, loudspeaker trucks and massive busing to ensure that overflow crowds appeared on the television news that night. Usually it worked.

```
F-13
5-14
3-15                    966-9353

    ① List of musts who must be
      mentioned & intro'd -  To RN
         by RN                CARDS

    ② Costumes ➡
             Down front

    ③ Never let RN appear to be
       late.

    ④ Be ready to stop when
       we arrive -
      ➤ Break thru crowd from
         the BACK (secret)

        (Crowd slow)

    ➤ Steps on crowd side w/ Pds -

Gibson
```

My notes of Nixon's instructions for a campaign rally.

```
WEDNESDAY 9-18-68  ④

8:00  RN departs
        To Cardinal
        McIntyre (:15)
8:15  baggage
8:15  Arrive
9:00  staff bus
9:30  Depart (:30)

10:00 - Arrive Airport
10:20 - Takeoff (:45)

11:05  Arrive Fresno
Bob Baker          Greeting
Bruce Jackson        Comm

11:20  Depart airport
11:40 - Arrive Del Webb
          Farmers for Nixon
12:10  Depart
```

California campaigning in 1968. In Fresno, Nixon got royally heckled by Chicano workers who weren't farmers for Nixon, and I got bawled out afterward. I was supposed to figure out how to prevent that sort of thing. Usually I couldn't.

Nixon stumps; when the Secret Service knew of death threats, that rostrum was filled with sandbags.

The 1969 inaugural. See the soldier, the policeman and the cameraman, lower left? My seat was behind them and the big pillar. I kept asking them to move so we could see Nixon sworn in, but they wouldn't.

The White House staff assembles in the East Room after the January 1973 inaugural to hear the President's plans for his second term (from Bob Haldeman, George Shultz and me). They are sitting on those spindly chairs which break with a loud snap if you lean back in them. For the sake of the Union, those chairs should be replaced. But they are protected by a Committee.

The senior staff gathers in the Roosevelt Room in the West Wing (with several guests) to have its picture taken: Rumsfeld, Haldeman, Shultz, Ziegler, Kissinger, Flannigan, Ehrlichman (looking serious and seriously overweight), Colson and MacGregor.

Aboard *Air Force One,* Haldeman gives me the word. Usually I sat across the aisle from Haldeman, sharing a worktable with Henry Kissinger.

In the Oval Office (taking notes). That ostentatious carpet was installed by the Nixons. It was bright blue and yellow; I always thought it made the room a trifle busy, but no one asked me.

So where is the President? Here I am in my ice cream suit, all ready to go. His San Clemente house was beyond the wall; our offices were off to the left, toward the ocean. The fellow holding the phone was one of Mel Laird's Signal Corps soldiers.

King Timahoe, Richard Nixon and I stroll the south grounds of the White House. The President has decided to mount an "incursion" of Cambodia, and he is telling me that for about two weeks he will be unavailable to deal with domestic problems. He intends to supervise the Cambodian operation personally, hour by hour, and I will have to make the domestic decisions for him until our troops withdraw from Cambodia. But the Kent State shootings and other protests made it impossible for him to focus on Cambodia alone.

A post-election meeting in November 1970 in the seldom-used office at Key Biscayne, Florida. From left, clockwise: Nixon, Rumsfeld, Mitchell, the author, Colson, Harlow, Haldeman and Finch. Nixon described a major Cabinet shuffle, but in this photo Harlow is saying he doesn't want to be Chairman of the Republican National Committee, thank you.

Tom Brokaw (left, doing Lamaze exercises) almost got Dan Rather's job; I made it impossible for CBS to fire Rather (but he's never thanked me).

UPI

UPI

TOP: Richard Nixon was Bob Finch's mentor; here they are playing Simon Says: Hands on Hips.

BELOW: Simon Says: Hands in Pockets. Finch wasn't as good at following Nixon's civil rights policy, though, and that led to Finch's moving from HEW to the White House.

Kent State students met with Richard Nixon in the Oval Office about twenty-four hours after the shootings on their campus. Ron Ziegler and their Congressman and I watched as the young men and Richard Nixon drank coffee and

looked at each other. The students had been passionate and articulate in my office, but the panoply and Richard Nixon caused them to "tie"; that happened often when citizens came to see the President.

Martha and John Mitchell arrive at the White House. Martha used to call me to complain about the way Mrs. Nixon and the Cabinet wives frustrated her attempts to organize projects for them all to do. Why she called me I don't know; maybe she was calling everyone.

John B. Connally, Richard Nixon's chosen successor, whose political career surely was blighted by his association with Nixon. As a Democrat he might have been President; I think he'd have been a good one.

George Romney, Secretary of Housing and Urban Development, who in 1972 deeply resented being sent to Wilkes-Barre, Pennsylvania, to unsnarl flood-relief efforts. Romney's wife wrote me a note asking that the President treat George better, but Nixon decided to fire him instead. After the 1972 Republican Convention, Nixon told him to leave, but Romney stayed until after the 1972 election.

UPI

Walter Hickel, Secretary of the Interior, was also fired by Nixon, but he didn't try to stay around. Nixon had decided to replace Hickel months before Hickel wrote a letter critical of Nixon's attitude toward young Vietnam war protesters. The letter actually prolonged Hickel's tenure, since Nixon didn't want it to appear that the Vietnam issue had caused him to fire Hickel.

UPI

Henry Kissinger and his young deputy, Colonel Al Haig. Henry and the President took some pleasure in advancing Haig in rank, over more senior officers. In five years Haig became a full general while working at the White House. Haig had also been an aide to General Douglas MacArthur and (in LBJ's White House) to Joseph Califano. His father-in-law was a general, too.

J. Edgar Hoover and his house. The President, John Mitchell and I went to dinner at Hoover's house in 1969. I suspect he had the same interior decorator as the Munster family.

Donald Nixon, the President's brother. Somehow I was put in charge of keeping Don out of trouble.

I did a better job at that, it would appear, than at keeping myself out of difficulty.

Spiro Agnew never seemed this sinister in real life. He smiled easily, always sat up straight and made little jokes in a high, sing-song voice. But he hated hard domestic-policy work, and he didn't like the President to tell him what to do.

"Do you think Agnew is insubordinate?" Nixon once asked me.

Ten photographers sat on the floor at the Senate Watergate hearings, their fingers on their shutter buttons, waiting for the witness to scratch his nose, shed tears or look ugly. I more than obliged them. Over the years, countless photo editors have used this one to illustrate what an arrogant and unpleasant fellow I am. I can't recall what I was reacting to; probably Sam Ervin's acting.

UPI

All through the Watergate cover-up trial I sketched and took notes. This is an early effort—John Sirica on the opening day of jury selection. Later we moved to a smaller courtroom with fewer microphones and judges' chairs.

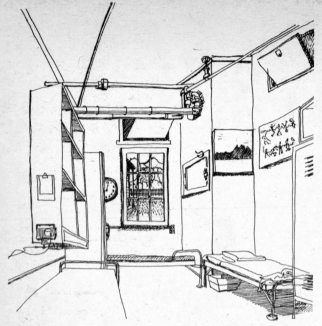

In a prison in Arizona I continued to paint and sketch. This is the little room I shared with two other inmates. The only windows were very high on the walls, so I painted that "window" at the far end to give us a view.

When I entered jail I had to shave the full beard I had grown when I moved to New Mexico. Then the Federal prison people changed the rules (they do keep changing their regulations a lot—it makes jobs for otherwise unemployable penologists), and I restored the mustache.

An Oliphant cartoon (c. 1969) which is one of my favorites. That's me, upper right, witnessing all those powerful fellows around Nixon.

At work at home in Santa Fe. The recording gear on the left was for a daily radio commentary I did for a couple of years for one of the networks. Our house, an adobe on a hill, overlooks the city, to the west. It has no square corners.

depending on local conditions. The Attorney General was also sending signals (doubtless inspired by the President) that the guidelines would be relaxed. It was never easy to tell exactly where Finch stood, but it was clear enough that he disagreed with Mitchell.

Almost from the beginning Finch's performance at HEW had been controversial. The American Medical Association opposed Finch's choice, Dr. John Knowles, for the post of Assistant Secretary of HEW for Health. All through that first summer (1969) Finch postponed sending Knowles's name to the President because he well knew Nixon would not ratify his choice of Knowles as long as the AMA objected. But the longer Finch delayed telling Knowles and the HEW hierarchy that he couldn't sell the nomination to the President, the greater grew the conflicting pressures. Meanwhile (and more than incidentally associated with Finch's loss in the Knowles fight), the President was moving closer to those friends and allies who wanted him to do something to stop HEW's zealous enforcement of school desegregation in the South.

As divergences of policy between Mitchell and Finch showed up in Nixon's news summaries, Nixon became increasingly disturbed. Bryce Harlow began conveying to Nixon the protests of powerful Southern committee chairmen in the Senate and House. In response Nixon demanded that Finch's people "get in line with Administration policy."

Harlow and I delivered the President's message to Leon Panetta at lunch one day at the White House. We tried to make clear to him that the President valued Bob Finch's advice and counsel when decisions were in a formative stage. But once the President reached a decision—which often was made up of considerations much broader than those HEW had weighed—then Finch and all his people were expected to support that decision. Panetta listened, but we didn't convince him.

In early July the Mitchell–Finch inconsistencies on guidelines and deadlines were resolved in a jointly prepared Presidential statement. Predictably, Mitchell won and Finch lost. Almost at once we heard that Leon Panetta was all over town undercutting the manifesto, leaking his unhappiness to the press and to Congressmen and their staffs.

The President was made well aware of Panetta's maneuvers. Bryce Harlow lost no opportunity to inform Nixon of the antagonism Finch's people were creating in the Congress and in the school districts of the South. Mitchell could send Nixon inside information from Finch's department because one of his good friends and ideological confederates was Robert Mardian, then the General Counsel at HEW. The President knew Leon Panetta's travel plans before Panetta's wife did, thanks to Bryce Harlow's Congressional pipelines. More than once I was given instructions to "tell Finch to keep that goddamned Panetta out of Atlanta" or some other Congressman's district.

On February 4, 1970, the President ran out of patience. He realized and finally admitted to himself that Bob Finch was in deep trouble; any other Cabinet Secretary would have felt the lash, but with increasing frequency Nixon was referring to Finch in our conversations as "poor Bob." Finch was being asked to do more than he was capable of doing, Nixon realized, and he blamed himself for putting his old friend in that predicament.

At last Nixon abruptly announced, during one of our routine meetings: "I accept Panetta's resignation." Leon Panetta had not resigned, of course, but Nixon was hearing more and more protests from Congressmen who were old friends and allies, men like Otto Passman of Louisiana, who came in to show the President a photograph of his "little golden-haired granddaughter" who was "bein' bused right past her neighborhood school," clear across town to a formerly all-black school. Nixon talked about Passman's granddaughter for days after that visit; she symbolized for him everything that was wrong with busing.

And Panetta symbolized the bureaucrat-ideologue who persisted in rubbing people's noses in a social mess that wasn't their fault. "In these race matters," Nixon explained to me, "one strong action is better than a lot of words. Firing Panetta is worth dozens of speeches and statements about integrating the schools."

I called Finch and reported that Panetta's resignation had been accepted. Bob laughed hollowly. "What now? What turned the Old Man on this morning?" There followed what Haldeman and I had come to refer to as "a finch"—a superwaffling, an evasion of such exquisite refinement that it could only be the result of genetic selection and a lifetime of practice. Finch finched.

But in this case Richard Nixon refused to be finched; as far as he was concerned, he had performed a symbolic act. Panetta was gone, and the only remaining question was who could replace him and be trusted to run the Office of Civil Rights as the President wanted it run. He telephoned me on February 12 to give me his specifications: he was looking for someone "tough and strong. Bill Casey would be okay for it; he's smart, strong and tough. We need such a person for Bob Finch's sake," Nixon explained: "I don't want Bob to look bad." Whoever replaced Panetta had to be good enough to keep Finch out of trouble.

Panetta left with a splash of accusation. He told the press that Haldeman, Harlow and I opposed civil rights for minorities and were out to get him personally. In fact, Panetta's problem was a little more basic: he refused to conform to the President's policies, and the President was out to get him.

On July 28, 1970, Bob Haldeman and I were at San Clemente with Nixon and the crisis of the moment was court-ordered school desegregation in Texas.

"Our people have got to quit bragging about school desegregation," Nixon demanded. "We do what the law requires—nothing more. This is politics, and I'm the judge of the politics of schools; believe me, all this bragging doesn't help. It doesn't cool the blacks. We'll just quietly do our job. Only Mitchell and [the new Secretary at HEW, Elliot] Richardson should be talking about schools, and they must not—they *will* not—be sucked into praising 'our great record.'"

Then Nixon decided to "lay out the line" on school desegregation for us, once more and finally:

- We carry out the law, and no more.
- We cooperate with local officials; we don't coerce them.
- Federal enforcers will not be sent into the South.
- Southerners will not be treated as second-class citizens.
- The school-desegregation problem will not be treated on a regional basis. It's a national problem.
- All Administration people who discuss the school problem must say flatly that we oppose busing; otherwise they will be fired. They must hit it squarely.

"Always remember," the President added: "on this subject a low profile is the key."

With all of that, Nixon personally involved himself in dozens of race-related meetings and projects.

The most disastrous meeting was one staged by Daniel P. Moynihan in the spring of the first year, 1969. In the Cabinet Room, Pat gathered Martin Luther King's putative successor, Dr. Ralph Abernathy; Dr. George Wiley, the welfare guru, and other black "leaders" from around the country. The plan was for Nixon and Moynihan to listen to constructive proposals for new approaches to minority problems.

Instead, Nixon was berated by his grandstanding guests until he finally stopped the harangue in disgust. He then delivered a short, grim sermon on the country's priorities as he saw them, with emphasis on foreign policy and ending the war.

Then, furious, Nixon got up and left the room. Moynihan did his best to salvage something, but predictably, Abernathy and the others went out and told the waiting press corps that the President didn't care about poor black folks.

For the next four years anyone who suggested that the President meet with a group of blacks could expect to hear about Moynihan's meeting with Ralph Abernathy and the leaders. "That was," Nixon would say, "one of my major mistakes in the first year."

Nineteen-seventy was our big year for race problems. A series of court decisions fell on North Carolina, Georgia, Texas and Virginia and even on a few Northern school districts. Almost every month the President called in the Attorney General and the Secretary of HEW for instructions to try to keep the departments from getting out ahead of him.

Nixon thought that Secretary of Labor George Shultz had shown great style in constructing a political dilemma for the labor union leaders and civil rights groups. Shultz persuaded Nixon to declare himself in favor of "the Philadelphia Plan," which required the unions to set goals for the admission of minority workers to unions when the union's members were on a Government job. The NAACP wanted a tougher requirement; the unions hated the whole thing. Before long, the AFL-CIO and the NAACP were locked in combat over one of the passionate issues of the day and the Nixon Administration was located in the sweet and reasonable middle.

After that, Shultz was just naturally invited in to help out with school desegregation. In fact, at one time or another almost everyone was in on it. Spiro Agnew was the titular head of a Cabinet committee on school desegregation. That committee's staff was led by Robert Mardian and Ed Morgan. Since Agnew was so exceedingly hard to work with, the committee staff soon was taking most of its orders from George Shultz. Bryce Harlow, Len Garment and Ray Price contributed substantially to the President's deliberations. But Bob Brown, the President's "liaison with the black community," was not included in most of the President's meetings; Nixon found it hard to talk freely with Brown around. Brown, of course, was black.

"We have good blacks working in this Administration," Nixon said to Mitchell, Shultz, Finch and me one February day in 1970. We'd been called to the yellow oval room on the family floor of The Residence to chew over the problem of schools once again.

"Bill Rogers is taking three of his black staff people to Africa with him," Finch said.

Nixon nodded. *"I'd* take one," he said earnestly.

Mississippi had just been hit with court orders. So had Georgia. The President was getting phone calls from Senator John Stennis and other Congressional allies. "John," Nixon said to Mitchell, "can we get these court orders to be more reasonable?"

In a long, rambling answer, Mitchell said no.

"You know," Nixon said, "in November, all the Democratic Congressional candidates are going to run against HEW and all the Republican candidates will run against the courts. Unfortunately, the average voter doesn't distinguish between the courts and the Administration. We're all the Government."

We talked about what we could do to ease the schools' transition. There was $200 million to improve school facilities. We could help with teacher training. With a few exceptions we were looking at Southern states; how about some tough enforcement in the North?

"No," Nixon instructed, "don't sue in the North. Try to get more time for Mississippi, Georgia, Alabama, Louisiana, Florida, South Carolina, Arkansas, Texas, Virginia and North Carolina. Let's explain the situation to Southern editors, business people, teachers and ministers."

George Shultz urged formation of groups of black and white citizens in the affected states to mediate the desegregation. He mentioned a recent memo by Pat Moynihan arguing that blacks were more antiwhite because they were now more affluent and better educated. "I doubt it," Shultz said drily.

Finch thought our worst year was behind us: "There have been changes."

Shultz nodded. "We've made some headway. Now we need small state committees. We need to give them a one-or-two-page statement of our goals. And we've got to keep saying to them, 'We care; we're with you.' And we've got to go there and be on TV and show them by what we do."

An article by Alexander Bickel argued that true desegregation would come only with fundamental economic equality among the races. "He says busing can't change the facts of life," Nixon paraphrased. "I have a hunch a lot of sensible people feel segregation is a bad thing but they feel busing to a different neighborhood school will do more harm to everyone. It's physically hard on the kids and it tears up the neighborhood."

Who should be speaking about school desegregation for the President? "That's tricky," Nixon said. "Agnew wants to. I'd rather have Finch and Shultz stepping up to busing than Agnew. Or I'll do it, rather than Agnew. Agnew can go too far, with a McCarthyite tinge."

Near the end of the summer of 1970, Agnew was included in one of the school-strategy meetings along with Finch and his successor, Elliot Richardson; Bryce Harlow; Len Garment; Treasury Secretary David Kennedy and Bob Haldeman.

Haldeman and I were sitting on the fireplace couches in the Oval Office listening. Mitchell, Agnew and Kennedy sat close to the President's desk. Harlow sat between Richardson and Finch to Nixon's right, Garment and Shultz to his left. Navy stewards came and went with coffee and soft drinks. We were treated to a long Nixonian monologue at the outset.

"There are no votes in the desegregation of Southern schools," Nixon declared. "It's a Washington issue. The NAACP would say my rhetoric was poor even if I gave the Sermon on the Mount. But I'm a firm believer that the law should and must be carried out. It is in our political interest to put the issue behind us now. If there are to be confrontations let's have them in 1970, not 1972. It's my philosophy that it's best to go with a low profile—I don't believe in kicking the South around; we'll do the job swiftly and fairly. Let Fritz Mondale be for busing—I'm not. We'll carry out the law. If there is *de facto* segregation, we'll tackle it as, if and when the Supreme Court rules on it. We'll have a low, effective profile; we won't brag or try to make political points from desegregation. Our enemies will attack us for not doing more. They want to hurt us—get us to hurt ourselves—by making more out of it. Remember: jobs are more important to Negroes than anything else."

On the subject of white-flight private schools, the President said: "The IRS shouldn't try to make cases or force the issue [of tax exemption]. I don't want the IRS rushing around. Let the policy be that if blacks apply to those schools they can be admitted.

"I want the public schools to be fair, but an artificial, forced integration on a quota basis is wrong. Kenneth Coleman has the other view; let him."

The Treasury Secretary assured the President he had the IRS under control. "Some regional directors might want to embarrass us, so I've pulled all the decision-making [on tax exemptions for private schools] into the Washington office."

Finch warned of future problems with new court orders.

"Bob," Nixon said, "I'm concerned about HEW's people rushing around the South. That's the wrong way to do it; we must wait and act on complaints. The people are going through an agony down there and we shouldn't make it worse for them; we've got to help them. I'm convinced that these high-profile, overly aggressive Federal actions can only worsen the situation. You people must keep your wild young horses in hand."

"Like Jerry Leonard [the Assistant Attorney General for Civil Rights]," Mitchell said helplessly. "I could wring his neck. He's got a hundred U.S. marshals out. Local public officials ought to be handling the situation."

"Local Federal officials want to make announcements all the time," Finch added. "Instead of just doing something, they want to issue a statement. There are code words they like to use, like 'monitor' and 'quota' and 'guidelines.' "

"Don't use the word 'guidelines' anymore," Nixon ordered.

"We're going through a profound social change," George Shultz said. "A lot is going to happen in a short while. To avoid an explosion is a management problem. We need small state and local groups running it. And we need to be well prepared here. The Southern Republican politicians may be our biggest problem. How do you communicate with them?"

Mitchell smiled his little smile. "Well, Strom Thurmond has desegregated more schools than HEW and Justice put together, but he has to deny it to survive. They have to take us on, and we just can't afford to react. Likewise, we've got to let the local law-enforcement people handle any flare-ups. Our marshals and FBI must not enforce the law."

Now Nixon was talking for the benefit of Elliot Richardson: "Attitude is very important; we aren't going to send some little snob down there [to the South] to say, 'Now, you shape up.' People have pride; they don't want to be thought of as racist. George Romney found out in Warren [Michigan] that there's as much racism in the North as in the South—they're as tough on blacks as they are in Jackson, Mississippi, or more so. So we just carry out the law. We don't insult people or create explosive situations. There is to be one standard, North and South. This problem is not limited to the South."

No one was going to be allowed to miss the point that day.

"I don't want a young attorney going down there being a big hero kicking a school superintendent around; that is not to be done. I'll not have such a pipsqueak, snot-nosed attitude from the bowels of HEW.

"Just remember, attitude is everything. The South is primitive, but in Harlem they are worse off. Let it permeate the bureaucracy: we are going to avoid an explosion. We may not avoid it, but our chances are improved by a low profile. Be helpful. Don't show superiority. . . . Big speeches won't do any good. There's already too much demagoguing."

Bryce Harlow chimed in to throw a little fuel on the fire: "Unfortunately, down South the government people are not doing what the President is saying here today."

Richardson was defensive. His HEW regional directors were Southerners; he'd seen to that. And the volume of busing was declining as desegregation took hold. There would be new money for education in the South.

Richardson's optimism provoked Spiro Agnew: "Some people are unrealistic. They view things in a sanitized atmosphere. The South is a powder keg. There is great danger there. I can't share [Richardson's] optimism. The South feels—rightly—that it's not being treated with an even hand. Pontificating 'opinion makers' are creating great resentment there. They are certainly not solving the problems of the Northern ghettos, and they are distorting the situation in the South. We've had two decades of such hypocrisy, and I'm very pessimistic about the situation. I think we're in deep trouble. We've got to start listening to the Southern politicians who are on our side, rather than to the bureaucrats in the machinery here in Washington."

Nixon closed the meeting with marching orders for everyone, but particularly for Elliot Richardson and John Mitchell:

—Do only what the law requires, not one thing more.
—Do nothing to the South that is not done to the North.
—When in doubt, call segregation *de facto,* not *de jure.*
—The eager beavers would like to screw us—the little pipsqueaks in the bureaucracy. Elliot and John, don't let them do it.
—Don't play to the galleries; keep discipline.
—Enlist the Southern politicians to help us.
—Don't invite the South's agony to the North just to be doing something. Insist on the same ratios, both North and South.
—Don't confuse integration and desegregation. There is separation in the all-black colleges, for example.

—Spend the money on the teachers—on education.

—Don't go looking for trouble.

Typically, Spiro Agnew introduced a prickly, rhetorical *non sequitur* just as everyone was ready to get up and leave: "How can we logically distinguish between racial discrimination and other forms of discrimination?" he asked. "People have different IQs, talents and other legacies. They are given different grades in school, aren't they?"

Symbolically, on July 23, 1970, *The Washington Post* published a picture of a yellow school bus on fire, black smoke pouring from its windows while firemen sprayed it with water. The caption read:

COUNCIL SESSION. The new Domestic Council met yesterday. Seated around the table from the left are: Secretary of Labor James Hodgson; Postmaster General Winston M. Blount; Advisers; the President; Caspar W. Weinberger, deputy director of the Office of Management and Budget; Secretary of Agriculture Clifford M. Hardin; Secretary of Housing and Urban Development George W. Romney; Bryce N. Harlow, counselor to the President, and John D. Ehrlichman, Assistant to the President for Domestic Affairs.

Busing was a virulent issue much of the time. The Federal courts were ordering the busing of white kids and black kids, and Richard Nixon wanted every one of their parents to know that he opposed it. My staff was trying to keep the Civil Rights Division at the Department of Justice under control and to keep the HEW zealots in step with the President. Delicate negotiations with Michigan's state officials were under way as we tried to work out a way to deal with judicial decisions ordering busing in and around Detroit. Unknown to me, one of Charles Colson's people was sent to make inflammatory antibusing speeches in Michigan, to the great distress of the local officials.

I called Bob Haldeman to find out why one of his staff members, Mike Balzano, was up in Michigan stirring up trouble. He made clear what I had already guessed: that Balzano was working for Colson. When I called Colson, he said he was operating in Michigan on the President's instructions. If I didn't like it, then I didn't understand what was good for Richard Nixon.

That afternoon I asked the President what he knew about Colson's man in Michigan.

"Oh—I don't know about that fellow," Nixon lied.

"You didn't send him up there?" I asked.

"No. Chuck [Colson] and I have talked a good deal about busing. But not specifically about Balzano going to Michigan."

"Do you want to tell Colson to pull him out of there, or shall I?" I asked.

"Oh, you can, if you want," Nixon said casually.

By the time I called Colson, Nixon had already talked to him. Balzano was out of Michigan before dark.*

The President was ambivalent about keeping a low profile on school desegregation. At times he made highly publicized appearances to ensure that people understood the President's position. When a Federal judge ordered Detroit to begin that huge exchange of students between the core city and suburbs, I was sent to meet with Governor William Milliken and have a press conference.

I went to Lansing with Ed Morgan and the Deputy Attorney General, met with the Governor and made the Michigan voters very much aware of the President's position on busing. (Then I went on to California to the wedding of my brilliant young staff secretary, John Campbell, to Bud Krogh's secretary, Jane Dart.)

Nineteen-seventy was the year George Shultz launched the biracial citizen committees in Southern states to ease the desegregation transition. We persuaded the President to attend the first session of the Louisiana committee, in a hotel in New Orleans' French Quarter.

When we were planning the meeting, Shultz proposed that the press be permitted in to photograph the President with the committee. Reluctantly, Nixon consented: "Well," he sighed, "it will be politically harmful, but it will help the schools, so we'll do it."

After the meeting, it was agreed, John Mitchell, Elliot Richardson and George Shultz would brief the press and the President would appear to make a brief prepared statement. "But I will not answer questions," Nixon declared, "and you must tell Elliot Richardson that he is not to make a headline. They are all to make no news."

Inevitably, the multiracial meeting with the President made news and then some. It was page one all over the country. The South was peacefully accomplishing a most profound social

---

* In listening to the Watergate tapes, I discovered a similar Nixon-Colson episode, involving clemency, that was far more serious than Michigan busing. See pp. 323–24.

change and Richard Nixon was there, helping Southerners to meet the demands of court orders with which he disagreed.

In fact, Nixon well knew that it was a big news story and that he was on the right side of the moral issue, but part of him hated every minute of it. His political compass told him to stay away from the whole subject of race. And if he could not stay out of it, the best political position was on the side of the white parents whose children were about to get on those hated buses.

In November 1970, running through his political rosary for me on the telephone from Camp David, the President ticked off what he wanted from the Domestic Council in the two years until the 1972 election. We could do things with labor, youth, the Catholics and even the Jews ("We won't get many, but don't write them off. We'll get most of the intelligent ones. Watch them play me off against the State Department [on Israel]").

He said he was aware we had only a "small chance of a breakthrough with the Negroes." But I was to convene Moynihan, Rumsfeld, Finch, Richardson and Shultz to plan a strategy to woo blacks. "Continue to pay attention to them," Nixon continued. "Do what is right. Keep some of them around. Let's help the Negro colleges. If we don't alienate them like Goldwater did, we should get about twenty percent of their vote."

In the summer of 1972, ninety days before the election, the Justice Department enraged Richard Nixon by filing or threatening to file civil rights cases against the cities of Los Angeles, Chicago, Boston and Birmingham.

Once again I was told to rebuke the Attorney General. Our telephone call went like this:

Text of a conversation with Attorney General Kleindienst, August 10, 1972

K KLEINDIENST
E EHRLICHMAN

E Good morning, General. Say, I'm told that you hauled off and sued Los Angeles and some place else for discriminating in hiring practices.

K Let me tell you about this, Johnnie. About six weeks or two months ago, just to get it all cleared out of the way before the summer wars came in, as a result of an investigation in one city on discrimination down in Birmingham on the hiring of firemen, I authorized some pilot complaints in four cities—Birmingham, Chicago, Los Angeles and Boston—to show that we weren't picking on the South on this problem, that it was a nationwide problem. They were all scheduled to go about a month ago at one time—you know, negotiation, etcetera. Then our United States Attorney down in Birmingham pulled a goddamn gun on it and filed his all by himself. We were in the process of negotiating out a settlement with Los Angeles and with Chicago without the necessity of filing a complaint. When they saw the goddamn complaint filed in Birmingham—which was a breach of discipline, really, down there—the negotiations just ceased in Chicago and Los Angeles. However, the violations were there. So I'm stuck with the goddamn program in the four cities.

E Why are you?

K Well, number one, because I set it in motion as a result of investigations of discrimination. They came up in a routine way. I'd authorized it six weeks ago.

E Well, the reason that I found out about it, other than just reading the news summary, is that Sam Yorty [the mayor of Los Angeles] called yesterday and pulled out of Democrats for Nixon.

K Jesus Christ. We had that one all negotiated out.

E Well, he's very, very upset because he felt that this was a lack of good faith and so on and so forth, and it's very embarrassing to him, so Connally heard from him and told the President, and so on and so forth.

K In Los Angeles the attorneys and the people with whom we are negotiating agreed. We had it worked out. And the City Council turned the goddamn thing down, you know, against the recommendations of their attorneys and everything else.

E How's chances for settling it?

K We had it settled.

E I know.

K The Council rejected it.

E Can you settle it now?

K I don't know.

E That's the President's desire.

K Sure—and the way I was hoping to handle it, you know, was to have settlement negotiations, until this jerk down in Birmingham filed the suit. Then I said to myself I'd hate like hell to get stuck as long as he did that.

E With just the South?

K Just picking out the South to avoid the criticism that we are just picking on Birmingham, Alabama, and incur the wrath of the South.

E What other cities have been sued?

K We are on the verge of filing a complaint in Chicago.

E Don't.

K And then we are talking, we're having our preliminary negotiations, in Boston, so that I had a—

E That I don't care about.

K Yeah.

E But Chicago, don't for now.

K Even though we're stuck with it in Los Angeles and Birmingham?

E Well, can you unstick Los Angeles somehow?

K I don't know. If they haven't filed a complaint I can, John.

E Find out, would you?

K If they filed a complaint then I can go back and try to negotiate. . . .

E Why don't you call the Mayor?

K Yorty?

E Yeah.

K I've never met that son-of-a-bitch. I'd be happy to.

E He's a wild man, and he's particularly wild today and yesterday.

K Yeah, I'm sure he would be.

E But see what you can do on that.

K I agree. It's a knotty goddamn problem.

E On those kinds of things, the more early warnings you can give us on something like that, the better. God, this thing just hit us after the fact like a thunderbolt.

K Just as a result of a precipitous action.

E Yeah, but I mean, for instance, filing against L.A.! Now, there you've got a key state and you know you're going to raise somebody's hackles. Let us know over here a day or two ahead if something like that has to be done.

K Okay. Thanks.

The President had expected Kleindienst to delay all such investigations—not to mention the lawsuits—until after the election. But Kleindienst allowed the investigations to go ahead, and demonstrably and foreseeably lost control of the litigation at the worst possible time. One or two episodes like that and Nixon lost confidence in someone like Kleindienst. After this episode it was only Mitchell's intervention that kept Kleindienst from being fired right after the election.

In November 1972 we began restaffing the Executive Branch, and the President wanted some blacks in prominent positions. In the first four years a number of talented blacks had served him well, but many of them were leaving for good jobs in industry and as consultants.

Sally Ann Payton, on my staff, was—in Nixon's words—"on the court track." He proposed that she be moved to a lawyer's job in one of the agencies until there was an opening on a Court of Appeals to which he could appoint her. Jewel La-Fontant of Chicago was destined for the Supreme Court. Fred Pearce could be the chairman of a commission.

The next Supreme Court vacancies would be filled with Catholics, women,* Southerners and blacks, Nixon told me. "Tell Burger," Nixon said, "to nudge Douglas and Marshall."

---

* But for sure, the nominee would not have been Rita Hauser. One morning in August 1970 the President saw an account of a comment by Miss Hauser, one of Nixon's longtime Jewish women supporters in New York City. Rita was an able, attractive lawyer who had held several influential positions in Nixon campaigns. She was quoted as being of the opinion that there were no Constitutional impediments to persons of the same sex marrying.

"Did you read that?" Nixon asked me. "There goes a Supreme Court

We needed their seats. Had either of them resigned in 1973, I think it unlikely that Mrs. LaFontant would have been nominated. Nixon's allies in the impeachment fight in the Congress would have been given a strong voice in naming the replacement. But absent Watergate, I think a black woman would have been the next nominee.

As the new 1972 Cabinet Secretaries paraded to Camp David for their obligatory meeting and photographed handshakes, Nixon urged each one to hire blacks for subcabinet jobs. He wanted Hispanics, Poles and Italians in those jobs, too. But in spite of his exhortation, few were actually hired. The list of blacks who had supported Nixon's reelection was short, and he refused to approve a black who was not a Nixon supporter.

The President was skeptical that he'd ever be thanked for his efforts by the black community. Even those who did thank us did it privately. My new friend Vernon Jordan was happy to take the millions of dollars in Federal funds we pumped into his Urban League, but he explained that he'd lose his credibility with his constituency if he openly praised the Nixon Administration. Every now and then Vernon would call to say, "I just wanted to let you know I'm going to kick you fellows."

"Where and when?" I'd ask.

"I'm speaking to the Baptists. I'm going to hit you Tuesday on the EEOC [Equal Employment Opportunity Commission]."

"Okay. I'll tell the President. How's our program going?"

"Thanks for your help with the Labor Department. We're going to put together a fine vocational-training program."

"Good. Thanks for calling." And I'd warn the President that his Wednesday news summary would include Vernon Jordan's attack.

The 1972 election and landslide vote were followed by an austere budget which threatened most of our racial initiatives of the first term. I argued that those cuts put the President's previous sincerity into question, but that remark drew only a look of amusement from Richard Nixon. A great many domestic initiatives were stifled by Watergate, but minority pro-

Justice! I can't go *that* far; that's the year 2000! Negroes [and whites], okay. But *that's* too far!"

Rita Hauser never again appeared on Nixon's working lists for the Supreme Court.

grams would have suffocated in Nixon's second term without the scandal, I believe. Peter Goldman's analysis in the February 19, 1973, *Newsweek* is a fair description:

Still, political power in America remains ultimately white power, and the election just past was a chastening experience for blacks. . . . they exist at the margin of national politics, an 11 percent minority overwhelmingly committed to one political party. Their almost monolithic loyalty typed the Democrats as the party of the blacks in November. The identification didn't help—not with an electorate inflamed over busing, quotas and law-and-order. . . .

None of this was lost on the President; he exploited the black connection to split first the South and then the hard-hat vote away from the Democrats and into his new majority. It is one measure of America's mood, and Mr. Nixon's reading of it, that he has felt impelled to soft-pedal the genuine efforts that his Administration has made on behalf of the blacks. The Nixonians desegregated Southern schools with greater dispatch and fewer bruises than their Democratic predecessors had caused. They expanded government hiring of blacks. They vastly increased Federal aid to minority businesses, banks and colleges and Federal spending on civil-rights enforcement. For all the President's austere rhetoric about his new budget, he sustained some important social programs at present levels or better; even the War on Poverty survived almost intact, its components hidden away in other bureaucracies and other budgets.

But other programs were dropped, scaled down or folded into revenue-sharing with no requirement that state and city governments continue them. Model cities was pinched off in the new budget; so were funds for housing, emergency public-service jobs for the unemployed and community-action programs—a keystone of the anti-poverty effort. The President backed away from his own innovative welfare-reform program last year and has postponed resubmitting it, at least until spring. . . . And Mr. Nixon has stood down even from the distant promise of integration as an object of public policy outside the South. 'We do not attempt to create social dislocation,' says one White House staffer—a polite way of saying the government will not force the issue any longer.

The domestic issues that poured into the White House came in a vast tide which never ebbed. As I rode to work every morning I leafed through the President's overnight news summary, which digested what television news, the papers and the newsmagazines had said in the previous twenty-four hours. I'd try to predict the domestic problems the President, my staff and I would be dealing with during the coming day.

Edwin Harper, my assistant director for policy and planning, made longer-range (and more rational) predictions based on "action-forcing events." A housing law will expire next year. We will be called upon to recommend to the President whether it should be eliminated, renewed or modified. Now, a year ahead, we must begin to gather the facts, audit its results and identify the political and social elements that will be involved in the decision and its effects.

Literally hundreds of questions like that had to be asked every month. While orderly work of that kind went on, coping with issues of rail transportation, commerce, urban decay, Indians, highway policy, veterans' care, tax reform, food and drug purity and a thousand other subjects, our daily routine was almost routinely derailed by some crisis of the moment. The shootings at Kent State and their aftermath required weeks of my time. The shooting of George Wallace, Hurricane Agnes, a California earthquake and Don Nixon's involvement in the sale of prefabricated housing to the Marine Corps took me away from the orderly management of our policy process.

Ken Cole, my deputy, Tod Hullin and Jana Hruska smoothly kept things going when the President pushed my button and I was urgently summoned to his office.

Harper, John Whitaker, Ed Morgan, Lew Engman and the other assistant directors of the Domestic Council staff kept the regular business going with very few helpers, although they too were subject to being pulled off their projects to fulfill some assignment from the President on a crash basis.

When Congress was in session, the President sent it a message and a legislative package—proposed bills, information and statistical data—about every ten days. We sent packages on crime, housing, tax reform, banking, health care, water quality and dozens of other issues. Working groups of people from the departments and agencies of Government and outside experts were put together by our staff to prepare the data from which the President chose the proposals he would make to the Congress.

Timing was critical. A legislative package on education, for example, was preceded by briefings for the Congressional committees involved. Our lobbyists made sure the key staff people on the Hill were forewarned. Elaborate press conferences were held to try to secure some early media attention for the President's initiatives. Then many of us would see columnists and specialized journalists for lengthy interviews to explain why the President had made the decisions he did.

Sometimes we had to convince the Federal bureaucracy, too; their hearts and minds were seldom ours for the asking. I staged countless meetings to explain to Federal employees what the President was proposing and why. We even had briefings for the wives of Federal executives so that they would understand our welfare-reform bill, our new economic policies and why we were for revenue sharing. I made many trips to the regional headquarters around the country to make similar explanations to the regional directors of the departments and agencies.

The working groups and the Domestic Council staff exerted extraordinary care in preparing the "option papers" that went to the President. I reviewed each one before it went "in" to make certain it answered all the questions the President might have. Sometimes a group had worked so deeply into an issue that its paper made assumptions or skipped over basic data which seemed obvious or simplistic. One of my functions was to insist that it give us the whole picture. I'd return the paper with "Why?" written in the margins.

In areas of my specific delegation I chose the options for Nixon, usually telling him what I'd done as soon as we had a chance to talk. Often I drew upon general guidance I'd taken from him long before. One reason I constantly kept detailed notes of our talks was that I wanted a record of even his most casual policy discussions.

Richard Nixon's domestic achievements, as Mark Antony predicted, will probably be interred with his bones. But there are those who remember pension reform, clean air, clean water, urban parks, the Alaska Native Claims innovations, the land-use initiatives and dramatic increases in support for the arts and humanities.

We tried for a reform of the archaic welfare situation, but Congress refused to act. Our alarums about energy were disregarded, too. But inflation never reached 7 percent, and our biggest budget was about $300 billion. We worked hard to keep food prices down too, with some success. We tried in vain to get Congress to put a lid on spending and reorganize the Executive Branch, but had a part in the reform of the Congressional budget and appropriation process.

Perhaps someday someone will notice that all the aspects of Watergate required only the tiniest percentage of the time and attention of the President and his staff. Then he may wonder what else was going on in 1972, 1973 and the years that went before. There will be occasion then for an archeological disinterment of all the domestic staff's efforts and a rediscovery of Nixon's creditable domestic work.

CHAPTER FOURTEEN

Economic Policy

ARTHUR BURNS LEFT the Cabinet to be Chairman of the Board of the Federal Reserve System in the fall of 1969, at a time when the President was convinced the Fed's monetary policy was the key to the nation's economy. Nixon was determined to control the Fed while maintaining the image of its independence from all politicians, including himself. He went about as far as he could, lecturing—even scolding—Arthur Burns about what the Fed must do to free up the money supply. But when he was upset with the Fed, much of the President's spleen was vented on the White House staff instead of Burns. Burns was one of Nixon's political fathers; he was never in real danger of being dominated by the President, rhetoric to the contrary notwithstanding.

Arthur Burns was born in Austria in 1904. He had been an economics professor at Rutgers and Columbia and one of President Eisenhower's leading economic advisers; he and Richard Nixon had usually been allies in the economic debates that took place in the fifties in that Administration.

Some economists who advise Presidents are oblivious to political reality, but Arthur Burns was every bit as much a politician as he was an economist. Appropriately, I first met him in the midst of the 1968 political campaign, when Arthur was in charge of a small staff that provided the candidate and his writers with position papers and research on the issues of the day. (Among his researchers then was Martin Anderson, a quiet young Ph.D. who was eventually to become Ronald Reagan's domestic-policy assistant.)

After the 1968 election Burns organized dozens of citizen Task Forces to make recommendations to President-elect

Nixon for action to solve a myriad of national problems. Burns did a good job of bringing these experts together and amassing their ideas. Some of their work became the foundation for our most notable reforms and initiatives in Nixon's first four years as President.

Burns was designated Counselor to the President, with Cabinet rank, and in the first week after the election it was originally thought that he would also be the President's principal domestic adviser. Burns had gathered around him a small staff to do the transition Task Force work, and he brought most of these people into the White House after the inauguration.

His was a group of conservatives, which was natural. Arthur Burns is a conservative, and he works at it. Had Arthur remained Nixon's principal domestic assistant it is likely that the Nixon Administration would have stayed very close to conventional conservative doctrine. That was Nixon's *a priori* view of most issues, and with Burns's reinforcement, Nixon would probably have rested there, content and unchallenged.

But challenge soon arrived in the person of Daniel Patrick Moynihan, a Democrat, Harvard professor, professed moderate, former protégé of the Kennedys. A betting man would have demanded long odds on any wager that Richard Nixon would hire Pat Moynihan for anything, much less as a high-level adviser on urban problems. But somehow Bob Finch persuaded Nixon that the problems of the time required Moynihan.

(As a measure of those problems, one of my early visitors during the transition was Warren Christopher, Lyndon Johnson's Deputy Attorney General. Christopher, who had been a year or two ahead of me at Stanford Law School, brought me a package of emergency proclamations and decrees and explained how to use them when big-city riots occurred. The Johnson White House was thoroughly prepared for civil unrest of every variety. Christopher, under Carter, was later to negotiate the release of the hostages in Iran.)

Moynihan had written extensively about urban problems, and particularly about the modern black American. He proposed that a Cabinet group be formed—an Urban Affairs Council—to mesh interdepartmental efforts to solve problems of unemployment, urban blight and racial tension. He had a bagful of imaginative and bold ideas. He was willing to remain mute on the subjects he and Nixon disagreed upon—notably the prosecution of the war in Vietnam—and he knew how to get good television and press for the President's domestic efforts.

It is understandable that Nixon liked Moynihan. I did too. Moynihan instinctively knew how to approach the President and the rest of us with his ideas. At the outset, Nixon was not a little pleased to have the services of genuine savants like Moynihan and Kissinger whom he could summon for unstructured conversation at his whim. And for their part, the university people—notably Burns, Moynihan, Kissinger and Shultz—served Nixon well.

But Arthur Burns and Pat Moynihan were rivals from the first day. At root they were ideological adversaries, but the competition went beyond doctrine. Arthur's staff was created in his conservative image, whereas Pat's was younger and much more liberal. The sniping back and forth by their staff members inevitably involved Burns and Moynihan. Their assignments were virtually coterminous; there was hardly a subject one began to deal with that the other wasn't involved in. At first Nixon played one off against the other; Burns's memoranda were sent to Moynihan for criticism, and vice versa. But both men were playing for keeps—they were arguing social philosophy they both cared about passionately, and the responsive criticism was often deadly.

Both men were old Washington hands, wise in the ways of the press leak and the bureaucracy. Before long each was seeing the President behind the back of the other, hoping to gain the final favorable decision on some disputed issue. Neither had an inside track, however. It was a fair, equal and brutal battle.

Pat Moynihan had the franchise to develop a comprehensive welfare-reform proposal, and he worked tirelessly to produce the Family Assistance Plan. At once Burns and his staff pounced on it, and Nixon found himself bombarded from both sides with conflicting and disputed analyses of how the plan would work. Burns argued that Pat's FAP plan would just give more money to the layabouts. Any reform, Burns said, should include a draconian work requirement. Nixon agreed with that, instinctively. Moynihan urged that the system be bottomed on incentives, not penalties. Nixon could also see the desirability of that.

Moreover, it was not just over welfare that the tug-of-war raged. The plight of the blue-collar worker was very much on Nixon's mind. Burns saw the problem in economist's terms. He proposed an end to social programs that taxed the factory worker and paid the unemployed black mother to have more children. He argued that the President should deeply cut Federal spending, cut taxes and restore that worker's buying power.

Moynihan, the radical sociologist, argued for a shift from the Federal delivery of welfare services to a cash strategy. Cut out the social workers (who were mostly Yale graduates with pangs of conscience) who pandered to black malingerers. Just send the entitled poor a check each month, Pat argued, and that blue-collar worker would begin to feel better.

Nixon soon began dreading his appointments with the antagonists. He was never one to enjoy being pulled and hauled upon by special pleaders, and Burns and Moynihan were experts. By the summer of 1969, Nixon was telling me that I would have to "coordinate" their controversies, which meant that he wanted me to become a buffer between the President and his two contending domestic advisers.

That was all right with me. Since returning from Europe in March 1969, I had been doing all sorts of odd jobs for the President and his family, far beyond the conventional and rather dull legal duties of the Counsel. So when I was interjected between the President and Burns vs. Moynihan, it seemed to be an opportunity to take part in substance. (At the same time, I had no ambition to create a policy niche for myself and had no reason then to think the President would move Burns or Moynihan to other duties.)

The Burns–Moynihan domestic operation contrasted markedly with the smooth and orderly operation of Henry Kissinger's National Security Council. The President began asking Roy Ash and the others who were studying the organization of the Executive Office of the President why he couldn't have a domestic-policy operation analogous to the NSC and as pain-free. As the Ash group met with the President and the Domestic Council evolved, Nixon began thinking about making some personnel changes along with the creation of new machinery.

One day Nixon called me in to talk about his unhappiness with William McChesney Martin, the longtime Chairman of the Board of the Federal Reserve System. As Nixon saw him, Martin was a stereotypical tennis-playing Eastern, Ivy League banker who considered himself wholly independent of the Nixon Administration. He had been Chairman of the Fed for more than eighteen years, during the terms of five Presidents. His tenure was due to expire in January 1970; but in the summer and early fall of 1969, Martin was virtually in sole command of the country's monetary policy from his cockpit at the Fed. By law the Fed is to be strictly independent, unbuffeted by political changes in the country; but the President and his economists found it difficult, if not impossible, to deal with economic problems without some handle on the monetary machinery. Nixon wanted his own man as head of the Fed. I was instructed to tell Martin that the President would soon be naming his replacement and wished the transition to begin as soon as possible.

Martin seemed a little surprised to be hearing from me about his retirement five months before his term expired, but he took it in good grace.

In October the President announced that Arthur Burns would be the new Chairman of the Board of Governors of the Federal Reserve System. About that same time Nixon decided to create the Domestic Council organization. Without Burns to balance Moynihan, Moynihan could not be put in charge of the domestic-policy apparatus; he'd run away with it. So someone else was needed to run the staff of the new Council, and something had to be found for Moynihan to do.

After much conversation it was decided to lump together the staff of Moynihan's Urban Affairs Council, Burns's doughty conservatives and my several young lawyers; call the conglomerate the Domestic Council Staff and put me in charge of it. Pat Moynihan would become the President's Counselor and resident thinker, to rove from subject to subject as he wished, stimulating our intellects and crying alarms. He would also shepherd his welfare reform through the Congress.

On October 23, 1969, about six days after his new appointment to the Fed was announced, Arthur Burns came in to see the President.

Nixon had decided to give a farewell dinner for William McChesney Martin and asked Burns to give the White House social secretary a list of banker friends of Burns's who should be invited.

"My relations with the Fed," Nixon said, "will be different than they were with Bill Martin there. He was always six months too late doing anything. I'm counting on you, Arthur, to keep us out of a recession."

"Yes, Mr. President," Burns said, lighting his pipe. "I don't like to be late."

Nixon continued: "The Fed and the money supply are more important than anything the Bureau of the Budget does."

Burns nodded.

"Arthur, I want you to come on over and see me privately

anytime. The Quadriad meetings are no substitute for private talks between us."

"Thank you, Mr. President," Burns said.

"I know there's the myth of the autonomous Fed . . ." Nixon barked a quick laugh. ". . . and when you go up for confirmation some Senator may ask you about your friendship with the President. Appearances are going to be important, so you can call Ehrlichman to get messages to me, and he'll call you."

Shortly before his confirmation Burns came to see the President again. He wanted to be certain that the members of his Federal Reserve Board of Governors would be receiving White House dinner invitations. "Can something be done to elevate their protocol rank?" Burns asked. "They are always so far down the list, it's embarrassing." I promised I'd see what I could do for them (and incidentally for Arthur, whose Cabinet rank was about to be lost).

"I'm afraid, Mr. President," Burns continued, his teeth clamped on his pipe, "that I'm not going to be able to effect the [Fed's] restrictive monetary policy until February, at the earliest. But there is much *you* can do now to cut the budget, beyond Bob Mayo's recommendations." Burns then rattled through his list: cut foreign assistance, reduce Federal pay increases to 3 percent, cut the White House staff 10 percent, eliminate White House conferences and suspend the Davis–Bacon Act. Nixon listened and nodded, but it was the monetary lever he wanted in his hands.

Burns was confirmed by the Senate in December, and he turned over to me Martin Anderson, Richard Burriss, Roger Freeman and the rest of his staff. Assimilating those wiry right-wingers along with some of Pat Moynihan's young liberals was enough to give a rock python indigestion. Most of Pat's people soon decided to move on to other things, but a couple stayed. Arthur's people stayed like in-laws.

The dinner for Bill Martin was scheduled for late January 1970. In the middle of that month, *New York Times* columnist James Reston wrote about the Martin-to-Burns transfer of power at the Fed. Reston implied that Burns had not been Nixon's first choice to succeed Martin. The next day I had a phone call from Arthur Burns, and I wrote the President a memorandum:

MEMORANDUM FOR THE PRESIDENT
INFORMATION
    William McChesney Martin
    Dinner

You will remember that I mentioned Arthur Burns' request that during this dinner party you take the occasion in a toast or in your remarks to make clear that he, Arthur Burns, was your first choice for Chairman of the Fed.

He wishes that this particular audience understand this to be the fact in view of the attached article by Scotty Reston which Arthur believes was based upon an interview with Bill Martin.

John D. Ehrlichman

From the outset of Burns's term I was one of the President's channels to the "independent" Fed. Peter Flanigan, Bob Haldeman and others also passed messages to and from Chairman Burns.

In mid-March, 1970, for example, I took these notes as instructions from the President:

Phone Arthur Burns—
Say: responsibility for a recession is directly on the Fed. It's a very tight situation.
They must free up construction money now or it will be too late.
The Fed has "saved the dollar" and caused recessions three times.
The President will take on the Fed publicly if its Open Market Committee retaliates.
Does the Fed want responsibility for a recession?

When I conveyed such a message to Burns he invariably said, "Well, I guess I'd better come over and talk to the President." So when I took these instructions I asked the President, "When do you want to see him?"

By the time Arthur Burns had been Chairman of the Fed for ten months, the President was, in his words, "very distressed" with Burns. On November 16, 1970, the President called me from Camp David to insist that I read a *Post* column by Hobart Rowan based on an interview with Chairman Burns. Arthur was quite plainly beating the drum for an "incomes policy" of wage controls to hold down inflation, and Richard

Nixon didn't like the public heat Burns's gambit was creating. It was pressure toward controls from a respected source, close to the President. Nixon wanted as much freedom of choice as he could get. Moreover, Burns was giving him advice in the newspapers instead of in private meetings.

"Burns will get it right in the chops!" Nixon yelled. "Is it time to take the Fed on in public? We won't take this! Shall we give the Fed a good kick now?"

I asked if the President wanted to see Burns.

"Tell him the President is very distressed before he comes in for a visit," Nixon said. "Tell him I'm considering a major statement about the Fed. He hasn't been too right about the economy, you know. Most of the economic advisers haven't. The only effect his 'incomes policy' talk will have is to hurt the business community, you know. You and George Shultz and Paul McCracken get together and talk about this Rowan interview before I see Arthur," Nixon directed.

That evening the President called me again. "I'll see Arthur, but you and George and Paul are to prepare for that meeting. Give me a line to use with Arthur."

Three days later the President convened a meeting of George Shultz, Paul McCracken, Herb Stein, Peter Flanigan and me to prepare him for his Arthur Burns meeting and also for a speech he intended to give to a convention of the National Association of Manufacturers. He was concerned that his economic policies were not working; he sensed a widespread public pessimism and a lack of buoyancy in the economy.

Paul McCracken was critical of the Fed: "They have a money-supply-expansion target of five percent, but they keep missing—undershooting it."

"Their New York manager, a man named Hayes, is opposed to Arthur Burns's policies and he frustrates them," Shultz added.

"What shall I say to Arthur?" Nixon asked.

Shultz suggested: "Ask him if he shares the President's objective of full employment by mid-1972."

"If he says yes," McCracken went on, "say that the Fed's monetary path can't and won't bring us to it."

"Arthur's personal philosophy is to spend to lick unemployment, I believe," Nixon said.

Herb Stein shook his head. "We can't get it all out of the Fed alone. A seven-percent monetary growth alone won't get us there. We need a package; that kind of monetary growth plus some fiscal devices. We've got to stimulate housing, for example. We've got to consider an interest subsidy."

"Is an incomes policy the wrong course?" Nixon asked.

"Ask Arthur Burns," Paul McCracken said drily, "specifically what he thinks should be done. I think he's making a hollow proposal, without anything in mind but that phrase. Does he want a price-and-income board? The Canadians have one and they've had a poor result."

"It doesn't work," said Stein.

They talked about the NAM speech. It should be a reassuring, jawboning statement of economic policy, everyone agreed. Our monetary policy is expansionist, Nixon would say to the NAM.

"Ask Arthur," Shultz suggested, "what there is in his 'incomes policy' that would keep down these wage increases. Anything with real impact is very sensitive politically. Arthur will have some things," he predicted, "but they'll be political suicide."

"Are things so bad," Nixon asked, "that we have to do what Arthur is demanding?"

Shultz shrugged. "Construction wages are up twenty-two percent."

Nixon shook his head. The NAM speech would be written by William Safire; it would explain what an "incomes policy" is, and it would explicitly reject it, he said grimly.

As the long meeting broke up, Herb Stein looked back as he left the President's office. "I just hope," he said, "that he doesn't nail us in. I'll talk to Safire."

The President met with Arthur Burns the next morning. They talked privately for about fifteen minutes before I was called in to join them. I assumed they'd discussed wage and price controls, because that subject was on the eight-item agenda I'd prepared for Nixon and it was not covered after I came in. Neither was the Fed's erratic performance in regulating the money supply.

There would soon be an opening on Arthur's board, and when I entered the Oval Office he and the President were talking about who might fill it.

They talked about construction-industry wages, the minimum wage, job training and productivity, but not controls. They talked about tax reform, consumer confidence and a wage-price board. They agreed to wait six months before deciding on the formation of such a board.

But there was no woodshedding that day, in my presence. If

Nixon chastised Arthur for advocating an incomes policy, it must have been in the first quarter-hour. It's my guess Nixon tried to buy him off with a promise to decide on controls very soon.

Ten days later, December 1, as he, Shultz and I were going over budget items, Nixon complained that he'd heard that Arthur Burns intended to make another speech about an incomes policy. The President's NAM speech would be December 4. Burns would speak on the seventh. "Arthur has persuaded Dave Kennedy that we ought to have controls," Nixon said. "Poor Dave just isn't well enough informed."

I was directed to send Arthur a memorandum. "More in sorrow than anger," Nixon instructed, "and you tell him the President is very surprised. Tell him he's going to see the President on Monday." Nixon hoped that might moderate whatever Burns might be tempted to say. "Say I thought—I expected that—especially before the November election—there would be nothing occurring which would chill economic confidence. There are some immediate effects of such a speech. A flattening would occur."

"I'm still waiting to hit the Fed," Shultz offered. "I still have my undelivered speech." George had written a speech blasting the Fed, but he'd never used it.

Nixon nodded. "Arthur just can't be out there speaking loosely about an 'incomes policy,' damn it. Save your speech, George. We may need it."

I sent the sorrowful, admonitory memo, but Arthur delayed his response to the summons until December 15—the same day the President returned Blue Lake to the Taos Indians. Unabashed, Arthur was still urging an "incomes policy"—"because, Mr. President, the people need a resurgence of confidence." What is that policy? Nixon demanded. Are you talking about a wage board? "Yes, Mr. President," Burns intoned. "The rate of inflation has not abated, and people worry."

Burns read Nixon an account of the Fed's progress in controlling the money supply. Interest rates were down sharply; the prime rate would soon be under 6 percent. Three-month Treasury bills were at 3 percent.

Evidently at their previous private meeting Nixon had charged that the Fed's New York money-supply man, Alfred Hayes, was disregarding Burns's orders. Now Burns reported smugly, "Hayes is under control, Mr. President. He's timid as a mouse."

Connally would soon be at Treasury. He would, Nixon confided, fire Charls Walker, David Kennedy's undersecretary.

"I hope he keeps Paul Volcker," Burns urged. "He's important to us abroad. We may have an international crisis."

Burns was about to leave to go to Europe with some of the Treasury officials. A serious problem of protocol was evidently preoccupying him and he needed the President's help. Secretary Kennedy ranked number one on this trip. And Assistant Secretary Samuels was ranked second. Arthur thought *he* should be number two and Samuels number three. Could the President persuade Kennedy to recommend a change in the pecking order? Nixon nodded to me wearily and I made a note to have Kissinger rearrange things.

Burns reported that France and Germany were requesting sizable gold purchases from the Treasury. Nixon approved France's request but instructed that the Germans' larger order be delayed. "We should give serious thought, Mr. President, to increasing the price of gold or embargoing its sale," Burns said. "Otherwise heavy requests could force a crisis; we are striking a delicate balance."

"It's a matter of timing," the President replied. "From a political standpoint, sooner is better than later—it shouldn't be close to 1972."

"But from an economic standpoint we're not ready," Burns said.

"Let me know when," Nixon said. "We'll do it. Domestically we should err on the side of a too-liberal monetary policy, Arthur. We should risk some inflation."

"That's a question of degree," Burns said evasively.

Nixon repeated: "Err toward inflation," his voice peremptory.

As the meeting ended, Burns was back to arguing that the only thing wrong with the economy was lack of consumer confidence, and an incomes policy would help that.

An hour earlier, Nixon had told George Shultz and me that he intended to be very tough in his meeting with Burns, and Shultz had urged Nixon to ask Burns what his objectives were for 1971 and the first half of 1972. "Arthur wants high interest rates," Nixon had said before the meeting, "because he fears investment money will all flow to the Swiss otherwise. I'll unload on him like he's never seen before. We'll take inflation if necessary, but we can't take unemployment. He's got to understand that." But as usual, no unloading occurred.

During the final weeks of 1970 we all labored to produce the Budget and the President's annual Economic Message. Burns's talk about popular confidence in the economy had an influence on Nixon. The budget and economic texts must be "optimistic, but not unreal," he said. "Arthur Burns is most pessimistic these days, you know. He is so volatile. He panics. He keeps telling me how that damn wage-price board is going to cure the national pessimism. The Fed's staff influences him, you know. And he gets a lot of business pressure. He wants to help us, but he gets sold one of these ideas and his vanity gets all wrapped up in it and it's a bad mixture."

Two months later, in February 1971, Burns was still pushing for a new economic policy. He was about to unload some Congressional testimony that would apply more pressure.

"Call Arthur," Nixon ordered Bob Haldeman. "Tell him that the President is furious. Say I've been meeting with John Connally and Shultz and Ehrlichman and we know just how Arthur's testimony will play in the press. Say I'm hurt and distressed, and when he asks for a meeting, say 'The President is unavailable.' "

A few days later, it was evident that Bob had made the call, and Arthur was feeling the heat for a change. During our daily meeting on Monday, the President mentioned that Burns had approached him at the White House church service the day before to ask for an appointment.

"Why does Arthur need to see me?" Nixon asked rhetorically. "You've talked to him, haven't you, George? And he was at the Quadriad meeting."

"He says we don't understand him," Shultz said. "He feels the White House is pushing him too hard."

"Well, seeing me won't help," Nixon said flatly. "He's still pushing that goddamned wage-price board. He knows the President opposes it, but he continues to leak it and advocate it. He can't have it both ways. If he's going to be for it, then he must be outside. We've been very good to Arthur; no one has taken on the Fed—yet. But I'm going to, by God. John Connally will do it first." Nixon hit his hand on the desk. "I'll see him [Arthur], but I won't butter him up anymore. That doesn't work with Arthur. He testifies Wednesday at the Congress on interest rates. I'll see him Thursday."

In March I delivered one of the President's stern admonitions to Dr. Burns. I was instructed to call him to say the President was deeply disappointed and I was to imply that the President found his conduct to be disloyal.

Arthur's response was so artfully ambiguous that I wrote it down: "You know the idea . . . the idea that I would ever let a conflict arise between what I think is right and my loyalty to Dick Nixon is outrageous."

In mid-August 1971, Arthur Burns got his incomes policy and then some. We were summoned to Camp David one weekend to put together the new economic policy. At the opening meeting I was surprised to hear Arthur Burns oppose a proposal to suspend the convertibility of the dollar into gold. In December of 1970, Arthur had been urging the suspension. In fact, he was the only one of our economists I had ever heard proposing an end to convertibility. I thought of asking Arthur what had changed his mind, but gold was a delicate issue up there that weekend and I decided to stay out of it. The new policy included wage and price boards, along with a ninety-day freeze on wage and price increases and some tax changes.

But in four or five months, as we began to phase out of the freeze, Burns became most unhappy with the operation of the wage board. He'd had high expectations for it, but in a January 1972 meeting he expressed his disappointment to the President and John Connally.

"Are you disappointed too?" Nixon asked George Shultz afterward.

"I didn't expect much. Arthur was unrealistic," Shultz answered. "Construction-industry wage increases are down to about ten percent, and to me that's progress, but to Arthur that's a failure."

"Everyone wants to replace the board chairman, George Boldt,"* Nixon noted. "And Frank Fitzsimmons of the Teamsters is unhappy with the public members of the board. Colson doesn't like Boldt either. Neither does Arthur."

"Well," said Shultz slowly, "in view of all that, maybe the board is working after all."

By February 1972, Burns was bad-mouthing the new economic policy all over town and Nixon was going through another get-Burns-under-control cycle. There would be a Burns meeting. I should take notes. After the meeting I should have a long talk with Arthur and say: The President made you Chairman of the Fed, Arthur. You are deeply in his debt. He expects you to be loyal. You were at Camp David in August and

---

* George Boldt, a Federal District Court judge from Tacoma, Washington, was one of my Uncle Ben's closest friends and business associates. Partly for that reason, I became one of his White House contacts and defenders when Big Labor tried to get him fired.

took part in shaping the new policy; now you should support the wage-price actions and other fiscal policies. You can't have it both ways, Arthur. The President is holding you personally responsible for monetary policy—for the money-supply situation.

"You see," Nixon said to me, "when Arthur criticizes our policy he creates uncertainty about it. A year ago he was for the value-added tax; now he instigates opposition to it. Schedule my meeting with him so there's not too much time available for him."

The President met with Burns as scheduled, but I did not. Nixon changed his mind about my scolding Arthur. And he changed his mind about chastising Arthur himself. As usual.

As everyone knows, John B. Connally was Nixon's darling boy. Of all his Cabinet and staff, Nixon saw only Connally as his potential successor.

Nixon was the third President whom John Connally had known well; years in the service of Lyndon Johnson had made Connally an old Washington hand. From the standpoint of experience and temperament, Connally could have been a good President from the first day he sat in the big chair. He would have been an inspirational leader, a strong executive and an able representative of the nation in world affairs.

Early in my White House time, Connally dropped by my office to talk about some innocuous piece of environmental business. Someone in Texas was having trouble with the Feds. I was surprised to find him so easygoing and friendly. He was then a Houston lawyer serving on the commission that was studying how to reorganize the President's staff. I saw him from time to time as I worked with the commission, and he was unfailingly cordial.

As Secretary of the Treasury, however, Connally was more difficult to deal with. He insisted on his prerogatives. For example, I was in the habit of delegating to my assistant directors the task of meeting with Cabinet Secretaries to work out substantive domestic problems. But Connally expected to deal with no underlings. If the President had words for him, he wanted to be called directly, not by Bob Haldeman or me. If I sent Bud Krogh to work with some of Connally's Customs people on legislation, Connally wanted me to get his permission first.

With anyone else, I'd have worked around all that formality and Nixon would have backed me. But with Connally, our orders were to do it the way he wanted it done.

One of Connally's friends explained to me that Big John was not as robust as he appeared. He tired easily, and when fatigued he was snappish and irritable. But overall, John Connally was as plain and warm as anyone I've known.*

In the pre-Connally days, the President yearned for an economic spokesman. "No one is speaking out with any confidence," he complained in the spring of 1970. "There is no one we can put on television—not Mayo, not Dave Kennedy or Agnew or Shultz. I want a real spokesman to replace Dave Kennedy at Treasury."

At that time his prospect list included Robert Anderson, Kenneth Rush and Pierre Rinfret, a glib economist who had impressed Nixon during a White House meeting on the economy.

"Rinfret is volatile," Nixon said, "but he might be able to give the market some reassurance. Mayo and Kennedy aren't a voice. Kennedy is a cipher. Stans has no credibility with the business community. Paul McCracken is just one voice." But Rinfret was only a passing and very controversial enthusiasm. Nixon wanted a big, forceful political spokesman, and he set out to recruit one. By the end of 1970 he had persuaded John Connally to become Dave Kennedy's successor.

Nixon had high expectations that Connally would solve a great many of the President's problems. In December 1970, Arthur Burns and the Fed were giving the President trouble. Now that we had John Connally, he would issue an economic statement that would get Arthur back in line. "He'll be tough," Nixon told George Shultz and me. "He'll take on the Fed and its monetary policy. He's one of the best."

Connally will soften up the Congress for comprehensive tax reform, Nixon told some governors a few days later. (Nixon and Nelson Rockefeller agreed at that meeting that the nation badly needed a value added tax, but it was not yet "credible" with the Congress. Rocky's college roommate, Congressman Herman Schnebele, reported that VAT had no chance of pas-

---

* During one working weekend at Camp David I had some of my family with me. At lunch my son Bob, then about 8, was seated next to Connally, and to my surprise, they found a lot to talk about. No one had ever taught Bob to shoot a gun, but it was something he had an 8-year-old's curiosity about. I could hear their conversation move from horses and cowboys to guns and shooting. And after lunch John Connally took Bob out to Camp David's skeet range and gave him an unforgettable introduction to shotguns. Connally did it because he was interested in Bob and wanted to do something for him, and although I didn't really care if any of my kids ever shot a gun, that meant a lot to me.

sage. But "We'll get VAT—I pledge," Nixon told Rockefeller.) "Connally is the toughest, most persuasive advocate," Nixon told the Republican governors. "Work with him. He'll get us some Democrats. We want some favorable reaction when he's announced as the new Secretary of the Treasury. You fellows"—Nixon pointed—"tell some other governors so there will be some good reaction."

Two months later, in February 1971, Connally was in place at Treasury and Nixon was giving him special assignments. He was to replace David Packard in dealing with the Lockheed–Rolls-Royce problem (their use of foreign-made engines), "because I'd like to see how he'll handle it."

"That Connally is a gut fighter and the total politician," Nixon told Kissinger and me a couple of days later. "I want to meet with him on the Arthur Burns problem."

Connally's advice was being heeded. That same day Nixon told me, "Connally wonders if we are pushing too hard for revenue sharing right now. Maybe we should compromise—if we can be sure our brand is on the result." (This reflected Congressional complaints Connally was hearing from Republican revenue-sharing opponents like John Byrnes of Wisconsin.) "You and Bob," Nixon said to me, "meet with Connally and plan our sales campaign for revenue sharing."

And, of course, Nixon had Connally in mind for an even bigger campaign. One day the President, Connally and I were discussing our legislative problems. Nixon remarked that over the years we had created a working coalition of Congressional conservatives and moderates which had in it as many Democrats as Republicans. Nixon and Connally speculated that Nixon had the support of millions of conservative Democratic voters too.

Looking ahead to 1980, Nixon and Connally began to daydream about forming a new political party which might attract voters all across the middle and right of the political spectrum.

They could realign the Congress, too. There would be a place in their new party for John Stennis, John McClellan and Joe Waggoner. Perhaps even Russell Long. What could they call such a coalition party of conservatives and moderates? We tossed out some names, borrowed from other countries. We talked about the true meaning of the labels "liberal" and "conservative."

Nixon speculated that he could get the new party started by calling a convention of the political leaders of the center and right. The Nixon people in each state could be formed into nuclei to create state parties. Nixon and Connally would be elected President and Vice President in 1972 by the new coalition party and could bring in with them a majority in both houses of the Congress.

Both Nixon and Connally had been in politics long enough to realize the near-impossibility of quickly creating such a realignment, but they were sufficiently intrigued with the notion that they wanted to have more thought given to it. Somewhere in the archives is a memorandum I did outlining the idea and the preliminary steps required to form the new party legally. I learned later that there had been a conversation between Nixon and Connally at which they agreed to wait until after the 1972 election to consider the new party further. But as far as they were concerned, it remained a possibility.

I wonder if 1974 might have seen the birth of a coalition party of everyone-except-the-damn-liberals had Watergate not intervened.

By the summer of 1971 it appeared that John Connally was indeed a strong economic spokesman, but the fact was that he was nearly drowned out by all our other economic spokesmen, who continued to speak out. Our economic message was cacophonous.

The last weekend in June was spent at Camp David with John Connally and George Shultz reviewing the budgets for the current and following years and planning what appropriations might be vetoed and how to cope with our mounting deficits. During those sessions Nixon adverted to the economic-spokesman problem several times.

"Well, if you want me to be the spokesman, Mr. President," said Connally, smiling, "you are going to have to order those other fellows to shut up. As it is now, no one knows who to believe."

Later Nixon called me to his den in Aspen Lodge. He'd been thinking about how to clear the way for Connally. The economists and the White House staff were going to be told plainly that we were all through speaking with many voices about the economy. (I was sent to tell George Shultz that in meetings with outsiders he was henceforth to defer to Connally. George didn't much like that.)

"Generally," Nixon said, "the Cabinet is incompetent and White House people should brief outside groups. But in this economic field, John Connally is the boss."

And Arthur Burns was to begin paying his calls on Connally

instead of the President to talk about economic issues. "Just tell Arthur to report to Connally," Nixon instructed. "The President won't see him.

"You know," Nixon went on in an afterthought, "I think Connally is anti-Semitic. It probably troubles him to deal with Herb Stein and Arthur Burns and Henry Kissinger and Safire and Garment. Too bad."

On Monday, June 28, Nixon summoned all the economic voices to the Cabinet Room. His three economic advisers; the Secretaries of Treasury, Commerce and Labor; George Shultz; Peter Flanigan and I were bidden to sit around the big table, to hear the riot act read. Nixon was in a harsh mood. That same day Daniel Ellsberg had admitted his theft and dissemination of the Pentagon Papers, and Kissinger was riding Nixon hard, urging revenge on Ellsberg.

The economists were told that John B. Connally was henceforth the Administration's one voice on subjects relating to the economy. And in the future, when Connally announced that some policy line would be taken, everyone was to hew to that line. "Or else," Nixon said brusquely, "you can quit."

To my surprise, Peter Flanigan and I were designated monitors. We would be watching how everyone performed and report to him, Nixon said. The meeting ended abruptly when Nixon walked out. And from that day, Connally was in fact the President's economic spokesman.

A month after the Cabinet Room meeting, on July 20, 1971, the President told me of Spiro Agnew's gaffes of the previous week during the Vice President's trip to Africa.* Nixon asked me my opinion of Agnew, and I told him it was my hope that the Vice President would resign soon. He was obviously not happy in the job, did not get on well with the President or the rest of us and was not suited to what he was expected to do.

"I talked to John Connally for three hours yesterday," Nixon told me. "I offered him the Vice Presidency or, if that's not possible, then Secretary of State. I want to position him as my logical successor." Nixon said Connally had told Bob Haldeman that he was leaving; he had decided to resign from the Cabinet because of the failure of some of the White House staff "to clear personnel appointments" with him, and so on. But Nixon had talked him out of resigning.

"Connally told me," Nixon said, "that he had no complaints about you or Bob [Haldeman]. But I want you to meet often

---

* The CIA reported that the Vice President had told African leaders he opposed our new friendly relations with China.

with Connally. You woo him. And I want you and Bob to meet with Connally and Bryce Harlow to figure out how the hell we can get Agnew to resign early."

John Mitchell took another view of all this. He saw Spiro Agnew as a loyal defender of Richard Nixon's right flank, and he saw John Connally as a turncoat Democrat who probably couldn't be confirmed by the Democrat-controlled Senate. Before long, Mitchell had talked with Nixon, and soon most of the Connally-for-Agnew stars had gone out of the President's eyes.

Still, in February of 1971 Nixon told Richard Kleindienst, Mitchell's successor as Attorney General: "There are going to be interdepartmental problems for you—like narcotics—where jurisdictions overlap. I want you to bend over backwards to keep in tune with John Connally. You call him—he's down in Texas today. You say the President suggested you call him."

That same day, in preparation for his absence during a foreign trip, the President gave instructions to George Shultz and me: "On the economy, you'll have Rumsfeld, Grayson and Boldt out talking about wages and prices. But you keep the policy making here. Connally is the chief spokesman, but he's so busy now! He wants to watch everything, but he lacks the staff to do it all.

"You fellows keep an oversight on wages and prices, but do it in such a way that Connally doesn't feel you are end-running or undercutting him. Talk to Connally. Develop policy with him, then bring the others in. Keep Rumsfeld under control. Prices are potent politics, remember. Either you fellows get Rumsfeld in or have John Connally do it, but keep him under control."

On May 15, 1972, the day George Wallace was shot, Nixon was busy shuffling people again. John Connally's resignation from the Treasury would be announced the next day. It was time he went back home, he said. (It had become evident that Nixon could not make him Secretary of State and was afraid to dump Agnew.) Shultz would move from OMB to Treasury, and Caspar Weinberger would take Shultz' place at OMB.

Connally's last cabinet meeting was on May 16. But after he returned to his law firm in Houston, he kept in close touch. When I was struggling with energy policy in late 1972 and early 1973 I often heard from him directly or through Nixon. It was obvious that they talked often.

During the tough Watergate days in March and April 1973,

Connally was one of Nixon's frequent advisers. In contrast with Bill Rogers, Henry Kissinger and Leonard Garment (and countless others), Connally gave longsighted, tough advice. He urged that the tapes be destroyed and not turned over to the courts, for example.

Had Richard Nixon listened to his instincts in 1972, Connally would have been Vice President instead of Spiro Agnew and Jerry Ford, and Connally would have been the President to follow Nixon. That's a missed fork in the road to conjure with.

CHAPTER FIFTEEN

The Press

THERE HAS BEEN some arrant nonsense written about Richard Nixon and the press, and some of it has been written by people who should know better.* Former newspaper people like Ray Price and Herb Klein argue that Nixon was the victim of a sort of transient, uncontrollable dementia where the press was concerned. That, as they saw it, accounts for his disregard of all their good advice. It is more likely that *most* of Nixon's conduct of his press relations was calculated and deliberate.

Before and during his Presidency, Nixon manifested no illusions about his press problems, although his well-rationalized reasons for journalists' dislike of him were unconvincing. All of his press world was divided into two parts, and the larger was made up of his enemies. "They hate me," Nixon would say, "because I have beaten them so often." He had nailed Alger Hiss, whom Nixon saw to be the darling of the press Establishment. The Checkers speech had frustrated their effort to sink him. He'd come back from his 1962 California defeat in spite of the media's universal political obituaries. In simplest terms, he believed that they were liberal and he was conservative and most of the people out in the country be-

---

* Nixon, interestingly, has not written much about the press in his memoirs.

lieved with him, not them. The press couldn't stand that, and so they were his sworn enemies.

During the years I worked for him, Nixon was usually capable of a passionless and penetrating analysis of his press opportunities. He was a talented media manipulator. I often watched him successfully plan how he or his spokesmen would dominate the evening news, capture the headlines and rightside columns of the front page of *The Washington Post* or the lead story in *Time* or *Newsweek*. Richard Nixon could think like an editor.

Nixon knew how to bait a hook to catch a columnist. Many of the most prominent columnists, including Hugh Sidey, Stewart and Joe Alsop, James Kilpatrick and Evans and Novak, have given Richard Nixon their allotted space, sometimes unwittingly, when he went after it.

As President, Nixon could also demand prime-time television for major policy statements and get it. He could speak to the people over the heads of the press and the commentators, commanding huge audiences which sometimes could find nothing but Richard Nixon to watch on their television sets.

Nixon was convinced that the vast majority of reporters and commentators would be unfair to him if left to their own devices. They had to be prevented from airing their biases, therefore, by whatever means were available. Television pictures of an event, a crowd or a person would preclude distorted comment; people could see a picture and could know what the truth was for themselves; so Nixon thought a lot about "visuals" and "photo opportunities." And he counted on the fact that most reporters would use handouts before they would dig for their own stories, because most Washington reporters were basically lazy or burned out. The prudent politician gives them well-written press releases full of facts, briefings, research and background information.*

Nixon believed in freezing out any reporter who revealed his or her bias against him. As President, he headed the most bountiful source of news in the nation. A reporter who was barred, so that he couldn't get news from the White House, was in trouble. Before long his assignment editor would move him out of there in favor of someone who could produce stories. Or at least, so the President believed.

---

* Later, Nixon and Charles Colson were to attempt more coercive tactics to counter media bias—including bringing direct influence to bear upon television-network executives.

Nixon came into the White House determined to exercise the fullest possible influence over what the press said about him and his Administration. He and Bob Haldeman shared the view that no previous President had properly organized and staffed the White House to manage the news. They set about constructing an apparatus that would appear to serve the White House press corps while, at the same time, sending volumes of information over their heads to small newspapers and television stations out in the hinterlands. For the first time the White House would systematically propagandize the general public.

It was Nixon's premise that the small group of old-timers who constituted the regulars in the White House press room were so jaded by their years of covering Presidents that they constricted the outward flow of news. If Nixon were to play with his dog—this is hypothetical, of course—there would be little or no coverage because Kennedy and Johnson had played with their dogs; dog-play was old stuff to the White House press corps. Therefore, the White House staff must include people who had the skills to have the President and his dog mentioned on evening television news. And there must be people who could write President-and-dog news releases and send them to the American Kennel Club newsletter for dissemination. A house photographer must take pictures of man and dog to be given exclusively to *People* magazine, the wire services, *Life* or the pet publications. A Navy film crew should be on hand to photograph dog-play footage which could be released to the television news organizations. And someone should write canned editorials about the President and Man's Best Friend for weekly newspapers and trade publications, to be disseminated by the hundreds.*

It took Bob Haldeman several months to get the propaganda mill fully staffed and in operation. Its first major project would be to counter a huge antiwar demonstration planned for mid-November 1969.

Bob Haldeman and Charles Colson were Nixon's principal

---

* There actually was a photo opportunity featuring Nixon and King Timahoe, his red setter, on the beach at San Clemente. Manolo, the President's valet, released the dog a hundred yards up the beach, and King Timahoe ran straight for Nixon, who opened his arms wide. But Timahoe was chasing a sea gull and ran right past the President and on down the beach half a mile, leaving Nixon unrequited (and unphotographed—except by me).

propaganda planners. They assembled a sizable staff and budget. Haldeman recruited Jeb Stuart Magruder, an ambitious young California businessman, to be his executor of the White House public relations plans. Herb Klein, too much of an old Nixon retainer to be wholly excluded, was designated "Director of Communications," but he was largely a figurehead. Jeb Magruder took his orders directly from Haldeman and Colson, and caused the Communications Office to produce the reams of news copy, the pictures and the editorials that poured out every day.

A couple of staff committees were formed to provide general advice to Haldeman, Colson and Magruder. The President's writers—Jim Keogh, Bill Safire, Pat Buchanan and the others—the scheduler, Dwight Chapin, the Press Secretary and occasionally some of us dealing with substantive matters were convened to "run it up the flagpole," "vet it" and "bounce it off the wall."

Most of these meetings were a waste of time, and I seldom attended. Richard Nixon would ultimately decide what would and wouldn't be done on these subjects, and it mattered little what any P.R. committees recommended. In the last analysis, Nixon would listen to Colson and Haldeman—and less often one of us others—and then do what he wanted to do.

I would estimate that Richard Nixon spent half his working time on the nonsubstantive aspects of the Presidency, and probably 40 percent of that half dealing with the problems of communication. (I recognize that a good argument can be made that communication *is* the substance of the Presidency. But from where I sat, George Shultz, Henry Kissinger and I were dealing in substance—policy and its implementation—while Bob Haldeman's element of the staff was concerned with process and appearances.) I have watched Nixon spend a morning designing Walter Cronkite's lead story for that evening, then send Ron Ziegler, Henry Kissinger or me out to a press briefing to deliver it in such a way that Cronkite couldn't ignore it.

Sometimes the subject matter alone would be enough to capture the top slot on the news. Other times we devised phrases or slogans to catch a news editor's attention. One day I was sent out to charge that the President was faced with an irresponsible "credit card Congress." Another time it was enough to call some appropriations bills "seven Trojan horses lumbering down Pennsylvania Avenue toward the White House."

In any Administration the Press Secretary's office grinds out

239

reams of handouts for its journalistic clientele. Mimeographed statements, announcements, proclamations, statistical collections, abstracts and analyses, photographs and schedules pour into the laps of the White House press. On most days the Press Secretary holds a "briefing" in the press room. The reporters may ask any questions they wish, but there are a couple of limitations. First, the television people may not photograph or sound-record most of these briefings. Second, there is no requirement that the Press Secretary must answer the questions.

An adroit Press Secretary can usually pump out into the nation's news columns the content that his President wants placed there. If the flow of the briefing didn't reach every subject Ron Ziegler wanted to peddle on a given day, he could call the wire-service reporters to his office and tell them what he wanted them to know. Ninety-nine percent of the time the wire services would dutifully carry the handout.

In February 1970 I was treated to a Nixon homily that emanated from his decision to veto a veterans' education bill. "Not on television," he instructed. He didn't want to be seen disapproving money for the vets. "You can do too much television, you know. You have to weigh giving news to the writing press or to television. It's not *what* Presidents do but how they do it that matters. That's what gives an Administration its personality—how the President works."

It wasn't until the end of this talk that Nixon used the word "image," but it was obviously what he had in mind as he ticked off a list of ingredients:

"—hard work, his guts, a restoration of dignity, the family, church, square," he said, looking at me as if expecting an argument. I looked back without expression. Nixon continued:

"He [the President; himself; Richard Nixon] came in with the press against him. They said he couldn't handle TV. Now there's been a complete shift in 'the man's' image."

"You know, it's been harder because I won't let Ziegler be a pimp for me like Jack Valenti was for Johnson. Instead we've built a mythology about the President."

"Teddy Roosevelt is a good example. Taft was a much more effective President than T.R. But Roosevelt is recorded by history as the 'greater' President. It's fine to be the good managers. But we've got to get the story out!"

"At press conferences I never have friendly questions planted. I never 'can' or memorize answers," Nixon added, gratuitously.

A month later, as we were discussing school desegregation, Nixon began to tell Bryce Harlow and me how his Presidential message on the subject should be news-planned. "It should have the broadest possible circulation," he began. "I want Fentress [of *Time*] backgrounded. You should brief [James] Kilpatrick and [Irving] Kristol. Call in black officials and preachers, including Reverend King. Brief our staff and Bill Rogers—he was Attorney General once, of course—and the Democrats in Congress, especially Stennis and Russell. Ed Brooke, too.

"I want them to understand what was possible. The object is to unite the country behind a program of desegregation that's *achievable*. Tell them how the statement was written: many people worked on it. My old law partner Len Garment was one. They sent me many alternative drafts. Twelve drafts. Say that I'm still making changes in it. You can cite them that phrase about 'stripping away hypocrisy, ignorance and prejudice' and tell them how carefully chosen it was.

"As in preparing the November 3 speech, the President has curious work habits," he dictated to us. "He reads, works, talks to the staff on the phone until midnight. The schedule the past three or four days has been brutal. [It hadn't been.] The President has slept only four hours a night. He goes to bed at eleven or twelve, then awakens at two and works from two to three. That's when he does his clearest thinking. Then he sleeps until seven-thirty."

Most of Nixon's speeches and statements were designed to reach beyond the press, directly to the people. A State of the Union address to a joint session of the Congress was a fully televised Presidential speech with a potential for high drama. Nixon prepared for this annual address with scrupulous care. It would ride the main line straight to the people.

On January 12, 1971, I had a series of Sunday phone calls from the President as he worked on the State of the Union he would give later that month. He had just received a proposed draft from Ray Price, the writer he'd assigned to help with that speech, and Nixon was not happy. His first call was to tell me that the proposed draft was terrible and that if *he* was to have to do this speech work, unassisted by competent writers, then we couldn't expect him to do any of the other chores around the office. "Tell everyone there's to be no further contact with the President for the next two days. Tell Henry [Kissinger] and Bob [Haldeman]. Henry wants to resign again. Tell him I just can't see him. I'm going to have to do this speech."

Two hours later he called again to explain that *his* speech would not be a "laundry list" of Administration proposals. He would have it short; the draft had to be boiled down. Each thousand words would be cut to one hundred. He would speak only of concepts; the details could be given later.

"I've read every inaugural speech ever given," Nixon said. "And I've read many of the State of the Union speeches. None of them that were over three thousand words were any good.

"This speech should be about ideals, goals and directions. You don't write one of these for the press; you explain it to them later. You just give the Congress a great concept and quit and get out.

"John," he went on, "you are probably unaware that I cut forty percent out of the State of the Union they [the writers] sent me last year. You have to take out all the details. It's much harder to write a conceptual speech; a clerk can write up a laundry list."

Nixon was always ambivalent about doing pure "P.R." events. He wanted the results—he wanted good press and public support—but he was reticent about doing most of the things his publicists and the other staff advisers urged him to do. Some of his mind knew that the President had to personify the Presidency, but the rest of him wished that that were not so. He kicked, bucked and dragged his feet when we suggested he get up from his desk and venture forth among the people. But paradoxically, he would sometimes do public things on impulse that demonstrated a latent love of the limelight and a good sense of the right thing to do.

When Wilkes-Barre, Pennsylvania, was devastated by a flood, Nixon called his man-on-the-scene, Frank Carlucci, to come to Camp David one Saturday for a firsthand report on Federal relief efforts. As Frank described the progress he'd made in emergency housing, cleanup and subsistence relief, Nixon began to think about going to Wilkes-Barre. He asked how long it would take to fly there from Camp David. It was the Jewish sabbath, he noted, so Pennsylvania Governor Milton Schapp would not be there to hog the limelight. Today would be the best day to go, to show the people that the President cared about them.

In five minutes I'd whistled up a helicopter and our Secret Service detail and we were off—just Nixon, Carlucci and I. And Nixon's personal photographer, Ollie Atkins, of course.

We landed in a schoolyard in Wilkes-Barre, drove to the flood-destroyed area in a borrowed police car and walked the streets among amazed citizens. At least once an hour the President devised some highly photogenic event that made me yearn for a network-television camera crew. He sat in the living room of someone's trailer and sympathized with old ladies about their tragedy. He talked with the workmen who were shoveling out mud and debris. At a town meeting he volunteered to buy the hot dogs for a community picnic for the flood workers. (We sent up hundreds of pounds of picnic food from the White House kitchen the next weekend.)

As we were leaving town, the President suddenly ordered our driver to stop the car in a suburban street. He had seen a bride and groom just coming out the doors of a church; he jumped out of our car and hurried across the street to them as their families and the minister were gathering on the church steps. Nixon visited with the wedding party for about fifteen minutes, posing with the bride and groom for the wedding photographer and Atkins. Then, putting $15 (of my money) into the Reverend's hand for the poor box, he bade the dazed crowd farewell and ran back to the car.

Flying back to a field near Camp David, Nixon dictated rapid-fire instructions to me. He was overflowing with ideas to help Wilkes-Barre. And he liked the little jet we were flying in. He would henceforth move around the country in a JetStar rather than *Air Force One*. He didn't need all the staff and press that usually went about with him. He would do more events on the spur of the moment. It was good to be out among real people.

But back at Camp David, the White House correspondents were raising hell. Their job was to cover the President, and they had been left at home. They lodged such a strong protest that Ron Ziegler promised they would never be left behind again. Then Ziegler came to Nixon to plead with him not to travel without at least a "death-watch" press pool, which could cover possible accidents or illness. Nixon reserved the right to escape the press, but from then on he would cite the inescapable need for a press pool as a good Catch-22 reason not to do some of the other worthwhile events that were proposed.

Sitting in the office, sheltered, Nixon told himself that he preferred not to go out to do such things. Once out among the people, he performed well and seemed to enjoy the interaction.

Perhaps it's fair to generalize in this way: Richard Nixon genuinely enjoyed the spontaneous. But he abhorred what he called "hokey" public-relations events, and would turn down about 90 percent of the P.R. proposals that came to him. With sixty or seventy reporters in train, almost anything a President does is devoid of spontaneity. Thus, the dilemma: When the press was around him, Richard Nixon was stiff and stagy. So reporters filed stories about the wooden, insensitive man who looked at his watch as he shook hands with well-wishers. In Wilkes-Barre he was sensitive, genuine and inspired as he moved about among the flood victims, unreported.

Occasionally a journalist got a glimpse of the unreported Nixon, but the resulting reportage usually alleged that Nixon had "changed," not that he was multifaceted. So Nixon's propagandists were dealing with a paradox. They were not unlike florists who were trying to sell a flower that would bloom only in absolute darkness.

Some of the White House press corps were lackluster journeymen who simply reported what they saw or were given in handouts. Others—a very few—evidently believed that it was their karma to affect national policy by what and how they wrote. And fewer still involved themselves actively in trying to change the course of events by becoming personally involved.

Mary McGrory was an approaching-middle-age spinster reporter and columnist for *The Evening Star* who had covered some of our campaigns. To read Mary's copy one would gather that every person is all good or all bad. All hats were white or black. Mary was (and, I gather, still is) given to consuming passions. At various stages she has written lovingly of Harold Hughes, Hubert Humphrey, Walter Mondale, Edward Kennedy and some of the antiwar activists. With equal passion she has hated-in-print Richard Nixon, Lyndon Johnson, Robert McNamara and countless hard-hats.

If she'd been a boy, Mary surely would have become a Jesuit priest. As a reporter she vigorously attacks the sinners according to her own narrow and unforgiving political theology.

Early in my White House tenure, Mary and I had a short conversation about the antiwar demonstrations. It was during the time that I was meeting secretly with individual students and campus leaders around the country, trying to understand better what it was we were up against. During that time I had conversations with Dennis Hayes from Stanford; Joe Rhodes, the student-body president at Cal Tech, and others, and in those talks I had learned some things I needed to know.

Mary McGrory suggested that it would do me good to talk to some of the leaders of the New Mobilization, and I said that I was sure she was right. She was obviously surprised. That reply didn't jibe with my stereotype.

A few days later Mary called to invite me to lunch at her apartment. She couldn't suppress the challenge in her tone:

"I've also invited Sam Brown, David Mixner and John O'Sullivan." I had to ask Mary who they were; at that time I didn't know.

Sam Brown and David Mixner had managed Eugene McCarthy's campaign in 1968, Mary told me. They were the architects of the McCarthy New Hampshire primary "victory" over Lyndon Johnson and were among the leaders of the great and bloody confrontation at the Democrats' Chicago convention that year.

Mary lived in one of those 1950's apartment houses along Rock Creek Park. I sat at her dinette table with her other guests and watched her play yenta and interlocutor for these bright young men. It was as if she were the teacher and they her prize pupils; she drew them out, to display their talents for the visitor. In response to her lead, they told me how they felt about Nixon and the war and the draft, and about defense budgets and what the country really needed. I asked about the legitimacy of making foreign policy in the streets, and they argued that the Establishment wouldn't listen unless they did it that way.

Then I asked about the McCarthy campaign. It seemed to me that none of them—the three young men or Mary—had any respect for Gene McCarthy. I saw ambition and a kind of lust gleaming in the young men's eyes as they recounted how McCarthy's candidacy had driven out a sitting President. That was power! How they seemed to love it! I realized that I had come to Mary's to meet bona fide ideologues but had encountered only three more young political engineers who were students of how to get it done with the tools at hand. They appeared to care only about techniques and power.

Gene McCarthy and Mary McGrory were just some of the tools they were working with.

After that luncheon I was never Mary McGrory's guest again. Maybe that's because we never invited her to our house. Maybe it's because I was so obviously turned off by her young power-lustful friends.

At the end of 1969, *The Wall Street Journal* ran a long article about the President's worsening press relations. Ron Ziegler came into the President's office with the newspaper one winter morning as the President was telling me what he wanted me to say about rumors that we would seek a value-added tax.

Nixon (who invariably professed indifference to the views of his critics) immediately read the *Journal* article. He looked up, partway through reading, and said to Ziegler, "You're doing just what you should. The press is hostile, and we'll continue to go over their heads to the public." At that moment Henry Kissinger walked in to join us. The President showed him the *Journal* article. Kissinger read the article, nodding. "Ron is the best press secretary in history, the members of the press corps tell me," Kissinger said.

We were then offered a Nixonian parable: "Henry, one time on a trip I had a long talk at a bar with an old-time White House reporter," Nixon began. "He was a little drunk, and he told me that everyone in the press hates the President. You know why? Because he goes right over their heads to the people, that's why. Seventy-five percent of them hate my guts because they don't like to be beaten. There was Alger Hiss, and Khrushchev in Moscow, and Caracas.

"Understand," Nixon went on, "the press's dislike of me is not personal. No, it's not personal. Their hate is based on the fact that they don't roll me very often. The only time they are nice to you is when they think you are finished."

The conversation moved to other subjects, but Nixon wanted to talk more about the press. Nixon was now talking to himself, not to the three of us in his office. "You know, in the Hiss battle I was alone. Ninety-five percent of the columns and news stories were against me. They all said Whittaker Chambers was lying."

Kissinger chimed in: "Hiss was the epitome of the Eastern Establishment, Mr. President. You and Chambers were outsiders. The wrongness of Hiss really rankled the press."

Nixon nodded. "Intellectuals can't stand a fight and they can't stand to lose."

In organizing the White House staff in late 1968, Nixon had decided there would be no press secretary in the pattern of Bill Moyers, George Christian or Jim Hagerty. Nixon wanted Ron Ziegler to run the press office, but it would be a far less important place than in the past. Ziegler would conduct the ministerial aspects of the office—the routine postings and announcements and press logistics—but he would have no discretionary functions. The President would hold his own press conferences from time to time to deal with policy matters. And in between, Ziegler would say what Nixon told him to say at regular press briefings.

Nixon had been President for six months when he instructed Kissinger, Burns, Moynihan and the rest of us to get busy and dominate the news. Herb Klein and Ron Ziegler were assigned to provide us with lists of the friendlies and un-friendlies among the media, which they dutifully did. In mid-July, I received a twenty-six-page catalogue of columnists, print-media reporters and radio/television reporters, listed by categories. "Those We Can Count On" was a short list. "Those We Can Never Count On" ran two and a half pages. Each reporter was described in a capsule biography:

4. **Richard Valeriani** - NBC - Unfriendly - *Valeriani,* if given a chance, will go with negative slant. Must be forced to the positive. . . .

6. **Bob Pierpoint** - CBS - Neutral - Pierpoint is admitted liberal Democrat but does report fairly, generally, except on matters relating to civil rights and liberal domestic matters. Tends to allow personal emotions to enter into reports. . . .

10. **Cliff Evans** - RKO General - Friendly - *Evans* very much leans to Administration. Often used to guide briefing questions. Unfortunately small audience. . . .

Herb Klein's personal report included:

ABC's Frank Reynolds is unpredictable. He is objective and on a few occasions when he has not been, I have worked on him through Jim Hagerty. . . .

ABC—Bill Gill—a sensationalist who is more negative than positive, and is not over-intelligent. He is just unpredictable and sometimes even friendly.

The most vindictive is Sander Vanocur. You know him. . . .

Klein wrote: "I don't have the opportunity to see television as much as I would like but I think we are getting a great deal of coverage, and our objective has been to decrease the negative. All the network executives are aware of the fact that we are watching and they hear from me both ways."

Richard Nixon was watching too. Among others, he was watching Henry Kissinger, and he outspokenly disapproved of Henry's self-aggrandizing leaks and posturing, but he almost never spoke to Henry about his unhappiness. Instead, he told Bob Haldeman to chastise Henry for his tête-à-têtes with Joseph Kraft, Henry Brandon and James Reston.

In my case Nixon was less reticent. Early in 1969 he told me flatly that I was never to see "Scotty" Reston of *The New York*

Times for any reason (and I did not). When I had given interviews to Hugh Sidey of *Time* or John Osborne of *The New Republic,* Nixon would patiently explain to me that these men were not our friends; I should favor our friends and freeze out our enemies among the press.

But John Osborne was the bell-cow of the White House press corps, and I had a good experience with him. He had covered Washington for years, for several news publications including *Time,* and he was a skilled practitioner of his art. He was always superbly prepared for an interview, but it was hard to see it. He asked questions like an old-time trial lawyer, obliquely, apologetically, behind enough of a smoke screen that the unwary would miss seeing the snare he'd laid by the path. John smoked constantly, mumbled and lost his notes, snuffled and snorted and seemed to ramble all over the place, but in ten or fifteen minutes he'd gotten me to tell him enough to permit him to write the most lucid, full-of-thought and genuinely perceptive column I'd see all week. In spite of Nixon's admonitions I continued to see Osborne, mostly because I liked to watch him work. Secondarily, I knew the other reporters talked to him a lot, and if I could convince John Osborne some domestic effort of ours was worthwhile, I was a long way toward finding approval in other reporters' news stories and columns.

In 1972 and 1973 I totally lost the right to see the reporters to whom I wanted to give interviews. Bob Haldeman told me that the President wanted all press contacts cleared with Ron Ziegler in advance, without exception.

From then on, routine requests for appointments with journalists were phoned to Ziegler when they came in. Often it took a day or two to get Ziegler's reply. I figured that in fact, Richard Nixon himself was passing advance judgment on my contacts. And I'm sure that he knew that I knew. The Ziegler fig leaf avoided an otherwise unpleasant confrontation with the President, which was all right with me. When I really wanted to see a reporter I just forgot to ask Ron.

Richard Nixon at times seemed to believe there was no national issue that was not susceptible to public-relations treatment. And he knew there were certain problems that were especially related to public attitudes.

After a 1970 year-end meeting with Dr. Arthur Burns, the President mulled over Burns's pessimistic report on consumer confidence. Christmas sales were down, while savings were the highest in history. General Motors was on strike. Shoppers were buying only inexpensive goods. There was a lack of confidence that there would be an economic recovery, Burns had said.

"What's the trouble?" Nixon asked me. "I doubt they're worried about inflation. Is it unemployment? There are ten days left until Christmas. I want to know how sales are going, regularly.

"We may need a media campaign about the economy," he continued. "All this recession talk can infect people, can't it? Can't there be a psychological recession? The question is, how can we un-create it?

"From 1961 to 1963 what did the three television networks say about recession?" Nixon asked, thinking back to the Kennedy years. "There was plenty of unemployment then. It was 6.7 percent in 1961. What was NBC saying then? You take responsibility for this," Nixon said to me. "How many stories did NBC run on the economy in 1961?"

A quick check disclosed that there had been no material difference in the television networks' concern for the economy ten years before. And Paul McCracken, George Shultz and our other economists felt the depressed consumer confidence they saw was based on much more than mere television talk.

But Nixon persisted in his feeling that a White House public-relations effort could affect the economy one way or the other.

When Arthur Burns and others persuaded the President to adopt an "incomes policy" and impose wage and price controls, it was from its inception to its fadeout as much public relations as it was substantive. And throughout, Richard Nixon was the architect of the P.R. aspects of wage and price controls. His theme was that Government was at last doing something about prices, inflation, the cost of living and buying power. The President stood for lower prices and fairness in the application of controls. Controls were only temporary. As soon as the "fire of inflation" abated, the controls would be removed and all Americans would realize the fruits of their sacrifice. If controls were largely an exercise in public relations, and if controls failed, the Nixonian syllogism would conclude that better P.R. would have made them succeed.

Toward the end of April 1971 I had gone to New York to do an interview with John Hart on his early-morning CBS news show. That involved traveling up from Washington the night before, going to sleep early and being at the CBS studio about six in the morning. During a break in the interview John Hart suggested that I stick around until he finished so we could have some breakfast and a visit.

So we went up to the Edwardian Room of the Plaza for breakfast, along with John's producer. About halfway through the eggs we were joined by John's boss Richard Salant, the President of CBS News. No one had said anything to me about Salant's joining us. But he was welcomed; I figured Hart had passed the word to Salant to join us, and that was all right with me.

Salant thanked me for coming up to do the interview and we talked a little about its content. Then he asked, "How are our people at the White House doing?" I took that to refer to Robert Pierpoint and Dan Rather, the two CBS Television regulars.

I'd had the quality of the CBS coverage on my mind at that time. A domestic-policy story they had recently carried was dead wrong. That was upsetting, but I was doubly upset because no one from CBS had checked the story in advance with my staff or me. If someone had, perhaps the story could have run correctly, or at least with two versions of the facts.

So when Salant asked me, I told him. I said, substantially, that I rarely heard from his people. I said it was my impression that Dan Rather was consistently critical of our domestic-policy initiatives. I said I had the impression that Dan Rather failed to check his stories, for one of two reasons: either he had a bias or he was lazy. From my standpoint, I said, it appeared that he was just lazy.

Salant replied that Rather had been brought to big-time television news from a Texas station as a result of diligent work during a hurricane. I had heard that story, I replied, and it had always seemed a long jump from covering a horse stranded in a flood to covering the White House. I made it clear that I didn't think much of Mr. Rather's diligence.

By way of contrast, the reporters for the other networks and many of the print journalists were in and out of my office all the time. Some had regular appointments to come in just before their filing deadlines to check their facts. Jack Sutherland of *U.S. News & World Report;* Herb Kaplow, then of NBC Television news; James Gannon of *The Wall Street Journal;* John Osborne of *The New Republic;* Joe Alsop; his brother Stewart; Lou Cannon of *The Washington Post;* John Leacocos; and George Herman of CBS Television, for example, were my regular visitors. But not Dan Rather.

My talk with Richard Salant has found its way into the folklore about Richard Nixon and the press as an incident in which the White House staff set out to get Dan Rather fired.

On June 8 a syndicated Washington political columnist, Marianne Means, erroneously reported that I had "paid a surprise visit on [Richard] Salant in his Manhattan office." There, she said, "President Nixon's principal assistant for domestic affairs demanded recently that CBS News President Richard Salant fire the network's veteran White House correspondent because the President did not like the way he reported the news. . . . Ehrlichman denounced CBS reporter Dan Rather as a biased observer who sounded like 'an arm of the Democratic National Committee' and who 'did not give sufficient emphasis to the President's accomplishments.'

"Ehrlichman insisted that Salant get rid of Rather. What Salant replied privately to Ehrlichman is not quite clear. . . ."

The New York Times, The Evening Star and *The Washington Post* got right on Marianne's story. A White House aide trying to get Rather fired would be a big story.

But alas, Marianne Means's story didn't check out; the CBS people who were interviewed agreed that I had done no such thing. The *Times* said:

The report, made in a syndicated column by Marianne Means and published in The Washington Star here today, was also denied emphatically by [CBS] network executives here.

The *Post* reported:

Both Ehrlichman and William Small, CBS Washington Bureau Chief, told essentially the same story of a meeting between Ehrlichman and Richard Salant, president of CBS news.
Small said that Ehrlichman was "very critical" of Rather but "at no time did he suggest that Rather be fired or transferred."

The *Star* (Marianne Means's home paper) carried my statement in full, in the longest story of the three. Its final paragraphs said:

William Small, CBS news director in Washington, confirmed Ehrlichman's version today after talking with Salant and Rather.
Small said, "at no time did Ehrlichman ask that Rather be fired."

Within minutes of my return to Washington from New York, I was told that my secretary had a call from Dan Rather saying he wanted to come see me. Bob Haldeman and I agreed that it would be a good idea for a third person to be present, and he volunteered. He was curious as to what Rather might say.

Haldeman felt I should know if Rather had ever requested to see me for an interview or to check a story, and whether or not I had turned him down. So I had Jana Hruska check the careful records she kept. They showed that Dan Rather had never made a request to see me and been turned down. Moreover, it had been more than a year since he'd asked to talk to me.

Rather was given an appointment, and came in. Haldeman and I talked with him for perhaps twenty minutes, during which I told him just how I had happened to talk with Salant, the question Salant had asked and just exactly what I had said in response. I told Rather I thought he was careless in what he reported on CBS, that the danger to the public was that he sounded as if he had checked his facts but that I knew he had not. I told him I was available—as I had always been—and that he could continue to feel free to call or come in to question me.

For the next two or three weeks, Rather did call or come in a couple of times a week. But in those contacts I could not help contrasting his professional ability with that of the real reporters among the White House regulars. John Osborne, for example, invariably came to an interview with such a depth of understanding of his subject that I found I could learn from him. And Osborne's technique reminded me of some of the great old cross-examiners I used to watch in the courtrooms back home.

I had the feeling that Dan Rather was asking his obvious questions because my talk with Salant had called his bluff. He was in my office because he had to be, to satisfy CBS, not because any sense of journalistic professionalism required it.

In a few weeks Rather stopped calling, and he went back to his old way of doing things.

But as Watergate heated up in the spring of 1973, the Salant-Ehrlichman story began to appear again. One magazine article carried Rather's version of his conversation with Haldeman and me, along with Rather's claim that he had not "seen much of Ehrlichman at the White House—because Ehrlichman would not see him."

Before long Rather was moving around the country (plugging a book he wrote with the help of a collaborator) telling interviewers that the Nixon White House had tried to get him fired. In spite of what Salant and the other CBS people had said, Rather found it to his advantage to adopt the discredited Marianne Means version of the episode, because by then, Rather had become a part of the Nixon story. His smart-aleck comments during White House press conferences had caused some professional journalists to criticize his obvious lack of objectivity. Rather's answer was that Nixon and his people had been out to get him for years, as evidenced by the Marianne Means story.

I hadn't really thought much about Dan Rather from the time I left the White House until after I got out of prison. During that time he'd been removed from the CBS White House assignment, and I had lost track of him.

But when I signed a contract with the Mutual Broadcasting System in the summer of 1978 I went to the Chicago convention of the National Association of Broadcasters. Mutual wanted to announce my upcoming series of commentary broadcasts there, to attract the maximum press attention. On August 20 I held a press conference and talked about what I hoped to accomplish with *The View from Here* on Mutual. About thirty reporters and six or seven television cameras were there, among them CBS Television news.

A print journalist asked me if it was true that I'd tried to get Dan Rather fired back in 1971. So I settled back and fully told the story of Salant's joining us at breakfast and of his question and my answer. I said I had not tried to get Rather fired; I felt then and had always felt that CBS had an absolute right to post anyone it wanted at the White House. But I also had a right to my opinion about the competence of the person the network chose. So when Salant asked me, I told him: his man Rather was slanted or lazy. Then I finished by telling about Rather's sudden but brief diligence after my talk with Salant.

At the end of the press conference several reporters came up to the table with follow-up questions. Finally, one of them leaned over and said quietly: "I'm from CBS Television [the reporter gave me his name]. I've worked with Rather for years. You're right. He's just plain lazy."

The questions and my answers at that press conference were carried widely. Some were about Nixon, some about the press and my new radio series; and some, of course, were about my opinion that as a White House correspondent, Dan Rather was lazy.

During this time—in fact, for two and a half years after my release—I was on parole. At first this meant that every time I left Santa Fe I had to obtain the permission of Norman Mugleston, my parole officer. And every time I returned home from a trip I was required to call him to check in.

When I returned from Chicago I was told to come to see my parole officer for a talk. This was the first and only time I had been called on the carpet as a parolee.

"I don't know any other way to tell you," Mugleston began, "except to give it to you straight out."

I couldn't imagine what he was leading up to, but he was more troubled than I had seen him before. "You had a press conference in Chicago three days ago."

"Yes," I said.

"Evidently it was very controversial." Mugleston leafed through some notes, then looked up at me.

"No, not really," I said.

"Well, I haven't read the transcript, nor do I intend to," he began.

"I'm pretty sure there wasn't one," I interrupted. "In any case, what does what I said in Chicago have to do with my parole?"

"The Parole Commission would be concerned if the travel which they permit you—like this trip to Chicago—involved conduct on your part which led to lawsuits. That kind of thing could be bad for your psyche—for your rehabilitation," Mugleston explained.

"What lawsuits? Who is going to sue me? What's this all about?"

"Did you make some charges against Dan Rather?" he asked. "He is complaining that you made false charges against him while you were on permitted travel in Chicago."

"Well"—I shook my head—"first, the answers I gave to the question about Rather were completely true. In fact, a colleague of his was there and agreed with what I said about him." I then told Mugleston about my chance meeting with Richard Salant nine years earlier and the substance of our conversation.

"As your parole officer, I would be very concerned if you became controversial," Mugleston said.

"Look, Norm, whatever I say or do is bound to be controversial. I've just signed a contract to be a radio commentator, and I'll be saying my opinion on the radio every day. And if someone asks me a question, I can't do less than answer it truthfully. What brought up all of this? Where does it come from?"

"Mr. Rather called the Parole Commission in Washington, D.C. They referred him to my boss and then Rather called me. I talked to him for quite a while."

"What does he want of you?" I asked. "Is he trying to get my parole revoked or is he merely interested in shutting me up?" I recalled with irony Rather's claim that I had tried to make trouble for him in 1971.

"Mr. Rather did not threaten you."

"Well, you have to admit there is a bit of coercion in all of this when you, in your official capacity as United States Parole Officer, call in one of your parolees and tell him that you are concerned about his conduct in criticizing Dan Rather. I think perhaps the chairman of the U.S. Parole Commission should write me a letter saying what limitations there are on my conduct—on my right to speak—on what I can and can't say about Dan Rather, or anything else."

Mugleston backed off a little. "The chairman is not involved in this."

"Well, whoever is involved, I'm feeling threatened; obviously, Rather called the Commission and then your boss and then you to make trouble for me. He's trying to shut me up, and he's using his clout with you and the rest of the Government to threaten me. What do you suggest I do?" I asked.

"You can do whatever you wish," he replied defensively. "I want you to understand that *I* do not intend to threaten you."

I told Mugleston I was upset because all my past dealings with him had been so satisfactory. It sounded as if he were letting Rather use him, and that bothered me. In any case, he could tell the Parole Commission or Rather or anyone else that unless my lawyer advised me otherwise, I intended to answer questions about Rather or any other subject as forthrightly and truthfully as I knew how, whatever the consequences.

Nothing more was heard from Rather, CBS or the U.S. Parole Commission about my voicing my dissatisfaction with Rather's past journalistic diligence or fairness.

But Tom Brokaw came to Santa Fe in the spring of 1979, about six months after the Rather-to-Mugleston episode. I taped an interview with Brokaw for the *Today* show (plugging my second novel, *The Whole Truth,* which had just been published), and then my wife Christy McLaurine, Brokaw and I went to dinner. Brokaw had been NBC's White House correspondent, in competition with Dan Rather, during some of the time I worked there. Tom and I reminisced some at dinner about those days and the people we had known, so I brought up Rather and told Brokaw of the CBS man who had come up to me after that Chicago press conference to corroborate what I'd said about Dan's laziness.

Brokaw nodded. "CBS approached me," he said. In 1971 CBS had decided to let Dan "move on" and had offered Brokaw a substantial sum to move over from NBC to cover the White House for CBS, in Rather's place.

Probably my comments to Salant saved Rather's job for him, as I now put the facts together. The CBS executives could not appear to be knuckling under to White House criticism, so once I'd spoken to Salant, they couldn't move Brokaw in and Rather out, whatever they thought of Rather.

Tom Brokaw said he and others had an impression that I was hostile to the press who covered the White House. It may be that I appeared that way. But in fact, I only wanted the press people covering the domestic side to be more diligent, more accurate and better informed. Perhaps I held them to a higher standard than that to which they held themselves.

The *Christian Science Monitor* ran a particularly incorrect editorial one day on some aspect of the budget for social programs. So I called Joseph Harsch, then the person in charge of the editorial page of the *Monitor,* and asked him to come talk about it the next time he was in Washington. As a Christian Scientist, I had more than ordinary interest in the performance of the *Monitor.* I was frequently available to Courtney Sheldon and Budge Sperling of its Washington bureau. (I once invited its prized columnist Richard Strout [also known as T.R.B.] to come in for a talk in 1969. I was disappointed to find him to be extraordinarily unpleasant and hostile; upon sitting down he announced that he was not a Christian Scientist—obviously he didn't approve of my religion—and he didn't think much of Richard Nixon, either. I said that at least some of that could be seen in his *Monitor* columns. I was interested in helping Strout understand what we were trying to do. I began to offer him whatever help I could, but it appeared he was interested only in antagonizing me. In his memoirs Strout contends that I tried to co-opt him during that brief session, but the fact is that his offensive personality so put me off that I decided to end the meeting quickly and to avoid Mr. Strout thereafter.)

When the *Monitor*'s editorialist, Joe Harsch, dropped by, I had a file of facts and figures ready for him. The Budget people had collected welfare statistics and other information on the subject of the *Monitor*'s recent editorial, and I invited Joe to take the data with him. I told him how greatly concerned I was that the *Monitor*—of all papers—be accurate in matters of this kind, and I wanted to help in any way I could.

Joe had his problems up there at the *Monitor* in Boston, and he began to share them with me. It is hard to be accurate when you are shorthanded to begin with and then some of your people are out (excuse the expression) sick.

"Maybe it would be better to just not print a doubtful editorial if you can't check the facts," I suggested.

"Listen," Joe said, "if we are right *half* the time, I've got to be satisfied." Joe didn't seem happy with the situation at the *Monitor,* but he was resigned to it.

I was to hear substantially that same surprising defense from Hugh Sidey in 1970. He was the Washington bureau chief for *Time* magazine when *Time* ran a long story on our health policy that was studded with errors. I met Hugh for lunch at the Hay-Adams Hotel to talk to him about our version of the facts. I had come armed with *Time*'s story pasted on sheets of paper with much of our data in the margins, annotating the story to show *Time*'s mistakes.

Sidey listened, but neither the facts nor I moved him. He began telling me about his impossible deadlines, the trouble his Washington people had with *Time*'s New York researchers and editors, and his difficulty getting access to Nixon people who would talk to his reporters about the facts. On balance, *Time* had run a pretty good story, Sidey said.

"But," I protested, "it's full of mistakes."

"Every story contains mistakes," he said. "A reporter on deadline just does the best he can. You have to expect mistakes."

It took a while, but eventually I did come to expect mistakes in reporting; but I never got to the point where I could join Sidey and Harsch in their passive tolerance of the errors.

I seldom criticized the press in a general way; I preferred to talk to individuals when I spotted mistakes. But one day in June 1972 in Los Angeles, Robert Abernathy asked me on NBC Television why the President was not holding more press conferences, and I made some general comments which really aroused the press. Abernathy noted that there had not been a televised Presidential press conference for many months, and he asked why.

I began my answer with approved doctrine: the President

used many avenues of communication to reach the American people. Of all of those, the televised East Room extravaganza was one of the poorest.

The Associated Press reported the details of the rest of my response this way:

NIXON AIDE SAYS REPORTERS ASK DUMB QUESTIONS

Los Angeles (AP) President Nixon's domestic affairs adviser says one reason the President has few news conferences is that newsmen ask dumb questions.

"He doesn't get very good questions at a press conference, frankly," said John D. Ehrlichman. "He goes in there for a half hour and gets a lot of flabby and fairly dumb questions and it doesn't really elucidate very much.

"I've seen him many times come off one of those things and go back in and say, 'Isn't it extraordinary how poor the quality of the questions are?'"

Asked during an interview taped Tuesday for showing on KNBC television Saturday why Nixon has had only one news conference this year, he said, "He's been very busy, and he communicates with the American people in a lot of different ways."

In a typical news conference, Ehrlichman said, "You have 300 people jumping up and yelling, 'Mr. President,' and all that kind of thing and it just isn't a very useful way of communicating with the American people. . . .

"I think some of them may be preoccupied with their own interests or their bureaus may have fed them things that they're asked to ask, but the long and short of it is that you don't get very much out of it.

"It seems to be a great deal more . . . could be developed as interesting news and valuable for the people out of a one-on-one with Dan Rather (CBS White House Correspondent), where he could follow up and press and so on."

Asked at one point whether he was accusing the Washington press corps of being flabby and dumb, Ehrlichman replied, "No—I said the questions are flabby and dumb."

Then, the next day, at another press conference, I took six or seven questions about what I'd said. Los Angeles reporters seemed very much upset that I had criticized their Washington colleagues. That led me to deliver a short remonstrance that resulted in this UPI story:

NIXON AIDE SAYS NEWSMEN LIKE
'INSECURE LADIES'

John D. Ehrlichman, one of President Nixon's top aides, Wednesday compared newsmen to "insecure young ladies" in love.

Ehrlichman, the White House domestic affairs adviser, was asked at a Los Angeles news conference about his remark the day before that President Nixon does not hold many news conferences because the reporters ask "a lot of flabby and fairly dumb questions."

Responded Ehrlichman: "When people at the White House get together with the press, newsmen are sort of like insecure young ladies and they keep asking us if we love them. Then, when we tell them the truth, there is a hurt feeling that sets in.

"It would be better if you didn't ask us if you didn't want to know."

By the time I returned to Washington, the White House press corps was lying in ambush for me. When the Secretary of Health, Education and Welfare, Elliot Richardson, joined me to announce an education bill the President had signed, I tried to defang the subject by saying, at the end of our press conference: "While I am here, I want to congratulate everyone on the apparent muscle tone and wit of the questions today."

The reporters laughed, but one of them called out, "We wish we could say the same for the answers."

Editorial writers all around the country picked up the "flabby and dumb" phrase to either blast Nixon for not having more press conferences or criticize the Washington press corps for their lack of diligence.

Finally, at his next in-the-office press conference, Nixon was asked:

QUESTION: Mr. President, is Mr. Ehrlichman correct when he says that you sometimes get irritated with us for our dumb and flabby questions, so-called?
THE PRESIDENT: You are not dumb and flabby. No, I noted that comment and expected a question on it. I am afraid if I begin to characterize the questions you will begin to characterize my answers, but you probably will anyway. In any event, as far as questions are concerned, I think what Mr. Ehrlichman was referring to was the tendency in the big East Room conferences for questions to come in from all over the place and no follow-up, as there can be in a conference like this.

Sometimes the questions may appear somewhat less relevant. I have found, for example, although we do not rule out the big conference where everybody gets to come, I have found that these smaller sessions do provide an opportunity for members of the regular White House press, who study these issues day by day and who know what is relevant and what is not relevant and who can follow up, I think that the possibility of dumb and flabby questions is much less and I don't, frankly, complain about it.

The other point that I should make is this: in looking over the transcripts of various press conferences, I have not seen many softballs, and I don't want any because it is only the hardball that you can hit or strike out on.

But on July 7, out at San Clemente, Nixon and I had an early-morning meeting to prepare for a session with his economists. He was disturbed by a report from the news summary editor, Mort Allin, that the media were being "soft" on George McGovern.

"They are biased, of course," the President said. "But I want Agnew kept out of the subject of media bias now. He is to make no public statements that the media is against us. Get others to do it." Agnew was too harsh and vindictive, Nixon said.

"Kicking the press is an art," Nixon continued. "Your flabby-and-dumb crack was good. You let them have it without rancor. That's what you have to do."

CHAPTER SIXTEEN

Nixon, Kissinger and Foreign Affairs

HENRY KISSINGER WORRIES about what the world thinks about him. He may care more than anyone else I know. And he works very hard to be sure that people—those who matter—think well of him. When someone is writing a book about Henry, he keeps track of the author, and especially to whom that author is talking. I've had several phone calls from Henry in the past three years because Seymour Hersh and others have asked me questions about Henry. I can't imagine how Kissinger knows to whom these authors are talking, but he does.

When we talk, Henry always reminds me that *he* is writing a book too, and that of course it must mention *me* to be complete. But, he assures me, I will be treated fairly—even in a kindly fashion—in his book. Then he asks me what kind of questions I was asked about him.

Henry and his wife, Nancy Maginnes, are the tenders of a flame: the historical reputation of Dr. Henry Alfred Kissinger, the Nobel laureate. When last I saw them, in 1979, I had the impression that they stand four-hour shifts, alert to attack, shielding the flame with their bodies and souls. Anything else they do is incidental to that life's work. Lately, I'd guess, they are spending more and more time gathering fuel to keep the flame alive. Henry explained to me that he is impelled these days by moral imperatives. When I asked him if he was having any fun, he didn't seem to understand the question.

Henry was not always so serious. In fact, most of my recollections of Henry during our White House years when he was an Assistant to the President involved good laughs (either with him or at him). I liked the personal, private Henry in those early days.

In 1975, when it was all over, he came to testify at my first trial (the Fielding break-in case), and that wasn't so funny. The judge was Gerhard Gesell, and the judge was determined that there would be a conviction. He would not let us examine Dr. Kissinger; he insisted my lawyer write out the questions he intended to ask. Then Gesell cut them back to six or eight innocuous queries. Gesell apparently didn't want to oppress the then Secretary of State. So my recollection of Henry at that trial had very little to do with Henry's testimony in the courtroom.

But I do remember his arrival and departure. To begin with, the trial itself was a media event. A considerable crowd gathered at the courthouse door each day to watch the witnesses come and go. There were five or six film crews, lights, twenty reporters and another twenty photographers hanging around on an ordinary day. The day Henry Kissinger came, the regular corps expanded to perhaps a hundred. Henry was never one to retire shyly in the face of journalistic interest. On this occasion he had worn his somber visage, with suit to match, and surrounded himself with a retinue worthy of an Arab king, a Mafia *capo* or a movie star. At his sides were eight

State Department security men, and the inner throng included Henry's lawyers and press representatives. I watched through an upstairs window as Henry alighted from his limousine, waited for his retainers to assemble, then stumped purposefully through the mass of reporters and cameras. When he got to the second floor of the Federal courthouse, Henry's team spread out to surround him as he moved along the wide corridor. It was impressive. I thought of Huey Long and Mussolini and J. P. Morgan and Barry Goldwater in 1964. (That year Goldwater had the biggest, roughest bodyguards I've ever seen. They threw people over couches in hotel lobbies when they got in Barry's way.) Henry swept out of the courthouse the same way he swept in. On his way he shook my hand and said, "I hope I've helped you," and I'm sure he meant it.

I first met Henry at the Hotel Pierre during Nixon's transition. Nelson Rockefeller, Henry's patron, had just given Henry $50,000, and everyone was wondering whether that should be mentioned in connection with Henry's appointment as Assistant to the President for National Security Affairs. In those days I was screening the Cabinet and other appointees for conflicts of interest, so I was given Dr. Kissinger's attention for a few minutes. He had no idea what assets he owned. He knew he had the $50,000, but a business manager looked after his holdings, even then, and provided him with a computer printout, quarterly.

Kissinger was not eager to tell people about his $50,000 gift, but we persuaded him that sooner or later it would become known. It was clear from Henry's balance sheet that his books on geopolitics had not been best-sellers; I thought it odd that such a modest financial corpus needed a manager.

I saw little of Kissinger again until we were in the White House after the inauguration. Then he and I worked together intensively, planning the President's February trip to eight European capitals.

At that time Henry's small office was in the basement of the West Wing, next to his communications center and the cramped little conference room that was called the Situation Room. The atmosphere down there was always frantic. Ten or eleven of Henry's staff sat at desks outside his door, and he rushed out and back constantly as we met in his office to plan the trip.

Once, when he went out to talk to one of his people, I noticed a wood carving of a bird on the windowsill. When I picked it up I realized it was hollow.

"Where did you get this?" I asked Henry when he returned.

"The Russian Ambassador, Dobrynin, gave that to me," Kissinger said. He sat down and we resumed work on the details of the President's trip. But my eyes kept coming back to that wood carving, which sat about four feet from Henry's desk.

I nodded toward the bird. "Have you had it looked at?" I asked. I kept remembering Henry Cabot Lodge showing the United Nations the microphones the Russians had hidden in the carved seal in our embassy.

Henry looked surprised, then annoyed. Kissinger's cultivated relationship with Dobrynin was extremely important to the workings of his operation. My suggestion was most unwelcome.*

Henry and I had our differences during that 1969 trip to Europe. My objectives were different from his, so our disputes were not remarkable, but they illustrate Henry's difficulty in joining Nixon's longtime staff at the beginning of the Administration. Some of us had been campaigning with Nixon ten years or more, while Henry was just arriving from the halls of Harvard.

During a political campaign, a candidate's staff is suspicious of the "locals." It's presumed that they have their own provincial objectives, which may not jibe with the candidate's electoral goals. In Europe I applied the same presumptions to the host nations and to our own embassy people as well. Our diplomats often seemed much more concerned with the host nation's desires than with our President's objectives.

Henry tended to side with the Foreign Service people. In England, Henry was deferential to our Ambassador, David Bruce, a venerable diplomat of great stature and wealth. I'm afraid I didn't know much about Bruce at the time, and he seemed a little over-the-hill to me. I was as blunt as Henry was sycophantic, and I insisted on arrangements that Bruce didn't like. He was looking at them as an Englishman would, and I was looking at how they would play on the evening news back home.

When we returned to the White House in early March, Bob Haldeman established some patterns which we then followed consistently from 1969 to 1973. At eight every weekday morn-

---

* Henry grabbed the wooden bird by the neck, jumped up and rolled through the door. In a moment he was back without it. "We will let someone else play with the bird," he said with finality.

ing there was a meeting in Haldeman's office. Over the years, Haldeman, Kissinger and I were charter members. Bryce Harlow was there the first couple of years. Ron Ziegler was added later. George Shultz attended after he moved from Labor to the White House. Usually there were four of us, seldom more than six.

Ostensibly, the meeting was held to plan the day. We sometimes reviewed the President's schedule and tried to anticipate his problems, but usually we ended up hashing over the crisis of the moment. Bad television or newspaper coverage, staff problems, ITT, Spiro Agnew, Vietnam, demonstrations, the Nixon family and Congress all were grist for the morning mill. If the President called one of us during the night with complaints or assignments, his gripes would become our agenda at the senior-staff meeting the next morning.

Kissinger often stayed in his office, eating his dietary eggs, during these 8 A.M. meetings. Sometimes he joined us later; his late arrivals were invariably greeted with sarcastic welcomes and jokes about his tardiness. Occasionally Haldeman phoned and demanded that Henry come down the hall to join in a discussion to which he was indispensable. On rare occasions Kissinger was there without invitation and participated enthusiastically in discussions, especially those that had nothing to do with national security or foreign affairs.

Over the years Henry became deeply involved in White House issues far outside his province. Partisan politics, the President's family and friends, our politics and logistics in response to the massive antiwar demonstrations, staff personnel changes, college unrest and the President's budget were all interesting to Henry. He freely entered into the President's conversations about hiring and firing, for example. William Rogers' was not the only tail Henry tried to tie a can to. An old academic rivalry had caused hard feelings between Henry and James Schlesinger. Schlesinger's rise from Deputy Director of OMB to Director of the CIA and Chairman of the Atomic Energy Commission occurred in spite of Henry's expressed opinion, not because of it. Henry was critical of Robert Mayo, Director of the Bureau of the Budget, too. Mayo had problems other than Kissinger's enmity, but Nixon's decision to make Mayo the first retiree from the Cabinet was unquestionably bolstered by Henry's opinion.

Henry even involved himself in Chappaquiddick. In early August 1969, he hurried to the President with an inside story he'd picked up in conversation with a person considered to be close to the Kennedys.

On August 7, I received this instruction from the President:

Talk to Kissinger on a very confidential basis with regard to a talk he had with J. K. Galbraith as to what really happened in the EMK matter. It is a fascinating story. I'm sure HAK will tell you the story and then you of course will know how to check it out and get it properly exploited.

Henry's hot tip turned out to be unverifiable gossip.

As freely as Henry expressed himself on subjects beyond his bailiwick, he was extremely reluctant to have any of the rest of us enter the National Security area. The only times I became involved in the Kissinger sphere were when the President specifically told me to. And at times, Henry objected so strenuously that Nixon backed down and pulled me out.

The President asked for network time in the summer of 1971 to announce that he would go to Peking for a summit meeting with the Chinese. I flew into Burbank, California, to watch the brief show. Euphoric, Nixon decided to break his rule against socializing with the staff and take a few of us out to dinner afterward, at Perino's. In the days when Nixon and I were growing up in Southern California, Perino's was the *ne plus ultra* of restaurants, but by 1971 it had been sold to a conglomerate chain and its former glory was somewhat faded.

With the President coming to dinner, the new owners recalled the aged Mr. Perino, in full evening dress, to greet us. He tottered about, showing us to a banquette in the main dining room. All the other diners looked as though they were just off the tour bus from Red Oak, Iowa. After we had been greeted by a series of captains, the President opened negotiations with the wine steward and Mr. Perino, seconded by Kissinger.

"Well, yes, that wine sounds interesting. What do you think, Henry?"

"I believe that '64 was a fine year, Mr. President. I believe that was a wet season," Kissinger bluffed.

"What about Château Lafite?" Nixon asked. "If we're having the beef that should go very well."

"We have a fine, rare selection," the steward said quickly. "Please let me select something for you."

So in a short while, a huge bottle was brought to us, dust-encrusted. It was the biggest bottle of wine I'd ever seen. There was a ceremonial opening, with much hovering about. Nixon sniffed it, swished it around in his glass and invited Henry's opinion while Bob Haldeman, Ron Ziegler and I tried to keep straight faces. At last the selection was approved and the steward poured for all of us. The bottle was the size of two tenpins, and the venerable Perino regaled us with its history as we tasted. To my uncultivated palate it seemed a bit sharp, but our two "experts," Nixon and Kissinger, proclaimed it outstanding. I had the feeling neither one knew what he was talking about.

After dinner both the President and Henry jumped up and began moving about the large dining room shaking hands with the other diners. The President's naval aide called me aside, looking very distressed.

"What shall I do, sir?" the Commander asked. "That old bandit [pointing to Perino] wants six hundred dollars for that bottle of wine!"

I suggested that the Commander raise his battle flags and offer the proprietor $300 spot cash. If he wanted more than that, let him make his demands to the President of the United States and leader of the free world, personally. The Commander did his duty and was able to settle for $300.

When we returned to the White House and resumed our normal routine, the President and I met each day to dispose of the domestic issues on my agenda. But he was full of the China trip and talked of it constantly.

On July 20, 1971, during one of these sessions, I broached the notion that I might "advance" his China trip, as I had done two years before in Europe. I suggested that he give the idea some thought. Nixon was noncommittal.

But that afternoon he called in Henry Kissinger and Bob Haldeman and told them that he had decided to have me lead the advance party to Peking. Kissinger was decidedly cool to the idea. He reminded Nixon of my bluntness. "You can't force the Chinese, you know," Henry said.

"Do you object to John doing it?" Nixon asked Henry directly.

"No," Kissinger replied. He said he wanted to think about it. So Nixon told me I was hired.

Within two weeks I heard from Bob Haldeman that Nixon had changed his mind. Kissinger had mounted a vigorous and successful campaign to keep me off the trip, Bob said, and his ultimate argument had been that since Henry and I were of equal rank, the Chinese would be hopelessly confused by my presence. What if, during the advance trip, I were granted an audience with Mao? Disastrous.

I was more than a little disappointed and was deeply resentful of Henry's campaign against me. I told Haldeman to tell Nixon that I wanted the President himself to rescind our arrangement, if anyone was going to do it. As far as I was concerned, I was still scheduled for the trip until *he* told me differently. Haldeman persuaded me that I was making things unnecessarily difficult for the President, and I was surely not going to help myself by insisting on embarrassing him.

For several weeks I found it difficult to be more than barely civil to Dr. Kissinger. I had a great deal of ego wrapped up in doing that advance trip to China. When the President told me I could do it I had confided in my wife and children, and it was difficult to explain to them why he'd changed his mind.

On July 23, during the morning senior-staff meeting, Henry and I had an argument. Without mentioning China, Kissinger delivered a sermonette about people on the White House staff trying to invade his province.

"As long as I am here," he intoned, "no one is going to go around me. They are not going around me on intelligence matters or narcotics or the budget or anything else."

I got the message, and it made me mad. "You are a damn bottleneck sometimes," I said. "Stuff can sit on your desk forever. We don't talk to you about narcotics enforcement because if we waited for your sign-off nothing would happen."

Henry flushed. "I cannot do everything. I have heavy responsibilities here. I work an eighteen-hour day as it is."

"Bullshit," I said with some heat. "You get here an hour later than the rest of us, and you're usually the first one to leave to go to some Georgetown party. Don't give us that eighteen-hour baloney."

Later in July, I called Henry and asked him to come to my office to explain to me why I would not be advancing the China trip. Our argument had strained relations, and I wanted to clear the air. Moreover, I didn't want him to believe he could knock me off the trip without any cost at all. In a few minutes he came in.

When Henry is faced with an awkward or embarrassing situation, his body betrays him. He clears his throat often, lips together tightly, nodding his head repeatedly. He found it difficult to look at me directly when he came in and sat down that day. Slowly, he explained his reasons for opposing me for the trip, his tone an octave lower than usual.

I said that in the future when we had a problem of this kind I would expect him to come to me directly, instead of campaigning against me behind my back.

"You are right," he said quietly. "Now if you will excuse me, I have people waiting for me," and he hurried out of my office.

Apparently Nixon was told of my profound disappointment. Before long he suggested that George Shultz and I take one of his (windowless) 707s to the Orient—to Vietnam, Japan, Hong Kong and Singapore—to do a few things for him. We took along wives, secretaries, aides and even Art Laffer, Shultz' young economist. In a way, that trip was a generous and unforgettable recompense for losing out on the China trip.

Henry Kissinger's well-chronicled feud with Secretary of State William Rogers was noisy. Kissinger often complained, "Rogers is stupid! Rogers is a danger to the world! Rogers is"—the ultimate insult—"an amateur!"

In response to most of this, Rogers maintained a decorous silence. Once in a while he made a phone call to Bob Haldeman when Henry had gone too far in public. But the more Rogers forbore, the worse Henry's complaints became. When there were serious international problems, Kissinger seldom missed an opportunity to attack the Secretary of State behind his back. It sometimes put extraordinary pressure on Richard Nixon.

In the summer of 1969, Nixon decided to go to Johnson Island in the Pacific, to be present when the first moon-landing astronauts returned to Earth. Henry Kissinger proposed that Nixon go on to make visits to several foreign countries and, incidentally, included himself in the Johnson Island contingent.

Now the Secretary of State had to be considered. "If Henry goes, I've got to take Bill," Nixon said to me.

But it rankled Nixon that he had to share this event with an entourage; this was to be *his* triumph, not *theirs*. "They can both come, but only the President goes out on the carrier to the splashdown," Nixon decided. "There will be no staff along, no doctor and only two Secret Service men," he instructed, watching to see if I was taking notes. "I suppose," he added, "I should take Munson." (Nixon invariably called Monzon, his Filipino valet, "Munson.") "Munson" could fix the President's meals, carry his suitcase and look after his other needs.

"There is to be no press pool on my helicopter," Nixon went on, playing that forlorn and impossible wishing game he liked so well. "You know, I'm inclined to take Bill Rogers out there and not Henry. It's a question of what is customary, you see. Bill is Secretary of State, after all, and Henry isn't. Adele Rogers' wife] could keep Pat company on Guam. Call Bill," he instructed me, "and see if he wants to go."

As he knew it would, Nixon's entourage at the splashdown included the full complement of bodyguards, a vast press contingent, the President's doctor, military aides, Haldeman, Haldeman's aide and, of course, both Rogers and Kissinger.

Nixon was never happy about Kissinger's feud with Rogers and the State Department. Nixon disapproved of State's "softness" and disloyalty, and he expected the White House staff to prevail over the departments (in his behalf), but he also hated acrimony.

In general, Nixon favored Henry and spoke to us of Rogers as "ineffectual, selfish and vain." But Kissinger made his case against Rogers many times over; the emotional tirades were overkill. At first Nixon tolerated them as the price of doing business with Henry, but before long the President was complaining to Bob Haldeman and to me (among others, I am sure) of Henry's tendency to waste great blocks of the President's time in childish and petty complaints against Rogers.

In August 1969, Nixon had delegated John Mitchell, Bob Haldeman and me to meet with Kissinger and hear his current grievances against Bill Rogers. Then we were all at San Clemente, ensconced in rental houses within a few blocks of the President's new home. Nixon hoped that the relaxed, informal atmosphere might help to calm Henry, and perhaps he thought our little committee would become a permanent sounding board for Henry, thereby relieving Nixon of some of the wear and tear.

Kissinger, Mitchell, Haldeman and I gathered at Mitchell's house to allow Henry to air his complaints. Henry produced a typewritten manifesto.

First, it said, Rogers could no longer be allowed to go around making policy speeches unless their content had first been cleared by "the White House"—which was to say, Henry Kissinger. (In fact, Rogers was cut out of so many policy decisions by Henry that it *was* dangerous for him to be speaking for the Administration. He was often uninformed.) Second, Henry demanded the right to deal with Rogers' State Department subordinates directly, without the Secretary's interference.

Henry regaled us with stories of Rogers' ineptness. "The man is a positive danger to the peace of the world," Henry said, slowly shaking his head. Kissinger demanded that Rogers be replaced. (I wondered who would accept the job if it became known that Kissinger did the hiring and firing.)

Mitchell volunteered to talk to Bill Rogers about Henry's demands. Mitchell said he would try to work out some ground rules between Bill and Henry to lubricate the friction. But all of us knew that Rogers couldn't agree to the kind of control Henry was proposing for himself. We'd given Henry a forum and we'd listened politely. Haldeman told the President about it, and nothing more was said about our three-man committee for nearly a year.

In January 1970, characteristically, Nixon considered solving the Kissinger–Rogers problem by moving people around. It made him feel better to think about new patterns. He would elevate Rogers—perhaps to the Supreme Court. Elliot Richardson could be Secretary of State. ("He gets along pretty well with Henry.") The State Department should be reorganized along with the CIA. ("Helms has to go.") But of course, both Rogers and Helms stayed for a long time after that.

One cold January morning in 1971, Henry Kissinger was late for the regular senior-staff meeting in Bob Haldeman's office. About nine the heavy door burst open and Henry stumped in and settled firmly into his chair. We began to tease him about his customary tardiness, but he cut us off in his deepest voice, usually reserved for major crises.

"I may return to Harvard, at once," he announced solemnly. Haldeman's face said: Now what? "That Rogers," Henry intoned, "has written a letter to the Egyptian Foreign Minister." Henry's continuing diatribe rehashed all his familiar grievances against Rogers. Having delivered us our daily ration, Henry left us. And we got back to work.

Henry went to work too. Within a few days he had the National Security Council staff amass a huge dossier to demonstrate Rogers' failures. A memorandum dated January 20, 1971, entitled "White House–State Department Relationships" was prepared by Al Haig for Henry, backed up with cables, "memcons" and letters. The National Security Agency furnished some of the evidence. It related to Chile, Germany and the Middle East primarily and featured some of Bill Rogers' own cables to demonstrate his "obstructionism and ineptness." Henry also cited a *Christian Science Monitor* story by Saville Davis that was in error. Henry had asked Davis for a letter admitting the mistake and saying his source was Rogers' State Department. All of this Henry unloaded on Richard Nixon.

Then Henry demanded a curtailment of Rogers' authority again, and the President asked us all to talk to Kissinger once more. This time Henry gave us Haig's huge dossier, and we heard a lot about the Middle East.

At the outset of his Administration, Nixon had assigned the Middle East to Bill Rogers and told Kissinger to stay out of it. Nixon explained more than once in my hearing that Henry, being Jewish, simply could not gain the required confidence from Arab leaders.

Kissinger felt strongly that the Middle East could not be separated from his other global responsibilities, and he took every opportunity to appeal for reconsideration of Nixon's ruling. At times he argued geopolitics; other times he asserted Rogers' general incompetence. He pounced on any mistake or setback in the Mideast to show Nixon that his Secretary of State couldn't handle the work. With continuing frequency Henry was threatening to quit, and his complaints about Rogers had taken on an unusually harsh tone.

We gathered in Bob Haldeman's office. Henry arrived at the meeting wearing that most solemn expression he reserved for discussions of his resignations. He had prepared another written ultimatum for us, and it was, typically, tough and unattributable. It had been typed on a single sheet of paper without heading, address or signature, and it said:

1. *Attacks on Kissinger—direct or indirect—must cease. An attack on HK is an attack on the President.*
2. *All cables with policy implications—including especially the Middle East—must be cleared in the White House. Sufficient time must be left for the clearance to operate properly.*
3. *All contacts with [Russian Ambassador Anatoly] Dobrynin must be cleared ahead of time. Talking points must be submitted before and a full report afterwards.*

We listened once again to Henry's grievances. Rogers was ruining the President's foreign-policy efforts. If we cared about Richard Nixon and his place in history, we would see to it that the President issued such a manifesto to Rogers. Otherwise, there would be a disaster. And Kissinger did not intend to stay around to see it.*

---

* Henry's anti-Rogers campaign continued beyond the 1972 election, up to the time Rogers' departure was finally scheduled for the summer of 1973.

On March 8, 1971, the senior White House staff was invited to dinner at Blair House so the public-relations experts among us could exhort the rest of us to employ more "anecdotal imagery" in our contacts with the press and public. We should, they said, tell stories about the President that illustrated his vigor, perspicacity, compassion, intellect, humanity, and so on.

Henry Kissinger drew me aside during the festivities, looking exceedingly dour. We went into the Lincoln parlor, just off the entry hall, and he closed the door.

"You have been a good friend to me, John," Henry said solemnly, "and I wanted you to know that tomorrow morning I intend to tell the President that I am leaving at once."

"What in the world, Henry? What's wrong?" I asked.

"I shall return to Harvard."

"What brought this on?"

"It's Rogers, of course. You will be sensitive to this, I know. You and I each have invoked necessary procedures to serve the President in an orderly way. Now Rogers has totally ignored National Security Council procedures. I've discovered he has been holding policy meetings on the Middle East over at the State Department. That I cannot tolerate."

I encouraged Henry to sleep on his decision and make time for more talk in the morning. When I got home I called Bob Haldeman to tell him of Henry's threat.

"So he got to you too?" Bob said. "I think Henry confided in everyone at the dinner tonight. Don't worry about it." That was in March. By early July, Henry was still on the payroll and on his way to his first secret meeting with the Chinese as the President's emissary.

In mid-June 1971, the Pentagon Papers case had caused Henry Kissinger deep concern; the episode touched him in many ways.

Daniel Ellsberg (who delivered the classified documents to newspapers) had been one of Henry Kissinger's collaborators during the transition and earliest White House days. Ellsberg had worked at Rand, the think tank, and was assigned to propose every possible Vietnam option. Eventually his work found its way into NSSM 1, Henry's first major decision paper for the President.

Henry's footprints were all over the Pentagon Papers themselves. He had been a part-time consultant to the Johnson Administration, and his name was prominent in some of the papers.

Kissinger had a legitimate concern that other countries with which he was in secret negotiation—notably the Chinese and Russians—would believe the United States was incapable of guarding its secrets. That argument, more than any other, persuaded me that the legal actions to restrain *The New York Times* and others from publication of the Pentagon Papers were worthwhile.

Richard Nixon's rationale was purely technical at first: *The New York Times* had violated the secrecy of *classified* documents. I feel sure that had some process removed the "TOP SECRET" stamps from those pages while they were in storage, Nixon would have had no objection to their publication. That long narrative of America's involvement in Vietnam called the Pentagon Papers all predated Nixon and embarrassed him in no way.

In 1969, when dealing with Lyndon Johnson's potentially scandalous last-minute peccadillo in creating the Austin Geriatric Center, Nixon suggested in a moment of hubris that we simply declassify all of Lyndon Johnson's papers with one stroke of the Presidential pen. Then the press could freely dig around in Johnson's archives down there in Austin and print anything they found. If they discovered irregularities involving LBJ and his cronies, that would be his problem, not ours. Such a blanket declassification never happened, of course. Johnson's Pentagon Papers remained classified. As Nixon saw it, that alone made them off limits to the *Times* and *The Washington Post* and all the others *unless* and *until* the President declassified them, and that was a law that any President was obliged to enforce if we were to be able to keep a single secret from a potential enemy.

And so we mobilized to prevent publication of Daniel Ellsberg's booty and punish those who were trying to erode the country's classification system.

Every day during that litigation a group gathered in my office to review the progress of the Government's investigation and its response. Kissinger was a leading participant in that group, which also included people from the Department of Justice. My secretary, Jana Hruska, took shorthand notes of those meetings. Somewhere deep in the archives are her transcriptions, demonstrating Kissinger's deep involvement in the formulation of the Pentagon Papers strategies.

Kissinger was passionate in his denunciation of Daniel Ellsberg. He knew quite a bit about Ellsberg's social proclivities (which Henry deplored) and Ellsberg's conduct in Vietnam. Henry urged that a thorough investigation of Ellsberg be pressed. Ellsberg knew a great many of the nation's most vital defense secrets, Henry said. Who knew what he might choose to disclose next?

In the two weeks before he left on his secret China trip, Kissinger fanned Richard Nixon's flame white-hot. Time after time Kissinger warned about the dire consequences of "letting them get away with this," of having Ellsberg running around loose and of permitting the Government "to leak like a sieve." Nixon was warned about Ellsberg. He was not the sort of fellow of whom Richard Nixon would approve. Henry dropped tidbits about Ellsberg's private life and his use of drugs.

At our daily Pentagon Papers meetings Henry exhorted us to act vigorously to stanch the flow of the nation's secrets. Without Henry's stimulus during the June 13–to–July 6 period, the President and the rest of us might have concluded that the Papers were Lyndon Johnson's problem, not ours. After all, there was not a word about Richard Nixon in any of the forty-three volumes.

The Congress soon wanted to know what all the shouting was about. Several committee chairmen demanded copies of the Pentagon Papers. After some initial hesitation, Nixon decided to send them duplicates of the set of the papers which the Defense Department held, but a few really sensitive secrets would be deleted.

In September 1971, I learned from Melvin Laird that along with the secrets, Henry had also caused every mention of his name to be deleted from the four unpublished volumes of the Pentagon Papers before they were forwarded to the Congress.

In December 1971, I was again invited into Henry's domain by an urgent phone call from General Haig, his principal deputy. The Jack Anderson column for December 14 contained a verbatim account of Henry Kissinger's remarks at a meeting of the Washington Special Action Group, Henry's super-secret committee which was supposed to be managing the country's response to the India–Pakistan war. Henry's quoted tirades were pro-Pakistan, intemperate and embarrassing. Worse, this was evidence that someone had given Jack Anderson the secret minutes of the meeting.

Within twenty-four hours Kissinger had persuaded the President to launch a full-scale investigation of Anderson's penetration of the WASAG committee's secrets. I selected David Young to lead the effort, reporting to Nixon through me.

David Young was a young lawyer from New York who had been recommended to Henry Kissinger by the Rockefellers.

Kissinger always had a young man on his staff who performed as a kind of combination administrative aide and servant to the Professor. No task that might be assigned such a man was too exalted or too menial. One moment he would be taking bachelor Henry's dirty underwear to the laundry and the next moment he would be with Henry and Chancellor Adenauer or some other world leader, taking notes. After Henry's first servitor, Larry Eagleburger, suffered a physical collapse in 1969, David Young had taken the job. Over a period of five years, Henry had five men arrive, pink-cheeked and eager. Most lasted only eleven or twelve months.

Within a week of Haig's call about the Anderson column, Young had assembled security experts and analyzed the Anderson leaks. Only a handful of people in the Government had been privy to the documents and meetings he had described. Most of the suspects were in the Defense Department, so the search began there. It ended at the very top, in the office of the Chairman of the Joint Chiefs of Staff, the highest-ranking military man in the nation.

Near the end of the week Young reported that a young Navy yeoman, Charles Radford, had admitted knowing Jack Anderson. While being polygraphed he also admitted stealing classified NSC documents. But he vehemently denied having delivered those documents to Anderson. Who got them? he was asked. *The Joint Chiefs of Staff,* he tearfully replied.

Yeoman Radford was the secretary to Admiral Robert O. Welander, the Joint Chiefs' liaison to Henry Kissinger and the National Security Council. Welander had an office among Henry Kissinger's people, in the Executive Office Building. There, with a White House pass, sat Yeoman Charles Radford, doing the Admiral's typing and office chores, and stealing Henry's papers.

Under questioning, Radford gave an extraordinary account of his career as a thief in the employ of the nation's military commanders. Radford was friendly with the NSC clerks and would loiter in the staff secretary's room leafing through the paperwork, copying anything that might be of interest to the military. He was especially encouraged to bring Welander and his previous boss, Admiral Rembrandt Robinson, memoranda of the President's conversations with Kissinger and Henry's comments about Nixon to others.

Yeoman Radford's greatest opportunity had come when Al Haig recommended that Henry take the yeoman along as his secretary on Kissinger's trip to Pakistan, from which Henry had made his first secret journey to Peking. On the long flight back from Pakistan, Radford had access to Henry's personal briefcase. The Joint Chiefs knew the secret details of the new China opening before most of the senior people in the White House did. The Joint Chiefs got copies of everything Henry dictated and even the papers he stuffed into the "burn bags" to be destroyed.

David Young suggested to me that Al Haig had probably planted Radford to help the military spy on Henry; but that did not seem logical to me because I assumed Haig had full access to Henry's papers and files. Young insisted that Haig constantly sold Henry out to the military, but I discounted much of what Young said about Haig. There was obviously bad blood between them.

There *was* a direct link between Yeoman Radford and Jack Anderson. Radford had been a secretary in the U.S. Embassy in India before his NSC espionage assignment. He was one of a small group of Mormons among the Americans there. When Jack Anderson's parents traveled to India they inquired at the embassy how they might find the Mormon Church in New Delhi. Yeoman Radford was introduced to them and became their part-time guide.

Once back in the United States, the senior Andersons called Radford's wife to tell her they had seen her husband, and when Charles Radford returned from India, he and his wife were invited to Thanksgiving dinner at the home of the elder Andersons' son Jack.

As a result of his acquaintance with India, Radford resented the Nixon-Kissinger policy, which favored a "tilt" toward Pakistan. Whether this had motivated Radford to seek revenge on Nixon and Kissinger or whether Anderson's cultivation of the boy had persuaded him to give the columnist documents we could never discover. From the beginning Anderson has denied that Radford was his source.

At 6 P.M. on December 21, Attorney General Mitchell and I met with the President and Bob Haldeman. I recounted all that Radford had confessed. Nixon listened closely, then said he wanted to know what Admiral Welander had to say in his own defense. I agreed to interview him the next day.

For an hour and a quarter the next afternoon David Young and I interrogated Rear Admiral Robert Welander in my office. I had met Welander once at Admiral Elmo Zumwalt's home, but on this occasion we didn't waste time with small talk. I had asked the White House Communications Agency for a recorder, and it sat on my coffee table in its bulky case. A large microphone on a stand stood on the table. I had also prepared a written statement, based on Radford's confession, for Welander to sign.

I turned on the machine, called the Admiral's attention to it and handed him the statement. I asked him to change it, if any parts were inaccurate, then sign it. After he'd read it, Welander refused to sign it. I was surprised. With his refusal, I thought we'd be in for a rough time. But Welander appeared contrite and completely willing to answer oral questions.

Welander confirmed that he'd regularly received NSC papers from Yeoman Radford, and specifically the contents of Henry Kissinger's briefcase from his China trip. He added that Radford had also accompanied Al Haig to Vietnam. The yeoman had also rifled Haig's papers and turned over the proceeds to Welander.

Welander confirmed that all the proceeds of the yeoman's efforts went directly to Admiral Thomas Moorer, our highest-ranking military officer. Welander explained that he had simply followed the procedures established by his predecessor, Admiral Robinson. I asked Welander to describe those procedures and asked him to acknowledge that he realized his answers were being recorded, which he did willingly.

When Welander left, I gave the tape to David Young and asked that he have it transcribed at once. Then he and I went to the President's hideaway office in the EOB to report what Welander had said. The President, John Mitchell and Bob Haldeman listened to us, then debated what should be done. It was a difficult problem, made more troublesome because the President did not trust his Secretary of Defense, Melvin Laird. Nixon explained to us that many of his instructions concerning Vietnam were transmitted through Moorer and the Joint Chiefs because he was not sure Laird would follow his orders. The President and Kissinger had invested much confidence in Moorer. Nixon said he feared that if he disciplined Moorer for conducting this espionage activity against the President and Henry, it would impair their vital "back channel" to the military. And it would give Laird a whip hand over the Joint Chiefs.

John Mitchell knew Thomas Moorer and liked him. Our bad news distressed the Attorney General greatly. I said I'd like to ask Admiral Robinson how all this spying had gotten started. The President nodded. I should have Robinson brought in, right after Christmas.

Meanwhile, the President sent John Mitchell to talk to Admiral Thomas Moorer about Welander and Radford. I would have preferred our interrogation of Admiral Robinson to come first, but Nixon couldn't be patient.

Mitchell reported to the President that Moorer denied knowing the material he received from Welander was stolen. He thought it was routine liaison material for his information, he said. If it was stolen, Welander should be punished, Moorer declared.

John Mitchell and I discussed David Young's recommendation that Yeoman Radford, Jack Anderson and some others be tapped to learn whether Radford had given documents to anyone besides his military boss. Mitchell foresaw some criminal prosecutions and felt taps were justified and advisable, but he wanted to talk to Nixon before tapping Jack Anderson. Nixon refused to authorize the Jack Anderson tap. But the FBI immediately began to listen to Radford's telephones at home and at work.

Through all of this, no one had told Henry Kissinger what was happening. At 3 P.M. on December 23, the President sent Bob Haldeman and me to tell Henry about Radford, Welander and Moorer.

Henry was calm, almost sleepy, as I recounted what we'd learned. His only reaction was to remark, almost indifferently, that the Joint Chiefs' liaison office must be closed at once.

As we left Henry's office I was full of questions. I had expected a huge eruption of emotion. Haldeman had told me that Henry was being a tremendous problem for the President that week. He had been mounting elaborate, daily tirades about Bill Rogers; Nixon, Haldeman reported, was nearly to the point of firing Henry, just to end the wear and tear.

That night our family had a Christmas-carol party for some of our neighbors and White House friends. About 10 P.M. Henry Kissinger called me at home on my Signal Corps telephone to say that he had fired Admiral Welander.

"John, do you have any hard evidence to support what you told me this afternoon?" Henry asked.

"There is a recording of what Welander told us," I replied. "You ought to listen to that. I'll play it for you."

"Yes, I'd like to hear it. Would it be all right if I bring Al Haig along?"

I said I'd play it for them right after the senior-staff meeting in the morning.

As soon as Kissinger hung up, I had a call from a badly shaken David Young. He had just been phoned by Al Haig. Haig was furious and had accused Young and me of "jobbing a fine military officer" on "nothing but flimsy circumstantial evidence." Haig had evidently called Melvin Laird, and Haig believed that our suspicion of Welander (and Moorer) rested only on Yeoman Radford's polygraph. Young did not tell Haig that we had interviewed Welander or that the Admiral had admitted everything on tape. I suggested to Young that he not attend in the morning when I played the tape for Henry and Haig.

For an hour and a half the next morning Kissinger and Haig listened to the Welander recording. It was obvious that they were both convinced. This time Henry wasn't so calm. When the tapes ended he began striding up and down loudly venting his complaints.

"He [Nixon] won't fire Moorer!" Henry shouted. "They can spy on him and spy on me and betray us and he won't fire them! If he won't fire Rogers—impose some discipline in this Administration—there is no reason to believe he'll fire Moorer. I assure you all this tolerance will lead to very serious consequences for this Administration!"

A couple of hours later I was with the President in the EOB office when Henry walked in, unbidden. In a very low, somber voice he spread gloom and doom. "I tell you, Mr. President, this is very serious. We cannot survive the kinds of internal weaknesses we are seeing."

The President, at his jocular worst, tried to give Henry some encouragement. Henry was suffering press attacks that week, based partly on his handling of the India–Pakistan war. The President's bucking up didn't seem to help. Henry left when he had delivered his load of melancholy.

The President wanted to talk to me at length about Henry, Rogers and the problem of Henry's mood swings. I suggested that some of the problem came from the fact that Henry had been mounting a big media campaign. He was trying to change the fact that during his WASAG meetings Henry had lost his objectivity and he'd been exceedingly intemperate in his attacks on India. But Bill Rogers and others at the State Department also had been busy making trouble for Henry with the media. Much of the press was being critical of Henry, and he didn't like it.

Nixon wondered aloud if Henry needed psychiatric care.

Henry Kissinger had always seemed to me to be very insecure. I'd never seen fingernails bitten so close to the quick as Henry's were during that time. He cared desperately what people wrote and said about him. Henry had erected a protective facade that was part self-deprecating humor and part intellectual showboating, but behind it he was devastated by press attacks on his professional competence. Henry did his best to deflect casual, personal conversation. When it appeared inescapable, he would sometimes open a chess book and small chessboard, moving pieces and muttering to himself as if he were studying. My assigned seat on *Air Force One* was across a table from Henry, and I watched this charade many times. Invariably, within five minutes the good Doctor would be sound asleep, the unread book open on his belly.

Once when he awoke I passed him a pad with a tic-tac-toe grid on it. "I think this is more your speed, Vudchopper,"* I said. The first game we played was a tie. I won the second and demanded that he sign the sheet in acknowledgment of my triumph over the Harvard mind.

The President seemed very sincere about Henry's seeing a psychiatrist. "Talk to him, John. And talk to Al Haig. He will listen to Al."

I could think of no way to talk to Henry about psychiatric care. I had no confidence that that was what would help Henry, nor could I bring myself to confront Henry with the President's apparent lack of confidence in his mental stability. Instead I had a long talk with General Al Haig.

On Christmas Eve afternoon I told Al Haig, "The President is very worried about Henry's frame of mind." Haig's reply went to the question of whether Nixon might fire Henry: "The President needs Henry." Al realized that it had come down to a question of whether Henry was dispensable. He knew the President was thinking of letting Kissinger go.

"You've got to realize," Haig continued, "that the President isn't doing his homework these days. It's only Henry who pulls us through the summit conferences."

Haig made a strong argument for tolerating Henry's moods and excesses. "Take the economic issues, for example. Nixon and Connally were letting them slide. It was Henry who forced the issue. He set the meetings with the United Kingdom, Germany and France to force a resolution of those issues. You can't get along without him."

Just before I went home on Christmas Eve, the FBI reported to David Young that at the last minute Yeoman Radford and his wife had declined their Christmas invitation from Jack Anderson and his family. On the telephone Radford had sounded very worried, the FBI said.

---

* Henry's Secret Service code name was Woodchopper. Mine was Wisdom; he usually called me *Weisheit*, the German translation.

At 11 A.M. on December 27, Admiral Rembrandt Robinson came to my office. Robinson was short and chunky, self-assured, in full uniform, complete with gold braid and battle stars. I had arranged the tape recorder on the coffee table in front of his chair, just as I had for Welander.

I asked him most of the same questions I'd asked Welander, but the answers were not the same. Volubly, Robinson denied everything.

I told Robinson that I couldn't reconcile his denials with the statements of Yeoman Radford and Admiral Welander. Did he have an explanation?

No, he didn't.

Two weeks later, Mel Laird summoned Admiral Welander to order the Admiral to turn over to Laird the contents of Welander's NSC-liaison safe. Welander called Al Haig to ask him what to do. Haig and I then talked. I told Haig to tell Welander that the President wanted any papers in his possession delivered to me. We assumed Welander still possessed copies of some of the material he'd sent to Moorer. Some of it might be dangerous in Mel Laird's hands.

On January 14, Al Haig delivered a sealed envelope which Tod Hullin marked and put in our safe. Supposedly it contained Welander's papers. I have no idea what was actually in it or where it is now.

Laird was a continuing problem. Nixon feared Laird intended to use the Radford episode to gain greater control over Moorer and the Joint Chiefs.

"Mitchell must tell Laird," Nixon said, "he's not to discuss the Joint Chiefs' actions on any basis with anyone."

And what about Jack Anderson? We had a pretty fair circumstantial case that Radford was the source of secret documents that had been printed. If Radford had been suborned to a breach of security, that might be a crime.

"We'll prosecute Anderson and the rest of them after the election," Nixon said. "Meanwhile, move the yeoman somewhere so he can't do any more damage. Lay off Anderson now and tell all our people, including Laird." Nixon, I sensed, had decided not to tackle Anderson, then or ever.

Jack Anderson was awarded the Pulitzer Prize for printing the WASAG documents about India and Pakistan. On May 3, 1972, when news of Anderson's prize reached Oregon, Yeoman Charles Radford broke his five-month silence to telephone Jack Anderson. It was their first conversation since the FBI had begun to cover Radford's calls.

Radford congratulated Anderson. Anderson commiserated with the yeoman about his removal from the Kissinger office and his transfer. Neither man mentioned Kissinger's purloined papers, but Radford expressed pride in the fact that Anderson's columns had won the Pulitzer. Their conversation was brief, but I read into it the link we had been looking for between Radford's thefts and the Anderson columns.*

In the pre-Watergate days, Henry massaged the press as no one else in the White House did. As I sat on the little terrace off my office at San Clemente I could hear Henry, on his terrace, playing host to the reporters and columnists who were invited to his office in a steady parade. There were so many that Henry often took them three at a time. His aide saw to it that the Navy stewards kept the coffee cups filled as Henry confided to his guests on "deep background."

I could not help hearing Henry's blandishments and his shameless self-congratulation. It surprised me that veteran journalists would let him get away with using them as they did. But James Reston, Marquis Childs, Richard Valeriani, the Kalb brothers and countless others came and went, congratulating themselves on having been the guests and confidants of Kissinger.

In the heat of Watergate, one of the nation's foremost columnists encountered an influential publisher at The Homestead, a spa in the mountains of Virginia. They talked about Nixon's troubles and about Haldeman's firing and mine. The publisher wondered about Kissinger's vulnerability. The columnist, one of Henry's frequent San Clemente guests, said, "I'm doing all I can to make certain nothing happens to Henry Kissinger."

"My God, yes," said the publisher. "Whatever becomes of Nixon, nothing must harm Henry. We must all see to that."

But Henry's good press relations had their price, too. There was constant tension between Henry and Richard Nixon because Nixon feared Henry's disloyalty. Over the years I conveyed many instructions from the President to Kissinger forbidding Henry to appear on television, to grant interviews on various subjects or to attend press functions. In May 1970, I

---

* Anderson came to Santa Fe in 1976 and we talked about the WASAG columns. He still denied that Radford was his source, but I don't believe his denials. The circumstantial evidence and that final, ambiguous phone call from Radford are enough to make me believe that both the Joint Chiefs and Jack Anderson were beneficiaries of Radford's rummaging in Henry's files and wastebaskets.

took lengthy notes on what Henry's forthcoming New York speech should contain. In summary, Henry was ordered to "leave out all the confusing ifs, ands and buts. The main point should be: the President was right. . . ."

In August 1970 the President *ordered* Henry to attend our senior-staff meetings regularly. Nixon was concerned that Henry was drifting off in his own direction. He was too independent. The rest of the staff should have a chance to gather him in each morning.

The next month Haldeman and I were instructed by Nixon to tell Henry that he was never to appear on television to discuss policy or "substance." Henceforth only the President and the Secretary of State would appear on television to discuss foreign policy. Occasionally the Vice President might speak on well-established policy—the Nixon Doctrine or Cambodia, for instance. But never Henry Kissinger.

Because Nixon would almost never deliver such an injunction in person, Kissinger might choose to believe that Haldeman or I had invented it to impair his popularity. Henry, a little insecure in his relations with the President, evidently preferred to believe Haldeman and I were out to get him, rather than that Nixon was increasingly unhappy with Henry's independent and self-serving press campaign.

During the Paris peace negotiations with the Vietnamese, Haldeman was handed a cable to be sent to Kissinger. "Oh, Bob," Nixon added, "tell Haig that when Henry has his picture taken with Le Duc Tho, he's not to smile."

Historians will be trying to define the Nixon–Kissinger relationship for years to come. Who was the conceptualist? Did Kissinger do more than simply articulate and carry out Nixon's foreign strategy? Was Haig correct—did Kissinger force events? And did he front for a Nixon who failed to do his homework?

Bob Haldeman once explained to me that Nixon had particularly wanted the White House taping system installed in order to demonstrate that the foreign-policy initiatives of his Presidency were in fact his own, not Henry's. I had many conversations with the President about his public and personal papers as we tried to create an estate plan that would provide for his widow and daughters.* But as many times as there were occasions for him to mention the existence of the tapes—

---

* Once Nixon proposed to me that his Presidential library rent his papers from him and his heirs for $200,000 a year.

which were analogous to the documents and other records we were discussing—he never told me of their existence.* Nixon intended to personally edit his papers and then leave them to his children. He planned to spend some of his retirement sitting in front of a fireplace, burning whatever might be embarrassing. Perhaps he intended to do the same with the tapes.

I had some insights into the way Nixon and Kissinger worked, but considering my proximity, the opportunities were remarkably few. On December 6, 1972, I was the President's guest at dinner in Aspen Lodge at Camp David. Henry was in Paris negotiating with the Vietnamese. That evening I saw, for the only time, the inner workings of that negotiation and something more of the Nixon–Kissinger relationship.

Henry had come home from Paris in late October 1972 after a series of negotiating sessions with Le Duc Tho. On October 8 the North Vietnamese had laid on the table a peace offer that was nearly acceptable to the United States, if not to the South Vietnamese.

On October 26, Kissinger held a press conference in which he used the fateful phrase "peace is at hand." The 1972 election was less than two weeks away. That announcement—taken by almost everyone in the country to mean that Henry's negotiations had in fact achieved an end to the war—surely helped our reelection campaign. But the phrase and its implications were Henry's alone. I know of no one who claims that the President told Henry to go out and say that to the press.

In fact, at the time, Nixon felt it would be better *not* to conclude a deal with the Vietnamese until after the election. Any agreement would become a target for potshots, no matter what it said.

After the election Henry was due to return to Paris. After his press conference, October 26, he had mounted a furious media blitz for several days, seeing Joe Kraft, Henry Brandon and a parade of other journalists. Kissinger, on background, described the course of the negotiations and repeated his prediction that one more negotiating session should wrap up the whole thing. It was as if he regretted the extravagance of his press-conference boast and were trying to buttress it with all the favorable comment he could generate.

---

* In March 1973 I learned that Nixon had taped a conversation with John Dean, but still no one told me of the continuous taping that had taken place. I learned of the taping system when everyone else did, during Alex Butterfield's testimony before the Senate Committee.

But before Henry could take off for Paris, the papers were full of quotations from an equally extravagant interview Henry had given Oriana Fallaci, an Italian writer. Henry genuinely thought he had detractors in the White House and State Department who made trouble for him by leaking unflattering descriptions of him to the press. But no one made as much trouble for Henry as he made for himself in that couple of weeks.

The Fallaci interview made him appear both egotistical and fatuous. He was the "lone cowboy" Americans loved, riding into town to dispatch the villains. This, he told her, accounted for his widespread popularity.

That was not exactly how Richard Nixon saw Henry. If there was a Lone Ranger handling foreign affairs, the President would have cast Henry, I suspect, as Tonto. Nor did it take much negotiating experience to predict that Le Duc Tho would take advantage of such comments as "peace is at hand," "just one more session" and "I'm the lonesome cowboy" when negotiations resumed. It is not remarkable that Tho and the North Vietnamese pulled the rug out from under Henry during the next sessions in Paris. The South Vietnamese evidently evaluated the situation the same way. They toughened their demands too.

Henry Kissinger has written* that during the late-November-and-early-December Paris talks Nixon retired to Camp David, where, surrounded by "amateurs and public relations experts," he sent Kissinger unhelpful cabled instructions. In fact, Nixon was at Camp David most of November and December 1972, engaged in restaffing the White House, the Cabinet and the Executive Branch departments and agencies, putting the finishing touches on the Federal Budget and preparing a State of the Union address.

The night of December 6 was snowy and cold at Camp David. Nixon rarely invited me to dinner at Aspen Lodge during our long sequestration there that winter. It was clear when I arrived that this was not to be a social occasion. We wouldn't be seeing *Around the World in 80 Days* again that night.†

At 6 P.M., Bob Haldeman greeted me with a handful of cables. Nixon was outside, swimming in his superheated pool.

---

* Kissinger, *The White House Years*. Boston: Little, Brown, 1979.

† While Nixon liked *Patton* and John Wayne movies, it was *Around the World in 80 Days* that he watched over and over. He knew every part of it by heart. "Watch—watch this!" he would say. "Here comes the elephant!"

One by one I was shown cables describing the tone and content of the Paris talks during that week. One of Kissinger's cables was obviously "for the record"; in it Henry advised the President that the North Vietnamese had drawn back from their October offer. Kissinger said he could either accept poorer terms than had been offered before or break off the talks, in which case the war would have to be intensified.

Kissinger proposed that the President go on prime-time television to explain why the negotiations were being broken off. Henry hoped that public support could be rallied for a resumption of the bombing of North Vietnam.

Haldeman then asked me the question Nixon evidently wanted me to be asked: "Do you agree with Henry? Should he [Nixon] go on TV now and explain the break-off?"

I shook my head. "The President should explain successes. The staff explains failures," I told him.

Then Haldeman showed me Henry's cables of December 4 and 5. They were pessimistic and predicted the failure of the current talks.

"I don't know if you realize it, but Henry was very 'down' when he left for Paris," Haldeman said. *"He's been under care.* And he's been doing some strange things. When he was in Saigon [in October], twice he cabled the North Vietnamese in the President's name to accept their October proposal. Henry did that over Al Haig's strong objection and beyond any Presidential authority."

"So what happens now? Do you call him home?" I asked.

"John Connally, Chuck Colson, Ron Ziegler and I have urged the Old Man to finesse the failure. We don't think he should go on television. Henry can come home and tell the press this is all just another Vietnamese maneuver."

The President, in a huge terry-cloth robe, came in from the terrace; I could see the clouds of steam rising from the pool. As Nixon dried his hair, Haldeman told him that I opposed Henry's proposed television broadcast.

"Three days ago," Nixon said, "we asked the Russians and Chinese for some help. Dobrynin gave Colonel Kennedy a note assuring us that they 'are working on it' and that we should try one more session in Paris. The South Vietnamese think Henry is weak now because of his press-conference statements. That damn 'peace is at hand'! And his Italian interview was debilitating for a negotiator. The North Vietnamese have sized him up; they know he has to either get a deal or lose face. That's why they've shifted to a harder position."

The President had dictated instructions to Colonel Richard

Kennedy, one of Henry's aides. Kennedy brought the typed draft to Aspen for Nixon's final review.

"I'm telling Henry to finesse," Nixon said. " 'Don't let yourself get painted into a corner. Don't give them any take-it-or-leave-it demands. Ask questions. Say you have to discuss it with the President. Then get up and come home.' " Nixon handed Kennedy the draft and a plastic dictation belt. "I've dictated maybe four or five pages of substantive material, Colonel. Combine it with the draft before you send it tonight."

After the Colonel left, Nixon sat looking into the fire. "There are no good choices, you know. But, by God, we won't let them humiliate us. Bob, have Ken Rush [Deputy Secretary of Defense] and the Colonel bring me those contingency plans tomorrow. We'll probably have to resume the bombing."

Haldeman made some notes.

Nixon talked to the fire. "There is no point in going on television to ask the American people to support more of the same in Vietnam. We can't rally them to support us when it's nothing new. Henry doesn't seem to understand that. Or does he? Maybe he just wants people to associate me with the failure."

I nodded. It seemed to me that that was precisely what Henry had in mind. His press conferences were full of the President when there was bad news, but Nixon was seldom mentioned when the news was good.

"John," Nixon asked, "how long do you think the Congress will appropriate money for South Vietnam after we begin bombing again? Six months?"

We were in the midst of the new, tough budget plan. "We're going to ask them to cut ten billion dollars from social programs in a few days," I said. "If they think Thieu and the South Vietnamese have obstructed peace they'll cut off the money in half that time."

Nixon nodded and stood. "I'll dry off and we'll have dinner," he said. "We've got to have support in the Congress. The people don't want us to trade the POWs for the South Vietnamese. If military and economic aid is cut off, the South Vietnamese are doomed. Do they understand that?"

In Paris, Kissinger negotiated fruitlessly for another week; then he and Haig came home. The so-called "Christmas bombing" began, and so did a near-hysterical attack by the nation's editorial writers, liberal Congressmen and other critics.

Things were made worse when *Time* magazine made the President *and* Henry Kissinger joint "Men of the Year."

Nixon was furious. It was simply another self-serving grab for publicity by Henry, which would weaken his negotiating position. When some columnists (incorrectly) asserted that Nixon had ordered the bombing resumption over Kissinger's opposition, the Nixon–Kissinger rift widened.

Around Christmas, the North Vietnamese signaled that talks should resume. On December 29, Nixon ordered a halt to the bombing. By mid-January, Henry had negotiated an agreement, and the South Vietnamese reluctantly ratified it, just after Nixon's second inauguration.

On January 23, the President announced the peace in a short, televised address. The next day I talked to Henry Kissinger briefly in the doorway of the Roosevelt Room. After congratulating him, I asked about the future. "How long do you figure the South Vietnamese can survive under this agreement?" I asked him. I expected Henry to give me some assurances. Instead he told me the truth, and it shook me badly.

"I think," Henry said, "that if they're lucky they can hold out for a year and a half."

Later, when I was far from Washington, watching the films of helicopters snatching desperate Americans from the roof of our Saigon embassy as the Northern invaders neared, I remembered Henry's cynical but accurate estimate.

Kissinger writes in the first volume of his memoirs that after initialing the Paris peace agreement: "I was at peace with myself, neither elated nor sad."

I wonder how that could have been.

CHAPTER SEVENTEEN

The Politician

RICHARD NIXON WAS a full-time politician, and he never let us forget it. At home and abroad, every day of the week and whatever the occasion, he (and we) looked after the politics.

Sometimes I had trouble getting the President to focus on my list of domestic problems, especially as the 1972 election campaign approached. He'd much rather have talked about

George McGovern. George McGovern was the perfect political opponent, Nixon felt, far to the left of center. If we did our job, McGovern would leave Nixon most of the moderates and independents. Nixon liked to talk about the McGovern strategy.

In early June 1972 I went to Stockholm as a member of the United States' delegation to the United Nations Conference on the Environment. The Chairman of the Council on Environmental Quality, Russell Train, and Christian Herter of the State Department had been planning for this meeting for many months. Over the course of a year or so they issued policy papers for us to read, and once there was a meeting and cocktail party for all thirty or forty of the delegation.

I was on the delegation to show that the White House (translation: the President) was behind the environmental cause all the way; but beyond symbolism, there was really nothing for me to do in Stockholm except attend an occasional meeting of the conference. I was expected to say nothing and stay out of the way. That was fine; Stockholm in June was a beautiful respite from the White House. Senators Howard Baker and Henry Jackson came to Stockholm for similar appearances, except that they held press conferences.

Shirley Temple Black was a U.S. delegate too. She and I had once lived in the same section of Santa Monica as children, but I had not met her before. She had become a matron of more than ample girth, and it was startling to see that memorable face from childhood movie matinees riding on a body from a girdle ad. During conversation with her at lunch, the depth of her political ambition also startled me. She lobbied me in no uncertain terms for a high-ranking Government job, preferably in foreign affairs.

Six or seven of the other U.S. delegates had been invited to go to Stockholm solely as a reward for their financial and political support of Richard Nixon. When I arrived at the luxurious waterfront hotel where we Americans were housed in Stockholm, I discovered that these Nixon loyalists were very unhappy. Our Government superstars had been assigned the best rooms and perquisites. Secretary of the Interior Rogers Morton, the Senators, the Congressmen and I had all been given limousines and drivers, for example. John Rollins and our other political supporters, who had given hundreds of hours and thousands of dollars to Nixon's campaigns, were to be found in the street in front of the hotel trying to hail taxis in rush-hour traffic. Train and Herter had lost sight of the President's priorities in their enthusiasm for the whales and birds and the rest of the ecology. All that was important, of course, but not as important as taking care of the President's political supporters.

I asked my assistant Tod Hullin to help the Nixon faithful. The next day he reported that logistics for the U.S. Delegation was being managed by the State Department. Tod had gone to the embassy to talk to the State Department fellow about cars, drivers and better rooms for John Rollins and the others. The answer was no. Sorry, but no.

So Tod and I had a meeting with our Ambassador, Jerome "Brud" Holland. He was one of our few black ambassadors, a former All-American football player and a plainspoken man. That week a Swedish mob had stormed the American Embassy. Most of the ground-floor windows of the chancery building were broken or missing. A few had been replaced with plywood and boards. We met the Ambassador behind taped windows.

The last thing Ambassador Holland needed was to be in the middle of a haggle between the State Department and the White House over cars and drivers. He was cordial, but he made it clear that the fellow running the delegation's operations was direct from State in Washington, not from his embassy staff.

Holland found me an embassy office to use, and I asked State's "operations" man to come in for a visit. I had a short, unpleasant interview with that short, unpleasant State Department bureaucrat, during which I explained to him the relative merits of taking care of the President's political supporters and taking care of officeholders and career State Department people. He said there was a shortage of cars, so I asked him some questions. When the gentleman from State admitted that one of the scarce automobiles was assigned to him, complete with driver, I became unfriendly.

Eventually I was able to motivate the fellow to hurry off to obtain better rooms, cars, theater tickets and other amenities for the President's political friends. But by then he had lost my confidence. I telephoned Henry Kissinger's office and asked that the State Department be told to recall its operations manager and send a replacement immediately. Henry was away, but one of his helpers promised to do what was required. I could stay in Stockholm for only the first third of the Conference and didn't feel comfortable leaving our delegation in the hands of State's operations fellow after I was gone. I assured Chris Herter that I would follow through when I got home.

My request was forwarded by Kissinger's office to the State

Department. As hot potatoes are, it was tossed up from one State Department level to the next until it landed on the desk of the Secretary himself, Bill Rogers.

Rogers, like Kissinger, had just returned from the President's trip to Russia and Iran. If you look at photographs of that trip, it's hard to find Bill Rogers in most of them. Henry Kissinger shared the limelight with the President wherever they went. The Secretary of State had been pushed aside by White House assistants (doubtless at Nixon's express instruction) throughout the trip. It must have been a difficult, even humiliating, time for Rogers.

My request for State's bureaucrat to be replaced in Stockholm must have looked to Bill Rogers like more arrogant White House high-handedness. But this time it was on his turf. He told his people to reply that no such replacement would be made.

Back in Washington I was met with the news that Secretary Rogers had countermanded my request that his operations man be taken off the Stockholm delegation assignment. And Jana Hruska, my secretary, greeted me with the President's instruction that I was to come to Camp David first thing the next morning.

I'd not seen Nixon or Haldeman for a couple of weeks. We met the next morning at eleven in the small den in the President's cabin, Aspen Lodge, at Camp David. Nixon was suffering badly from hay fever; at such times his large nose became red, swollen and fluent.*

Nixon greeted me warmly and asked about Stockholm. I told him at once about my bout with the State Department's operations man and Bill Rogers' response. It had given me great sympathy, I said, for Henry Kissinger's problems with State.

Nixon wanted to hear every detail. The hay fever had subdued him to some extent, but he became angry, especially at "Rogers always backing up his goddamned bureaucrats."

Rogers had to go. The President hated to say it, but he'd known it for a long time. Confidentially, Nixon said, he had already decided on Kenneth Rush to replace Rogers.

Nixon told Haldeman that I had been absolutely right to

---

* My notes of this Camp David meeting were somehow misfiled; as a result, the FBI did not capture them. I discovered them in 1980 in a box of dinner menus and other mementos. Thus, I have a record of what was said and done on that occasion which is not to be found in the Archives or on tape.

look after Rollins and our other political friends and fat cats. He instructed Haldeman to make clear to Rogers that the President, personally, was ordering the recall of Rogers' minion from Stockholm. Forthwith. Today. Nixon could see I was pleased. The President backed me up; that made me feel wonderful. But I never did follow up to find out if the man was brought home.*

At the precise time Nixon, Haldeman and I were meeting at Camp David, Ron Ziegler's deputy, Jerry Warren, was conducting the daily press briefing at the White House.

Jerry is a spare, laconic newsman of complete integrity. As a professional, he must have found it difficult to be in the middle, between the working press and Ron Ziegler, who was not an experienced professional. Ordinarily Richard Nixon and Bob Haldeman (and sometimes I) programmed Ziegler. Then Ziegler would set the "line" that Jerry Warren was expected to take in the briefings Ziegler didn't want to do himself. I felt great sympathy for Warren as he struggled with the dilemmas this system created for him.

On June 9, Warren opened his briefing:

MR. WARREN: The President will be meeting this morning at Camp David with John Ehrlichman, who returned late yesterday afternoon from the Environmental Conference in Stockholm. The President asked Mr. Ehrlichman to come up this morning and brief him on that conference and also to discuss with him a variety of domestic matters which the President has been concentrating on throughout the week in Camp David.

Undoubtedly they will be talking about the Higher Education bill, the conference report of which has now passed the House. They will be discussing revenue sharing legislation, which will be acted on by the House next week. And they will be discussing H.R. 1, the welfare reform, as it is now moving through the Senate, and other matters.

I would like to call your attention to a number of matters which Mrs. Stuart's office has posted on the board. Monday, at 10:00, Tricia Nixon Cox will present the 1972 Scholastic Achievement Award for the Reporting of [Recording for?] the Blind, Incorporated, in a ceremony in the East Garden and there will be coverage of that.

---

* At dinner in Santa Fe in 1980, Chris Herter told me the State Department's man was suddenly recalled after I went back to Washington.

Following that, in the East Room, at 11:15, the President will participate in the swearing in of Richard Kleindienst as Attorney General, George Shultz as Secretary of the Treasury, and Caspar Weinberger as Director of the Office of Management and Budget. There will be full coverage of that ceremony.

Those are all the announcements we have.

Then there were questions from the press:

Q: Jerry, in the House yesterday in the debate on the Higher Education bill, the Administration leader, the House Minority leader, Gerald Ford, made a strong speech against passage of the bill. Not the least of what he pointed out was it would lead to metropolitan area school districts.

Is this an indication that the President is not going to sign the bill?

MR. WARREN: Bob, we have had a number of discussions in this room and there have been a number of discussions on the Hill about the Higher Education bill. The President feels, as we have said, and Mr. Ehrlichman said last month, that the so-called busing provisions, attached to the Higher Education bill in the conference, are not effective, will not be effective.

The President feels that the busing legislation which he submitted, the moratorium, is the way to resolve this matter in a fast, final and fair—to quote Mr. Ehrlichman—manner. The President still believes that. He still urges the Congress to hold hearings and discuss the moratorium legislation. He believes it is important to do this prior to school opening in September and he also believes that Congress should begin to discuss and consider the more substantive legislation, the Equal Education Opportunities Act.

Having said that, on the matter of the bill itself, it will receive careful review in the White House, as all important bills do, and then will go to the President for his decision. However, I would not want to leave you with the impression that there is an active consideration of veto of the bill.

Q: Jerry, you mentioned that the President had been concentrating on domestic issues. Who else has been up there besides John Ehrlichman and in what way is he concentrating on it?

MR. WARREN: The President took with him, according to one of the many reliable wire services which report out of Washington, "bulging briefcases," so he had a number of things to review. He has been working up there and has been in consultation with Mr. Haldeman, in person, and of course he has been on the telephone with advisers and assistants here in the White House.

Q: Is Mr. Rebozo up there?

MR. WARREN: No, he is not.

Q: Is he on his way?

MR. WARREN: Not to my knowledge.

Q: How long will the President stay there?

MR. WARREN: I can't tell you that at this point, Don. I do not know his plans on return. Mrs. Nixon, as you know, is there. She went up yesterday afternoon.

Q: He is obviously returning Monday; right?

MR. WARREN: He will be here Monday morning at 11:15, yes.

Q: Has the President decided on a nominee for the Assistant Attorney General in charge of the Anti-Trust Division?

MR. WARREN: There is consideration being given to that matter obviously, and we hope to have something to announce to you on that fairly soon.

Q: Today, perhaps?

MR. WARREN: I can't say that, but we hope to have an announcement on that very soon.

Q: What about Deputy Attorney General?

MR. WARREN: That is a matter which also is under consideration by the new Attorney General and I just have nothing to give you on that today.

Q: Did the President call Mr. Kleindienst after the confirmation vote yesterday?

MR. WARREN: I believe he did, but I would like to check on that before I make that firm.

Q: Where is Mr. Ziegler these days?

MR. WARREN: He is in a meeting this morning and that is why I am here.

Q: Jerry, is election year politics one of the domestic issues that the President is concentrating on?

MR. WARREN: I think the President made his position very clear on that and I don't think that I need to restate it.

Q: He said he wasn't going to comment about it. He didn't say he wasn't going to think about it. (Laughter)

At Camp David there was no sign of those "bulging briefcases." We talked briefly about the details of Kleindienst's swearing-in as Attorney General. His confirmation hearings had been long, tough and bloody, with much embarrassing testimony about ITT, Dita Beard and political payoffs.

The President instructed Haldeman to have Chief Justice Warren Burger come down to swear in Kleindienst, and also George Shultz and Caspar Weinberger.

Nixon had phoned Kleindienst when he heard of the Senate's confirmation vote. Kleindienst talked to him briefly about who he'd like to have as his Deputy Attorney General. John Mitchell was pushing for William Ruckelshaus, then head of the Environmental Protection Agency and formerly Mitchell's assistant. Another Mitchell assistant, Jerris Leonard, was lobbying hard for the job.

Nixon asked our opinion of James Lynn, then number two man in the Commerce Department. I said I didn't think Lynn and Kleindienst would work well together, although I admired Lynn.

Haldeman said Clark MacGregor was also pressing very hard to leave the White House to become Deputy Attorney General. MacGregor wanted to become Attorney General someday and figured this was his best way to maneuver it.

During the years MacGregor had been a Congressman from Minnesota, before Hubert Humphrey defeated him for the Senate, he had learned how to use the Washington press. When it had become known that Attorney General Mitchell was going to retire, the Washington columns began reporting that Nixon was seriously considering MacGregor for Attorney General. In fact, other than at this one meeting in June, 1972, I never heard Nixon seriously discuss Clark MacGregor for any Cabinet or subcabinet job.

The President had made it clear more than once that he considered MacGregor to be of limited capacity—suited to his job of lobbying the Congress for the White House, but unqualified for more weighty responsibility.

By way of explaining why he would not select Bill Ruckelshaus to be Kleindienst's deputy, Nixon said he had decided to veto the Water Quality bill the Congress had enacted because it had been distorted with a number of very expensive add-ons. Bill Ruckelshaus was perceived to be the Administration's front man for clean water and air. If Ruckelshaus were to be transferred from his job running the Environmental Protection Agency to Deputy Attorney General at the same time he vetoed the water bill, Nixon would be accused of opposing clean water. He opposed overspending, not clean water, but the veto alone was going to be hard enough to explain. So Ruckelshaus would not get the job, and Nixon said it was up to me to explain to John Mitchell why his boy was being passed over.

Thinking about his conversation with Kleindienst, Nixon warned me: "He's going to pull end runs around you if he can. I told him he was to clear everything with you, but you had better get him in and handle him."

I made a note to see Kleindienst the next day. Instead, we talked briefly at Langley High School's graduation that Saturday when my son Tom and one of Kleindienst's sons received awards and diplomas.

I asked Nixon what he'd decided about that Higher Education bill, over which at that moment the press and Jerry Warren were skirmishing back at the White House. My staff and I had prepared a long memorandum for the President to review when he returned from his Russian trip, outlining his options and asking for an early decision.

Nixon said he'd decided to sign the bill but he wanted a tough "signing statement" to be released at the same time, making clear his position on busing and school integration.

Moreover, he wanted me to begin work at once on the busing plank for the Republican Party Platform. That delicate project was not to be left for the Platform Committee or the Convention.

Then, with busing on his mind, Nixon began to talk about Warren Burger and the other changes the President had wrought in the Supreme Court. Nixon liked the looks and the performance of Burger and the other Justices he'd picked. They were exactly what he had promised the people when he ran in 1968. That, he told Haldeman, should be "played" more in our P.R. It was a strong 1972 campaign argument.

We went back to the Higher Education bill; he'd sign it, but we'd "come down hard" on busing. Ed Morgan and I were to be sure the platform plank and the signing statement did that. We were to keep up the fight for Nixon's proposed law imposing a moratorium on court-ordered busing, too.

We should, Nixon said, come out strongly for a Constitutional amendment prohibiting busing-to-achieve-racial-balance, but the timing on that was important. "Find out when school starts next fall," he instructed me. "We'll be ready to go with a Constitutional amendment between then and the election."

The cost of the Higher Education bill bothered the President. There must be cuts in the next budget in expenditures for education. He was distressed at the prediction that the education budget would rise drastically in fiscal year 1973 (our staff memo had exposed him to the subject of the education budget).

Treasury Secretary George Shultz; Cap Weinberger, the new head of the Office of Management and Budget, and I were to bring some realism into the budget—there had to be cuts.

"How about cuts in defense?" I asked. "Since the [just-completed] Moscow trip, everything is now wonderful with the Russians, I've been reading." Nixon laughed. There were to be no defense cuts right now. Perhaps later.

Then I took him on a short trip over the domestic landscape, to get his guidance on some of our other problems: Is the decision on the Water Quality bill final? Yes, Nixon said. Get a veto message ready.

"The Congress may override you on a veto of the clean-water bill," I reported. "If they do," he said, "let's set up the Congress to take the blame for a tax increase. They have overspent the budget on water and these other things, so we will have no choice but to change our position and ask for a necessary tax increase. Let them go home and explain that to the folks."

The veterans' bills coming soon from the Congress would be very expensive. "Do you want to cut there?" I asked. "No," he said, "we can't veto those. Go see Congressman Teague and see if you can make some kind of deal to save some money on veterans some other way."

Welfare reform? "There's to be a hard line on our legislation," he said. "No giving in. We'll stick with the bill we've got."

"Elliot Richardson [then Secretary of Health, Education and Welfare] doesn't know how to take a hard line with the Congress on anything," I said. "He'll give away the store."

"Get him in!" Nixon said. "I'll see the son-of-a-bitch and give him some backbone!"

Haldeman said Richardson was away and would return Tuesday. Nixon would have time to see him Thursday.

"Rural-development bills will be costly too," I continued.

Nixon nodded and nursed his painful nose. He had had enough of my domestic problems. It was time for politics. "What about the cost of the Democrats' and McGovern's proposals?" he asked. "Use what they are advocating as the basis for calculations and put *those* huge numbers out for people to think about. We have budget problems. Let him share the grief.

"The fact sheets we are putting out are too factual and dull," he said. "We need more catchy slogans in them like 'get people off the welfare rolls and onto payrolls.' There should be more 'savage attack lines' in our literature.

"McGovern advocates amnesty for draft-dodgers. Put in there that it may cost a billion dollars just to buy enough white flags for this country. You, John, must coordinate all of this.

"We must put out an attack on McGovern in the foreign field, too.

"Pick four major thrusts," Nixon instructed. "For example, McGovern's for surrender. He's for amnesty. Here's a phrase—these are like cheer lines in a speech: 'Thousands died for their choice; now the living must live with their choice.' He's for left-wing extremism. And he is for increased taxes.

"McGovern must be handled with attack. Agnew, Connally and the other surrogates must attack him. Don't create too many issues; drum three or four major themes. Review the transcripts of the Presidential press conferences and pick out three or four major things to get across.

"Don't ever let any of our people say, 'McGovern has changed his position.' Rather, say that there is absolutely no question where he stands. The conservative cares about consistency. Look at William Buckley, for example. Liberals have idealism, but they are pragmatic. They want to win. A conservative would rather lose than change his position.

"That's why the Communists win, you know? They are pragmatic. They know what power is.

"Attack McGovern on his wildest, most radical position. We must always stay with his worst positions, keeping him over on the left. He is always to appear to be a fanatical, dedicated leftist extremist.

"Oh, he has a pleasant manner, of course, we say. To get power he is sailing under false colors. Let's see, what's the record? What is his ADA rating?

"Abbie Hoffman, Jerry Rubin and Angela Davis are around McGovern's neck.

"Left-wingers will always compromise to win. For example, they'll wear American flags and ride in police cars and be for law enforcement right up until the election. Then the flags come off.

"The issues are radicalism; peace-at-any-price; a second-rate United States; running down the United States; square America versus radical America.

"We've got to open up on McGovern right now. We can't wait. We are in a race with his effort to clean himself up.

"Editorial backgrounders and those kinds of things aren't worth spending time on. You've got to do television. Put on veterans, Democrats and labor leaders—they are our best representatives if we can get them.

"Ehrlichman, ask Colson if McGovern is able to control what is in the Democratic Party platform.

"Timing is important. The 'Ten O'Clock Group'* should get together on timing—when to open up on McGovern. Ask Finch what he thinks.

"McGovern—this is the line—McGovern is left-wing; ADA left-wing. He is a dedicated radical, pacifist left-winger."

Nixon paused to nurse his inflamed nose with his handkerchief, so I decided to try to bring him back to the list of domestic questions my staff needed to have answered so that our work could go on.

"Have you decided," I asked, "what you want to do about aid to parochial schools?"

"Wait," he nodded. "Say nothing for now. At the Republican Convention, put a pro-aid plank in the platform. It looks [from the content of our staff memorandum] as though we can't do anything else right now."

---

* The public-relations committee of the White House staff.

Haldeman had things to talk about too. He always received advance word of forthcoming Gallup polls. There would be one in mid-June comparing Nixon's 1968 lead over Humphrey with Nixon's 1972 margin over McGovern. Gallup would say they were virtually the same.

Nixon nodded, reminiscing: "Between September and November in 1968 there was the bombing halt and Humphrey's Salt Lake speech. They cut our lead ninety percent. Ours was a better campaign, you know. We were better organized, and we spent as much money as they did, but Humphrey did something right and we did something wrong.

"Pat Buchanan and John Sears have the theory that you have to keep up your momentum—that you have to go all around the country making speeches even when you have that kind of a lead.

"There was something wrong with that 1968 campaign. Of course, the press was building Humphrey and hurting me. The Efron book* shows the media was ten to one against us."

Haldeman: "Yep."

"How can we cope with that kind of press bias?" Nixon asked rhetorically. Nixon turned to me. "Have you anything else?"

I had the problem of the President's position on repeal of the Davis-Bacon Act. Nixon had read our memorandum. He asked me to have Mitchell cool off Senator John Tower's effort to repeal it. He should tell Tower that the unions would put Nixon on the spot if Tower kept beating the drum. The President would be forced to be for the unions if Tower didn't lay off.

Nixon emerged from that 1972 election with a huge plurality and with the unfounded belief that he had at last wounded his adversaries. His virulent antipathy toward the press (and vice versa) had reached the point where some society reporters from the *Post* were turned away from White House parties, and the President ordered an investigation of a reporter who was doing a story about Julie Eisenhower's teaching job in Florida. The *Post* and some of the others were running stories about campaign dirty tricks and slush funds that reached into the White House, naming Dwight Chapin and Bob Haldeman.

---

* Efron, Edith, *The News Twisters.* Los Angeles: Nash Publishing Company, 1971.

Nixon was convinced his aides were under attack because the press hated Richard Nixon, pure and simple.

Just before the election, Katharine Graham, publisher of *The Washington Post,* had written a letter—addressed to me, but plainly for the President to see—denying any personal animosity.

November 3, 1972

Dear John:

A short while back you threw me a message over the fence, and I genuinely appreciated it. Here is a message I want to send to you.

Among the charges that have been flying over the past few weeks, many have disturbed me for the general misunderstanding they suggest of the *Post's* purposes in printing the stories we do. But none has disturbed me more than an allegation Senator [Robert] Dole made the other day. It was that the *Post's* point of view on certain substantive issues was explained by me as proceeding from the simple fact that I "hate" the President.

There are so many things wrong with this "anecdote," that one hardly knows where to begin in correcting them. But I would begin with the fact that I cannot imagine that the episode ever took place at all or that I ever expressed such a childish and mindless statement—since it is one that I do not feel.

I want you to know that. And I also want you to know that the fiction doesn't stop there. For the story suggests, as well, that somehow editorial positions on public issues are taken and decisions on news made on the basis of the publisher's personal feelings and tastes. This is not true, even when the sentiments attributed to me—unlike this alleged and unworthy "hate" for the President—may be real.

What appears in the *Post* is not a reflection of my personal feelings. And by the same token, I would add that my continuing and genuine pride in the paper's performance over the past few months—the period that seems to be at issue—does not proceed from some sense that it has gratified my personal whim. It proceeds from my belief that the editors and reporters have fulfilled the highest standards of professional duty and responsibility.

On this I know we disagree. I am writing this note because I think we have enough such areas of sharp and honest disagreement between us not to need a harmful and destructive overlay

of personal animosity that I, for one, don't feel and don't wish to
see perpetuated by misquotation! (My turn, it seems.)

Best regards to you and Jean,
Kay

Mr. John D. Ehrlichman
Assistant to the President for Domestic Affairs
The White House
Washington, DC 20500

KG/mlr
PERSONAL & CONFIDENTIAL
BY HAND

I asked Nixon to consider inviting Kay Graham in for a
conversation. I showed him her letter, and suggested that such
a meeting might benefit them both; at the very least, it might
dampen some of the heat we were getting from the *Post*.
Nixon patiently explained to me that Mrs. Graham had written the letter because it was obvious that the President would
win reelection. Our unfriendliness toward the *Post* was beginning to hurt them, and it would hurt them a great deal more
before we were through. (Nixon gave an exclusive interview to
a *Star* political writer not long after.)

Nothing, Nixon asserted, would ever be gained by showing
friendliness toward the *Post*. He would not waste time with
Kay Graham, under any circumstances.

After Bob Haldeman and I left the White House, the President began to depend on others for the services he had once
received from Haldeman and me. He talked to William
Rogers, Garment and some of his writers. And almost by default, Ron Ziegler began to perform many of the ministerial
tasks Bob Haldeman had done.

Ziegler passed instructions, called to ask questions, summoned people the President wanted to see. Someone had to sit
there across the desk from Nixon and listen to his rambling,
instruction-studded conversation for hours on end, as Haldeman used to do. Ziegler filled the vacuum. In that process
Ziegler became a confidant, eventually even an adviser.

Ron Ziegler had been the White House mouth for nearly
five years by then. He combined a talent for articulation and a
feral instinct for survival that usually kept him out of deep
trouble in press briefings.

But Ziegler was ill-suited to the role of confidant and adviser to a President in terminal trouble. Although Nixon

needed someone of wisdom and experience, he chose a very young man whose principal employments had been as a junior advertising executive, and as the fellow who gives the spiels while he runs the little boat through the plastic hippos and cannibals on the Jungle River Cruise at Disneyland.

Because Nixon was well aware of all this, Ziegler lacked leverage with him. Nixon had programmed Ron, day after day, for years. Asking Ron for advice was like asking, "Mirror, mirror on the wall / Who is the fairest of them all?"*

The Washington Post's only local competitor was *The Evening Star*. The *Star* was published afternoons by the Kauffman and Noyes families, who were disposed to be friendly to Richard Nixon and his Administration. For his part, Nixon longed to see the *Star* infused with millions of new dollars and a livelier management, to give the *Post* some real competition.

An aggressive Washington newspaper can virtually set the Federal (hence the national) agenda. It is read by everyone in the White House, the Congress and the Supreme Court, so such a paper can, by drumfire, move hunger or air pollution or aid to Namibia to the top of every action list in town. It can elevate obscure individuals to social and political status. It can vest or destroy credibility overnight.

At times of extreme difficulty with the *Post,* Nixon searched about for a friendly and wealthy buyer for the *Star.* Once it looked as if one of the Mellon heirs might agree to buy out the Kauffmans and Noyeses, and another time Nixon talked to Walter Annenberg about buying the *Star.*

But all through his Presidency, Nixon saw the *Post* grow and the *Star* wane.

Then, a couple of days before his second inauguration, Richard Nixon received a letter from Newbold Noyes, an editor and part owner of the *Star.* Nixon had recently come down from Camp David, where he had spent virtually all of November and December, sifting through the Cabinet and staff, planning a radical reorganization of the Executive Branch and putting the finishing touches on the new budget. The new Cabinet appointments had been announced, one by one, and

---

* I had no chance to watch Ziegler in action during the months from May 1973 to Nixon's retreat to San Clemente, but I am told by some who were there that he became fiercely protective and as reclusive as his President. If that is so, it may account for some of Nixon's otherwise inexplicable end-play moves. For example, it will be interesting to learn what part Ziegler actually played in Nixon's decision to preserve the White House tapes, rather than destroy them the same week Alex Butterfield disclosed their existence.

word of Nixon's austere second-term plans was seeping around Washington. The new Secretaries hadn't inspired much enthusiasm. Tough budget cuts had Washington worried.

Nixon had gone to Florida to put the finishing touches on his State of the Union address and get a little tan for the television cameras. Noyes's letter reached him there, and it concerned him. It couldn't be brushed off like Kay Graham's olive branch. This one was from a friend, and it contained a serious threat.

Nixon had Ron Ziegler read Newby Noyes's letter to me over the telephone. I turned on my dictating machine and recorded it as Ron read it slowly.* Noyes had written to Nixon:

When someone is worried about a friend and finds himself in anguish as to what is going on, the friend is entitled to be told.

He should not learn it secondhand. He should not read it in the papers. He should have the benefit of the friend's report which he can consider privately. This letter is such a report to you. I have thought and prayed hard before deciding to send it, and I hope you will feel at least that it is not wrong for me to have done so.

You know that we at the *Star* endorsed you editorially for re-election and in general have supported you in your major decisions abroad and at home. Since the election, however, it seems to us things are developing not at all as we hoped they would and felt they should. In a way, that dims the bright promise of your victory.

We are saddened and frightened by what we see. The issue is not your decision to renew bombing of North Vietnam, which seemed to us wrong and on which we have already expressed ourselves in print. Whatever your reasons for starting the bombing, you made a courageous decision in stopping it. I know you want to bring peace in Southeast Asia at the earliest possible moment. There is no doubt you will succeed.

The concerns I want to express run to other areas, involving the whole picture of your second term that seems to be emerging.

I had thought it would be so different. I had told myself and my colleagues that having seen an end to the fighting abroad, after the election you would immediately turn full of hope and

---

* This standard "phone" attachment on my standard dictating machine was the only recording device in my office throughout my entire tenure. Once I had special equipment brought in for a specific conversation—with Admiral Welander. News stories about permanent recording gear being "found" there by my successors either were false or described microphones I was unaware of.

energy to another battle here at home, trying to inspire a new spirit of purpose and unity in the American people. It is a sad fact, Mr. President, that in the recent election many of us voted our negative feelings on domestic problems. Feelings of frustration, weariness, even reaction. You must recognize that you benefited to a degree from an unhappy, unhealthy mood. A portion of your mandate grew out of forces unworthy of you and the things you stand for. It seemed to me that the question, with all respect, was whether you would cater to this trend or whether you would choose to lead us onto higher ground.

I believed fervently that you would take the latter course, but I must report you have badly shaken this belief. Some of my associates tried to reassure me with the thought that it is too early to tell what you want for your second term. I hope they are right. It seems to me, however, that there have been a great many signs as to the intended direction, almost all pointing the wrong way.

One of these, ironically, was your talk with Jack Horner, and I'm sure you know how much we appreciated your granting that interview. But, Mr. President, do you really mean to convey the impression that to your mind the main thing this country needs is a more responsible attitude on the part of its disadvantaged citizens? Do you really believe that the awful problems of our cities—the poverty, ignorance, ill health, rotten housing—that all of these festering disaster areas will disappear if we just keep our cool and resolve not to throw dollars at them? I think a fair-minded person could infer from the Horner interview that this is your basic position.

If it is, this country is going to be in desperate shape by 1976, in this conservative's opinion. I know we have to operate under tight budget restraints. I know the big problems in the world do not yield to pat, theoretical, expensive answers. Certainly not the answers offered these many years past by liberal sociologists and politicians. I know it is cruel deception to pretend that all of our ills or perhaps any of them can be solved by government.

But I also know the President of the United States, more than anyone else, is responsible for the moral tone, the mood and spirit of the American people, and right now that spirit is not good. If you do not move energetically to improve it, and soon, I'm afraid you, your party and your country will come to regret the notion that it is possible, let alone wise, to sit on a mandate for four years, even a mandate as comfortable as yours.

What seems to be necessary is not a lot of vast new programs you obviously shy away from. It is more a matter of attitude, a commitment that there will be the hard effort to make headway against the social ills of this country. And leadership to instill the feeling of hope in a discouraged and turned-off citizenry. I'm not going to load you down with an argumentative recital of the evidence that makes me question whether this is the direction in which you are going. You have already begun to get plenty of heat along this line from our friends in the Eastern Establishment press.

What we have to go on is all very impressionistic. The Cabinet changes, one would suppose, provide the firmest clues available. Let me just confess that I find myself agreeing with someone, maybe it was Stewart Alsop, who wrote that too many of the people who dealt imaginatively with problems and ideas are leaving. And that they are being replaced by bland administrative types whose instinct is just to keep things running smoothly. I think that is a reasonable comment, with ominous implications.

Summarizing my complaint rather crudely, it looks as though you have decided to go along with what I believe is a transitory, negative trend in our politics, instead of leading us along the high, progressive road that alone can take us to a worthwhile future. I am sick at heart about this because your current situation has precisely the security and strength which permits you to do the necessary.

Obviously, Mr. President, sometime soon I must face the question whether the views I am expressing here should not be elaborated in some sort of major editorial effort in the *Star;* one which would put us in the painful position of eating a lot of words. I've been thinking the Inaugural might be the logical occasion, unless, in the meantime, something happened to convince me my impressions were unfounded. Perhaps you do not care about this sort of criticism. Certainly a person in your position gets a bellyful of it. And from sources far more qualified and influential than this one.

The thing I want to be sure you understand, sir, is that this does not come from some traditional journalistic adversary of yours anxious to score a few brownie points with the Georgetown set by laying another one on you. I am your guy around here. When you were Vice President and came back from being spat on in Venezuela or wherever it was, I wrote a front-page editorial in the *Star* urging everyone to get out in the streets and let you know you were appreciated, and then I went out and stood there myself shouting greetings as you drove by. I covered the Hiss trial, and I greatly admired back then and still do how you blew the whistle on that liar. (I am wearing the Presidential cuff links you sent me as I write this.) I say these things only so you will know I mean you well. I do not want anything from you except the performance that I and like-minded supporters can be proud of.

I think you are in a uniquely favorable position to confound your detractors and win a most honored place in history by turning things around and leading us into a new era of progress at home and peace abroad.

I'm afraid you're getting ready instead to settle for small-minded, short-range, timid political maneuvering which in the end will not even have the merit of achieving its cramped objectives. I hope to God you prove me the wrongest man in Washington.

Noyes's letter obviously had some immediate effect on the President. Whether it was the force of his sincere argument or Noyes's not-so-veiled threat to write some critical editorials in the *Star,* Nixon's State of the Union address was amended to say:

We have the chance today to do more than ever before in our history to make life better in America—to ensure better education, better health, better housing, better transportation, a cleaner environment—to restore respect for law, to make our communities more livable—and to ensure the God-given right of every American to full and equal opportunity.

That was, in Nixon's phrase, the laundry list.

I urged Nixon to invite Newby Noyes in for a talk. Noyes had written of concerns that I shared, and I hoped that he might be able to persuade Nixon to moderate some of his attitudes. I had been able to save Revenue Sharing from extinction in the new budget, but only temporarily. I could see big defense budgets ahead, but only tough and doubtful battles for money to solve domestic problems.

And I hoped that a meeting with Noyes would keep the *Star* friendly. It was that argument which finally persuaded Nixon to see him early in March 1973.

When Richard Nixon was on the defensive in a face-to-face encounter, his instinctive tactic was to talk, endlessly, about anything and everything except the subject he was feeling defensive about. That is what he did the day Noyes came in. I was designated to arrange the meeting and sit with the President and his guest during their "conversation."

In truth, it was a Nixon monologue. He talked at length about Vietnam; in late January he and Henry Kissinger had wrapped up a peace settlement after managing to persuade the South Vietnamese to acquiesce. Nixon told Newbold Noyes a lot about Henry's Paris negotiations with the North Vietnamese.

Noyes proffered an apology for having been so critical in his letter, but his apology was less a statement of regret than an attempt to change the conversational subject. Nixon brushed off the attempt. It was clear that the President did not intend to explore Noyes's unhappiness on the merits.

On the way out I thanked the editor for the try, and offered to talk with him about the subjects of his concern. He thought that might be a good idea; but we never did get together.

In looking back, I think the Graham and Noyes letters offered the President two opportunities which he badly missed. If Nixon had engaged in quiet, open conversations with Kay Graham and Newbold Noyes, separately, perhaps something fundamental and dramatic might have occurred on both sides. Perhaps not. Much would have depended upon Nixon's frame of mind, the setting and who had spoken to him last, just before such talks. (By then Nixon had sufficiently lost confidence in Charles Colson that he'd decided that Colson must resign.)

If Nixon had listened to Noyes instead of haranguing him, or if I had been willing to use up my usefulness by insisting that he do so, perhaps Nixon might have been encouraged to more openness.

From January through April 1973, as he became increasingly defensive, Nixon reacted like some sea anemone which recoils and closes when it is threatened. With each new development in the growing Watergate scandal the President agreed with me when I talked about the need to make a full disclosure. But he could not bring himself to take the first step, nor could he permit those close to him to step out and say that which needed saying if the Nixon Presidency was to be saved.

It's hard to recognize turning points as they occur, especially if no one tries to begin a turning. But Nixon's rejection of Kay Graham's little olive branch and his filibuster of Newbold Noyes were probably his last best chances for openness and reconciliation before he began his long, tortured slide down that greased chute to his resignation.

By then, Richard Nixon's genius for politics had become entangled in the more personal struggle that has come to be called Watergate.

Part IV

CHAPTER EIGHTEEN

Watergate

I DIDN'T BEGIN to understand "Watergate" until long after I'd been fired in the spring of 1973. Which is not to say that I completely understand Watergate today.

A half-hundred secrets which remain locked in the memories of a dozen men are needed to answer all the remaining questions, but I don't suppose we'll ever know them.

James McCord knows more than he's said, I'd guess. My wife, Christy, and I were standing in a ticket line in the Seattle-Tacoma airport in 1979 when McCord came up and introduced himself. He and I had never met. "Why did you fellows break into the Watergate?" Christy asked bluntly. McCord turned and retreated, mumbling an evasive reply.

My wife and I had been talking about Watergate secrets a few weeks earlier. I'd said it would take ten or eleven selected people sworn to candor to answer the unanswered; it would take a dedication to an illumination of the facts and a common pooling of the bits and pieces. Christy proposed a colloquium, led by some disinterested student of the facts, attended by the Keepers of the Secrets—and no one else.

McCord, Howard Hunt and Gordon Liddy can explain part of the break-in, but John Dean, John Mitchell and others must provide the precedent details. Maybe some CIA people need to be in that group too. I don't know.

The "cover-up" of Watergate could be explained by John Dean, if he'd tell the truth. He was at its center from the second day after the break-in. Others who could contribute vital bits and pieces of uncovered information on Watergate include Herb Kalmbach, John Mitchell, H. R. Haldeman, Richard Nixon, Henry Kissinger, Richard Moore, Richard Kleindienst, Pat Gray, Vernon Walters, Robert Mardian, Al Haig and Charles Colson.

It is clear from the record that Richard Nixon didn't confide everything in everyone. Charles Colson knows a great deal more about Richard Nixon and the origins of the Plumbers than I do. But I knew some things Colson didn't. Bob Haldeman said nothing to the rest of us about $350,000 the President had him skim off the top of the 1972 campaign funds to be held in a safe-deposit box (by Alex Butterfield) for "emergencies." Most of us operated in watertight compartments, unaware of what Nixon was ordering our colleagues to do.

I have answered the hundreds of thousands of questions asked of me by all the lawyers and investigators as truthfully as I could. And more important, I have answered the questions I've asked of myself. In some cases my answers were dead wrong, but I didn't know that at the time. It has turned out that as much as I knew, there was more that I didn't know—and didn't even suspect.

I knew about the break-in at Dr. Fielding's office (he was Daniel Ellsberg's psychiatrist) in Beverly Hills, California. I learned of it in 1971 a few hours after it occurred. I didn't report the burglary to the Beverly Hills police, nor did I cause Egil Krogh, David Young, Howard Hunt or Gordon Liddy to be arrested. At the time, I didn't know who had ordered them to do the break-in; but I think I do now.

In 1972 I knew money was being given to the Watergate burglary defendants. Some of it came from Richard Nixon's own cache of surplus campaign funds being held in trust by Herbert Kalmbach in California. The defendants needed to support their families and pay attorneys, and no one at the reelection committee or at the White House wanted Hunt or McCord or any of the others to become so unhappy that they would embarrass the President's reelection campaign.

In March 1973, I heard that Howard Hunt was threatening to implicate me in the Fielding break-in unless he was paid more money. That deeply shook me, but I did nothing about it. I knew John Mitchell and others were finding money for Hunt. I felt some comfort from the fact that the President had declared that subject to be a matter of "national security" that was not to be discussed.

When I was indicted in 1974, I was accused of a number of crimes, some of which I did not in fact commit. The perjury charges were particularly difficult for me to view calmly. I had always taken pride in my "good word," my reputation as a lawyer whose representations could always be believed. Now the prosecutor charged that I had intentionally lied to the FBI* and several grand juries.

The grand-jury allegations were based only on the conflicting testimony of other witnesses, notably John Dean. The trial jury was being invited to convict me on the uncorroborated story of John Dean! I felt sure I'd be acquitted because I knew I'd told the truth. It is some measure of the feverish mood of Washington in those days that the jury found me guilty on every single count.

Other charges rested on the White House tapes. Between February 15 and April 30, 1973, I participated in dozens of conversations with Richard Nixon and others about aspects of Watergate. Day after day the President called me to his office to hash over the alternatives left to him, as the Senate Committee hearings drew nearer.

During that same time, Nixon spent many hours alone with John Dean.

In retrospect, it seems that most, if not all, of the President's problems would have evaporated had he stepped out, forthrightly, and told the American people everything he had known or suspected in February or March 1973. But Nixon couldn't bring himself to do that.

During my last ninety days with Nixon my great crime was not forcing him to make a full disclosure. Perhaps if I had threatened to go into the press room myself, I might have manipulated him into speaking out. All the time, in advance of the Senate hearings and before Dean's plea bargaining, I felt that only such a Presidential disclosure could put an end to Nixon's trouble.

Several times I told Nixon just that. But all my suggestions to him were made in the established context of our relationship within the Nixon White House. It was the President of the United States taking counsel from aides, most of whom did not realize that they had as much at stake as the President. For many years each of us had relied on Richard Nixon to arrive at the wisest, most prudent and proper decision. The President ultimately would decide, and as we'd been doing for years, we would then abide.

In this case Nixon temporized and vacillated, and his failure to decide became his decision. He defaulted the initiative, and it passed to John Dean and the Senate.

---

* The lying-to-the-FBI charge was thrown out by the trial judge.

During February, March and April 1973 everyone had his secrets. Some people told what they knew to save their skins when it became evident that Nixon's catatonia was permanent. Others told lies.

Thanks to the Nixon tapes, I now know a little more of what Nixon was saying and doing with some of the other people than I would have known without hearing some of the tapes.

There is some question as to what I knew about the President's taping system. The fact is I was totally unaware it existed. Because one of the tapes has me referring to the President's recording of a conversation with John Dean, some commentators deduced that I knew about the whole system. In fact, Bob Haldeman, alluding to Nixon's fear that he might have said something self-incriminating to Dean in one of their March 1973 meetings, had just told me, "We have Dean on tape in that one." I didn't dream that *everything* I'd been saying and hearing in the President's office for years had been recorded.

My reaction to the news that there was a taping system is perhaps a measure of how little I understood of Watergate. "That's great," I said to a reporter on my front lawn when he informed me of Alex Butterfield's disclosure. "Now all the innuendos and questions will be answered with some hard evidence." I was confident the tapes would help, not hurt.

I was convicted in two criminal trials. In the months between them, the Special Prosecutor was required by law to let my lawyers and me listen to any and all of the tapes that might be used in the second trial. (No tapes had been played during the first Fielding break-in trial.)

My lawyers, William Frates and Andrew Hall, tried to listen to some of the tapes, but they simply couldn't understand them. The prosecution said it had called upon electronics experts to assemble the finest available playback equipment, but even with the most sensitive earphones it was nearly impossible at times to guess what people were saying.

The prosecution and the FBI had prepared written "transcripts" of the tapes, copies of which were given to us to read along with the tapes. I knew the voices and had been present during some of the conversations, so I was elected by my lawyers to monitor the tapes in order to evaluate the accuracy of the transcripts. Some passages I replayed a dozen times, fast and slowly.

The fidelity of the tapes was terrible. If Judge John Sirica had required the jury to listen to them without benefit of written transcripts, those poor people could not have had a clue to what was being said or done. Moreover, as I sat in the Special Prosecutor's listening room looking at the written text and playing the tapes, I immediately understood that the authors of the transcript didn't know the players. The text often attributed Haldeman's words to me, Nixon's to Haldeman, Dean's to Haldeman and many phrases to "unknown."

I had been listening to Richard Nixon for years; I knew his voice and I also knew his syntax and speaking rhythm. It was obvious that the transcribers did not.* Also, literally dozens of phrases the FBI put into the transcript were not to be heard on the tapes.

There is a conversation taped the afternoon of March 22, 1973, involving five people. The transcript indicates I said the classic phrase "It's a modified limited hang out." Writers on Watergate have pointed to the passage as evidence I proposed that the President make a sham disclosure. In fact, all through that meeting, as attested by the tapes, I was advocating that everything except a few FBI summaries be included in a report by Dean to be published or turned over to Senator Sam Ervin. But at page 287 of the transcript, I suddenly seem to shift to a "modified limited hang out." In fact I am not the person who speaks those phrases. (The voice in question isn't mine; I believe it is Bob Haldeman's.) The FBI transcripts are full of important errors of that kind.†

As I sat in the Special Prosecutor's hot little listening room, playing the hard-to-hear passages over and over, I experienced

---

* The problem is not limited to listening. In a handwriting-analysis book published during Watergate, the author deeply analyzes Richard Nixon's character from "his" writing. The only trouble is that the Nixon samples are my writing, not Nixon's.

† When Sirica ruled that he'd let the jury listen to the tapes, my lawyers pointed out that the proposed transcripts were not accurate. The prosecutor said they had all been checked by Alexander Butterfield, one of Haldeman's assistants, and urged that each juror be given a text—so that they could understand what they were hearing in their earphones!

Sirica, typically, solved the problem by allowing each juror to have one of the inaccurate transcripts to refer to as he or she listened, but then he required that the texts be returned to him without being admitted into evidence.

Later the defendants put Alex Butterfield on the stand and proved by his testimony that there were egregious errors in the text. But by then the jury had heard the tapes and read the transcripts, and the damage was done. Sirica made it as hard as possible to impeach the transcript texts. He liked them.

a kind of revelation. I heard how people had talked about me in the President's office when I wasn't there; for example, I heard the President tell people to keep secrets from me. And I heard Nixon agree with Haldeman that there must be a meeting with the CIA's Richard Helms and Vernon Walters on June 23, 1972, to try to block an FBI investigation. Mitchell and Dean inspired the cover-up idea. Haldeman says on one of the tapes:

Mitchell came up with [a plan] yesterday, and John Dean analyzed [it] very carefully last night and concludes, concurs now with Mitchell's recommendation that the only way to solve this, and we're really set up beautifully to do it . . . is for us to have Walters [of the CIA] call Pat Gray [Director of the FBI] and just say, "Stay the hell out of this. . . ."

Haldeman says the White House must order the CIA officials to contact Pat Gray and turn off the FBI Watergate investigation. And here's where I come into Mitchell's plan: Haldeman says to Nixon:

And the proposal would be that Ehrlichman (cough) and I call them in.

Nixon says:

All right, fine. . . . How do you call him in? I mean you just well, we protected Helms from one hell of a lot of things.

And Haldeman is heard to reply, "That's what Ehrlichman says," although I have no idea to what this refers. I was not aware that "we" protected Helms from anything except the publication of the Marchetti book which threatened to spill many CIA secrets.

I attended the subsequent Helms-Walters meeting, but as all three of the others testified, I didn't say much. One reason I was quiet was that I simply didn't know why we were having the meeting and I didn't really know why I was attending it, beyond the fact that Haldeman had told me the President wanted me to sit in on it.

That meeting took place six days after the burglars went into the Democratic Headquarters in the Watergate Office Building, and Nixon's role in that part of the cover-up was a vital element in his ultimate resignation. It was to be nearly two years before I heard the June 23, 1972, tapes and began to understand why the meeting took place.

The President had gone to his home at Key Biscayne, Florida, on Friday, June 16, 1972. Bob Haldeman and Ron Ziegler had gone with him. Charles Colson stayed in Washington, and John Dean was in the Philippines on a junket. I was at home in suburban Virginia.

At 4 A.M. Saturday, June 17, some of the burglars were arrested in the Democrats' office at the Watergate. About thirteen hours later I received a telephone call from a Secret Service agent who had a police report alleging that when arrested, one of the burglars possessed one of Howard Hunt's checks and his White House telephone number.

At that time I'd totally lost track of Howard Hunt. I'd met him only once, when Charles Colson was urging the White House to hire him in 1971, but after the break-in at Dr. Fielding's office in California and the disbanding of the Plumbers in September 1971, I'd heard little or nothing about him.

In my mind, Hunt was Colson's man. I didn't like the deduction that was shaping up from that Secret Service phone call: (1) a burglar is doing a campaign job on the Democrats and (2) he carries Hunt's phone number; (3) Hunt is close to Colson, who (4) is close to Richard Nixon. (5) Hunt does jobs for Colson and (6) Colson does jobs for Nixon. We are in the June before the November 1972 election, with less than 150 days to deal with this burglary, *if* it is a Colson production. That is a very short time.

I called Colson and asked what had ever become of that fellow Howard Hunt. Colson wanted to know why I was asking. I told him Hunt's name had turned up on a Watergate burglar. Colson said Hunt was working for a lobbyist and had been there at Bennett & Associates for some months. "Is he all through at the White House? Did we terminate him?" I asked. Colson assured me there was no connection. "Why does Hunt have a White House phone?" I asked. Colson said he didn't know.

I called Key Biscayne next. Haldeman was out, so I told Ron Ziegler of my talks with the Secret Service and Colson.

The next day, Sunday, I talked to Haldeman on the phone briefly and expressed my concern that Colson might be involved in the Watergate burglary. We agreed that I'd turn the question over to our Counsel, John Dean, the next day.

I saw Dean on Monday at noon and asked him to find out how the break-in had occurred. Two hours later he and I met briefly with Attorney General Richard Kleindienst, who promised to keep us fully informed on the progress of the investigation.

In his ghostwritten book, Dean (or the ghost, Taylor Branch, or both) alleges he told me that morning that he'd already met with Gordon Liddy and Liddy had admitted to him that the burglary was his project. That is untrue. Had I suspected Liddy was the manager of the break-in, my suspicions would have turned immediately to John Mitchell, his boss. But when the President returned the next day from Florida, my prime nominee was still Charles Colson.

Dean also manufactured the story that I had instructed him to have Howard Hunt flee the country. Dean claimed I committed that bizarre felony in front of three witnesses at a meeting in my office at 4 P.M. Monday (June 19). The others at that session, Bruce Kehrli and Charles Colson, do not corroborate Dean; in fact, Colson tells me (and has sworn in court) that Dean told him that he, Dean, told Hunt to flee without any instructions from anyone. I am certain that I did not have any part in any such instructions to Hunt.

At that afternoon meeting with Kehrli and the others I had discovered that Howard Hunt was still shown on current White House records as Charles Colson's employee. Worse, he still kept an office at the White House, and in that office was a locked safe with God-knew-what inside. I suggested that Bruce Kehrli have the GSA open the safe and that Dean observe the opening to inventory and preserve the contents.

The next morning the President was back in his office, but I didn't see him until 10:30 A.M. From nine until ten, Haldeman and I met with John Mitchell, John Dean and Richard Kleindienst. Kleindienst assured us that any leaks to the papers about the Watergate break-in (and there were many) were coming from the local police, not the Justice Department. So far Kleindienst saw no White House involvement in the break-in. He believed that Colson was guiltless. The purpose of the meeting was to agree on how the White House, the Justice Department and the reelection committee could coordinate press releases and other statements. We decided that Mitchell's press man would carry the burden and the in-Government people would keep comments to a minimum.

At ten-thirty I went over to the Executive Office Building to talk to the President alone, for the first time since the break-in. We had problems with the Higher Education bill, busing (the Broomfield Amendment) and welfare reform.

In the middle of my review of the busing amendment to the Higher Education bill, Nixon began to talk about the unfairness of the Watergate accusations. "We've reduced the number of wiretaps by fifty percent in this Administration," he said. "Robert Kennedy tapped the most when he was Attorney General. It's been a steady downtrend since then."

He was trying out a possible press "line" on me, obviously. But I waited to see how he would tie together the statistics on Government tapping with political spying by Hunt and the others. Maybe he knew something I didn't.

"Our primary interest is in the foreign contacts made by domestic subversive groups," the President continued. "As the President said a year and a half ago, it is the policy of this Administration to use taps sparingly. Tapping has been a practice of every Administration since World War II."

I waited for him to close the circle, but that was all he said about Watergate at our first meeting after the break-in. "I want a one-minute statement prepared," he continued, returning to the amendment, "making the point that busing is an inadequate answer to the problem of school segregation."

The rest of our meeting dealt with my other substantive questions. He then gave me marching orders to negotiate changes in our proposed Welfare Reform Act, and I headed for Congressional meetings on the Hill. I did not see the President alone again until we flew to Harrisburg, Pennsylvania, the next Saturday to inspect flood damage caused by Hurricane Agnes.

The Potomac River flooded that week too, threatening John Dean's town house near the Alexandria waterfront. Dean stayed home to sandbag his yard and move his furniture upstairs. As a result, I saw nothing of him after Wednesday, June 21, until the following week.

The meeting with Haldeman, Helms and Walters on June 23 was at 1 P.M., in the midst of a heavy day. I sat in on Haldeman's meeting with the CIA, cold. I'd been told to be there, but beyond that I had no idea what Haldeman intended to do. Haldeman told Vernon Walters and Richard Helms in effect that "the White House" would like the CIA to tell the FBI to keep away from the question of money flowing through Mexico to some of the Watergate burglars. When Haldeman hinted that the trail might lead to the Bay of Pigs, Richard Helms yelled like a scalded cat. "We're not afraid of that!" he said with more animation than I'd ever seen in that urbane gentleman before. Richard Helms was not attractive when he got excited, I thought at the time, and the Bay of Pigs was obviously a very touchy subject. Helms had become CIA Director at least in part because he had put much distance between the Bay of Pigs debacle and himself. But the Agency was still very touchy about its part in the failure, and I think Helms's distress that day was institutional, not individual. Both Helms and Vernon Walters* seemed to get Haldeman's message, and neither objected.

That meeting—ultimately so important in the outcome of Watergate—was the focus of the taped "smoking gun" conversations between Nixon and Haldeman, held both before we met the CIA officials and afterward, when our meeting was described by Haldeman to Nixon (on tape) as a success.

I've been given (or heard) three different explanations of that June 23 meeting from Richard Nixon. The first was an absolutely false story he told me at San Clemente two weeks later. At the time I believed it completely.

I testified before several Congressional committees in 1973 and 1974 that I knew the June 23 meeting was an innocent, good-faith effort to avoid conflict between the CIA and the FBI. The basis for my testimony, I told them, was that explanation the President had given me a few days later at San Clemente.

The second came a couple of years later, in the prosecutor's hot little listening room when I heard those June 23 conversations between Nixon and Haldeman. I realized then that I'd been conned. I felt used and stupid and very angry. And I realized that Richard Nixon—within six days of the break-in—had been actively covering up for Mitchell or Colson or someone.

We—my attorneys and I—were preparing for trial when I heard those tapes. At that point, our trial defense strategy changed. My lawyers began demanding that Richard Nixon be a witness at the trial, and we kept demanding it right up to the last minute before the verdict. We said that if he was really laid up with phlebitis then we'd pay to have all the lawyers

---

* Vernon Walters was a high-ranking military attaché, a flawless interpreter in a half-dozen languages and one of our country's ablest spies. Nixon made him Deputy Director of the CIA. Walters' memoranda of the June 23 meeting and subsequent events (written about a week later) are striking examples of selective recollection and ass-covering.

flown to San Clemente for a videotaped deposition, but we wanted Nixon's admissions and denials in front of the jury. The jury ought to know that Nixon had been engineering the cover-up in the summer of 1972 and had lied to *me* about it at San Clemente two weeks later.

But the President didn't want to appear. Nixon fought it tooth and nail, claiming his phlebitis was life-threatening. And John J. Sirica didn't want the appearance either. He stalled and stalled, refusing to rule on our request. He sent some doctors to San Clemente to look at Nixon, and they said it would be perfectly safe to take Nixon's deposition anytime after January 6. So just before New Year's Day, Sirica finally ruled; he refused to delay the trial (which had been going since September) a week to permit the lawyers to travel to California and back and take Nixon's deposition. Sirica by then was in a pellmell rush to judgment that had nothing to do with judicial probity. It had to do with fame and public pressure.

The third Nixon explanation of the June 23 meeting might have been Nixon's court testimony, including rigorous cross-examination; but thanks to Sirica's judicial incapacity, it was not.

Instead, we find the third account in Nixon's published memoirs. There he explains that he and Haldeman feared disclosure of Howard Hunt's political "activities" for Charles Colson, so they wanted the CIA to deflect the FBI's investigation lest the trail lead to Hunt.

In the two weeks between that June 23 CIA meeting and Nixon's first explanation to me at San Clemente, I spent only three days at the White House: June 26, 27 and 28. On both the twenty-sixth and the twenty-eighth I saw John Dean. At the President's urging, I had Dean in on the twenty-sixth to explain to me why preparation of the Nixons' estate plan was lagging. Weeks had passed without Dean's delivering the wills he was supposed to be getting prepared for the Nixons. After he'd given me an account of his problems with the New York lawyers who were studying Nixon's tax situation, Dean digressed to say he was wondering what to do with the contents of Hunt's safe. Some of the papers he'd found there were classified, he said, and some were potentially embarrassing.* He feared the FBI or the police would leak what it was that Col-

---

* Hunt had been doing work for Colson on the Kennedys' involvement in the Vietnamese war, and he'd collected cables and other State Department papers.

son had Hunt doing.* Dean suggested he might just turn everything over to Pat Gray, the acting FBI Director. He could do it in such a way as to make it Gray's responsibility to ensure that there were no leaks. I said that sounded fine.

On Friday, two days later, as I was having a meeting with Pat Gray at the President's direction to express our concern about leaks to the press from the FBI, Dean came to my office and gave Gray a large envelope. He told Gray it contained "politically sensitive" documents from Hunt's safe. I had just been talking to Gray about the President's unhappiness with the FBI. I said, in effect, that the reason Dean was giving the envelope to Gray personally was to be sure the contents didn't get leaked by his subordinates at the FBI. But nothing anyone said could have given Gray the impression that the package was to be destroyed—yet we discovered later that that is what he did with it.

When I left on June 29 for a trip to Michigan, Illinois and California, I was convinced that John Mitchell should be removed as director of the reelection campaign. On the twenty-eighth, I'd told Haldeman that I thought Mitchell should leave quickly, before the break-in scandal damaged the President's reelection any more. I had no hard information of Mitchell's personal involvement, but by then we all believed Liddy had been the organizer of the break-in, and simple deduction brought Liddy home to Mitchell's door. Haldeman proposed also replacing Mitchell's deputy, Jeb Magruder, with Fred Malek. He offered several possible replacements for Mitchell: Herb Kalmbach, Don Rumsfeld or Clark MacGregor. I voted for MacGregor, with some reservations.

That day—June 28—Haldeman said Nixon wanted me to travel with him during the 1972 campaign—although he didn't intend to leave the White House much—to look after "issues" and deal with local politicians. I agreed to do that.

Three days later Mitchell resigned, just as I arrived at San Clemente, where the President intended to remain until after the Democratic Convention took place, about three weeks later.

---

* Dean contrived a story about this conversation when he was bargaining to avoid prosecution. He alleged I'd advised him to "deep-six" the Hunt materials—throw them off a bridge into the Potomac. That I never said. Evidence at the trial later showed that Dean had in fact destroyed some of Hunt's things before June 23, without anyone's suggestion or direction. He involved me to explain why he had done so.

Just after the Fourth of July the new reelection-campaign leaders—MacGregor and Malek—came west for a meeting with the President. When I went to see the President in his office early on July 6, he told me that MacGregor had delivered an oral message to him from Pat Gray, asking that the President telephone Gray. Gray had then told Nixon on the phone that General Walters had sent him a note saying the CIA had "no interest" in the Mexican money channel the FBI had discovered during its investigation of the Watergate break-in.

"John," Nixon said excitedly, "they are just protecting their people down below. They will hurt the President if the people around the President try to cover for their subordinates." I didn't understand the real reason Nixon was upset; from what he said to me, I figured he knew the CIA was involved in moving Mexican money and that the President knew Walters' note was false.

Nixon was unhappy about the way he got Gray's message, too. "MacGregor is not discreet, you know. MacGregor must never talk to the President about Watergate again!" he exclaimed. "You and Bob [Haldeman] talk to MacGregor and tell him that; but you must not raise hell with Pat Gray or Walters. We may take some heat as a result of this, but it won't be that bad." I misunderstood that remark, too. I thought he meant that CIA money channels now might be exposed by FBI investigation. But Nixon knew then that far more "heat" could result.

When we met with MacGregor and Malek later, Nixon said to them, "Move into your jobs with decisiveness, but I don't want you doing anything to embarrass John Mitchell. Jeb Magruder [who had not yet been fired] is not a good manager. Oversee him."

The next morning, July 7, I was called to the President's office a few minutes before a meeting on the economy. Bob Haldeman was taking a few days off, so Nixon gave me some instructions of the sort he ordinarily would have given to Haldeman. Nixon was thinking of going back to Washington earlier than planned. He wanted media bias studied by Mort Allin.

"You know," he began on a new tangent, "the release of the Pentagon Papers has led to a demand for declassification of a lot of secret documents and may lead to grave consequences for the CIA and its former officials. They have to worry about the Bay of Pigs and [Vietnamese President] Diem's assassination and other things. Haldeman has Tom Huston's study of this. Howard Hunt was privy to most of the CIA's problems, you know. It all will blow! We tried, but we can't have this followed up. Gray and Walters must tell people that there is no effort to cover up either by the White House or the Committee to Re-elect. A cover-up is the worst thing; cover-up is how I nailed Truman. It can hurt deeply."

The next day this conversation continued, first just after noon and later during a long beach walk after a swim at Red Beach, on the Camp Pendleton property. "We can't even *appear* to have a cover-up of anything," Nixon began. "Not a whiff of it. We must get out to the press the enthusiastic nature of the investigation [of the Watergate break-in] that's going on—the FBI, the grand jury. The President said, 'Do it fully; let the chips fall where they may. There is to be no cover-up.'

"No one in the White House is involved. Our own investigation is completed, and that's the finding." (He was spinning out what his spokesman should be saying. I wondered what investigation he was talking about, because I wasn't aware of any that could be called "ours.") He continued: "At the Committee to Re-elect, there is a possible involvement of a few lower-level officials."

Then Nixon turned from press relations to his concern about Howard Hunt. The papers had been full of Hunt for two days, and obviously Nixon had been talking to Colson about his friend: "Chuck is close to Hunt, you know, and he's concerned about what Hunt might do too. He's wondering about offering Hunt immunity in return for his silence."

That appalled me, and I said so. "The whole idea is for you to keep separate from that burglary; we've got to keep the White House staff and you isolated from it."

Nixon seemed to agree. "You'd better ask Chuck if he's had any recent contact with Hunt. Ask: 'Have you seen him?' Tell him: 'Don't see him.'"

The President knew a great many things about Hunt that I didn't know. "His lawyer is Bittman," Nixon told me. "Do you think we could enlist him to be sure Hunt doesn't blow national secrets? Or what about Sirica? Would he help?"

I said I doubted it.

That afternoon we talked further about keeping distance between the White House and the burglars. I said, "You're concerned about Hunt trying to save himself by telling the CIA's secrets, or by blowing some covert CIA operation, and sooner or later someone is going to come to you with the proposition that you pardon Hunt to keep that from happening. Probably Colson." We were walking side by side along a desolate stretch of Camp Pendleton's beautiful beach, the ocean on our left. We'd been swimming at Red Beach, a mile to the south. "You simply can't let anyone talk to you about clemency," I repeated. "A conversation like that will bring it all into your lap."

Nixon nodded agreement, but he didn't want to close the door on clemency. He argued that worse criminals had been pardoned. A lot of crooks were never prosecuted. He would not promise anyone clemency, but after the trial and after the election, when the smoke cleared, it would be the right thing to do. Perhaps, after the election, he could pardon McGovern people who might be arrested too. He could pardon both sides evenhandedly and get Mitchell's reelection people off that way.

"Don't even think about it," I protested. "Let's agree that that whole subject is off limits for everyone in the White House. When 'the smoke clears' will be time enough to raise the subject again if you want to."

At the end of that day I thought I had Nixon's agreement that henceforth any clemency or pardon suggestion would be summarily rebuffed. I was wrong again. Two years later I heard an early-1973 tape of Nixon and Colson talking about offering clemency to Howard Hunt in return for his silence. I had told Colson never to raise the subject, but obviously it had been raised by one or the other of them before the taped conversation took place.

During that beach walk, Nixon and I talked about Jeb Magruder too. John Dean had told me Magruder would be called as a witness and would probably plead the Fifth Amendment to avoid incriminating himself. Magruder was a Haldeman man, and such a plea would raise some difficult implications that we had to anticipate. (As it turned out, Magruder testified, lied through his teeth and was praised from the bench by John J. Sirica as a fine example of young American manhood.)

On that same walk on the beach, Nixon and I also talked about Hunt's and Liddy's involvement in the Fielding break-in. In his memoir Nixon places the conversation in his office on July 6, but I'm sure it was two days later, on the beach. He refers to the topic in his book in vague terms:

... activities which were perfectly legitimate but which would be hard to explain in investigating the Ellsberg case, the Bay of Pigs, and the other matters where we had an imperative need to get the facts.*

To be plain about it, that day we discussed the Howard Hunt problem—what he'd done and what he knew—and that included his California burglary, his attempts to prove that John Kennedy had caused the failure at the Bay of Pigs and his similar project involving the assassination of Diem. From that day forward Nixon knew everything I knew about Howard Hunt's activities.

The Hunt problem cut several ways. The CIA had to worry about him and so did the White House. Colson was his leader, as I saw it. At the time Nixon and I strolled along the beach, I honestly did not have the slightest tingle of personal concern about the Fielding break-in. I knew I had not participated in it, and I thought I had done the right thing in stopping any further "operations" by Hunt and Liddy. Nor did I suspect that Richard Nixon had had any part in the Fielding operation.

As we returned from San Clemente to Washington, I believed that Nixon was genuinely concerned that the Watergate investigation might uncover CIA secrets. Two years later, I heard on the June 23 tape that Mitchell and Dean had cooked up that pretext to give Pat Gray a reason to restrict the investigation, and I heard Richard Nixon order implementation of that cover-up.

In his memoirs Nixon describes the problem with the FBI investigation:

As I understood it, unless we could find some way to limit the investigation, the trail would lead directly to the CRP [the campaign committee], and our political containment would go by the boards.

Haldeman said that Mitchell and John Dean had come up with an idea on how to deal with this problem.... General Vernon Walters, the Deputy Director of the CIA, was to call Pat Gray and tell him to 'stay the hell out of this ... business here ...!'

Nixon writes that he's the one who suggested to Haldeman that Howard Hunt knew many CIA secrets:

I told Haldeman to say that we felt it would be very detrimental to have the investigation go any further, alluding to the Cubans, to

---

* *RN*. New York: Grosset & Dunlap, 1978.

Hunt and to "a lot of hanky-panky that we have nothing to do with ourselves. . . ."

If the CIA would deflect the FBI from Hunt, they would thereby protect us from the only White House vulnerability involving Watergate that I was worried about exposing—not the break-in, but the political activities Hunt had undertaken for Colson.

I returned from San Clemente with the President on July 18 and was interviewed by two FBI agents about three days later. I told them in answer to their questions that I had known nothing of the Watergate break-in before it happened, had never met Gordon Liddy and had seen Hunt only once, for five minutes, in 1971. They thanked me and left.

John Dean, Fred Fielding and Bud Krogh had come to my office to prepare me for that interrogation a couple of hours earlier. They urged that I volunteer nothing about Hunt and Liddy's California break-in of Dr. Fielding's office in 1971. If I was asked about it directly, Dean would instruct me, he said, not to answer. Dean was in regular touch with his friend Henry Petersen, the Assistant Attorney General in charge of the Criminal Division, and Petersen was telling Dean in advance who would be visited by the FBI. Dean was confident that the questioning would be brief and without surprises, and he was right.

For the next ten days I was immersed in substantive work. I didn't talk to Dean or anyone else about Watergate. But on July 31, Dean and I had lunch at the Justice Department with Attorney General Richard Kleindienst. I'd been asked over because the President had instructed me to involve myself in the U.S. Attorney's demand that Commerce Secretary Maurice Stans appear before a grand jury. The President saw no reason why Stans should be paraded into a grand-jury room. A Justice Department lawyer, Nixon instructed, could take his sworn testimony and that could be read to the grand jury.

I had passed the President's word to Dean, who later insisted that I talk to Petersen myself. I did, and Petersen didn't like it much. But when I suggested that I could arrange to have Petersen come in and take the instruction direct, from the President himself, face to face, he acquiesced.

Shortly thereafter I had Kleindienst's invitation to lunch. As I'd guessed, Petersen had complained to him. "Just call me, not my assistants," Kleindienst urged. He would have Petersen take Stans' statement, but Stans would have to be a witness at the burglary trial. The trail of money ran right across the Secretary's hands, Kleindienst said.

The good news was that the burglary trial would take place after the November election. Hunt, Liddy and the others would be indicted September 15. The investigation, Kleindienst said, had been conducted "with vigor, thoroughness and scope." There were no White House people involved. Colson had been cleared of any complicity.

The agreed Watergate counterstrategy was always "containment," and a big part of that effort was to delay the trial until after the election. Another element was to drumbeat that no White House people had been involved. Committee for the Re-Election people might have done wrong, we'd concede, but no one near the President.

Yet John Dean almost systematically involved White House people from the beginning. Fred Fielding, his assistant, was apparently told about most of Dean's hush-money operation. Dean dropped in on Bob Haldeman frequently to tell him how things were going. I saw Dean eighteen times from August 1 to the end of 1972.*

I was gently eased into the cover-up, along with the others, without ever realizing the legal consequences. For example, when Mitchell and Dean decided to requisition Herb Kalmbach's Nixon trust funds in California for money to pay Hunt and the others, I heard about it. Kalmbach told me during a visit to his Newport Beach office that he had Tony Ulaciewicz carrying cash back to someone in Washington. I wasn't asked for any reaction to the fact, nor did I give any. Even before that, I had heard of the arrangements from Dean.

Herb Kalmbach had come to Haldeman and me when Maury Stans became Nixon's finance chairman in 1972; Herb felt sure Maury would ask him to do fund raising for him, and Herb was looking for our protection. He asked that we agree to let him tell Stans that he was doing only special fund raising for the President. He would do only those projects the President specifically wanted him to do, as confirmed by Haldeman or me. We said, "Sure, why not?" and left it at that.

When Dean called Herb and asked him to raise money—a

---

* Some of those meetings involved the Watergate break-in, but others dealt with the President's estate plan, convention arrangements, the restaffing of the Justice Department and the grain sale to Russia. The majority of our meetings involved three or more people, according to White House records.

"humanitarian fund"—for the burglars and their families, Herb ducked. He did things only with the President's okay. Ask Haldeman or Ehrlichman. So Dean asked me to call Herb and give him the green light. When I did that, I crossed an invisible but vitally important line in the law.* I gave it no thought; it seemed no different from a dozen political requests I'd relayed to Kalmbach from others over the years. But that's all it takes to become a co-conspirator these days.

The Republican Convention was held in Florida in mid-August 1972, and surely Florida in August would be punishment enough for most wrongdoing. I went there early to help the Platform Committee find its way to a Presidentially approved result. While there, I urged our new campaign chairman, Clark MacGregor, to step out and make a clean breast of the campaign's involvement in Watergate. He, after all, was pure and clean and could put the whole thing behind us. To my surprise, that was not a popular proposal. John Mitchell explained to me, as to a child, that such a statement could prejudice the rights of the burglary defendants, to say nothing of some truly innocent individuals who might be mentioned in any press conference MacGregor would hold.

The President was to go to Hawaii at the end of August, I argued. While he was there making high-level news with the Japanese Prime Minister, a statement by MacGregor would be a separate story and might help people to see Watergate as a problem apart from Richard Nixon. But Bob Haldeman didn't like the idea either. MacGregor clearly didn't want to have anything to do with it. MacGregor did do a sort of press conference while we were in Hawaii, but to be on the safe side he merely made a brief announcement and refused to take questions.

On the eve of our departure for Hawaii the President held a midday press conference. In answer to a Watergate question he said, with finality, that he'd had John Dean investigate every lead and Dean had reported that no one in the White House had any complicity in the Watergate affair. That certainly came as a welcome surprise; I hadn't known Dean was doing an investigation. (In fact, he hadn't done more than sit in at FBI interviews and read the FBI reports Pat Gray gave him.)

---

* I became Herb Kalmbach's co-conspirator in an obstruction of justice; but worse, the law considered that I technically conspired with those Herb dealt with, even though I had no contact with them or knowledge of what they were doing.

We returned to San Clemente from Hawaii, then went to San Francisco on our way back to Washington. In a couple of days—on September 9—the Justice Department announced with a fanfare that its vast investigation of Watergate was complete. Indictments were expected soon.

The following Tuesday, September 12, Richard Kleindienst spoke to a White House breakfast meeting of the Cabinet and the Republican Congressional leaders. He said categorically that culpability in Watergate reached no higher than Gordon Liddy and James McCord. He described the thousands of man-hours and unlimited funds which had been devoted to uncovering the facts of the case. No one in the White House and no one at the Committee above Liddy was involved. Three days later—right on schedule—the seven burglars, including Hunt, were indicted.

CHAPTER NINETEEN

More Watergate

ON SEPTEMBER 20, 1972, the President summoned Caspar Weinberger and me to Camp David for a two-hour monologue on how he intended to change things in his second term. This meeting was a landmark in several respects. First, it set radical and austere budget levels for fiscal 1973. Second, it presaged the wholesale restaffing Nixon did after the election. And it shifted his domestic priorities, from race and the economy and the other political issues to the President's capture of the Executive Branch. We would reorganize as completely as the law allowed. We would repopulate the bureaucracy with our people. We would seek new laws to permit the dead (and disloyal) wood to be cast out.

Weinberger was to figure out how to cut the expenditures. I was to plan the renascence of the Executive Branch. Everything was to be ready to go in about forty-five days—right after the election. Go!

For the second time, the President told me that day to stay out of the Watergate problem; I had plenty to do. I assured him that I had no desire to be involved and that I had not been since before the convention in August.

Throughout the fall I was devoting a large part of my time to reviewing the President's campaign speeches and statements and the issue literature that was coming out of the campaign committee.

I met with Dean later in September to assign him the task of defining the legal limits on reorganizing and restaffing the Executive Branch. We didn't talk about Watergate. My only Watergate exposure was at the weekly meetings of the re-election-campaign strategy committee, which I recorded in my notes as H_2M_2CE (Harlow, Haldeman, Mitchell, MacGregor, Colson and me. Mitchell quit attending those sessions in mid-September). The group met thirty times from May to November, and at some of those meetings we talked about Watergate-the-campaign-issue.

The reorganization project needed my time. And I was called on to give some speeches and do the Sunday-morning network talk shows.

On Sunday, October 15, I went to the office very early to read the Sunday papers and review the thick briefing book my staff had prepared for me. Then I rode over to ABC to appear on *Issues and Answers*. The election was three weeks away, and the questioning was tough.

When I returned to the White House, I found that some of the writers, the senior staff and Ron Ziegler were in an emergency meeting in the Roosevelt Room. I joined them because they were trying to figure out how to respond to the morning headlines accusing Dwight Chapin of masterminding Donald Segretti's "campaign dirty tricks and sabotage." That was the first serious charge to reach into the White House itself.

The following week, as Ziegler declared "There is no spy chief in the White House," I was sitting up nights with a Congress that insisted on spending more money on water quality than could possibly be spent. We had asked Congress to impose a spending limit on itself, but on October 17 it turned us down. Later that night, as I sat in the Senate gallery, it passed a Water Quality bill the President had promised to veto.

At 11:30 P.M. I went back to the White House and held a press conference to explain why Nixon would veto the bill.

All that week those of us in Weinberger's "budget-cut group" met to prepare our post-election recommendations. On October 20 we holed up at Camp David to get away from the headlines, which were full of Segretti and Chapin and last-minute campaign charges back and forth.

On Tuesday, October 24, there was another what-shall-we-say? meeting in the Roosevelt Room; but this time it was because Wednesday's *Post* would charge Haldeman with doling out a secret fund of money. Haldeman told us it was untrue, and the next day Ziegler issued an angry denial. George McGovern made a speech about morality in government and Haldeman's fund.

On October 30 a reporter discovered that the FBI was gathering political-issue information at the various places where the President was making campaign stops. Its findings were coming to my staff, to be included in the President's political briefing book for each visit. The news story said this was being done "at John Ehrlichman's request."

I did some checking, then went downstairs to use Ron Ziegler's press room. The story was mostly true, I told the press corps. I had not asked the FBI for the service. But the Justice Department had admitted to me that the FBI was in fact doing the political chore.

"That was a mistake," I said. "We're stopping it now, with an admonition to the overzealous partisan at Justice who started it."

My confession was all it took to damp the story down. It ran for another day and that was all. Although Watergate had other dimensions, I think an equally forthright response, early in the game, could have ended Watergate long before it got away from us.

At the end of October, a strange shudder—a premonition?—went through the people near the President. Our campaign trip to Chicago was canceled on Tuesday—Halloween—because a commuter train was wrecked there, with many killed and injured. As Haldeman and the schedulers began to arrange for the President to go to Chicago on another day, Richard Nixon resisted the idea. He had been getting messages via Rose Woods from Billy Graham and Jeane Dixon, among others, warning that his life was in danger.

Nixon had been extremely reluctant to do a campaign motorcade in Ohio the previous weekend because of these predictions. He was still under their cloud when he decided that the Chicago trip would be canceled altogether. Chuck Colson, Clark MacGregor and Bob Haldeman finally convinced him he might lose Illinois to McGovern if he didn't go, but any thought of an elaborate parade through the Loop was discarded. On Friday, November 3, Nixon appeared briefly at the Chicago airport, then quickly went on to Oklahoma and Rhode Island. The soothsayers had him worried.

Nixon took us to San Clemente for the election, then back to the White House for one day, November 8. In quick succession the President met with the White House staff, the Cabinet and all the agency directors. He made a brief, perfunctory statement of thanks to each group, then turned things over to genial Bob Haldeman, who asked for everyone's resignation.

I had decided to leave before the 1972 convention, but the President and Haldeman had persuaded me to stay on until the fall or winter of 1973, so I figured my resignation wasn't going to be accepted. But others were thunderstruck. It had been a rough fall; from the convention on, everyone was feeling the effect of the harsh political attack on our Administration, and the Segretti-Chapin-Haldeman charges had made us defensive. Weinberger and I had imposed heavy demands on the staff to complete the President's second-term assignment by election day, and many people had worked long nights to finish it. Now Haldeman was telling them they were all fired. Thanks for nothing.

That afternoon the President flew off to Florida, and I was told to come too. Since November 3, I had been to Illinois, Oklahoma, Rhode Island, North Carolina, New Mexico, California and Washington. It was to be weeks before I spent a full seven days at home. We were five days in Florida, and the minute we returned to Washington we went to Camp David for five days. For the next two months I'd spend one or two nights at home and then four or five at Camp David. Occasionally the President took us off to Florida for three or four days in the sun; then it was back to Camp David and the fenced-in snow. Through all of this, Haldeman and I worked long hours with Nixon on the reorganization plan and on totally repopulating his Cabinet and staff.

Once in a while during this time—twice, or three times at the most—I was involved in conversations about Watergate. Dean came to Florida once to tell us how deeply Chapin and Segretti were in trouble, and he played a tape recording of his interview with Segretti to demonstrate the extent of Chapin's involvement. Another time Dean and Walter Minnick of my staff came to Camp David to review the legal problems involved in the proposed reorganization of the Executive Branch. Dean claimed later that he played a tape concerning Hunt for Haldeman and me then, but he didn't. Haldeman told me of spasmodic reports that the burglary defendants had money problems, but there was nothing for me to do about that.

In mid-December I took a two-week vacation. Our family went to Sun Valley for Christmas, and I skied, sketched and loafed. It was a boisterous and active family Christmas, with a minimum of contact with the White House.

But when I returned to Washington on Wednesday, January 3, it was evident that the problems had not taken a holiday. The first morning was a series of meetings—with the domestic-policy staff, the three new Counselors to the President, the senior staff—Roy Ash, Haldeman, Shultz, *et al*—and the energy-policy group.

At noon John Dean came in to say Colson was having serious problems with Howard Hunt. At Dean's urging, I agreed to meet them at the end of the day.

Meetings at the White House continued all afternoon. At about 7 P.M., Colson and Dean came in. Colson had been talking to Howard Hunt's lawyer, William Bittman, and Bittman reported that Hunt's morale was very low. His wife had been killed in an airplane crash, and he was worried about his children. If he was jailed for a long stretch, his family would suffer badly. What, Bittman asked Colson, was the White House going to do for Hunt? The implication was that if something weren't done, Hunt would tell "his secrets."

Colson also made a strong pitch to me on compassionate grounds; he felt sorry for his friend and wanted us to help.

I said as plainly as I could that Colson could not say anything to Bittman that even hinted at clemency. I said the President had decided that right after the burglary.

Colson understood, he said. Perhaps he could offer to look after Hunt's kids. I shrugged. Anything like that was fine. But not a whiff about pardons.

Later Colson told me about his conversation with Bittman. He'd made a long memorandum of what he'd said, and he was sure he'd been skillful in how he'd offered reassurances to Hunt. He'd not violated my injunction, he said.

Many months later, listening to the tapes, I discovered that Colson had gone behind my back and gotten Nixon's consent to talk clemency with Bittman. (John Dean/Taylor Branch imply in their book *Blind Ambition* that I *knew* Colson had discussed clemency with Bittman. I did not.)

At the time, I thought I had handled the Colson-Hunt clemency episode pretty well. I had, I believed, rebuffed Hunt's demand but caused Colson to tender him "compassion" to prevent Hunt from telling all those secrets that worried the President so much. That's what I reported to the President, and he gave me no indication he'd given Colson any other instructions. He did ask me to find out from Kleindienst what the burglars' sentences were likely to be.

So Dean and I had lunch with Kleindienst on January 4. Kleindienst subsequently sent word back through Dean that the sentences would probably be heavy; Sirica was called "Maximum John" because of his knee-jerk practice of throwing the longest possible sentence at every criminal defendant.

Nixon was inaugurated for his second term on January 20—the same week Daniel Ellsberg's retrial* began and four of the Watergate burglars pleaded guilty. The Daniel Ellsberg prosecution bothered me. I had several times urged the President to call it off. The charges were technical, it seemed, and did not go to the heart of his Pentagon Papers offense. But more important, the trial gave Ellsberg high visibility. We were giving him a soapbox from which to blast the President and his Vietnam policies.

At the time of Ellsberg's first trial I had proposed that the Justice Department simply announce that the Government had concluded that he was *not* the person responsible for taking and disseminating the Pentagon Papers. Ellsberg was all over, making speeches, collecting big lecture fees, becoming a counterculture hero. Just say he's innocent and that knocks the props out from under him, I argued. Ellsberg could scramble around yelling "I did it, I did it," but he'd be much less interesting.

At one time Nixon agreed with me, and I passed his decision on to the Attorney General: the prosecution should be dropped. But Mitchell and Kleindienst thought my idea was just awful. We were a law-and-order Administration, by God. We couldn't let Ellsberg go! What would our constituents say? Nixon caved in, and the case went to trial. At the time, I didn't foresee any of the subsequent relationships between the Ellsberg case and Watergate,† so I just chalked that loss up to experience.

In January 1973 I had two meetings with Senator Sam Ervin to explain the President's reorganization plan and his stand on executive privilege and the impounding of appropriated funds. Those issues were being hotly debated in the press, and Ervin, the Senate's "Constitutional law expert," was being quoted often. I found him to be less of an expert than I had hoped,

---

* The first attempt to try Ellsberg had ended in a mistrial.

† The circumstances of the Fielding break-in (he was Ellsberg's psychiatrist) were allowed as evidence against me in the Watergate trial by Sirica, although I'd already been tried and convicted for it in Gesell's court.

and ardently partisan. I'd never met him before and had expected to encounter a better intellect than I did. But I left him some legal memoranda to read (or have his staff read) and departed with the impression that he could be expected to hew to the opposing political line on those issues rather than to be persuaded by any Constitutional argument.

On February 6 there was a White House staff meeting to review the Democrats' move in the Senate to probe Watergate. Two days later the Senate voted to create an investigating committee, and that evening the President and some of the staff went to San Clemente for a long weekend.

The next day, Friday, February 9, the President asked what was being done to prepare for the Senate Watergate hearings. "Who is in charge?" was Nixon's favorite question in such a situation. Bob Haldeman and I described a meeting we'd attended three days earlier with Bryce Harlow, John Mitchell, Bill Timmons, John Dean and Dick Moore. "I'd say Dean and Moore are in charge, if anyone is, but I'm not sure anyone is," I concluded.

"Well, what do they say?" Nixon asked. Who was going to be on the committee? What about its staff? What about its subpoena power and rules?

We didn't know.

For months I'd been comfortable with Nixon's injunction to "stay out of Watergate." Now he was demanding that Bob Haldeman and I get into it, all the way. Nixon said we should spend the weekend with Moore and Dean and learn everything we could about the Senate's plans. And we'd better find out how much trouble that committee could make for us. What does Dean say? There have been a lot of headlines about White House people lately. Bob Haldeman's aide Gordon Strachan was called a "spy net link" that week. Is the White House likely to be involved? Has the containment strategy collapsed?

We sent for Moore and Dean and spent parts of two days with them at the La Costa resort, where the staff stayed when the President was at San Clemente. In that series of meetings I heard enough to trouble me deeply. Dean described some of the maneuvers he'd employed to keep money flowing to the defendants for their attorneys and families. He spelled out White House connections the Senate committee could explore—Hunt to Colson, and Liddy to Jeb Magruder to Gordon Strachan, for example. Haldeman and his aide Larry Higby both denied that Haldeman had actually received any of Liddy's political-intelligence reports, but the Senate com-

335

mittee would surely ask. And there was the Segretti-to-Chapin link, which loomed as a much larger problem then than it actually was later.

After our La Costa sessions, Nixon wanted to know everything Moore and Dean had told us, and typically, he asked a hundred questions we'd not thought to ask Moore and Dean. I finally said, in exasperation, that the President ought to be talking to Dean directly. Dean obviously knew more than he was telling us, and the President was going to want to call the shots, so he should know everything. Haldeman agreed. Almost as soon as we returned from San Clemente (where the weather was terrible) the President left for Florida to find the sun. In between, he nominated Pat Gray to be permanent Director of the FBI.

As soon as he returned from Florida, the President began his series of fateful meetings with John Dean over the following thirty days. Nixon decided then to take personal control of Watergate and clean it up, and I thought that was wonderful; I'd come to the conclusion that there was no one who could do it for him.

On Friday, February 23, Nixon asked me for a draft statement he could issue on the subject of the doctrine of Executive Privilege. He said he would meet with Kleindienst alone about Watergate; I need not arrange it. From now on he intended to work through John Dean. Nixon saw Senator Howard Baker alone to talk about the Senate committee. The next day, Saturday, the President told me again that Dean would be his exclusive contact with the Justice Department *and with Colson** with respect to the Senate committee on Watergate. Just in case I'd missed the point, he repeated it during a call on Sunday: Haldeman and Ehrlichman were to stay out of matters relating to the Senate committee; Dean and Kleindienst would handle it.

I went to Detroit and New York on Monday, but on Tuesday at 6:15 P.M. I met with the President to revise the Executive Privilege statement he'd asked for. Again I was told to "stay out of" preparations for the Senate hearings. The Governors' Conference was in Washington that week, and I had a long and difficult two and a half hours there explaining the President's austere budget.

Every day the news was freighted with new accusations. Ed Nixon was charged with carrying a $200,000 cash "contribu-

---

* Colson had resigned and returned to a private law practice.

tion" from Robert Vesco to the President. Dean had FBI Watergate files he shouldn't have seen. Colson had masterminded Hunt's escapades. I read all of this in the papers, but I was not called on to deal with it. I became heavily involved in the development of an energy message to Congress,* the President's new economic initiative and many new contacts with the Congress.

On Monday, March 12, we issued the President's definitive statement on Executive Privilege. White House aides (such as John Dean, who was about to be subpoenaed to testify at Pat Gray's confirmation hearings), said the statement, would not testify, but the President would informally make appropriate information available to the Congress. The next day Dean refused to appear before the Senate Judiciary Committee but offered to write a response to written questions.

I was seeing the President every day, but he wasn't talking to me about Watergate. In connection with the Executive Privilege statement, he said, "I want no cover-up. We'll cooperate, but I can't send [the Senate] witnesses. That might be a precedent." He was gearing up to refuse Ervin the members of the White House staff.

On March 19, Ervin threatened to send the Senate's Sergeant-at-Arms to arrest White House aides who didn't come to testify before his committee. We didn't take him seriously, but the Washington papers gave him the headlines he was looking for.

On March 20, my birthday, the President and I met with George Bush, who was then Chairman of the Republican National Committee. Bush argued that the only way to blunt the current onslaught in the newspapers and on television was for the President to be totally forthcoming—to tell everything he knew about all aspects of Watergate. Nixon seemed to agree. He had just had a letter from an old colleague from the Eisenhower days, Gabriel Hauge, who became president of Manufacturers Hanover Trust Company in New York; the letter had deeply affected Nixon. It also called on Nixon to come forward with the facts. It was clear from the letter that Nixon was about to lose a staunch supporter if he didn't.

Nixon evidently was not ready to go public all the way; we need a full statement prepared by John Dean, he said in sub-

---

* Our first energy message, a pretty accurate forecast of the country's future troubles, went to the Congress in 1971, but there was no Congressional action in response to it. In 1973 we renewed our call for legislation and a comprehensive energy policy.

stance, that deals with all the issues. Then I can give a copy to George [Bush] and Gabe Hauge and Ziegler. And we can give the FBI our findings, too. It would be a comprehensive review, but it would *not* be made public.

It was agreed that I would talk to Dean about doing a full report. He had been talking to the President, I knew, but I was not sure what he'd told Nixon. They had talked about immunity apparently, because I was asked to get Dean's idea for immunizing grand-jury witnesses to encourage them to come forward to testify.

Haldeman and I met with Dean briefly before seeing the President in the late afternoon of March 21. I told Dean about the President's support for a statement to be prepared by Dean on all the aspects of Watergate. Dean said it would result in the indictments of Gordon Strachan, Dwight Chapin and perhaps even Bob Haldeman. I caught an implication that it might make trouble for others, perhaps Dean himself. We talked briefly about Dean's notion that everyone with any facts to contribute could be granted immunity from prosecution in return for testimony before a special panel of investigators or the grand jury.

At our meeting with the President that day I said I thought the immunity idea wouldn't "wash." I didn't think the public would stand for it. For forty minutes we debated the idea of a Dean statement. I urged it without reservation, and Dean opposed it as vigorously. (That conversation is all on tape, and anyone can listen to it for himself. The written transcript of that tape has some major bloopers, but the tape is reasonably audible.)

The next day the headlines from the Pat Gray confirmation hearings focused on John Dean, and Dean was tense at a meeting with Haldeman, Mitchell and me that morning. I left them after a few minutes to fetch George Shultz at the airport and to talk with him about the wage-and-price-control phase-out.

When Haldeman, Mitchell, Dean and I met with the President, from about two to three forty-five that afternoon, the subject again was a report from Dean, and again I was urging it. Soon the President was also pressing Dean to go to Camp David and ". . . see what you come up with."

"That would be my scenario," I said: "that, that he presents it to you [the President] as, at your request. And you then publish it." Dean and Mitchell protested that it might prejudice some people's rights. "I know that," I said, "but I don't care." I was thinking of the President's need to make a full disclosure. That, it seemed to me, transcended other considerations.

Dean was uncomfortable: "I was everywhere—everywhere they look they are going to find Dean." (Just after that statement the tape is garbled.)

Soon Haldeman and I left the President's office. Dean, Mitchell and the President continued talking; then Dean left. At the time I left I believed the President really wanted Dean to prepare some kind of detailed statement. I expected that we would get a chance to expand it before it was published, but I thought this first step was going to be taken at once.

But when they were alone, Nixon and Mitchell praised Dean for his handling of a "son-of-a-bitching tough thing." Nixon then told Mitchell how he really felt: "I want you all to stonewall it, let them plead the Fifth Amendment, cover up or anything else, if it will save it—save the [?]. That's the whole point." On the other hand, Nixon said, he'd like to do it "the other way," presumably by making a disclosure, particularly if the whole story was going to come out anyway.

Nixon and Mitchell apparently hoped a statement prepared by Dean and tendered to the Senate committee could persuade the Senators to conduct their investigation in executive session rather than in public. Thus a lot was riding on Dean's statement.

Within twenty-four hours John Dean went to Camp David, at the President's urging, to draft a Watergate report. But early in the effort he realized that his report could never be delivered to Nixon. "If my notes should fall into the wrong hands," his book says about his realization, "I would have confessed my own involvement in the cover-up."

There seems to be some question as to whether or not there ever was a Dean Report. There was and there is. It is Exhibit 39 in the court files of the Watergate cover-up case tried before Judge Sirica, and it is Dean's notes and his typewritten synopsis of who did what when. On its third page Dean says:

During the days and weeks that followed [the Watergate break-in] I discussed the incident with everyone who I thought might have any knowledge or involvement. Set forth below are the findings from these conversations.

The report then relates talks with Colson, Krogh, Young and others, but not with me. At the trial, Dean said in effect that his notes and the typed synopsis were lies, but his plea-bargaining statements to the U.S. Attorney were more truthful. One need only compare the Dean Report, Dean's testimony before the Senate committee and the tapes which subsequently became available to see their vast and material divergence. His "image" as a young man with a flawless memory is undeserved.

Dean's time at Camp David from March 23 to 26 was a turning point. Once he'd written out his own vulnerability, he decided to hire a lawyer and try to bargain for leniency or immunity.

While Dean was at work on his report, I was in San Francisco at a church meeting and Haldeman was in Florida with the President. Just before I left Washington, Kleindienst sent me a copy of the letter James McCord sent Judge Sirica charging that Dean had had advance knowledge of the break-in and that many witnesses in the burglary trial had been pressured to lie.

On my first day back from California the President issued a statement saying he had "total confidence" in Dean; but that was not so. Dean's "strategy of containment" was in a shambles. Howard Hunt was appearing before the grand jury; Magruder was saying Liddy's break-in had been a White House operation; Paul O'Brien—the former CIA agent who was the Reelection Committee's lawyer—was calling for John Mitchell to confess everything to take the heat off innocent people. Haldeman knew Dean was hiring a criminal lawyer, but he believed Dean was hiring someone to counsel everyone at the White House; no one realized Dean was hiring a personal attorney. Haldeman told the President that day, March 27, about Liddy's early meetings with Mitchell and Dean when he had proposed espionage plans, code-named "Gemstone," to learn the Democrats' campaign secrets.

Once he realized that the Dean Report would not be delivered, the President began thinking of securing a similar report from an investigating commission to be headed by William Rogers. But he wasn't sure Rogers would agree to do the job.

I spent the first half of the week of March 26 dealing with Indians, parks, energy policy and foreign economics. On Wednesday, the twenty-eighth, John Connally called to warn that the Shah of Iran would soon expropriate all U.S. oil companies' interests in Iranian oil fields if we didn't do something fast. The companies had cut a sweeter deal with the Saudis than with Iran, and the Shah was mad. "The President has got to start saying more about Watergate," Connally added. "He's got to speak out."

On top of everything else, our Senate-watchers reported that Pat Gray's nomination was in very serious trouble. Gray had been a poor witness, but beyond that, he'd been revealed as a very flexible tool of the White House, not the independent FBI Director the Senate wanted. On March 29 I had a long session with the President during which he debated the pros and cons of abandoning his old retainer Pat Gray. After two hours of vacillation, he decided to withdraw Gray's nomination, "but not today."

The next day Nixon called me to his office at noon to say he'd lost confidence in John Dean. I had no idea what he and Dean had been saying to each other in their many private sessions, but I assumed Dean's failure to produce the report the President wanted had led to Nixon's change of heart. Would I, he asked, step in and try to find out the true facts? Evidently there would be no Rogers Commission. It was up to me.

I realize now that at that moment the President knew virtually everything about the burglary and the cover-up; he certainly knew far more than I. If I'd been adroit, I'd have asked him to tell me everything Dean had told him. But I didn't think of that. I was concerned that someone like Sam Ervin might ask for the fruits of my investigation, so I drafted a letter for Nixon to sign which I hoped would create an attorney–client relationship between the President and me. If Nixon was ever charged with wrongdoing, I thought, my work product might be privileged, although I was by no means certain of that.

That afternoon we went to San Clemente again. Nixon was to meet there with President Thieu of South Vietnam, but it was also going to be nice to escape Washington's poisonous atmosphere. Before departing Washington, the President, in an effort to take some of the heat off the White House, directed a change in the policy on Executive Privilege. The President decided he would allow his aides to testify before a grand jury.

The next day the President asked me to talk secretly to Senator Ervin to try to negotiate favorable ground rules for White House people in return for a Presidential decision that his staff might also testify at the Senate hearings.

After the Thieu visit Haldeman told me he'd had a call from Dean. Dean was talking to the U.S. Attorney about Watergate, and he was trying to arrange immunity; but Haldeman need not worry, Dean said. "Neither you nor Ehrlichman are targets," Dean reassured him.

Taking the President's assignment seriously, I began to investigate Watergate, trying to piece together both how the burglary had begun and what had taken place afterward. I talked for nearly three hours with Paul O'Brien, who had an encyclopedic knowledge of the facts and a strong bias against John Mitchell. As attorney for the Committee for the Re-election, O'Brien had reconstructed the early Dean-Mitchell-Liddy meetings where intelligence gathering was proposed. A stubby, bluff and direct man, O'Brien insisted that Mitchell had been involved from the first. He had approved Liddy's budget, seen the fruits of Liddy's phone taps on the Democrats and sent Liddy back to the Watergate for better results. Much of what O'Brien told me was new information to me. I took detailed notes and filed them away.

Nixon sat in his office playing who-will-replace-Gray games. The Attorney General came for a talk on March 31 and reluctantly acquiesced in Nixon's decision to withdraw Gray's nomination. About that time I told Dean on the phone that Gray was still our nominee in name, but in fact was "twisting slowly, slowly in the wind" because the President had decided irrevocably to nominate someone else. (While that classic phrase *is* mine, I must acknowledge my debt to Aldous Huxley, whose last lines in *Brave New World* paint a similar scene more artfully.)

Attorney General Kleindienst telephoned a few days later to suggest that the President nominate Federal District Judge Matthew Byrne of Los Angeles to head the FBI. The President liked the idea; Byrne was young, and a Democrat, and had done a good job with the Scranton Commission. It would be good to put a judge at the FBI. Would he take the job? I should call and get him down to San Clemente for a talk, Nixon said.

None of us—Kleindienst, Nixon or I—discussed the fact that Byrne was then Daniel Ellsberg's trial judge. I knew that he was, but I had no idea where things stood in that long trial. I believed it was nearing its end, and I knew that Al Haig had been a sur-rebuttal witness, but I had to ask the Judge on the telephone whether our talking would be awkward for him. I told him I needed to talk with him about his availability for an important appointment. But I said it could wait if his trial made it inappropriate. He said he'd like to have a visit and he could come to San Clemente the next day, April 5.

He arrived right on time, at 4 P.M. I suggested that we walk out to the bluff overlooking the ocean. "If at any time," I said, "what I'm saying makes it awkward or embarrassing for you,

ust turn around and leave. I'll understand, and we can talk
ater instead." He assured me that he would.

As we talked, I told him that Gray's nomination would be
vithdrawn and the President was considering several people
or FBI Director. I asked if the Judge was available for consid-
ration. Immediately he said he was. He had many ideas for
eform of the FBI that he'd like to put to work. I was noncom-
nittal, but said I'd tell the President of his interest. As we
valked back toward the office building, Nixon came out onto
he lawn to greet Byrne. As they talked, I noticed Bob Halde-
nan taking a movie of us from the patio by his office. The
President's conversation with the Judge was small talk; noth-
ng was said about the FBI job.

The next day, Friday, Gray's nomination was withdrawn.
About 3 P.M. the President talked to Gray on the phone. He
asked Gray to stay on at the FBI until a successor qualified.
He explained that unless Gray's name were withdrawn, the
confirmation hearings "could ride along for eight months. In
he end we could get you confirmed," Nixon told Gray, "but
we can't let it ride like that. You're an innocent victim, as
we're all aware."

When he hung up, Nixon said to me: "He's a broken man.
But he wasn't a POW for seven years, was he? It's all relative,
sn't it?"

I had a telephone call from Judge Byrne that same day ask-
ng for a second meeting. I agreed to meet with him in Santa
Monica. I was due to have dinner there with my mother on
Saturday, so I drove up early. Byrne and I met in Palisades
Park about 3 P.M. for a brief talk. He wanted the President to
know of his *very* strong interest in the FBI job, now that
Gray's nomination was actually withdrawn. I asked him some
questions about his availability, and he said he couldn't predict how soon he'd be finished with the Ellsberg trial. A lot
depended on what the verdict was. He promised to keep me
informed as the case wound up.

The next day, Sunday, I returned to Washington with the
President. In flight, the President asked Haldeman and me to
see Dean at once and tell him that he was free to testify before
the grand jury but he was not to testify before the Senate
committee. Nixon wanted to bargain with Sam Ervin. He
didn't want anyone agreeing to testify until he could strike a
deal. Haldeman summoned Dean to Andrews Air Force Base,
and we stood in the aisle of *Air Force One,* after everyone had
gotten off, giving Dean Nixon's message.

As we talked I asked Dean about John Mitchell's earl[y] meetings with Liddy. Dean was one of the people I intended t[o] question as part of my inquiry. Paul O'Brien had told m[e] about the espionage proposals Liddy had made to Mitchell a[t] the three or four meetings Dean had attended before th[e] break-in. Dean confirmed that the meetings had taken place but said Mitchell had turned down Liddy's proposals. Some—whores and houseboats at the Democratic Convention—we[re] outlandish. Others were too expensive.

The following week, I met secretly on two occasions wit[h] Senators Ervin and Baker at Blair House, across Pennsylvani[a] Avenue from the White House. The President sent me to offe[r] an exchange: he would allow White House people to testif[y] before their committee provided the hearings were not tele—vised. During the next week there were serious negotiation[s] with both Ervin and Baker, but ultimately Baker told me tha[t] Senator Ervin would not make a deal.

While the attempt to negotiate was fading into failure, [I] continued to interview people who might help me understan[d] the true dimensions of Watergate. In Washington I talked wit[h] Gordon Strachan, Haldeman's aide; Charles Colson and, fi—nally, John Dean again. The night of April 13 I couldn't slee[p;] the information I'd picked up during the previous two week[s] had fallen into a pattern, and I had a sense that time was run—ning out. If the President was ever going to make a disclosur[e] that would help him get out in front of the growing scandal, h[e] would have to do it during the coming weekend. A grand jur[y] was hearing people like Strachan, who knew about the pay—ment of huge sums of money, for example. Colson had warne[d] that John Dean was trying to trade other people's heads for hi[s] freedom and had begun to talk to news people to put pressur[e] on the U.S. Attorney to force him to make a deal with Dean[.]

I got out of bed and spent the next two hours drafting a re—port* for the President:

In late March you requested that I undertake to determine th[e] facts and applicable law relating to the Watergate break-in and tr[y] to put myself in position to advise you as matters unfolded. I hav[e] as you know, devoted nearly full time to this assignment since largely spending it in interviews with some people with knowledg[e] of the facts.

I think it is now essential to tell you what I have been told. Since

---

* A copy is to be found among the Nixon papers in the National Archives[.]

so much of this is hearsay I cannot vouch for its ultimate truth. But where I have been presented with doubtful assertions I have attempted to sift them out.

Findings re the Watergate burglary:

Although JNM [Mitchell], JSM [Magruder], GL [Liddy] and JD III [Dean] met several times in early 1972 while JNM was still A/G [Attorney General] to discuss "intelligence" activities I believe these meetings ended without agreement by JNM as to the course or plan to be followed. JD III says he expressly objected to GL's proposals as improper and even illegal. And so nothing happened. Some time later in the spring Liddy and Hunt complained to Colson that JSM [Magruder] would not authorize the funds for them to do the work necessary to gather information requested by Colson. At about that time HRH [Haldeman] and Colson wanted specific information about Dem [Democratic] primary candidates, their schedules, speech content, etc. Apparently the material requested by the W.H. [White House] was pretty innocuous. When "intelligence" was said by Hunt and Liddy they meant different information—harder, less properly come by.

Colson called JSM—with whom he was having trouble in securing other performance in the campaign, *e.g.* ethnic activities; Colson demanded that JSM move ahead with "intelligence."

Subsequently JSM and GL conferred, and a memorandum was prepared and submitted to JNM asking him to "pick the targets" for electronic surveillance and other intelligence gathering. JNM did so in the belief that the operatives would be two or three people removed from any CREP [Committee for the Re-Election of the President] personnel.

JSM then authorized Sloan to give GL funds to procure equipment and people.

Watergate Democratic offices were first entered in May and bugs were planted. I am told (unreliably) that the equipment was purchased in April in New York from a man who was told by McCord that it was for Watergate. He promptly told Larry O'Brien, either directly or through a third person.

When the plant was performing badly* Liddy was told to go back in and fix it, also to photograph some documents. Liddy ad-

---

* Liddy prepared three rather obscure synopses of what was heard over the bugs. A vague attribution to "a reliable source" or a "sophisticated political source" or some such was used. The paper did not indicate facts from which one could deduce that there was a bug in DNC headquarters apparently. JSM sent one carbon of each to Strachan. He, in turn, digested the contents of at least one for HRH [Haldeman].

...unt they had to do it, in spite of Hunt's protests, because Mitchell insisted.

Of course they were apprehended in June. Thereafter began an effort to insure that the five burglars (4 Cubans and McCord) and Hunt and Liddy did not implicate anyone else.

John Dean was enlisted by John Mitchell to seek help from the White House in raising money to pay subsistence and attorneys' fees. Dean transmitted messages but was unsuccessful in securing aid. The best he could get was a referral to Herb Kalmbach who may have helped. As a result of his transmittal, however, a number of White House people became aware of JNM's effort, including Dean, HRH, Colson, Moore and me. Probably all of those named knew of some specific aspects of this activity; only Dean was in possession of most of the facts. With the exception of Dean, I don't know that any White House people were aware of any specific acts of obstruction of justice or sought to procure any person's testimonial silence. In Dean's case, he was not an actor but may have joined in a concerted effort which eventually led to such procurement by others.

JNM, Mardian, LaRue, Attorneys O'Brien, Parkinson and Bittman have been given to me as names of participants in this effort but I cannot say whether this is factual. I have not tried to get far into this aspect.

The Segretti Affair

This is entirely separate from the Watergate burglary in substance. Hunt became Segretti's contact at CREP at some point in time, but S had no part in the burglary.

S was recruited by Chapin and Strachan to be our Dick Tuck.* They sold the general idea to HRH who authorized Chapin to draw salary and expenses from the funds held by Kalmbach from 1970.

HRH exercised no control over S. Chapin did, I think, to a limited degree. Strachan did not to any material degree.

Segretti apparently violated mail or campaign laws in failing to properly designate mailings, etc. He was cruelly effective on Muskie. Some of his stunts were hilarious. Some were crude and unworthy. He recruited at least three operatives whose names are known to investigators and countless others who are still unknown. They also hit HHH [Humphrey], Jackson and McGovern and EMK [Kennedy] as well.†

---

* Tuck was the Democrats' unofficial campaign dirty-trickster.

† Segretti and Chapin were both eventually sent to prison for alleged crimes as a result of these dirty tricks.

Chapin had S come to Portland [Oregon] while you were there on a trip and S observed how a political trip is staffed, advanced and conducted. He called Chapin at times and mailed him clippings describing his triumphs. While the "Cannuck letter" is credited to S or one of his operatives by some, I can't establish it.

At some point CREP took over the full supervision and support of S.

Status and Course of the Investigation and Prosecution:

I believe JSM, Hunt, Liddy (?) and Fred LaRue are willing to make full disclosure in the coming week. Hunt is, for sure, on Monday. Mitchell and Mardian still are not. Liddy apparently has remained silent on JNM's assurance that he would be given a pardon.

If and when JSM is recalled (he may not be; the U.S. Attorney can probably indict him without his further testimony) he will implicate JNM, Dean and Strachan, and probably others.

Dean is also ready to testify and would involve JNM and JSM.

Dean believes the jury may not have enough facts to indict JNM and JSM but I question whether it does. Hunt alone adds mostly hearsay with *res gestae* adverse to JNM.

As he apparently has [been] for literally months, JNM is the key to a full disclosure of the facts of the Watergate matter. JSM is a somewhat smaller key—he would provide fewer facts.

JNM is also the target of the Vesco Grand Jury in New York and of the Klein Grand Jury in Washington, D.C. I do not know the degree of jeopardy he has in these investigations. Colson avers that both are serious. Should he [Mitchell] be indicted in any of these cases Attorney General Kleindienst and his assistant, Henry Peterson, will decline to exercise the prosecutorial discretion required. Someone else will have to be designated to do so.

White House Counsel

John Dean has not involved himself in this matter as your counsel for several months, and properly so.

I should not continue to fill in for him for several reasons, including the impermissible demands on my time that result.

You need a full-time special counsel to follow these related problems, who can advise you of the legal niceties from his experience in constitutional, criminal and governmental practice.

I will be happy to continue to consult with the special counsel and Ron [Ziegler] as often as necessary.

I do not recommend that Dean take a leave. That is neither in nor out. He has involved himself to the extent described above. Either that requires dismissal or it does not, and that choice should be made at once. If he is discharged, the U.S. Attorney and Grand Jury may treat him differently.

The next morning I handed the report to Nixon. He handed it back and asked me to read it aloud to him and Haldeman. When I finished reading, the President had Haldeman summon John Mitchell from New York and asked me to tell Mitchell that if he had any information, he should not remain silent out of loyalty to the President.

When Mitchell subsequently told me flatly that he had nothing to contribute, I interviewed Jeb Magruder, who came to my office with his lawyers. Jeb was very forthcoming, and he added information about how the break-in was originally authorized. He and Fred LaRue had met Mitchell in Florida, he said, and presented Liddy's plan for bugging three places, including Larry O'Brien's office at the Watergate. Mitchell gave his approval, Jeb told me. When Liddy's original effort produced nothing, Mitchell called and "chewed him out." So Liddy, on his own, ordered the reentry during which the burglars were caught. Dean had later suborned Magruder to perjury, Magruder said, and told Jeb to destroy his diary.

Dean had told me a day earlier that the U.S. Attorney had assured him no one in the White House—including Dean himself—was a target of the grand jury, but after hearing Magruder, I found that hard to believe.

I immediately went to the President's office to tell Nixon what Magruder had said, and we agreed that I should tell the Attorney General what I'd learned. I called Kleindienst from the President's office and told him I'd been interviewing people for the President for two weeks and had gathered a substantial amount of information. He thanked me for calling and said he'd be in touch with me if he needed what I had, but no one from Justice ever asked for it.

The next day the President met with Henry Petersen, the head of the Justice Department's Criminal Division.* Petersen

---

* Why Henry Petersen? He had impressed Nixon at several Cabinet-committee meetings in 1971 and 1972. With Mitchell under suspicion, Kleindienst unwilling to get involved and both John Dean and me the subjects of probable prosecution, Nixon needed advice from some lawyer, and he chose the lawyer who might decide who *else* might be pursued. The President curried favor with the prosecutor, probably unaware that Petersen had strong alliances with people who were not Nixon's friends.

Kleindienst recommended Petersen to Nixon, and in April and May of 1973 the President chose him over Leonard Garment, Richard Moore and other lawyers on his staff as his principal legal adviser. Later Nixon re-

relayed to the President some of Dean's "disclosures" which Dean had offered to the U.S. Attorney for the District of Columbia as bargaining chips. I was accused of a whole shower of crimes.*

For several weeks Dean had tried to persuade Nixon to authorize immunity for any White House staff person who went before the grand jury to testify. I opposed such immunity; I thought we should go voluntarily without that kind of inducement. I suppose Dean thought I was trying to put him in a crack, but actually I was thinking of the President. How could he justify such favoritism for his staff and survive?

After hearing the President's account of Petersen's April 15 report I went home heartsick. About 9 P.M. Bebe Rebozo called and asked me to hurry back to the White House; the President wanted to talk to Haldeman and me. As I drove along the George Washington Parkway, I was overcome with foreboding caused by the cumulative effect of the accusations and a feeling that the President had completely lost control of the situation. I had told him Dean's accusations were false, but I wasn't sure he had heard or believed me.

When I arrived, Bob Haldeman was already there. We'd been called back, Nixon said, because he'd just been told by Henry Petersen about the contents of Hunt's safe. Had I turned them over to Pat Gray? He was obviously very much concerned about the material that had been in that safe. Colson no longer worked at the White House, but I got a whiff of the Nixon-Colson-Hunt linkage. Nixon was agitated by the thought that Hunt's safe contained documents which might lead to Colson and to the President.

I said I'd seen Dean give Gray a large envelope in my office. Dean had said the contents were from Hunt's safe. We'd have

---

cruited Fred Buzhardt, James St. Clair, James Wright and others to help him.

Petersen and Kleindienst intended to form a law partnership when the time came to leave Justice for private life, although I didn't know that then. And there was some close connection between Dean and Petersen which I could never define. Petersen, according to Dean, was Dean's willing source of inside information.

* Later, when it came out that Dean had destroyed Hunt's diaries and papers, I understood Dean's inspiration for his allegation that I'd told him to "deep-six" some of Hunt's belongings. And when Jack Caulfield testified that Dean had sent him to offer James McCord clemency, I saw why Dean had falsely told the U.S. Attorney I'd authorized clemency for the burglars. Had someone told Hunt to flee the country? Colson said Dean had, but Dean falsely told the U.S. Attorney that I'd issued the order. Dean tried to cover his own acts and tracks by putting blame on others.

to ask Gray where the contents were now. The President urged me to do so immediately, and I called Gray in Connecticut on the President's phone. I couldn't believe Gray's answer: he'd taken the papers to Connecticut and recently burned them, he said. He'd thought they were very sensitive and that that was the best thing to do. I was dumbfounded at this bizarre action. But Nixon was immeasurably relieved. He evidently knew what it was that Gray had destroyed, even if I did not.

I now know some of what was running through Nixon's mind in mid-April 1973, because I have heard the tape recording of his conversation with Richard Moore that went from 3:45 to 5 P.M. on April 19. Evidently no transcript of that talk has ever been released. In it Nixon and Moore compare their knowledge of what had taken place.

Moore had learned that he would be called to testify before the Senate committee; he assured Nixon he would say he had known nothing of the break-in or cover-up until February of 1973.

"Dean kept telling us no one in the White House was involved," Nixon said. "He denied he was involved. He said John Mitchell was the culprit. It's all about getting money for the [Watergate] defendants. Ziegler talked to Dean in California August 29, and Dean told him 'No one in the White House is involved.' Dean was covering for John Mitchell, you see."

Moore and Nixon talked about an early meeting with Dean. Nixon thought Moore had been at the meeting. Moore was sure he had not.

"I needed a report from Dean in order to 'get it all out,' " Nixon said.

"But Dean said, 'I can't put this together,' " Moore rejoined. Dean had known all about Gordon Liddy's plan—the kidnapping and all the rest—from the first. His report would be self-incriminating.

"I can't give Dean the immunity he wants," Nixon said. "He's gunning for Haldeman and Ehrlichman."

Nixon told Moore that Dean was accusing Haldeman of complicity in the Segretti dirty-tricks operation and a $350,000 fund paid to the burglars. Dean was saying Ehrlichman ran "the Plumbers" in an operation "in the national-security area," as Nixon put it. "Dean was vague, but he said Krogh has a problem too. I told Petersen they can't go into that national-security area. It's about Ellsberg."

Moore told Nixon of our La Costa meeting in February: "We weren't organized [to counter Sam Ervin's Senate Select

Committee]. We had no organization, no people, no research—we agreed it was a job for the [reelection] committee to hire lawyers and other people. I [Moore] was to go to New York to get input from John Mitchell, fill him in and get him to hire the needed people.

"The second day at La Costa," Moore continued, "Dean said there was a need for more money for those fellows [the Watergate defendants]. Haldeman or Ehrlichman told him to get it from Fred LaRue.

"I didn't ask the purpose of the money," Moore said. "I surely didn't believe it was a payoff. But when I went to New York, I didn't tell Mitchell to raise the money."

Then Nixon told Moore his motive for replacing Dean with me during the fateful month after March 23: "I took Dean off and put Ehrlichman on it. I didn't put somebody else on it because I didn't want anybody to nail me.

"Dean told me it would take a million dollars," Nixon told Moore, "and I said you can't do that. I wasn't prepared to pay blackmail."

Later in the long meeting, Nixon said of his "million-dollar" conversation with Dean: "The only thing I'm concerned about is my knowledge of that particular thing. The suggestion came *ex parte* from Dean. But I didn't notify the U.S. Attorney or anyone. I intended that we investigate it ourselves."

My lawyers wanted to interview Dick Moore, especially about his recollection of the La Costa meetings and who had said what about money for the burglars. Moore was reluctant to talk to anyone. Nixon said to him: "Talk to Haldeman's and Ehrlichman's attorneys about La Costa. I wouldn't want to suggest any subornation of perjury, but I would just be very damn hazy."

Moore said: "I would say they [Haldeman and Ehrlichman] didn't do anything."

"Well," said Nixon, "I'm going to forget whatever I know about that."

"I am going to forget everything too," Moore replied.

"Will it do any good to talk to Dean?" Nixon asked.

"He's out to save himself," Moore said. "He wants immunity. His story is that he was led by Haldeman and Ehrlichman."

"Should there be resignations?" Nixon asked.

"The Attorney General [Kleindienst]," Moore said. "Mitchell should step forward. Then Haldeman and Ehrlichman should go, to satisfy the vultures."

"I don't know how much Petersen levels with me," Nixon

said. "I was unaware of the three-hundred-and-fifty-thousand-dollar fund and the payoffs [to the Watergate defendants]," Nixon told Moore. "It was stupid to bug the Democrats. I couldn't believe John Mitchell had done it. As for Haldeman's and Ehrlichman's obstruction of justice, they never had a money problem."

On that clanging *non sequitur* my notes of the taped conversation end.

CHAPTER TWENTY

The Firings

EASTER WEEK WAS worse. Haldeman and I had just hired an attorney, John J. Wilson, to represent us, and we spent endless hours with him and his partner, Frank Strickler, going over the facts and Dean's allegations against us. Howard Baker called to say the Senate hearings would be televised. Colson phoned to warn that Jeb Magruder was talking to the press. The President and Attorney General Kleindienst spiced up a Cabinet meeting with a bitter argument over Watergate. (The President accused Kleindienst's prosecutors of leaking grand-jury proceedings to the press, and Kleindienst denied it.) It was a lively time until the President went to Florida for Easter. Pointedly he suggested that Haldeman and I use Camp David while he was gone, instead of coming with him. Nixon had begun to cut us loose.

Easter Sunday's papers, reflecting Dean's systematic press campaign,* finally zeroed in on Haldeman and me. Over the weekend Nixon did his best to keep John Dean "on the team" with a phone call ("You're still my Counsel, John"), but when Nixon returned to the White House, it was obvious he'd become very much personally concerned about Dean. He and

---

* For an account of Dean's extraordinary bargaining with the press, see David Halberstam, *The Powers That Be* (New York: Knopf, 1979), pp. 690 *et seq.*

Haldeman spent hours together reviewing the kinds of problems Dean could make for the President. When they talked to me, I suggested that if in fact the President had a recording of what he'd said to Dean (as Haldeman had told me he did), he'd better listen to it.

"From what I've been told by you, it sounds to me like the talks with Dean could result in the President's *impeachment,*" I said. That was like dropping a dead cat into the Kool-Aid. The tapes show that after I left the room, Nixon dramatically recoiled from my remark. I guess that was the first time anyone had used the word "impeachment" in Nixon's presence.

Wednesday, Ron Ziegler met with Haldeman and me to try to persuade us to resign and leave the White House. He said he'd been talking with John Connally, William Rogers and Al Haig, all of whom felt it would "move the problem away from the President" if we resigned. "If you two remain, it will be impossible for the President to disengage from it and move on with the business of the Presidency," Ziegler parroted. That was Nixon talking. I'd delivered so many messages like it in the previous four years that I couldn't be wrong. "Because of the weight of public opinion and the direction it's going, they [the advisers] think you should make a voluntary departure," Ziegler said in his stilted style.

"That's odd," Haldeman replied; "when I've talked to those three men that's not what they've recommended to me. They all say to me they don't know what I should do."

Ziegler turned a deep red, and his voice tightened: "Connally says you should leave, Bob. I've got the notes of our conversation."

Ziegler and Haldeman haggled for a long time over what Connally and the others advised, while I sat and listened. The Presidency is in some lot of trouble, I thought, if Ron Ziegler has become Lord Chamberlain.

Haldeman and I argued that Nixon might be in bigger trouble with us gone than if we stayed. Our departure might tend to imply that Nixon knew and had known what was going on, if we knew.

"I don't know what Henry Petersen told him down there," Ziegler finally said, nodding toward the President's office, "but you two are under a cloud and that's what did it."

I was very angry. All of the secondhand Dean-to-Petersen-to-Nixon charges I'd heard made against me up until then were false. If I was going to be sent away because I was "under a cloud," then a long list of other people ought to be sent as well. There were a great many clouds overhead. I dashed off a list headed *"If any [go], these should go: . . ."* It contained the names of seventeen people on the White House staff who I believed had committed crimes or who had been accused of serious wrongdoing by the newspapers. Ziegler's name was fourth from the bottom.

After the warm-up with Ziegler that morning, we met with the President to discuss his proposal that we take a leave of absence while we cleared up the charges against us. (I later learned that at that time Henry Petersen was insisting the President fire Haldeman and me but leave Dean in his position.)

Although our lawyers had visited with Nixon and assured him they could see no legal substance to the charges Dean was making, Nixon was worried about the money Kalmbach had funneled to the burglars and the other Dean allegations. "This is the Mitchell–Ehrlichman feud, too," Nixon said. "There could be trouble from him; Mitchell may lie to save himself. Anyone who touched that money—the accusations will be believed. They'll be guilty in the public mind. If you leave, it will only avoid some of the future problems. You'll be presumed guilty and everyone will think the President knew it. But the truth will out in the long run. You have a short-term vulnerability to Mitchell and Dean." That was an infuriating *non sequitur*. No one—not even Dean—was accusing me of dealing in the hush money that Nixon and the others were worried about.

Nixon pressed me to decide quickly. "Decide now and I'll live with it. The President has a duty to stand by you."

The President was expecting Henry Petersen to come see him at 5:30 P.M. Nixon was troubled over what he might have said to Dean. Bob Haldeman, Nixon said, would listen to the recording of one of his meetings with Dean. "We can't run the risk of Dean attacking the President," he added with feeling.

Nixon reopened the question of granting Dean the immunity he wanted so much. I said I thought that would be seen as simply another cover-up. "Well, I can let him go; he disserved me. I could mount a crusade to clean up campaigning. We could change the structure," Nixon said vaguely.

"Did you ever talk to anyone about clemency?" I asked.

"Only you and Colson," Nixon replied. "Never John Mitchell."

After some other talk about his meetings with Dean, I asked Nixon, "Why has there been so much coddling of Dean up to now?"

Nixon said, "Henry Petersen has asked me to wait before doing anything."

"It's wrong to put us in the same bag with Dean," I said.

"But he says Haldeman and Ehrlichman knew everything, every inch of the way," Nixon replied.

"Not true," I said hopelessly. "Do you think I knew he was going around suborning perjury? That all came to us in the past few weeks; in March."

After more of that kind of fruitless conversation, Nixon listed the arguments for our taking a leave of absence. How long a leave? I asked. "Let's see what Dean does say," Nixon replied. "Until the grand jury acts, the President won't judge it. And whatever you do, I'll treat Dean the same."

"I have a list of fifteen others who should go too," I said. "They are people who knew about the alleged crimes; they are no different from Haldeman and me. Ron Ziegler checked with Dean by the hour," I said. Nixon shrugged. "He knew what was going on," I added.

"Our resignation will be quite a headline," Haldeman predicted.

"It would be good in that it will say I'm cleaning house," Nixon said.

"I think it will be bad," Haldeman said, shaking his head.

"Henry [Kissinger] says the staff must have the President's confidence," Nixon said in conclusion. The handwriting was on the wall. I went home to tell my family that I was about to resign.

"If you're not guilty, why is he asking you to leave?" one of my children asked. I tried to explain that the President felt it would move the trouble away from him. That answer didn't convince anyone.

The next day, April 26, when they were alone, the President enjoined Haldeman from "telling Ehrlichman that the office was taped." That day he was so genuinely afraid of the damage Dean could do that he even proposed that Dick Moore be sent to offer Dean clemency in return for silence; but Haldeman talked Nixon out of that idea.

Friday, April 27, was a very bad day for me. The *Los Angeles Times* carried a totally false story that I had tried to help Robert Vesco secure preferential treatment abroad. John Mitchell had in fact sent Vesco's agents to see me to ask for favors, but after the meeting I had cabled our embassy in Lebanon not to help Vesco. The cable was on file in the State Department and I could prove exactly what I had done, but I couldn't catch up with the story once it had run. To this day the falsehood persists.

That day the President took Haldeman and me to Meridian,

Mississippi, where he was to dedicate a memorial to Senator John Stennis. We were to fly over some severe flood damage on the way, and I had gone to the flight deck of *Air Force One* to stand behind the pilots, where I could look out the front windshield to see it.

As I stood there, I was taken with the realization that I could end everyone's troubles by throwing myself against the controls, wedging myself between the pilot's control yoke and the pilot. We'd all be gone in about a minute and a half. I stood there chatting with the navigator, measuring my chances for a moment; then turned and went back to my seat.

When we returned to the White House, there were two FBI agents waiting for me in my office. They asked me a few questions about the FBI bugging and tape logs Bob Mardian had brought us a year or so earlier. Ironically, the agents had to wait a few minutes for me while the President and I met with William Ruckelshaus in the Oval Office to tell him that he'd been selected to be the new acting FBI Director.

On Sunday, April 29, Haldeman phoned to say that he and I were to go to Camp David for a 2 P.M. meeting with the President. Ziegler had called Bob; the President had finally decided to ask for our resignations. I was at the same time angry and very sad. I felt I was being falsely accused—convicted solely on the word of John Dean, and being lumped with Bob Haldeman, who had some real troubles with hush money which I did not share. Worse, no one had the class or courtesy to deal with me directly.

"When you talk to Ziegler," I said, "tell him I won't agree to a mass meeting. If I'm going to get fired, it's going to have to be one-on-one." Haldeman said he'd tell Ziegler.

I ordered a White House car and rode to the Pentagon helicopter pad. I was overwhelmed with self-pity. I was being disgraced, and it was unfair.

I was barely civil to Haldeman when we took off, but as we flew low over the Maryland landscape, which was turning a bright spring green, I eased up. As we chatted, Bob told me Nixon had been meeting with Bill Rogers, taking his advice as to what to do with us. I could imagine Nixon suggesting to Rogers that he talk to us, just as the President had so often asked me to do his dirty work for him.

At Camp David, we were taken to Laurel Lodge in a Navy car. Haldeman went to Aspen Lodge first, and I sat alone on Laurel's terrace. I telephoned my Christian Science practitioner and teacher, who had been helping me through those difficult times, to tell him what was about to happen.

In about forty minutes Haldeman came out to the terrace, looking grim. He hooked his thumb toward Aspen: "Your turn."

"How did it go?"

"About as we thought."

I walked the two hundred yards to Aspen and entered the living room without knocking. Nixon, in a checked sports coat, came into the room from his bedroom. Neither of us sat. His eyes were red-rimmed and he looked small and drawn. It was impossible for me to remain composed as he told me he had hoped and prayed he might die during the night. "It is like cutting off my arm," he began, and he could not continue. He began crying uncontrollably, and I put my arm on his shoulder to comfort him. He walked away, out the door to the terrace, to pull himself together. The Camp was in full spring bloom out there, I noticed. All the bulbs were up and out.

"You'll have to resign," Nixon said at last.

I nodded.

"You've been my conscience all through this mess," he said. "You were right about a lot of things—you were right about Colson and you were right about Mitchell.

"It's like cutting off my arms," he said. "You and Bob. You'll need money; I have some—Bebe has it—and you can have it."

I shook my head. "That would just make things worse." I was near tears myself. "You can do one thing for me, though, sometime." It was hard for me to talk. "Just explain all this to my kids, will you? Tell them why you had to do this?" I turned and left, wiping my eyes with my handkerchief.

When I arrived back at Laurel Lodge, Haldeman said we had to wait for Bill Rogers to return to work out the details of our resignations. We waited nearly two hours, until 5:20 P.M., and then we were ushered back to Aspen by Ron Ziegler. I used the interval to make very detailed notes of what Nixon and I had said to each other.

Rogers, Nixon and Ziegler suggested that we tender our resignations the next day, but that we take our time leaving. We could stay around for three or four weeks of paid transition if we wished.

I asked about Dean. He would be fired and Kleindienst (who refused to prosecute Mitchell) would resign at the same time we resigned, we were told. That made me feel a little better. I guessed that Rogers had been in Washington engineering that resignation while we waited for him.

The long trip back in the helicopter was difficult. Haldeman and I didn't compare notes on what Nixon had said to us alone. It was getting dark when we landed and drove to our homes to tell our families what had happened.

CHAPTER TWENTY-ONE

Hearings and Trials

As SOON AS my "resignation" was announced by the President, I was fair game for every investigation in town. Three grand juries in Washington and one in Los Angeles wanted me, over and over again. I stopped counting after the fifteenth appearance. Three Congressional committees wanted testimony about the CIA, the President's taxes and campaign "abuses." May and June brought me teams of FBI men asking about a dozen subjects, many of them involving outlandish charges against Nixon. For example, someone in Pennsylvania accused Nixon of taking a bribe to award a GSA contract to some contractor.

Haldeman and I collaborated to some degree in preparing for the Senate Watergate Hearings, scheduled to reach us in late July 1973. We had the same lawyers, John Wilson and Frank Strickler, and they guided us in what we should expect. But I wrote my opening and closing statements at home, without help.

I got ready for those hearings as I used to prepare for the trial of a lawsuit. I spent hours going over the few records I'd not lost when the FBI seized the contents of my office.* My preparation was badly hampered by the lack of some of my files.

The Senate Committee's staff insisted on interviewing me on May 4 and several times in June. Senator Lowell Weicker

---

* The day after Nixon fired me at Camp David, Attorney General Elliot Richardson had moved the FBI into my office to box up and cart off everything—family pictures, files, diaries—even my pencils and letter opener.

came in to listen to our first session, and I knew what he was there for. Weicker was the source of most of the leaks from the Committee. He gave out whatever information he could pick up at these interview sessions to curry favor with reporters, or to make himself look good. Weicker had inexplicable Presidential ambitions, and he was missing no opportunity to build credit with reporters and others who might help him later.

I watched the televised testimony of John Dean and the other witnesses who preceded me. As I sat at home watching and listening to the hearings, I came to consider old Sam Ervin as opposing counsel. His manner reminded me of an old trial lawyer I'd run into a number of times trying cases in the counties north of Seattle. His playacting could be exposed, but it had to be punctured early and often. It bothered me that all the witnesses and their attorneys were letting Ervin get away with his very unfair tactics. It also bothered me that Ervin was so transparently, but successfully, playing to the grandstand.

When it was my turn, I responded as I would have in trying a tough lawsuit, cramming the facts down their throats and not letting Ervin get away with his phony country-lawyer act. I came on hard.

Haldeman, the fellow with the reputation for Prussian hardness, was a real pussycat by comparison. He niced them, smiled and deferred at every opportunity and came away with the great American public thinking he didn't deserve his reputation as a martinet.

My opening and closing statements reflected how I saw my role at that time: I was there as the President's advocate. It wasn't until months later that I realized how much I had failed myself in the process. I attacked my accusers—Dean and the Committee and its staff—and I defended the whole Nixon White House. I had not yet heard any of the tapes; I still believed all of what Nixon had told me. And I thought the Senators a shabby collection of posturers and politicians, winding themselves in swaddles of self-righteousness.

The television lights were brutally hot and bright, and a horde of still photographers sat on the floor between the Committee and the witness chair, Nikons poised, waiting for me to scratch my nose or look unpleasant. I felt like a bug on a pin for all of the five days.

The hearing was television theater. Senators like Herman Talmadge and Joe Montoya had to climb over cables and through a maze of electronic equipment to get to their places. The hearing room was dominated by the lighting towers and camera platforms. Television was a massive presence. The

Senatorial actors were playing their parts without much regard for consequences beyond their own careers. Senator Daniel Inouye, for example, dramatically called me a liar during the third day. My doughty old lawyer John Wilson reacted with anger, because he knew that I was facing imminent indictment and a jury trial in which my credibility would be vital. Inouye's offhand crack could hurt me badly with every prospective juror who was watching on television. Unfortunately, John went out into the hall and vented his spleen against "that little Jap" in a network interview, which gave us a problem with Inouye we didn't need. But my biggest problem was my own style.

For years afterward I'd be told how tough, cold and arrogant I appeared during those hearings. But I was far less concerned with my "image" than with refuting the charges the Committee and its witnesses had made. I had my eye on the evidence and the record and I saw myself in a hostile environment, so I struck out as I would have in a courtroom back home. I disregarded the "hot" television medium, and that was a mistake. It's as much how you say it as what you say on television, and I was oblivious to that fact as I dueled with the Committee.

Those five days on television made my face instantly recognizable wherever I went (or would go), forevermore. As soon as I'd finished my testimony, our family jumped into our station wagon and we headed for Seattle; and as we drove across the country, I was dumbfounded to discover that every gas-station attendant and motel clerk recognized me instantly. It took me a long time to learn to live with that phenomenon.

As we crossed the prairies our car radio couldn't pick up all of Kleindienst's testimony, and we missed parts of Henry Petersen, too; but I heard enough. Petersen was a bureaucrat with a cause; I suspect that his objective was always Richard Nixon's ruin. If I were required to make a nomination for "Deep Throat," Henry Petersen would be mine.

Seattle was a headache. At our old home we were besieged by local and national reporters wanting to file a he-returns-home story. They came from far away to badger and bother my good neighbors, and the stuff they wrote was lugubrious and mostly wrong.

For the next year we survived on my very thin law practice and the bounty of friends. My wife was working too, and we scraped and borrowed. And some Seattle people raised a modest defense fund, which helped to pay for lawyers and their expenses during the two criminal trials.

The State of California indicted me for the Fielding break-in at about the same time as did the Special Prosecutor in the District of Columbia. It was obvious that Leon Jaworski and the Los Angeles District Attorney wanted to make my job of defense just that much more costly and difficult. After the Federal case was over, the Los Angeles District Attorney quietly dropped his prosecution; it had served its purpose. But while it lasted I was compelled to make many trips to Los Angeles for pretrial motions, because the trial judge there insisted upon my being present at every hearing. He seemed to enjoy the attention of the press, which swarmed around whenever I showed up.

The first criminal trial in Washington, D.C., the Fielding case, was very different from the later Watergate cover-up trial. The first judge, Gerhard Gesell, was very bright and quick, in contrast to Judge John Sirica. Both seemed determined to achieve the popular result, but Gesell was much more obvious in his hostility toward me. In fact, a number of spectators at that trial gave us affidavits describing Gesell's facial reactions and gestures, which seemed intended to indicate to the jury how he felt about me and my attorneys. Since he was careful, for the record, about what words he spoke, these affidavits were our only way of recording* what Gesell had done.

The five lawyers Leon Jaworski assigned to prosecute me in the Fielding case were dispassionate and professional. (They were a marked contrast to the huge coterie of lawyers who prosecuted the later Watergate cover-up trial. The cover-up prosecutors displayed an ambitious zeal which seemed to me to take them far beyond the bounds of propriety. Any judge in control of his courtroom would have slapped them down for their asides and mugging to the jury, for example; but little James Neal had his way with Judge Sirica all through the trial. As far as Sirica was concerned, the prosecutors could do no wrong.)

I'd retained William Frates of Miami to represent me. He was a very experienced trial lawyer who was also my friend. He urged me to retain co-counsel who were black, because

---

* The Court of Appeals said we made our record too late. We were obliged to confront the judge, it ruled, at the moment of his actions, not at the close of all the evidence.

Frates was obviously a white Southerner and the Washington, D.C., juries were predominantly black. We hired two black lawyers, one of whom badly disappointed us. It's hard to say whether that attorney's handling of much of the trial work made any difference in the outcome, but the poor man became the target of much of Gesell's venom. Gesell does not suffer fools, Watergate defendants or slow talkers.

As we approached trial, my lawyers demanded that the Government make my White House files available to us. President Nixon refused to release them. So we moved that the indictment be dismissed because the Government was denying me a chance to prepare my defense. For a time it looked as if Gesell would grant our motion. But suddenly the Prosecutor produced an affidavit from Fred Buzhardt, Nixon's new Counsel, attesting that there was nothing in the files which might be material to my defense. When we attempted to telephone Buzhardt, we were told he had suddenly suffered a heart attack and was in the hospital in intensive care. Gesell immediately denied our motion for dismissal, basing his ruling on the Buzhardt affidavit alone (in spite of our citing many dozens of documents which we offered to show him were material), and we went to trial.

The lingering mystery about that trial is why Fred Buzhardt gave Prosecutor Jaworski that affidavit saying that he'd examined the tens of thousands of documents in the White House files and found nothing there which might be material to my defense. In fact, hundreds of the documents would have been helpful. But I have no idea how Jaworski persuaded poor Fred Buzhardt to sign it just before his heart attack.

On the basis of that affidavit, Judge Gesell ruled as a matter of law that I was obliged to stand trial without access to my White House files and the other documents the FBI had taken from my office. With that ruling, much of the steam went out of our defense. We wanted to show all the circumstances that had led to the investigation of the Pentagon Papers theft and Ellsberg, but we couldn't. We were allowed to ask Henry Kissinger only a few questions. When I testified, Gesell sent clear signals to the jury that *he* didn't buy what I was telling them about my ignorance of the plan to break into the psychiatrist's office.

A criminal defendant is entitled to call character witnesses to bolster his credibility, and I had asked a number of people who knew me well to come and testify to my "reputation for truth and veracity." One of them was a Congressman from the

Midwest who had been my neighbor in suburban Virginia. On the day he was due to testify he slipped into court unnoticed, but at the recess he insisted on talking to Bill Frates and me. "This is a break-in case?" he exclaimed. "And that's your judge? I can't believe it! When my wife and I first came to Washington," the Congressman said excitedly, "Gerhard Gesell was assigned by his law firm to help us to get located. I was a new Congressman and he was a lawyer in private practice; he took us around town and even helped us choose a house. One place we were to look at was all locked up, and the real estate lady didn't show up. So Gesell went down to the basement door and—guess what?—he broke a window with his elbow and reached the doorknob and let us in! How's that for a coincidence?"

We debated for about thirty seconds whether we should remind the judge of his very own break-in. Considering all the trouble we were already having with Gesell, we decided to forget it.

In the months between the Fielding break-in trial and the Watergate cover-up trial, I listened to the Nixon tapes the Special Prosecutor intended to use in the second trial. As a result of what I heard on the tapes, my attorneys and I felt it essential that Richard Nixon appear as a witness, either in person or by filmed deposition. Neither Bob Haldeman nor John Mitchell was enthusiastic about putting Nixon through that ordeal. My strategic disagreement with the other defendants was fundamental, but I left it to the lawyers to argue it. I had been through the Fielding trial, and my attitude toward the second trial was very different from that of my co-defendants.

I was deeply pessimistic all through that second trial; I had seen a District of Columbia judge and jury at work in the first case. Neither Sirica nor the new jury looked any better. My co-defendants displayed much of the optimism I'd had in that first trial, but I couldn't share it.

John J. Sirica lived up to his reputation when he tried the second, "cover-up" case. As a lawyer I've tried hundreds of jury cases before all kinds of judges in the seventeen years I was at the bar. I know a good judge from an inept one, and I'm compelled to say Sirica was not good. I often felt that the *Star, Post,* and TV networks were having an undue influence on his conduct of the trial. Furthermore, his methods of jury selection were hasty, careless and capricious. As a result his *voir dire* failed to disclose that one juror was a close friend of an employee of the Prosecutor. Another juror wrote a note confessing her bias partway through the trial. But Sirica left her on the jury, in spite of our objections.

Nevertheless, I'm not able to say I could have been acquitted under different circumstances. There was no question that I had known money was going to the burglars and I had abetted its flow. I had failed to have Krogh, Young, Hunt and Liddy arrested when I learned of the Fielding break-in. That's an obstruction of justice, Judge Gesell said, and he was sustained on appeal. Perhaps, in the twilight of my advanced years, I will quarrel with that and some of the other accusations, if I have nothing better to do. I may flip through those old trial notes someday and rehash all of that; but that seems a foolish use of my time right now.

CHAPTER TWENTY-TWO

Retrospection

IF THE 1971 California break-in at Dr. Lewis Fielding's office by Howard Hunt and Gordon Liddy was the seminal Watergate episode, as I believe it was, then historians should continue to inquire into its origins. Judge Gerhard Gesell's rushed trial of the criminal case left many questions unanswered.

Historians may believe that Hunt and Liddy went to California, sent for a Cuban team of break-in artists* to join them and rifled Daniel Ellsberg's psychiatrist's files merely on Bud Krogh's orders, as Gordon Liddy claims.

They may believe that Krogh or David Young told me that Hunt and Liddy were going to burglarize Fielding and that I approved the plan. That is the story David Young traded for his freedom.

Or they may believe that Charles Colson encouraged Howard Hunt, his old friend, to get Ellsberg's secrets from his psychiatrist's files. Since Colson pleaded guilty to the strange

---

* One of the Cubans told me at our joint trial that he had performed over two hundred break-ins for the CIA, all over the United States and in Cuba, Canada and other countries.

charge of obstructing justice by conspiring to defame Ellsberg, there is no room for doubt that he would have been happy to have whatever derogatory information Hunt might have brought him.

It seems clear that Hunt and Liddy first proposed the Fielding break-in. But without high-level approval and a budget they would not have pulled it off, they both agree. Liddy's book *Will* merely *implied* that I had given that approval, but the fact is I did not. I'd never met Liddy. I'd seen Howard Hunt only for five minutes the day Colson hired him, and never again. Krogh and Young were always their go-betweens to me. Bud Krogh came to me in the summer of 1971 complaining that the FBI was not vigorously investigating Daniel Ellsberg. Krogh made the extraordinary proposal that White House employees Howard Hunt and Gordon Liddy be permitted to investigate Ellsberg. The President had been putting on the heat; Krogh's suggestion responded to that Presidential pressure. A day or two later, when Nixon was demanding to know what was being done, I asked the President how he felt about White House employees' acting as investigators. I told Nixon that Krogh and John Mitchell were having trouble with Hoover at the FBI. I said that Krogh felt Liddy and Hunt might be able to answer some of the questions Henry Kissinger and Nixon had raised about Ellsberg, about what he might do in the future.

Nixon nodded. It was direct action that he wanted. "If Krogh thinks they can do it, let's go ahead," he said.

I passed that affirmative word to Krogh, with my own admonition that these fellows were not to call themselves "White House investigators." I thought it would be unfortunate to read in some paper that the President had created his own secret police force which was going around flashing White House credentials.

I don't know what Krogh intended at that moment. Hunt and Liddy were going to California to investigate; everyone agreed to that. Krogh has confirmed to me many times since then that he never told me a break-in was contemplated. That was his testimony in a long, carefully written affidavit in 1973. But the affidavit was only part of it; Krogh recanted some of that testimony after Leon Jaworski had him thrown into a jail tank with some big, tough blacks out in Maryland, so there is sworn Krogh testimony going both ways on a number of important questions.

When Krogh phoned just after Labor Day 1971 to tell me that there had been a break-in at Dr. Fielding's office, I was shocked. He was calling to ask me how I felt about a new Hunt-Liddy proposal: Fielding's files on Ellsberg were not in his office; they might be in his home.

I flatly refused to approve the proposed break-in of Fielding's apartment, and I was openly critical of the office break-in. "Get them away from there," I told Krogh, "and never send them back." Krogh tried to reassure me by adding that Hunt and Liddy had not personally engaged in the break-in. "Get them back anyway," I said.

I knew I had not authorized that office break-in. Who did?

In *The Ends of Power*, Haldeman sheds some light on the subject:

Not to be outmaneuvered or left in the cold from anything as potentially juicy as this [Ellsberg investigation] appeared to be, Chuck Colson hastily got involved too—recommending the hiring of Howard Hunt to augment the Plumbers' staff.

Haldeman then goes on to describe a remarkable talk he had with Nixon in November *1976:*

I found Nixon in his armchair in his [San Clemente] office. Once again he wanted to probe my memory for details of various Watergate events for use in his book. The subject today was the Plumbers, and the Ellsberg break-in.

The more Nixon spoke, the more I realized something strange. Nixon was worried that he had personally ordered the Ellsberg break-in. This came as a surprise to me because I remembered all of those Oval Office conferences in 1973 when he appeared so stunned—and even hurt—by the Ellsberg break-in. At that time, he called it absurd, bizarre.

And I was remembering Ehrlichman, face red, saying to me during our trial, "Nixon didn't even make a deposition at my Ellsberg trial. He let me go right down the tube and never lifted a hand." But even in that moment of anger, Ehrlichman hadn't told me Nixon ordered the break-in. Which meant Ehrlichman was a patsy, if Nixon had really told Krogh—who worked for Ehrlichman—to do the break-in without informing Ehrlichman. And Ehrlichman took the rap.

Nixon said, "Krogh told me he didn't believe I ordered—or even knew about—the break-in."

Haldeman's book came out while I was an inmate at the Federal Prison Camp at Safford, Arizona. This passage astonished me. It described a meeting that took place a month after I'd entered prison to begin serving my sentence for that break-in. It appeared possible that Nixon was sitting in comfort at San Clemente while I was doing jail time for something *he*, not I, had done. In 1974 and 1975 I had testified that so far as I knew, President Nixon had not ordered the Fielding break-in. That is what I believed then. Now I believe he ordered it.

Time magazine commissioned me to write a review of Haldeman's book. I had the privilege of using the pay phone in jail, so I telephoned several people near to Nixon to ask if they had anything to add to Haldeman's account of his extraordinary conversation with Nixon about the Fielding break-in. Eventually, after the book review was published, I found two people who corroborated Haldeman's impression: Privately, Nixon now admits what he formerly denied. He knew of the Fielding break-in before it occurred, and he encouraged it. One of my informants was then on Nixon's payroll, the other had been; both had talked to Nixon about the Ellsberg-Fielding break-in. Both were convinced that Nixon had caused it to occur.

The second person I talked to was much more precise: "He [Nixon] now recalls that he's the one who put all that [the break-in] into motion," he told me.

In his memoirs Nixon avoided the question:

On Labor Day weekend, 1971, Krogh's group organized a break-in at the office of Ellsberg's psychiatrist in an attempt to get information from his files on his motivation, his further intentions, and any possible co-conspirators.

I do not believe I was told about the break-in at the time, but it is clear that it was at least in part an outgrowth of my sense of urgency about discrediting what Ellsberg had done and finding out what he might do next. Given the temper of those tense and bitter times and the peril I perceived, I cannot say that had I been informed of it beforehand, I would have automatically considered it unprecedented, unwarranted or unthinkable. Ehrlichman says that he did not know of it in advance, but that he told me about it after the fact in 1972. I do not recall this, and the tapes of the June–July, 1972 period indicate that I was not conscious of it then, but I cannot rule it out.

Today the break-in at Ellsberg's psychiatrist's office seems wrong and excessive. But I do not accept that it was as wrong or excessive as what Daniel Ellsberg did, and I still believe that it is a tragedy of circumstances that Bud Krogh and John Ehrlichman went to jail and Daniel Ellsberg went free.*

If Nixon *did* approve the Hunt-Liddy plan, as his colleagues tell me he now believes he did, who presented it to him and passed the word back to Krogh, Young, Hunt or Liddy? Haldeman says it was not he. I know it was not I. The logical alternative suspect is Charles Colson, of course. He was Hunt's sponsor, close friend and confidant. Who knows for sure? Well, apparently Richard Nixon's memory is much better than it was during my first criminal trial. He knows; Colson knows. And if the green light was given to Krogh, then Krogh knows.

Many times Krogh has said I did not approve the break-in. John Dean claims that Krogh told him that approval came "from the Oval Office." When all the tapes surface and Nixon, Colson, Krogh and Hunt have given their last testaments to the historians of their choice, I think it will appear that Howard Hunt took the Hunt-Liddy break-in proposal to Charles Colson. Hunt and Liddy said they needed several thousand dollars for equipment. And they needed Colson's help for a second reason. Krogh had imposed my unwitting injunction that Hunt and Liddy must not be *directly* involved in the Ellsberg investigation. Krogh construed that to apply to break-ins as well. Hunt and Liddy wanted "action," so if Hunt appealed Krogh's prohibition to Colson, Colson could have topped my orders by going to Nixon.

Nixon would not have restrained Hunt and his confederates. Nixon was demanding action. Once before, when Nixon was in such a mood, Colson had planned to firebomb the Brookings Institution to get at its cache of secret documents. Nixon knew about that plan in advance too, as I discovered after I ordered it stopped.

In those days Charles Colson and Richard Nixon had few secrets from each other. It is beyond my imagination that Colson knew of Hunt's proposed Ellsberg operation and kept it secret from Nixon. It is undisputed that Colson raised the money Hunt and Liddy asked for and Colson gave it to Krogh. I can't visualize Colson keeping all of that juicy evidence of his diligence from the President when Nixon was calling him at all hours demanding to know who was doing

---

* I find this passage notable, too, as the only known expression of regret by Richard Nixon on the subject of my going to jail. At no time before, during or since have I heard from him directly.

what to "get" Daniel Ellsberg. The probabilities corroborate Haldeman's account of Nixon's hint to him, and the two ex-employees are even more categorical. I'm now convinced that Nixon perpetrated the Fielding break-in.

I made a profound decision when Krogh was telling me on the telephone that the Fielding break-in had occurred. Knowing that the President himself had approved their trip to California and their investigation of Ellsberg (but not knowing the President may have authorized the break-in), I barely considered the notion that Hunt, Liddy and their Cubans should be exposed. Later it was not hard to rationalize my decision to keep the break-in secret; I knew that copies of the top secret Pentagon Papers had been given to the Russians and Japanese. Someone was betraying national secrets. Hunt and Liddy did what the FBI had been doing in such cases for years with the blessing of the Attorney General and the President. A Nixon man didn't expose FBI black-bag jobs either.

Years later, at my first trial, the judge and prosecutors insisted that it had been my legal duty to call the Beverly Hills Police Department and report the Fielding burglary. That was an idea that never entered my mind at the time. I conceived my job as being to protect the President, not to expose him.

There was a secondary consideration, however. I felt that Krogh and David Young deserved protection. I was not sure then how deeply they were involved. David Young had presented me with their joint proposal (as the middle item in a memorandum containing a long series of requests for approval) for Hunt and Liddy to go to California. Young and Hunt had asked the CIA for a second "psychological profile" of Daniel Ellsberg. "Henry gets them all the time on people," Young said. Young and the others weren't happy with the CIA's first try on Ellsberg. The CIA psychologists said they needed more information to do a better profile. Hunt and Liddy knew of the psychiatric help Ellsberg had been getting; they proposed to try to find out what the psychiatrist knew about Ellsberg, and to feed that information to the CIA's profilers.

I was asked to specifically approve such an investigation, and I did—with the injunction that Hunt and Liddy were not to pass themselves off as "White House cops." There was nothing about a burglary in the long paper Young brought me, but when the Special Prosecutor began to threaten David Young with prison he was persuaded to implicate me.

Among Young's plea-bargaining suggestions was the notion

that I had actually *seen* the burglary plan that Hunt and Liddy had written up and passed on to Krogh and Young for approval. But alas for David, I was on vacation on Cape Cod at the time. I had an alibi.

The only time I met with Leon Jaworski, he accused me of taking a razor blade to White House records to excise the references to Hunt and Liddy's investigation. In the strongest terms I denied doing so,* and we were later able to prove that Young had done that document tampering himself, in his own interest.

At no time following Krogh's revelation of the Fielding burglary did I consider that I was in jeopardy. I knew I hadn't known of it in advance. Nor did I think there was anything wrong with failing to call the police, given the context in which it occurred. Until the verdict in the Fielding-burglary trial was delivered, I thought I'd be acquitted. I had badly underestimated the many factors which brought about that result.

Nixon writes that he cannot recall our 1972 conversation about the Fielding break-in. I can. We two walked the beach south of the Western White House, on the Marine reservation at Camp Pendleton, in early July of 1972. The Watergate break-in had occurred less than a month before. We talked at great length about Hunt and Liddy.

Nixon talked about raising money to help in the defense of the Watergate burglars; he thought Herb Kalmbach's trust fund could be used to cover their legal expenses. Nixon raised the possibility of clemency or pardons in the event the burglars were convicted. I objected to such an obvious and direct link between the defendants and the President. Then I told the President that Hunt and Liddy might want a very broad par-

---

* Jaworski says in his book that this was the only accusation I denied: "*That* I did not do," he quotes me. The implication is that I was thereby admitting his other allegations. In fact, I'd been advised by my attorneys to stay silent throughout. But this razor-blade charge angered me so that I disobeyed them. Poor Jaworski was so befuddled all through that meeting that I'm surprised he recalls the incident. Repeatedly during that session Jaworski had his facts wrong, and was continually corrected by the staff he had inherited from Archibald Cox. For example, he assured us that he'd arranged for Bud Krogh to keep his license to practice law in the State of Washington. I knew that was not so, and I challenged Jaworski. His staff corrected Leon; Krogh would be disbarred as a result of his plea-bargain, they told him. I formed the impression that Jaworski had passed his prime; his confusion and ignorance of the facts were surprising to me in view of all the publicity about his steely efficiency.

don—one broad enough to cover the Ellsberg-Fielding break-in as well.

Nixon asked me no questions about that break-in; but he reluctantly agreed with me that no one should even *hint* at the possibility of clemency for the Watergate burglars.

Nine months later, on April 18, 1973, at Aspen Lodge at Camp David, I was present when Richard Nixon telephoned explicit instructions to Assistant Attorney General Henry Petersen that there was to be no investigation of the Fielding break-in. John Dean had told the U.S. Attorney about it, as part of his *quid pro quo* during his plea-bargaining. Dean was trying to get immunity from prosecution in return for implicating others.

"I know about that," Nixon told Henry Petersen, "and it is so involved with national security that I don't want it opened up. Keep the hell out of it!"

Nixon hung up the telephone and turned to me. "That should keep them out of it. There is no reason for them to get into it. What those fellows did was no crime; they ought to get a medal for going after Ellsberg."

On May 2, 1973, in the week after I was fired, the President and I had our last face-to-face conversation, in his office. He told me about Spiro Agnew's coming troubles. Then he turned to the reason he'd called me in. He had to decide what to do with Bud Krogh (who since January had been Undersecretary of Transportation). Ellsberg was on trial in California. Henry Petersen had recommended that the Justice Department disclose the Fielding break-in to Ellsberg's lawyer and the judge. Petersen was asking for an affidavit from Krogh setting forth all the facts. Krogh was asking whether or not he should resign.

At about 3 P.M. on May 2, 1973, Nixon was trying to tell me that as soon as he had heard about the Fielding break-in he'd talked to the Justice Department about it. It occurred to me, from the way he was putting leading questions to me, that he might be recording our conversation. (I didn't know then that he was recording everything.)

"In March [1973] I learned some things [from Dean]," Nixon said. "But [late in April] when the Attorney General confirmed it [Fielding], I acted instantly. I said to Kleindienst and Petersen: 'By all means, get it to the prosecutor or Dean will hold it over your head.' As soon as it came to my attention—that's the important point—it was relayed to California."

Ever the wet blanket, I asked: "What about that phone call to Henry Petersen on April 18 when you told him to stay out of it—that it was a national-security matter? You obviously knew a lot about it then."

Nixon changed the subject. Krogh should resign toward the end of the week. I should tell the new Attorney General, Elliot Richardson, that the President had caused the Fielding information to be sent out to Ellsberg's judge in California.

I stood. "You know," I said, "it would be terribly unjust if Krogh were punished for this Fielding thing. Please promise me you won't let him go to jail for it—after all, he was just doing what you wanted him to."

"You mean a pardon?" Nixon asked.

"Yes."

"All right," he promised.*

He looked up at me from his desk. "Did I know about it sooner?"

I nodded my head silently.

"Well, if I did, it evidently didn't make an impression on me. I didn't remember it."

I stepped outside and made a note of that final episode. Richard Nixon and I have never spoken face to face since.

All through 1973 and early 1974, after we were fired, Bob Haldeman stayed in touch with the President and his new Chief of Staff, General Alexander Haig. I did not. Other than a call from Nixon on Christmas Eve 1973, I heard nothing from the President or Haig. But I talked with Haldeman frequently, and he told me much of what Nixon and Haig were saying to *him*. In that way I followed the battle for the tapes, the tightening noose of impeachment and the debate over whether Nixon should resign.

As Nixon's resignation became more likely, Haldeman urged Nixon to grant clemency to everyone facing conviction or already convicted for "Watergate" crimes. He and his lawyers prepared a convincing brief for pardon. They argued that Vietnam draft-evaders should be pardoned by Nixon at the same time, to give incoming President Ford an absolutely clean slate.

Haldeman's petition to Nixon said:

---

* Krogh served about seven months in a federal prison camp in Pennsylvania.

It is submitted that all acts and things done by petitioners during that period were either:

    (1) at the President's direction

    (2) with the President's knowledge and approval

    (3) under a general Presidential authorization or direction

    (4) or done for the President's personal, political or institutional use or benefit.

In no event were such acts done for the personal enrichment or benefit of petitioners.

In equity and in recognition of the derivative nature of petitioners' actions, the President should relieve them of liability.

The petition went on to argue that it was in the national interest to "close the Watergate Book." And the Nixon Administration's files, records and papers could be "preserved" only if future prosecutions were blocked.

Then Haldeman took the long view for Nixon:

IV. The probability of contemporary and historical approval of such clemency is high

  A. Public policy justifies it—

    (1) It insures an end to the current turmoil

    (2) It offers some assurance to future presidential appointees that they can follow presidential instructions without undue jeopardy

    (3) It saves millions of dollars

    (4) It permits the wrongs and rights to be adjudicated in the "court of history" rather than in the highly prejudiced political crucible of Washington, D.C. courts

    (5) It strengthens the tattered doctrine of Executive Confidentiality

  B. It adds to the image of Richard Nixon

    (1) He seeks to assume the historic judgment of responsibility under circumstances where all know he need not have done so

    (2) He is loyal to his colleagues and expresses gratitude, compassion, friendship, unselfishness

    (3) He seeks to do justice when he knows the judicial process cannot or will not

    (4) He ascribes good motives to those who sought to serve him and attempts to mitigate somewhat the enormous costs of that service to his colleagues

  C. It permits those pardoned to set straight the garbled record of the Administration without fear of future jeopardy

D. The *contra* argument: That by this act the President assumes the sins of all those whom he pardons is
   (1) probably moot—those who would so reason have already imputed these sins to the President
   (2) specious reasoning: like imputing one's wrongs to his judge
   (3) either historically true (i.e., the President is responsible for wrongs done) or it is not. History will judge the President regardless of the act of clemency.
   (4) Assumes the President's resignation will not sate the appetites of the persecutors; the probability is that Congress is willing to grant the President immunity rather than seek the last drop of blood.

Late on the afternoon of August 7, 1974, Haldeman called me to read me his petition. It had gone to the White House, addressed to the President, but Al Haig, not Nixon, had called him in response. Haldeman was troubled that he had not heard from the President.

"Pardons for everyone have been extensively considered," Haig said (according to Haldeman), "and the idea has been rejected as impossible; it can't be done."

"Is there any appeal?" Haldeman asked. Haldeman felt Nixon had neither seen his petition nor made the decision to reject it. "Did you receive our written petition from our attorneys?" Haldeman asked Haig. (I don't know who joined Haldeman in this petition; I know I did not.)

"I don't know," Haig said. "I'll check on it and get back to you."

"When does he plan to resign?" Haldeman asked.

"His resignation is not sure. His family is arguing strongly against it," Haig said.

Haldeman sensed that Haig was in favor of Nixon's resigning. "I thought resignation was a certainty," Haldeman said.

"The situation has changed many times," Haig replied.

"Once his decision is final," Haldeman went on, "there will be a rush to do a lot of things. I want to get our points on clemency in to him now. Later he will have enormous regrets if he doesn't do it."

Haig was noncommittal about Haldeman's talking directly to Nixon. Haldeman called me to see if I could help put him in direct touch with Richard Nixon.

"You have much better relations with the family than I do," Haldeman said. "Do you think you could reach one of them—Julie would be best—and ask her to have her father

all me? Give her my number so the Old Man could dial me
lirect?"

I said I'd be glad to try. The idea that Haig was intercepting
ll Haldeman's calls to Nixon both bothered and amused me.
t was not a little ironic that Haldeman's own screening system
vas working so well to keep his calls from the President. I
alled Julie at the White House and asked her to give Bob's
nessage to the President.

I told Julie that Bob wanted to talk about pardons. I said
hat for friendship, if for no other reason, the President ought
o call Haldeman.

Contrary to printed accounts of that call, I did *not* ask Julie
o seek a pardon for me. In fact, right after Haldeman's call I
phoned my lawyer William Frates to tell him about Halde-
nan's petition. We agreed that I should not join in it. In ac-
epting a pardon, I would be admitting guilt.

When I finished talking to Julie Eisenhower I called Halde-
nan to tell him that Julie had promised to give his message to
ler father. Evidently she did; Nixon and Haldeman talked be-
ore the resignation, and Nixon said he'd given no thought at
ll to the question of pardons for others. Nor had he seen Hal-
leman's petition.

It's my guess that Richard Nixon was giving a great deal of
hought to a pardon for himself at that time. I've never known
lim to take a major step without thoroughly outlining its con-
equences. I can't visualize Nixon resigning without thinking
hrough the benefits. He would have carefully weighed impeachment versus resignation. If he were to resign, he would
lave considered the consequences—including criminal prose-
ution.

I know nothing of Haig's role as a go-between from Nixon
o Ford, and I've read all the denials issued by Nixon, Ford
nd Haig. But I *do* know Richard Nixon. I'd bet that Jerry
ord promised to pardon Richard Nixon, and that the prom-
se was made before Nixon's resignation.

There is room for me to be wrong; there were advantages for
Vixon in resignation whether he was pardoned or not. It put
n end to the threat of impeachment. Given Jaworski's weaknesses, Nixon's resignation probably obviated prosecution,
oo. Jaworski was certainly less than a vigorous and energetic
prosecutor. Resignation preserved all the ex-President's perquisites and pensions, the guards and cars and staff and
noney.

But the pardon ended *all* the risk and would make possible a
gradual rehabilitation of Nixon's influence and image. If one

cared about one's place in history, the pardon route was the best. And Richard Nixon cared deeply about his place in history.

Whether Nixon's pardon was the product of a "deal" or not, I think Jerry Ford did the right thing, for the nation's good. Had Nixon been prosecuted after leaving office, Ford's White House would have been paralyzed. Documents, personnel like Al Haig, even Ford himself might have been haled into court by one side or the other. Surely Dean, Haldeman and the rest of us would have been key witnesses. The country would have been torn and torn again as the trials progressed. And very little constructive purpose would have been served.

At that time I was not parsing out the pros and cons of a pardon. But in retrospect there were some good reasons for me to accept a pardon, if it had been offered.

There had been some pre-trial exposure of Judge Gerhard Gesell's angry preconceptions that bothered me, but I was optimistic that he would settle down and try the break-in case fairly. But now, from this perspective, it seems that all that optimism was nonsense. As far as I am concerned, Gesell was determined to effect a conviction, and he did everything possible to achieve that result.

The trials—the Fielding prosecution and the Watergate cover-up—were long, intense and difficult, very expensive and personally destructive. They were as publicized as any in history, I guess, and put my whole family into the harsh limelight day after day.

The convictions resulted in my disbarment; a pardon might not have saved my license to practice law, but there is a possibility it could have.

On the other hand, the trials, conviction and imprisonment forced me to confront some very stark and surprising realities about myself. Much good has come from that process. A pardon would have permitted me to escape that confrontation; had I been granted a pardon, I surely would have eschewed the difficult realizations and decisions the prosecutions and punishment forced upon me.

The whole episode from March 1973 on was the subject of the most intensive prayer on my part. When Jesus prayed in the Garden of Gethsemane he was facing a trial and crucifixion, and he prayed that the bitter cup of that experience be taken from him if it was God's will that he be relieved of it. I can recall times during the days when a pardon was a possibility when I was trying to know God's will too. I was putting myself into God's hands, saying "not my will, but Thine be done." Knowing that I was not blameless, I wasn't praying for a loophole. I was asking only for God's perfect result, whatever that might be.

And now, from my present standpoint, I have a little better view of how all of that works. I can count great blessings which have grown side by side with the tares.

CHAPTER TWENTY-THREE

A New Beginning

WHEN I WENT to jail—nearly two years after the cover-up trial—I had a big self-esteem problem. I was a felon, shorn and scorned, clumping around in a ragged old Army uniform doing pick-and-shovel work out on the desert. I wondered if anyone thought I was worth anything.

But the news stories and pictures about my incarceration caused a flood of mail to come to me from all kinds of people, and it helped. Religious folks said they were praying for me. Some Arizona people offered to visit.

Before long, some of my correspondents did come for visits. A family from Phoenix began bringing picnics on the weekends. A man from Tucson used to arrive with bulging grocery bags of deli food. He'd been a lawyer in the East, and I looked forward to his visits and to hearing about his business adventures in Arizona. After my Scrabble-playing friend John Bishop was paroled, his parents kept coming to Safford to visit me. And old friends from California, Washington and Seattle came there in a steady stream to give me encouragement.

A few of my correspondents were famous, but most of them I'd never heard of. Clare Boothe Luce wrote me a kind letter. Norman Mailer advised me not to eat the bread they serve in jail; when he was in one time, he had gained twelve pounds, he said. And Mrs. W. E. Woody of Atlanta sent cards and letters full of uplifting thoughts.

There were the girls, too. To the extent that my lack of self-esteem had to do with the fact that I was a portly, middle-aged and balding fellow whose marriage was on the rocks, the letters from the girls did help a lot. I'd heard from a few of them before I went to prison, but most of them were comely and lively strangers, who sent me their pictures in swimsuits or low-cut gowns and suggested future frolics. While mail of that kind has its frustrating aspects, there are redeeming features too. I answered the most literate and forwarded a couple of the others to Pete McCloskey for attention.

I also seemed to need some affirmation of my intellectual capacity, and my literary agent and editor gave me that as I sent them chapters of the novel I was writing. My children gave me essential support of a different kind. They visited me when they could afford to make the long trip from Seattle to Arizona, and I realized with joy that we were growing closer. I was open to them now, accessible and not at all the forbidding father I once had been. Whenever one of them came to visit we sat in the sun at Safford and talked for six or seven hours without stopping. I don't think I'd ever talked with any of them like that before.

For years I had been able to sweep most of my shortcomings and failures under the rug and not face them. But during the two long criminal trials I spent my days listening to prosecutors tell juries what a bad fellow I was. Then at night I'd go back to a hotel room and sit alone, thinking about what was happening to me.

During that time I began to take stock.

I'd felt for a long time—since we'd moved to Washington— that Jeanne and I didn't have a real marriage, but I had successfully avoided admitting it to myself. During the interminable Watergate trials we were apart most of the time. She stayed in Seattle, as we had agreed, to try to keep the family on an even keel. Several of our children were going through very rough times and needed Jeanne as much as I did or more. I knew that it was right for her to be at home.

But I was fatally lonely during the long second trial. It seemed a hopeless time.

Before the second trial was over I'd had my first affair. I was deeply affected by it—I'd never come close to infidelity before—yet even so, it was essentially symbolic. I was telling myself I had no marriage in terms that I couldn't blink away. I was also responding to someone who was willing to say, "Regardless of what they are saying about you in the papers or in court or behind your back, I will take you into my arms." I needed that.

In the midst of that brief encounter, everything went into a ailspin. I was convicted of more felonies, my wife heard from ne of my infidelity and I was suspended from practicing law.

My wife came to Washington for the last days of the trial, and we returned home to Seattle in turmoil. Jeanne felt betrayed; worse, she didn't know what she wanted from me by way of expiation. I didn't know if I had anything to give her; worse, I wasn't at all sure I was interested in trying to put our marriage back together. We didn't talk; she cried and I yelled. Some of the children yelled, too.

That was not, I told myself, what I was entitled to expect from these people in my family. I had been back East being beaten up by a bunch of paid assassins and in a few weeks I was going to be sentenced to prison. I was out of work, exhausted and feeling indescribable pressure. Somehow I had to figure out where we were all headed, and all that yelling and crying wasn't helping.

Whereupon, for the second time in recent weeks, I followed my instincts. I threw some clothes into a car and left. I don't think I'd ever before just gotten into a car and driven away without knowing where I was going, let alone how far, or for how long.

It was winter, cold and windy, and I remembered having once stayed at a place on the Oregon coast where one could sit in his room and feel the waves hitting the rocks below. When I got there, I discovered that the hotel had been expanded and remodeled by a Miami Beach architect who liked purple plastic minarets and sequined white plaster. So I drove on into new territory and came to a quiet wood lodge offering long stretches of secluded beach.

I stayed there about two weeks. Every day I read the Bible, walked on the beach and sat in front of my fireplace thinking and sketching, with no outline or agenda. I had no idea where all this was leading or what answers I'd find. Most of the time I didn't even know what the questions were; I just watched and listened.

I was wiped out. I had nothing left that had been of value to me—honor, credibility, virtue, recognition, profession—nor did I have the allegiance of my family. I had managed to lose that too. It was all gone, and it seemed hopeless to expect that I could ever get any of it back. But I realized that—unless I was willing to just kill myself—I had to begin to *move;* I had to go slowly in some direction, a step at a time. I wasn't sure that I could take a step and then another, but it was clear to me that I had to try, or die.

By the time I left the Oregon coast I knew I had to begin in a new context, untethered by the societal bonds that had he[ld] me in place in Seattle. Unsure beyond that, I delivered myse[lf] to a friend in an Eastern city, hoping I could begin again i[n] partial shelter. But, being a friend, the friend turned me out t[o] take the steps alone.

That was a time of horrible buffeting from aunts, friend[s,] even my religious mentor. No one approved of my leavin[g] Seattle and going off on my own. But one friend understoo[d] and urged me to start over in the Southwest.

Just before I was sentenced, I began to talk to a new ac[-] quaintance, Ira Lowe, an iconoclastic Washington lawyer wh[o] was an advocate of "alternative sentencing." He believed tha[t] only dangerous criminals should be put in prison, and poten[-] tially productive defendants should be alternatively sentence[d] to public-service work or to make other forms of restitution[.]

Lowe urged me to allow my sentencing by the two judges t[o] become a showcase for his idea. I realized that the propos[al] was doomed, and it was, but it received wide notice in th[e] press. Tom Wicker wrote a thoughtful column about sentenc[-] ing. The judges refused to let me "do time" helping Indians i[n] New Mexico, but because of all the publicity about my offe[r,] when I moved to Santa Fe to await the outcome of my appea[l,] many Indians, Hispanics and Anglos came to me for help.

Once settled there, I didn't want to leave. Beneath its Ol[d] Worid facade, which is both charming and utilitarian, Sant[a] Fe has a community tradition very congenial for a refuge[e.] People let you alone. More than that, most of them seem t[o] understand.

I lived alone there for two years, taking one step at a time[,] looking back each time to say, "I did that; it's an accomplish[-] ment. Congratulations." Then I'd venture another step. Goin[g] to prison in my own time,* in my own way, was one of thos[e] steps.

When I came out I'd bought a house in Santa Fe (with Pet[e] McCloskey's help, since a Federal prisoner can't buy or se[ll] property on the outside). And I'd persuaded Jeanne that [I] could never come back.

Twice during my eighteen months in prison, business ha[d] brought Jeanne to Arizona and she had come by Safford to se[e] me. Those visits just reinforced my feelings. By the time I wa[s] released, I was no longer anyone's husband. By then I ha[d] been away from our marriage for about four years. It re[-]

---

* I entered prison while my appeal was still pending.

mained for a lawyer and judge to go through the motions of divorce.

I have no feeling that I lost my marriage to Jeanne because my wife did or failed to do anything. Had both of us done things differently from 1968 on, perhaps we'd still be married. But somehow along the line our marriage was allowed simply to die, like a garden when people neglect it. I'm sorry it happened. My leaving was hard on the children (who by then were quite grown up) and on some other people I love. If I'd known how to spare them, I would have.

Now Santa Fe is home. I don't know where I'll be in ten years or even five, but I don't need to know that kind of thing anymore.

Nor do I worry anymore about what people-I-don't-know believe about me. I realize that they can't really know me. It is hard enough to form an accurate picture of anyone we know well. It's impossible to truly understand those we only see on television and read about. I'm aware that images created by the televised Ervin hearings, and the fact that I'm a (Dan Rather's favorite descriptive phrase) "convicted felon" have made adamant what some people think of me. I can't affect that, nor will I try. In the past few years people I have met for the first time have often said, "Well, you're not the person I thought you were. Not at all." That is simply some measure of the vast distance between the real aspects of a publicized person and the public's perception of him, views that are usually frozen at some point in the past.

I can't say that the public perception of me was wholly in error. I confess that when I watched the PBS videotapes of my testimony before the Senate Committee I didn't like what I saw. When I listened to the President's secret tapes I wasn't proud of some of the harsh, cynical and even cruel things I heard myself saying.

I was in many respects a person I can neither defend nor condone, nor do I try. The things that happened can't be wished away; but the way I was then has become a picture of a person I barely know, far away. I surely can't blame people who saw me then for remembering me as they saw me. I don't try to reach those people and change their minds because it is hopeless to try. And there are too many better ways to spend my time and energy these days.

Since about 1975, I've begun to learn to see myself, and I care what I perceive about my integrity, my capacity to love—and be loved—and my essential worth. There are a couple of small handfuls of people whose opinions I'm concerned about, and I care very much how they see me. This account is written for them, primarily, so that they will know how it was for me then.

Just now, as they know, it's a good time, and I'm grateful for that.

I don't miss Richard Nixon very much. He epitomizes both good and bad interludes in my life, although surely it is evident that not all of my bad times were Richard Nixon's fault.

Each of us who was implicated in Watergate must bear his own measure of blame.

Richard Nixon probably doesn't much miss me either, and I can understand that. I've made no effort to be in touch. We had a professional relationship that went as sour as a relationship can, and no one likes to be reminded of bad times.

Those interludes—the Nixon episodes in my life—have ended. In a paradoxical way I'm grateful for them. Somehow I had to see all of that and grow to understand it in order to arrive at the place where I find myself now.

Index

THE MAN WHO KEPT THE SECRETS

RICHARD HELMS AND THE CIA

From operator, spymaster, planner, and plotter
to Agency Director, the story of Richard Helms
is the story of the C.I.A. Read it now—in Pulitzer
Prize-winner Thomas Powers' incisive, uncen-
sored, and balanced portrait of **THE MAN
WHO KEPT THE SECRETS.**

THOMAS POWERS

POCKET BOOKS

THE FALCON AND THE SNOWMAN

A TRUE STORY OF FRIENDSHIP AND ESPIONAGE

ROBERT LINDSEY

Christopher Boyce and Andrew Lee were typical American teenagers from an upper middle class community in southern California. Devout Catholics and altar boys, they grew up together, played high school football together, and cemented their friendship in their mutual love of falconry. Seeking the American Dream, Chris drifted from college to college, and Andrew dealt drugs. And when the American Dream didn't work out for either of them, they found another solution.

They sold their country's secrets to the enemy.

With a never-before-published update on the Falcon's escape from prison!